KPMG

PERSONAL TAX PLANNING GUIDE

1996

Prepared by

KPMG

Co-Editors

S. Brian Fisher, CA
Partner
Waterloo

Paul B. Hickey, CA
Partner
Toronto

Contributing KPMG Editors

Joanne Ivanski, CA
Montréal

Benita Loughlin, CA
Burnaby/New Westminster

Mark Worrall, CA
Vancouver

Dereka Thibault, CA
Edmonton

Deborah Goch, CA
Toronto

CARSWELL
Thomson Professional Publishing

Canadian Cataloguing in Publication Data

Main entry under title:
1996 Canadian Personal Tax Planning Guide

Annual.
1990/91 - prepared by KPMG Peat Marwick Thorne.
ISSN 0838-6064.
ISBN 0-459-57448-5 (1996)

1. Tax planning - Canada - Popular works - Periodicals.
2. Income tax - Canada - Popular works - Periodicals. I. KPMG Peat Marwick Thorne (Firm).

KE5759.C43 343.7105'2'05 C88-031025-1
KF6499.ZA2C36

Printed in Canada

CARSWELL
Thomson Professional Publishing

One Corporate Plaza
2075 Kennedy Road
Scarborough, Ontario
M1T 3V4

Customer service:
Toronto 1-416-609-3800
Elsewhere in Canada/U.S. 1-800-387-5164
Fax 1-416-298-5094

This book has been printed on text paper which meets Environmental Canada's and the Canadian Standards Association's "Environmental Choice Program" guidelines for recycled fibre content and environmentally safe manufacturing processes.

Overview

Introduction

Chapter 1/ **Tips for your Tax Return**

Chapter 2/ **RRSPs and Other Tax Deferral Plans**

Chapter 3/ **Income Splitting**

Chapter 4/ **Capital Gains and Losses**

Chapter 5/ **Investments and Tax Shelters**

Chapter 6/ **If You Are Employed**

Chapter 7/ **If You Are Self-Employed**

Chapter 8/ **If You Have Your Own Corporation**

Chapter 9/ **Farming**

Chapter 10/ **Professionals**

Chapter 11/ **Minimum Tax**

Chapter 12/ **Estate Planning**

Chapter 13/ **Dealing with Revenue Canada**

Chapter 14/ **Québec Taxation**

Chapter 15/ **U.S. Citizens**

Chapter 16/ **U.S. Residency and Ownership of U.S. Property**

Chapter 17/ **The Goods and Services Tax**

Appendices

Index

Table of Contents

Introduction/1

1. Tips for Your Tax Return/3
   - 1.1 Background/3
     - 1.1.1 The tax calculation/3
     - 1.1.2 Deduction versus credit/4
   - 1.2 Deductions/5
     - 1.2.1 Alimony and maintenance/5
     - 1.2.2 Moving expenses/7
     - 1.2.3 Child-care expenses/8
     - 1.2.4 Attendant for disabled person/9
     - 1.2.5 Legal fees/10
     - 1.2.6 Northern residents/10
     - 1.2.7 Other deductions/10
   - 1.3 Non-refundable credits with provincial component/10
     - 1.3.1 Personal and dependant credits/11
     - 1.3.2 Age credit/11
     - 1.3.3 Disability credit/11
     - 1.3.4 Charitable donations/12
     - 1.3.5 Medical expenses/12
     - 1.3.6 Tuition fees and educational status/13
     - 1.3.7 Pension income credit/14
     - 1.3.8 CPP/QPP contributions and UIC premiums/14
     - 1.3.9 Other credits/14
   - 1.4 Non-refundable credits — federal only/15
     - 1.4.1 Political contributions/15
     - 1.4.2 Other credits/15
   - 1.5 Refundable credits — federal only/15
     - 1.5.1 Child Tax Benefit/15
     - 1.5.2 Goods and Services Tax Credit/16
     - 1.5.3 GST rebate/16
   - 1.6 Old Age Security and UI benefits clawback/16
   - 1.7 Planning opportunities/17
     - 1.7.1 Claim married-equivalent credit/17
     - 1.7.2 Family planning/17
     - 1.7.3 Claim moving expenses/18
     - 1.7.4 Higher-income spouse claim credits to reduce high-income surtax/18
     - 1.7.5 Medical expense credit — spouse and year-end options/18
     - 1.7.6 Medical expenses — claim for dependants/19

1.7.7 If you are separating/19
1.7.8 Investigate whether you can claim the disability credit/20
1.7.9 Plan for at least $1,000 of pension income per person/20
1.7.10 Political contributions/20
1.7.11 Charitable donations/20
1.8. References/21

2. RRSPS AND OTHER TAX DEFERRAL PLANS/23
2.1 Registered Retirement Savings Plans — RRSPs/23
2.1.1 What is an RRSP?/23
2.1.2 How do you set up an RRSP?/24
2.1.3 How much can you contribute?/24
2.1.4 What is your contribution worth?/27
2.1.5 What happens to the funds in the RRSP?/28
2.1.6 How do you get money out of an RRSP?/31
2.1.6.1 Withdraw the funds/31
2.1.6.2 Purchase an annuity/31
2.1.6.3 Convert RRSP to RRIF/31
2.1.6.4 Convert locked-in RRSP to Line Income Fund (LIF)/32
2.1.7 Special RRSP rules/32
2.1.7.1 Spousal plans/32
2.1.7.2 Transfers to and from RRSPs/33
2.1.7.3 Death/34
2.1.7.4 Overcontributions/34
2.1.8 The Home buyers' plan/35
2.2 Registered Pension Plan — RPPs/38
2.2.1 Ordinary RPPs/38
2.2.2 Individual Pension Plans — IPPs/38
2.3 Deferred Profit-Sharing Plans — DPSPs/39
2.4 Registered Education Savings Plans — RESPs/40
2.5 Planning opportunities/40
2.5.1 RRSP: contribute early and often/41
2.5.2 Consider a self-directed RRSP/41
2.5.3 Consider a labour-sponsored venture capital corporation/43
2.5.4 Consider RRSP rather than additional RPP contributions/43
2.5.5 Contribute to spouse's RRSP/43
2.5.6 Transfer retiring allowance or severance pay to RRSP/44
2.5.7 Consider non-deductible contribution of $2,000 to RRSP/44
2.5.8 Planning for the home buyer's plan/44
2.5.9 RRSP withdrawals in low-income years/45
2.5.10 When you turn 71/46
2.5.11 Consider an Individual Pension Plan/46
2.5.12 Vesting of RPP benefits/47

2.5.13 Consider an RESP/47

2.6 References/47

3. INCOME SPLITTING/49

3.1 Why Income Splitting?/49

3.2 Rules that prevent income splitting/50

3.2.1 Indirect payments/50

3.2.2 Attribution between spouses/50

3.2.3 Attribution with respect to minor children/52

3.2.4 Attribution on loans to adult family members/52

3.2.5 Special anti-avoidance rules/53

3.3 Planning opportunities/54

3.3.1 Higher-income spouse should pay expenses/54

3.3.2 Salary or consulting fee to spouse and children/54

3.3.3 Loans of business assets/54

3.3.4 Loans on which interest is charged/55

3.3.5 Pay interest on spousal loans/55

3.3.6 Transfers for fair market value/55

3.3.7 Reinvestment of attributed income/56

3.3.8 Child tax benefit payments/56

3.3.9 Transferring future capital gains to children/56

3.3.10 Payment of spouse's taxes/57

3.3.11 Payment of capital dividends/57

3.3.12 Spousal RRSP/58

3.3.13 Children 17 and older/58

3.3.14 Allow children to invest the funds they earn/59

3.3.15 Assignment of CPP benefit payments/59

3.3.16 Transfer of tax credits to spouse/60

3.3.17 Pay children over 18 for child care/60

3.4 References/60

4. CAPITAL GAINS AND LOSSES/61

4.1 What is capital?/61

4.2 Capital gains/62

4.3 Capital losses/63

4.3.1 Ordinary capital losses/63

4.3.2 Allowable business investment losses/64

4.4 The capital gains exemption/65

4.4.1 Qualified small business corporation shares/65

4.4.2 Qualified farm property/66

4.4.3 Restrictions on use of the exemption/67

4.4.3.1 Capital losses deducted against regular income/67

4.4.3.2 Cumulative net investment loss (CNIL)/67

4.4.4 The $100,000 exemption and the election as of February 22, 1994/69

4.5 Special cases/71

4.5.1 Pre-1972 property/71

4.5.2 Reserves/71

4.5.3 Principal residence/71

4.5.4 Death/72

4.5.5 Other rules/73

4.6 Planning opportunities/74

4.6.1 Gains and losses — income or capital/74

4.6.2 Canadian securities election/75

4.6.3 Use loss carryforward and carryback/75

4.6.4 Consider filing late election to use capital gains exemption/75

4.6.5 Delay all or part of an asset sale until after year-end/77

4.6.6 Transfer securities to RRSP/77

4.6.7 Claim capital gains reserve/77

4.6.8 Change principal residence ownership/78

4.6.9 Use exemption for qualified small business corporation shares/78

4.6.10 Make election to treat rented-out property as principal residence/78

4.6.11 Emigration — elect to trigger exemption/79

4.6.12 Plan around your CNIL balance/79

4.6.13 Keep at least 1 unit of investments with exempt capital gains balance/79

4.7 References/80

5. Investments and Tax Shelters/83

5.1 Dividends/83

5.1.1 What is a dividend?/83

5.1.2 How is a dividend taxed?/83

5.1.3 Special cases/84

5.1.3.1 Stock dividends/84

5.1.3.2 Capital dividends/85

5.1.3.3 Dividends received by a corporation/85

5.1.3.4 Mutual funds/85

5.1.3.5 Election to transfer dividends from spouse/85

5.2 Interest income/86

5.2.1 General rule/86

5.2.2 Accruing interest/86

5.2.3 Stripped bonds and clipped coupons/87

5.3 Deductibility of interest expense/87

5.4 Tax shelters/88

5.4.1 Tax shelter identification number/89
5.4.2 Limited partnerships/89
5.4.3 Limited partnerships used to finance mutual fund commissions/90
5.4.4 Films and television productions/91
5.4.5 Resource activities/92
5.4.6 Business ventures/92
5.4.7 Commodity straddles/93
5.4.8 Real estate investments/93
5.4.9 Labour-sponsored venture capital corporations/93

5.5 Trusts/94

5.6 Exempt life insurance contracts/94

5.7 Planning opportunities/94
5.7.1 Structure investments to make interest deductible/94
5.7.2 Acquire investments to mature after year-end/95
5.7.3 Buy preferred shares/95
5.7.4 Set up trust for children/95
5.7.5 Consider investments in tax shelters/96
5.7.6 Look into investing in a labour-sponsored venture capital corporation/96
5.7.7 Acquire an exempt life insurance contract/97
5.7.8 Use exempt capital gains balance for mutual funds/97

5.8 References/97

6. IF YOU ARE EMPLOYED/999

6.1 Employment benefits/99
6.1.1 Non-taxable employment benefits/99
6.1.2 Taxable employment benefits/100

6.2 Loans to employees/101

6.3 Stock option plans/103

6.4 Company automobiles/104

6.5 Deferred compensation/105

6.6 Retiring allowances and severance pay/106

6.7 Death benefits/106

6.8 Overseas employment tax credit/106

6.9 Deductions from employment income/107
6.9.1 Using your own automobile for employment/107
6.9.2 Travelling expenses/109
6.9.3 Commission sales person's expenses/109
6.9.4 Supplies, assistant's salary and home office/110
6.9.5 Union and professional dues/110
6.9.6 Legal fees/110

6.9.7 Musicians' instruments/111
6.9.8 Artists' expenses/111
6.9.9 Northern employees/111

6.10 Planning Opportunities/112
6.10.1 Arrange to get non-taxable benefits/112
6.10.2 Where possible, request reduction of source withholdings/112
6.10.3 Pay interest owing on loan from employer within 30 days of end of year/113
6.10.4 Consider employees' profit-sharing plan/113
6.10.5 Transfer retiring allowances to an RRSP/113
6.10.6 Set up stock option plan/114
6.10.7 Consider a stock purchase plan/114
6.10.8 Consider a phantom stock plan/114
6.10.9 Keep track of business use of car/115
6.10.10 Take steps to minimize taxable benefit from car operating costs/115
6.10.11 Avoid expensive employer-owned vehicles/115
6.10.12 Reduce time company car is available for personal use/116
6.10.13 Maximize employment-related use of car/116

6.11 References/116

7. If You Are Self-Employed/119
7.1 Employee or independent contractor?/119
7.2 Taxation of the business/121
7.2.1 Business year-end/121
7.2.2 Business income and expenses/122
7.2.3 UI, CPP and other payroll taxes/123
7.2.4 Capital cost allowance/124
7.2.5 Automobiles/124
7.2.6 Meals and entertainment/125
7.2.7 Home office expenses/126
7.2.8 Capital gains/127
7.2.9 Investment tax credits/127

7.3 Partnership/128
7.3.1 How partnership income is taxed/128
7.3.2 Adjustment of partnership allocation/128
7.3.3 Capital gains/129
7.3.4 Allocation of investment tax credits/129
7.3.5 Gain or loss on partnership interest/129
7.3.6 Assessment of partnership/130

7.4 Business losses/130

7.5 Planning opportunities/131
7.5.1 Arrange to be a consultant rather than employed/131

7.5.2 Maximize income for "stub period" ending December 31, 1995/131
7.5.3 Deduct transportation expenses/132
7.5.4 Automobile planning tips/132
7.5.5 Claim business meals and entertainment expenses/133
7.5.6 Write off home office expenses/133
7.5.7 Pay salary or consulting fee to spouse or children, or bring spouse into partnership/133
7.5.8 Use loss carryovers/133
7.5.9 Acquire capital assets before year-end/133
7.5.10 Consider claiming less CCA than the maximum/134
7.6 References/134

8. IF YOU HAVE YOUR OWN CORPORATION/137
8.1 Taxation of the corporation/137
8.2 Ways of extracting funds from the corporation/138
8.2.1 Dividends/138
8.2.2 Salary/139
8.2.3 Payments on loans from shareholders/139
8.2.4 Capital dividends/140
8.2.5 Repayment of capital/140
8.2.6 Loan to shareholder/141
8.2.7 Deemed dividends/142
8.2.8 Shareholder appropriations/142
8.3 Effect of having a holding company/142
8.4 Shareholders' agreements/143
8.5 Pension plans for small business owners/144
8.6 Investment income earned in a corporation/144
8.7 Selling the business/144
8.8 Planning opportunities/145
8.8.1 Pay salary to spouse and children/145
8.8.2 Defer income to the next calendar year by accruing bonuses/145
8.8.3 Calculate optimum salary/dividend mix/146
8.8.4 Maximize capital dividend payments/146
8.8.5 Consider repayment of capital/146
8.8.6 Keep the corporation a small business corporation, or crystallize your capital gains exemption/147
8.8.7 Consider a holding corporation/147
8.8.8 Consider corporate partnerships/148
8.8.9 Multiply capital gains exemption/148
8.8.10 Consider an individual pension plan/148
8.8.11 Be cautious about keeping investments in a corporation/149
8.9 References/149

9. FARMING/151
- 9.1 Farming — a business or not?/151
- 9.2 Computing farming income/152
  - 9.2.1 The cash method/152
  - 9.2.2 Purchase of inventory/153
  - 9.2.3 Cost of improving land for farming/153
  - 9.2.4 Sales of livestock in a drought region/153
  - 9.2.5 Forced destruction of livestock/154
  - 9.2.6 Net income stabilization account (NISA)/154
- 9.3 Farming losses/154
  - 9.3.1 Ordinary farm losses/154
  - 9.3.2 Restricted farm losses/154
- 9.4 Investment tax credits/155
- 9.5 Transfers of farming assets/155
  - 9.5.1 Capital gains exemption/155
  - 9.5.2 Transfer to children or grandchildren/155
  - 9.5.3 Principal residence exemption/156
  - 9.5.4 Capital gains reserve on sale of farm to child/156
- 9.6 Planning opportunities/157
  - 9.6.1 Establish that your business has a reasonable expectation of profit/157
  - 9.6.2 Classify farming as chief source of income/157
  - 9.6.3 Claim deductions available for the self-employed/157
  - 9.6.4 Make use of special rules for calculating farm income/157
  - 9.6.5 Use the $500,000 capital gains exemption/157
  - 9.6.6 Take advantage of intergenerational transfer rules/158
  - 9.6.7 Claim alternative principal residence exemption where appropriate/158
- 9.7 References/158

10. PROFESSIONALS/161
- 10.1 Specific rules that apply to professionals/161
  - 10.1.1 The modified accrual method of accounting for income/161
  - 10.1.2 1971 receivables/162
  - 10.1.3 Professional corporations/163
- 10.2 Specific rules that apply to partnerships/163
  - 10.2.1 Deductibility of interest paid by the partnership/163
  - 10.2.2 Income payments to retired partners/163
- 10.3 Planning opportunities/164
  - 10.3.1 Elect the modified accrual method/164
  - 10.3.2 Adjust billings and drawings to maximize 1971 receivables/164
  - 10.3.3 Maximize interest deductibility/165

10.3.4 Pay retiring partner income or capital as appropriate/165
10.3.5 Considering paying club dues at partnership level/165
10.3.6 Incorporate your business if you work on certain overseas projects/166
10.4 References/166

11. MINIMUM TAX/167
11.1 Outline/167
11.2 Calculating the tax/167
11.3 Minimum tax carryover/168
11.4 Planning considerations/169
11.4.1 Have 35 cents regular income for each $1 in exempt capital gains/169
11.4.2 Continue generating interest expense and business losses/169
11.4.3 Watch out for RRSP deductions/169
11.4.4 Limit "tainted" tax shelter deductions/170
11.5 References/170

12. ESTATE PLANNING/171
12.1 Taxes on death/171
12.1.1 Tax payable by the estate/171
12.1.2 Deemed disposition of capital property/172
12.1.3 Probate fees/173
12.1.4 Death benefits/174
12.2 The Will/174
12.2.1 Purpose of a will/174
12.2.2 The Executor/174
12.3 Trusts/175
12.3.1 What is a trust?/175
12.3.2 What kinds of trusts are there?/176
12.3.3 Why would I use a trust?/176
12.3.4 How is a trust taxed?/176
12.4 Family law/177
12.5 Estate freezing/178
12.5.1 What is an estate freeze?/178
12.5.2 How does one freeze an estate?/178
12.5.3 Benefits of an estate freeze/179
12.6 Life insurance/180
12.7 Charitable gifts and bequests/181
12.7.1 The tax credit for charitable donations/181
12.7.2 Gifts to the Crown/182
12.7.3 Gifts in kind/182

12.7.4 Gifts of cultural property / 183
12.7.5 Gifts of life insurance / 183
12.7.6 Purchasing an annuity from a charity / 184
12.7.7 Charitable issued annuity / 184
12.7.8 Charitable remainder trusts / 185

12.8 Planning opportunities / 185
12.8.1 Make a will (or review your existing will) / 186
12.8.2 Consider an estate freeze / 187
12.8.3 Consider setting up a family trust / 187
12.8.4 Take steps to minimize probate fees / 188
12.8.5 Make sure you have sufficient insurance / 188
12.8.6 Consider planning charitable gifts or bequests / 189
12.8.7 Plan for the succession of your business / 189
12.8.8 Consider effects of foreign estate taxes / 190

12.9 References / 190

13. Dealing with Revenue Canada / 193

13.1 Tax returns / 193
13.1.1 General / 193
13.1.2 Electronic filing of tax returns (EFILE) / 194

13.2 Payment of tax / 194
13.2.1 Source withholdings / 194
13.2.2 Instalments / 195
13.2.3 Payment of balance / 196
13.2.4 "Direct deposit" of refunds / 196

13.3 Interest / 197

13.4 Assessment, audit and reassessment / 198
13.4.1 "Quick" assessment / 198
13.4.2 Audit / 198
13.4.3 Reassessment / 199

13.5 Objections and appeals / 199
13.5.1 Notice of Objection / 199
13.5.2 Appeal to the Tax Court / 200
13.5.3 Appeal beyond the Tax Court / 200

13.6 Planning opportunities / 201
13.6.1 File return even if you can't pay balance; pay balance by April 30 even if filing late / 201
13.6.2 File with EFILE for quick refund / 201
13.6.3 Be aware of interest rates and compounding / 201
13.6.4 Consider prepayments of instalments / 202
13.6.5 File notice of objection where appropriate / 202
13.6.6 Claim changes when return reopened on reassessment / 202

13.6.7 Sign a waiver only to the extent necessary/202
13.6.8 Be sure you understand the legal issues when appealing/203
13.6.9 Consider paying balance even when objecting or appealing/203
13.7 References/204

14. QUÉBEC TAXATION/205
14.1 Québec income tax rates/205
14.2 Differences from federal tax/205
14.2.1 Child-care expenses/206
14.2.2 Legal fees re variance of alimony payments/206
14.2.3 Senior citizens/207
14.2.4 Charitable donations/207
14.2.5 Tuition fees/208
14.2.6 Person living alone/208
14.2.7 Adults housing "direct ascendants"/208
14.2.8 Allowance for children/209
14.2.9 Adoption expenses/209
14.2.10 Medical expenses/209
14.2.11 Political contributions/210
14.2.12 Real estate tax refund/210
14.2.13 Registered Home Ownership Savings Plans (RHOSPs)/210
14.2.14 "First home" refundable tax credit/211
14.2.15 Québec sales credit/212
14.2.16 Cumulative net investment loss/212
14.2.17 Resource exploration expenses/213
14.2.18 Employer-paid health insurance/213
14.2.19 Overseas employment tax deduction/213
14.2.20 Artists' deduction from copyright income/214
14.2.21 Rental expenses — documentation/214
14.2.22 Minimum tax/214
14.2.23 Instalments/214
14.2.24 Health services fund contribution/215
14.3 Special Québec incentives/215
14.3.1 Québec Stock Savings Plan (QSSP or REA)/215
14.3.1.1 What is a QSSP?/215
14.3.1.2 What kinds of shares qualify?/216
14.3.1.3 How much can you deduct?/216
14.3.1.4 What happens when you sell the shares?/217
14.3.1.5 Investment clubs and investment funds/217
14.3.2 Québec Business Investment Companies (QBIC or SPEQ)/217
14.3.2.1 What is a QBIC?/217
14.3.2.2 What can a QBIC invest in?/218
14.3.2.3 How much can you deduct?/218

14.3.3 Cooperative investment plans (CIP or RIC)/219
14.3.4 Labour-sponsored venture capital corporation (FSTQ or FTQ)/219
14.3.5 Worker gain sharing plans/220

14.4 Québec sales tax/220
14.4.1 The tax rate/221
14.4.2 Categories of sales/221
14.4.3 Input tax refunds/221
14.4.4 Administration/222
14.4.5 Miscellaneous rules/222

14.5 Planning opportunities/223
14.5.1 Be aware of differences in the tax systems/223
14.5.2 Purchase home furnishings with RHOSP funds/224
14.5.3 Invest in FSTQ or the new CNTU fund and transfer shares to RRSP/224
14.5.4 Claim credit for housing "direct ascendants"/224
14.5.5 Claim refundable credit if you adopt a child/224
14.5.6 Senior citizens — consider hiring domestic help/224
14.5.7 Claim refundable credit for "first-time" home buyers/225

14.6 References/225

15. U.S. CITIZENS/227

15.1 Two systems of taxation/227

15.2 Basic mechanisms for avoiding double taxation/229
15.2.1 Foreign earned income exclusion (U.S. tax law)/229
15.2.2 Foreign tax credit (both U.S. and Canadian law)/230
15.2.3 Canada-U.S. tax treaty/231

15.3 Differences in calculating income/232
15.3.1 Deductions on U.S. return that are not available in Canada/232
15.3.2 Deductions on Canadian return that are not available in the U.S./232
15.3.3 Limitations on U.S. deductions for high-income taxpayers/233
15.3.4 Retirement and profit-sharing plans/234
15.3.5 Dividends/235
15.3.6 Charitable donations/235
15.3.7 Moving expenses/235

15.4 Differences in taxation of capital gains/236
15.4.1 Basic calculation/236
15.4.2 Use of capital losses/236
15.4.3 The Canadian capital gains exemption/237
15.4.4 Reserves vs. instalment sales/237
15.4.5 Foreign exchange gains or losses/237
15.4.6 Pre-1972 holdings/238

15.4.7 Principal residence/238
15.4.8 Immigration to and emigration from Canada/239
15.4.9 Other capital gains differences/240

15.5 Minimum tax/240

15.6 Income earned by children/241
15.6.1 Effect on dependant rules/241
15.6.2 Attribution rules/241

15.7 U.S. filing requirements/242
15.7.1 Joint return or not?/242
15.7.2 Time requirements for filing/242
15.7.3 Estimated taxes/243
15.7.4 Disclosure requirements/243
15.7.5 U.S. passport renewals/244

15.8 U.S. estate and gift taxes/244
15.8.1 Estate tax/244
15.8.2 Gift tax/245

15.9 Planning opportunities/246
15.9.1 File joint return where appropriate/246
15.9.2 Review income splitting arrangements to prevent double taxation/246
15.9.3 Watch out for Canadian ownership of Canadian mutual funds or other Canadian corporations earning passive income/246
15.9.4 Keep records of expenses deductible on your U.S. return/247
15.9.5 Claim foreign earned income exclusion if beneficial/247
15.9.6 Aim for maximum foreign tax credit/247
15.9.7 Watch out for AMT liability/248
15.9.8 Elect out of instalment sale rules where appropriate/248
15.9.9 Be cautious of using the $500,000 capital gains exemption/248
15.9.10 Consider steps to take on departure from Canada/248
15.9.11 Plan for U.S. estate and gift taxes/249
15.9.12 Watch shareholder-corporation transactions/249
15.9.13 Beware of differences in rules governing retirement income/249
15.9.14 Seek professional tax advice before moving to Canada/249

15.10 References/250

16. U.S. RESIDENCY AND OWNERSHIP OF U.S. PROPERTY/253

16.1 Income from U.S. properties/253
16.1.1 Rent from real estate/254
16.1.2 Dividends and interest from U.S. corporations/254

16.2 Sale of U.S. properties/254
16.2.1 Sale of real estate/254
16.2.1.1 Withholding tax (FIRPTA)/254
16.2.1.2 Income tax/255

16.2.2 Sales of U.S. stocks and bonds/256

16.3 Snowbirds — U.S. residency rules/256

16.4 U.S. estate taxes on death/257

16.4.1 Determination of property subject to estate tax/257

16.4.2 U.S. federal estate tax rates/258

16.4.3 Unified credit/258

16.4.4 Interaction with Canadian tax/259

16.5 Planning opportunities/261

16.5.1 Elect net rental income method/261

16.5.2 Sell real estate to buyer who will occupy it as principal residence/262

16.5.3 Apply for U.S. withholding certificate on sale of real estate/262

16.5.4 Be cautious about keeping artwork and other assets in the U.S./262

16.5.5 Be cautious when acquiring shares in U.S. corporations/262

16.5.6 Hold property through Canadian corporation/263

16.5.7 Leave property to spouse or qualified domestic trust/263

16.5.8 Acquire property jointly with spouse or other person/264

16.5.9 Sell U.S. property before death/264

16.5.10 Take out life insurance to cover estate taxes/265

16.5.11 Mortgage property (non-recourse) to reduce value of U.S. real estate/265

16.5.12 Acquire the U.S. property through irrevocable Canadian trust/266

16.5.13 Consider the effects of the protocol in your situation/266

16.5.14 Avoid becoming a U.S. resident while visiting/266

16.6 References/266

17. THE GOODS AND SERVICES TAX/269

17.1 How does the GST work?/269

17.2 What does GST not cover?/271

17.2.1 Zero-rated supplies/271

17.2.2 Exempt supplies/271

17.2.3 Small suppliers/272

17.3 GST and business/273

17.3.1 Claiming input tax credits/273

17.3.2 The "quick method" and simplified accounting/273

17.3.3 Other miscellaneous rules/274

17.4 Rebates/275

17.5 Administration/277

17.6 Provincial sales taxes/277

17.7 Importing goods/278

17.8 Transitional rules/278

17.9 Planning tips/278

17.9.1 If you own a business/278
17.9.2 Consider GST when purchasing a home/279
17.9.3 If you own rental real estate/279
17.9.4 Employees and partners should claim GST rebates/280
17.9.5 Planning around GST on employment benefits/280
17.9.6 Get credit for GST when trading in a used car/280
17.9.7 Purchases from small suppliers/281
17.9.8 Be aware of GST on food/281
17.9.9 If you have friends or relatives visiting from outside Canada/281
17.9.10 Claim the GST credit/282

17.10 References/282

APPENDICES/281

Appendix I —1995 Personal Tax Credits/281

Appendix II —1995 Federal Income Tax Rates/283
1995 Provincial Income Tax Rates/283

Appendix III—1995 Québec Provincial Income Tax Rates/285
1995 Combined Federal and Québec Tax Rates/285

Appendix IV—Worksheets for Estimating 1995 Tax Liability/287
Schedule 1— Estimated 1995 Net Income/287
Schedule 2— Estimated 1995 Tax Payable/288
Schedule 3— Calculation of Tax on OAS Benefits/289
Schedule 4— Calculation of Personal Tax Credits/290
Schedule 5— Tax Credits Transferred from Other Taxpayers/291
Schedule 6— Estimated 1995 Minimum Tax Exposure/292

Appendix V —1995 Dividend/Interest Yield Comparison/293

TOPICAL INDEX/295

QUICK LOOKUP TABLE—DOLLAR AMOUNTS/311

INTRODUCTION

What is tax planning?

Tax planning is a perfectly legitimate activity. It is neither illegal nor immoral. You are entitled to arrange your affairs, within the limits of the law, so that you pay a minimum amount of tax. The government accepts this principle.

Tax planning is not **tax evasion.** Evasion is illegal. You are evading tax if you fail to report income or if you misstate facts so as to claim deductions or credits to which you are not entitled. If you evade tax, you will be subject to interest, penalties, fines and possibly imprisonment as well as being required to pay the tax owing.

Tax avoidance is the somewhat nebulous activity of using the tax system in a way in which it was not intended. The *Income Tax Act* contains a general anti-avoidance rule (GAAR), which can apply to avoidance activities. If you misuse or abuse the provisions of the *Income Tax Act*, you may run into GAAR. The line between tax planning and tax avoidance is not always clear.

Note that Revenue Canada does *not* make the law. The *Income Tax Act* is enacted and amended by Parliament. Revenue Canada's role is to administer and enforce the Act. In this book we will occasionally refer to "Revenue Canada's position" on a particular matter, to indicate that this is an administrative position rather than a matter of law.

If you disagree with Revenue Canada's interpretation of a particular rule, and you have a good legal basis for doing so, you are perfectly within your rights to object to an assessment or reassessment by filing a Notice of Objection, and, if you wish, appealing the case to the Tax Court of Canada.

What can this book do for you?

In this book we have set out the most common rules and tax planning techniques available to individuals. Tax planning is a **year-round** activity, not something you do just in February or April. You will find that a few hours invested in reading this book and understanding the tax system can pay off substantially in tax savings and in the organization of your financial affairs.

The book is organized into 17 chapters. In each chapter we present an explanation of the topic covered, followed by tax planning tips. You may wish to skip the detail and go directly to the "Planning opportunities" section. We feel, however, that you can best understand the effectiveness of planning techniques only if you *first* understand the underlying rules.

At the end of each chapter we include references to Revenue Canada publications that are available from your local District Taxation Office (or, for GST publications, from your local Regional Excise Office). These publications are a good source of more detailed information on the topics discussed.

At the end of the book are Appendices that will let you work out an estimate of your 1995 tax, taking provincial taxation into account.

What can this book not do?

This book cannot replace your tax adviser. Even if your affairs are relatively simple, you should consult a qualified tax professional (not just a tax return preparer). You will likely find the savings far outweigh the fees.

This book deals only in general terms. The Canadian tax system is horrendously complex, far more than the book makes it appear. The details fill shelves, not a thin book. You can consult the reference materials for more information, but you should also consult your tax adviser with respect to any planned activities.

The book does not go very far in dealing with the tax treatment of businesses, whether incorporated or unincorporated. Only brief treatment is given to this topic in Chapters 7 and 8. If you carry on your own business, or manage a corporation, you will benefit greatly from personalized professional advice.

The income tax system has been subjected to massive and rapid change over the past few years, and the process continues. If you thought you knew the rules a couple of years ago, you may find they have changed. We also cannot predict what changes are in store for the future. This book is current to August 31, 1995, and reflects the law and publicly-announced proposals for change as of that date.

KPMG Peat Marwick Thorne

Chartered Accountants

1 Tips for Your Tax Return

Planning Tips

- Claim married-equivalent credit
- Family planning
- Claim moving expenses
- Higher-income spouse should claim credits to reduce high-income surtaxes
- Medical expense credit—spouse and year-end options
- Medical expenses—claim for dependants
- Minimize joint tax bill if you are separating
- Investigate whether you can claim the disability credit
- Plan for at least $1,000 of pension income per person
- Political contributions
- Charitable donations

In this chapter we highlight both the most commonly available, and the sometimes not well known, deductions and credits that can be claimed on your income tax return.

1.1 Background

1.1.1 The tax calculation

To understand how deductions and credits function, you need to understand the basic tax calculation. We'll describe it briefly here. (For Québec residents, the *provincial* tax calculation is completely separate and not as described below. See Chapter 14.)

You start by adding up your various kinds of income: employment, business, interest, grossed-up dividends, taxable capital gains, etc. This gives you **total income**. From this figure you subtract certain deductions, some of which we'll look at in 1.2, and reach **net income**. The net income figure is used for certain purposes later. Then some additional deductions are allowed, primarily loss carryforwards and the capital gains deduction (see 4.4), giving you **taxable income**.

You then look up your **federal tax** in the tax table, or calculate it using the formula shown on Schedule 1 of your tax return. Then you subtract various **non-refundable tax credits** (see 1.3), and certain others such as the dividend tax credit (see 5.1). This gives you **basic federal tax**.

To the basic federal tax figure you add the **federal surtax** (3% of basic federal tax, plus an additional surtax of 5% for high-income earners). You also add the **provincial or territorial tax**, which is a percentage (anywhere from 45% to 69%, varying by province or territory) *of the basic federal tax*. Then, depending on the province, you may also have to add a provincial surtax and/or flat tax. If you are self-employed, you may also be required to add your Canada Pension Plan contribution on your self-employment income at this point.

Next, you claim as a credit any other non-refundable credits that are federal only (see 1.4), and you end up with two figures: your federal tax for the year and your provincial tax for the year.

Finally, you record all source deductions of tax (withheld by your employer, for example) and instalments paid, both of which are credited to your account. Along with these are the **refundable credits** (see 1.5), which are given the same treatment so that they can effectively be refunded to you even if you pay no tax for the year. (Some of the provinces also provide refundable tax credits.) The bottom line is your **balance due** or **refund claimed**, and that will be the cheque you send in on April 30 or receive when your return is assessed.

You can see why the non-refundable credits are given that name. They can reduce your tax to zero, but they are not paid to you if you have no tax to pay for the year. They *can* trigger a refund, however, in the sense of refunding tax that was taken off at source or paid by instalment.

1.1.2 DEDUCTION VERSUS CREDIT

Before we get into the specific deductions and credits available, you need to understand the different effects of a deduction and a credit. You can refer back to the calculation in 1.1.1 as we go through this.

A **deduction** reduces your taxable income, on which your federal tax is calculated. The combined effect of the federal and provincial taxes and surtaxes means that, as long as you are still paying some tax, a deduction is worth about 27% where your taxable income is under $29,590; about 41% where it is between $29,590 and $59,180; and about 50% where it is over $59,180.

In other words, a $100 writeoff (of, say, deductible moving or child-care expenses) is worth about $27 to $50 in tax savings, depending on your tax bracket.

A **credit**, on the other hand, is a direct reduction in tax. $100 of a credit such as the credit for political contributions (1.4.1 below) is worth exactly $100 to you.

There is a twist, however. Most of the credits are calculated as part of getting to basic federal tax, *before provincial tax and federal surtax are calculated*. As a result, these credits are worth about 50-75% more than they would otherwise be, because the provincial tax, provincial surtaxes and federal surtax are reduced as well.

EXAMPLE

*Richard calculates his federal tax for 1995 as being $6,000. Federal surtax is 3% of federal tax. Richard lives in Ontario where the provincial tax is 58% of the federal tax, so his total tax bill is **$9,660** ($6,000 federal tax, $180 federal surtax and $3,480 provincial tax).*

*Richard discovers that he is able to claim an additional credit, which he had not thought of. The credit is $100 against federal tax. Now his federal tax is $5,900, the 3% surtax is only $177 and his provincial tax is 58% of $5,900, or $3,422. His total tax bill is now **$9,499**.*

As you can see, the $100 federal credit is actually worth $161 because of the reduced surtax and provincial tax—even though there is no explicit provincial credit to be claimed. The additional $61 is actually 3% + 58% (the federal surtax and provincial tax rate) on the $100. (The impact of provincial surtaxes can magnify this effect still more.)

Finally, note the distinction between refundable and non-refundable credits. Because they are treated as having been paid by you, just like source withholdings and instalments, refundable credits are always worth what they say they are. Non-refundable credits, like deductions, become worthless once you reach the point of paying no tax at all for the year.

1.2 Deductions

We'll now look at a selected group of deductions—worth anywhere from 27% to over 50% (depending on your income and your province of residence) of the amount you deduct.

1.2.1 Alimony and maintenance

Alimony and maintenance payments (including spousal and child support) are *deductible* to the payer and *taxable* to the recipient if they meet a number of well-defined and strict criteria. This is generally of benefit to the separating or divorcing couple, since the person making the payments is often in a higher tax bracket than the recipient.

Note that your ability to claim a deduction does not depend on whether the recipient actually reports the income. Provided you meet all of the requirements, you can go ahead and claim the deduction, and it is up to Revenue Canada to take action if the recipient does not include the payments for tax purposes.

To be deductible, any payments must be an *allowance* which has been established in advance as a recurring payment. The amounts payable must be predetermined. (However, if they are required to be adjusted for inflation, they can still be considered predetermined.)

The further requirements are:

- the allowance must be paid under a written agreement or under a decree, order or judgment of a competent tribunal; and
- it must be payable on a periodic basis for the maintenance of the recipient (your spouse or ex-spouse) and/or the children of the marriage; and
- you must be living apart from your spouse or ex-spouse, at the time the payment is made and throughout the rest of the year. If the payments are alimony (rather than maintenance) and the marriage breakdown occurred before 1993, you must also be separated pursuant to a divorce, judicial separation or a written separation agreement.

Payments to former **common-law spouses** may be deducted on the same basis, where the recipient is an individual of the opposite sex who cohabited with you "in a conjugal relationship" or you are the natural parent of that person's child. However, if the common-law breakup occurred before 1993, the maintenance payments must be paid under a court order to be deductible.

Note that the "periodic basis" requirement excludes one-time payments and transfers of property in settlement of rights of the marriage.

Payments made directly to third parties, rather than to your spouse or ex-spouse, are allowed in limited circumstances. Such payments can include medical bills, tuition fees and mortgage payments for your spouse or ex-spouse's home. Among other requirements, the court order or written separation agreement must specifically provide for the payments and must specifically provide that the relevant provisions of the *Income Tax Act* will apply, to make the payments deductible to you and taxable to your spouse or ex-spouse. For court orders and agreements made after 1992, these rules also apply to most common-law relationships.

In general, you also may deduct payments made **before obtaining a court order or signing a written separation agreement**, provided the order or agreement is signed by the end of the year following the year in which the payment is made, and that it specifically provides that the amounts paid earlier are to be considered as paid and received pursuant to the agreement.

If you pay alimony or maintenance to a **non-resident** of Canada, you must withhold a percentage of each payment (up to 25%, depending on the recipient's country of residence and the terms of any tax treaty between Canada and that country) and remit it to Revenue Canada.

If you **receive** alimony or maintenance payments in circumstances where they are deductible to the payer, they are taxable to you (subject to change resulting from the *Thibaudeau* case, as discussed below). If you receive child support from a resident of the **United States**, however, it will not be taxed due to the Canada-U.S. tax treaty (see 15.2.3).

In May 1994, the Federal Court of Appeal ruled, in the *Thibaudeau* case, that the rule requiring child support to be included into income was a violation of the *Charter of Rights* and therefore unconstitutional. However, on May 25, 1995, the Supreme Court of Canada reversed that decision. Thus, you must include child support into income as required by the *Income Tax Act.* However, proposals for change to the system of taxation of support payments may soon be released by the federal government.

1.2.2 Moving expenses

Moving expenses are often overlooked as a deduction. If you start working at a new location of employment, or start a new business, and you move to a home that is 40 km closer to your new work location than was your old home (to the new work location), you can deduct very substantial amounts for tax purposes. However, expenses incurred in moving from another country to Canada, or from Canada to another country, are not deductible for Canadian tax purposes.

Except to the extent you are reimbursed by your employer, you can deduct the following:

- reasonable travelling costs, including meals and lodging, to move you and the members of your household
- the moving costs for your household effects, including storage charges
- the cost of meals and lodging near either the old or the new home for up to 15 days
- lease cancellation costs
- selling costs in respect of your old home, *including real estate commissions*
- where you are selling your old home, the legal fees and land transfer tax payable when you buy a new home. (GST was allowable as well, but due to a retroactive change introduced in April 1995, any GST you pay on buying your new home will not be allowed, even for past years going back to 1991.)

The real estate commissions alone can easily run into many thousands of dollars.

Students can also claim moving expenses, if they move when they begin a job (including a summer job) or start a business. If they are moving to attend full-time post-secondary education (whether or not in Canada), they can deduct the expenses, but only to the extent they have scholarship or research grant income.

1.2.3 CHILD-CARE EXPENSES

Subject to various limitations, child-care expenses can be deducted, usually by the spouse with the **lower income**. (The assumption is that the lower-income spouse would otherwise stay home with the children.) Child-care expenses include babysitting, day nursery services, day camps, boarding schools and camps.

For child-care expenses to be claimed, they have to have been made to allow you or your spouse to work, to carry on business, to take an occupational training course or to carry on grant-funded research.

Assuming you are the lower-income spouse, the deduction for child-care expenses is limited to $5,000 times the number of your children who are under seven at the end of the year, plus $3,000 times the number of children seven and over but under 14. It is also limited to two-thirds of your "earned income" (basically salary and business income). The deduction is based on when the services are provided rather than when the amounts are paid, so prepaying in December does not give you the deduction a year earlier.

Payments to a boarding school or camp are limited to $150 per week that the child attends the school or camp, for children under seven, and $90 per week for children over seven but under 14.

EXAMPLE

Rick and Arlene are married and have two children under seven. Rick earns $70,000 and Arlene earns $21,000. They pay $12,000 in 1995 to a nanny to take care of their children while they are working.

Arlene must be the one to claim the expenses, since she is the lower-income spouse. Her deduction is the least of: (a) the amount paid—$12,000; (b) $5,000 per child—$10,000; and (c) two-thirds of her earned income—$14,000. She can therefore claim $10,000 as a deduction against her $21,000 of employment income. This will reduce her tax bill by about $2,700.

Where a child aged seven or over is **disabled**, special rules allow a deduction as though the child were under seven. The age 14 limit also does not apply.

There are also special circumstances where the lower-income spouse is not expected to care for the children. These are: where the spouse is **disabled**; where the spouse is in **prison** or **hospital**, or confined to **bed** or a **wheelchair**, for at least two weeks; where the spouse attends full-time **post-secondary education**; or where the spouses have **separated**. In such cases, the higher-income spouse can claim the deduction for up to $150 per child under seven ($90 per child seven and over) for each week that the condition continues.

Common-law couples who meet certain criteria are treated the same as spouses for purposes of calculating child-care expenses, as well as for all other purposes of the *Income Tax Act*. See 1.3.1.

In the past, some taxpayers claimed child-care expenses as business expenses, based on a 1989 Federal Court decision (the *Symes* case). The Supreme Court of Canada ruled in that case in December 1993 that child care cannot be claimed as business expenses. If you made this claim in past years, expect it to be disallowed by Revenue Canada if it is found on audit.

1.2.4 ATTENDANT FOR DISABLED PERSON

There is a deduction of up to $5,000 for the costs of an attendant needed to allow a disabled person to earn income. The deduction is limited to two-thirds of the disabled person's "earned income" (basically salary and business income). As an alternative, expenses of an attendant can generally be claimed for purposes of the medical expense credit (see 1.3.5), even where the disabled person is not earning income.

For disabled people with income over about $30,000, the deduction is more useful than claiming the attendant as a medical expense. At a high level of income, a deduction from income is worth more than a 27% credit against taxes payable (see 1.1.2). However, because of the $5,000 limit, a full-time attendant is generally more usefully claimed as a medical expense credit. (For example, a 27% credit on $15,000 is more valuable than a deduction worth 50% of $5,000.)

1.2.5 LEGAL FEES

The tax treatment of legal fees you pay depends on why you are paying them.

First, legal fees are generally deductible if they are paid for the purpose of earning income from business or property. Legal fees to acquire or preserve a capital asset are normally not deductible, though there are a number of exceptions.

Second, legal fees associated with an objection or appeal of your income tax assessment (see 13.5) are deductible. This includes the costs of negotiations with Revenue Canada officials prior to filing a formal Notice of Objection. The fees are also deductible if you are appealing a Québec income tax assessment or an income tax assessment of a foreign government, or an Unemployment Insurance or Canada/Québec Pension Plan decision.

Third, legal fees to collect unpaid salary or wages owed to you by your employer or former employer are deductible.

Fourth, legal fees can be deducted where they are incurred to obtain a "retiring allowance" (including severance pay) or a pension benefit (see 6.9.6), but only up to a limit of your income from those sources (in the current year or past years).

Finally, legal fees to enforce an existing right to alimony or maintenance that is taxable in your hands (see 1.2.1 above) are deductible. They are not deductible, however, when incurred to *establish* a right to alimony or maintenance, except for maintenance for which you must sue your spouse or former spouse in a Family Court or under certain provincial legislation.

1.2.6 NORTHERN RESIDENTS

If you live in northern Canada, a special deduction is available to help offset the higher costs of living and the hardship and isolation relative to the more populated parts of the country. The deduction is limited to 20% of your net income.

If you live in the "prescribed northern zone", the deduction is $15 per day ($5,475 per year). If you live somewhat further south, in the "prescribed intermediate zone", you can only claim half as much. As well, if your employer pays the cost of travel for you and your family (e.g., an annual trip to southern Canada), a deduction is available to offset part or all of the taxable benefit that is thereby included in your income. See 6.9.9.

1.2.7 OTHER DEDUCTIONS

Some other common deductions are covered in other chapters. See, for example, 2.1.3 (contributions to RRSPs), 4.3.2 (allowable business investment losses), 4.4 (capital gains deduction), 5.3 (interest paid) and 6.9 (deductions available to employees). Some of the deductions relating to self-employment (carrying on business) are discussed in Chapter 7.

1.3 NON-REFUNDABLE CREDITS WITH PROVINCIAL COMPONENT

Each of the credits in 1.3.1 to 1.3.3 below is actually worth about 1.6 times the amount stated, after the effect of the credit on provincial tax and on the federal surtax have been taken into account. A table summarizing the credits can be found in Appendix I.

Most of the credits are worded in terms of 17% of something. That is because 17% is the rate of federal tax that applies to the first $29,590 of income. A credit of 17% of, say, tuition fees is worth about 27% including provincial tax, and is equivalent to a deduction if you are in the lowest tax bracket. When you complete your tax return, you will find that you total up a number of "amounts" and then take 17% of the total.

Some of the credits outlined below can be transferred between spouses if not otherwise usable. See Schedule 2 to the T1 General income tax return.

1.3.1 PERSONAL AND DEPENDANT CREDITS

Every individual gets a basic federal credit of $1,098, which offsets the federal tax on your first $6,456 of taxable income. (On your income tax return, it is a claim for a "basic personal amount" of $6,456, which you later multiply by 17%.) You can claim a further federal credit of $915 if your **spouse's** income is under $538, or a reduced amount if your spouse has income between $538 and $5,820.

If you are not married or are separated, and you support another family member (such as a child) in your home, you can claim that person under the "**equivalent-to-married**" credit. This will allow you the same claim as if that person were your spouse. (It cannot be used to claim a common-law spouse, however.)

There is no credit available for **dependent children** under 18. (This was eliminated in 1993 with the introduction of the Child Tax Benefit described in 1.5.1.) However, there is a $269 credit for disabled dependants aged 18 and over.

Common-law spouses who meet certain criteria (below) are treated identically to regular spouses for all purposes relating to income tax. This means that the spousal credit can be claimed for a dependent common-law spouse. It also means that a taxpayer who has a common-law spouse cannot claim the "equivalent-to-married" credit for a child.

Common-law spouses are treated as spouses if they are two people of the opposite sex who "cohabit in a conjugal relationship", where either they have had a child together, or they have cohabited for at least 12 continuous months. Separation is not considered to terminate this "cohabiting" unless the couple separates for at least 90 days because of a breakdown in their relationship.

1.3.2 AGE CREDIT

If you are 65 or older by the end of the year, you get an additional federal credit of $592. However, this credit is now linked to your income. It is phased out by 2.55 cents for each dollar that your net income (see 1.1.1) exceeds $25,921. Thus, the credit completely disappears once your net income reaches $49,134. (Your spouse's net income does not affect this calculation.)

1.3.3 DISABILITY CREDIT

If you suffer from a **severe and prolonged mental or physical impairment**, you get an additional federal credit of $720. Your status must be certified by a medical doctor (or alternatively, for a visual impairment, by an optometrist).

To qualify as having a severe and prolonged impairment, your ability to perform a "basic activity of daily living" must be "markedly restricted", and the impairment must have lasted or be expected to last for at least a year. The *Income Tax Act* has specific definitions to determine whether you qualify. The rules can be found on Revenue Canada's disability credit certificate, Form T2201. However, it is often difficult to determine whether one qualifies or not, and the Tax Court of Canada has recently issued a large number of decisions interpreting these rules.

If you have a dependent child who qualifies for the disability credit but does not earn enough income to be able to use all of it, the child's unused credit can be transferred to your return. As well, if you support a dependent child age 18 or over who is disabled, you can claim an additional federal credit of $269.

1.3.4 CHARITABLE DONATIONS

Charitable donations entitle you to a two-tier credit. The first $200 of donations for the year (total to all charities) gives you a 17% federal tax credit, worth about 27% when provincial tax is taken into account. All donations above that level give you a 29% federal tax credit, worth about 50% when provincial tax is factored in.

Charitable donations above $200 for the year are therefore given the same treatment as if they were deductible, if you are in the top tax bracket (over $59,180 in taxable income). If you are in a lower bracket, the credit for large donations is worth far more than a deduction.

To claim charitable donations, you must submit official receipts which show the recipient organization's charitable registration number. Revenue Canada's administrative policy is to allow you to claim receipts made out in either your name or your spouse's (including a qualifying common-law spouse; see 1.3.1).

The donations you claim in the year may not exceed 20% of your net income. To the extent you have receipts for more than this amount, or if you choose not to claim a donation for any other reason, you can save the receipts and claim the credit in any of the following five years.

A number of special rules relating to charitable donations, and creative techniques for use of the credit for donations, are discussed in 12.7, in the chapter on Estate Planning.

1.3.5 MEDICAL EXPENSES

Medical expenses over a certain threshold entitle you to a tax credit. The threshold is 3% of your net income, or, if your net income exceeds $53,800, a flat $1,614. All qualifying medical expenses above this amount give rise to a 17% federal credit, worth about 27% when provincial tax is counted.

EXAMPLE

Ben's net income is $30,000. He spends $1,500 on qualifying medical expenses in 1995.

3% of Ben's net income is $900, so the remaining $600 qualifies for the medical expense credit. The federal credit is 17% of that, or $102. Ben's provincial tax and federal surtax will be reduced by about $60 as a result. So of his $1,500 in medical expenses, he will get back about $162 in tax.

All expenses claimed for any given year must have been paid within one 12-month period ending in the year. You can claim expenses for yourself, your spouse and any close relative dependent on you for support. However, to the extent any dependant you claim has net income over $6,456, any claim for medical expenses will be reduced.

The list of qualifying medical expenses is very long, and you should refer to Revenue Canada's Interpretation Bulletin (see 1.8) if you need specific details. The list includes:

- payments to medical practitioners, dentists and nurses
- hospital fees not covered by public health insurance
- diagnostic procedures
- prescription drugs
- premiums to a drug or dental plan
- travelling expenses and meals and lodging, in some cases
- institutional care (e.g., nursing home)
- attendant for disabled person
- guide dogs (both purchase cost and upkeep cost)
- eyeglasses and hearing aids
- dentures
- home renovations required for someone with a mobility impairment
- a long list of specific devices, ranging from crutches to insulin needles, wheelchair lifts, speech synthesizers, visual fire alarm indicators and TDD devices for the deaf.

1.3.6 TUITION FEES AND EDUCATIONAL STATUS

Tuition fees qualify for a 17% federal credit if you pay them for yourself. Tuition fees paid for your child or other person cannot be claimed, subject to the transfer rules discussed below.

To be eligible for a credit, the fees must be paid to a Canadian university, college or other post-secondary educational institution, or to an institution certified by Employment and Immigration Canada. Fees paid to post-secondary institutions in other countries may qualify as well. Any fees you claim must total more than $100 per institution.

Note that fees paid to private schools for grade-school or high-school education will not entitle you to a tax credit. However, religious private schools are generally able to provide a tax receipt for all or most of your tuition fees, treating that amount as a charitable donation (see 1.3.4) made toward the school's religious instruction.

As a separate credit from the tuition fees, you are entitled to a further **educational status** credit of $13.60 (federal) per month during which you are in *full-time* attendance at a post-secondary educational institution. Disabled students qualify for this credit even if they attend the institution only part-time.

If you are not able to use your tuition and education credits (because you have no tax to pay), up to $680 in federal credits for the two combined may normally be transferred to your spouse or to a parent or grandparent.

1.3.7 PENSION INCOME CREDIT

You are entitled to a federal tax credit of 17% of your pension income, up to $1,000 of pension income for the year.

Pension income does not include Canada Pension Plan (CPP), Old Age Security or Guaranteed Income Supplement payments. It basically means private pension income received through a life annuity. If you are over 65 or are receiving payments as a result of your spouse's death, it also includes annuities out of an RRSP or DPSP, a payment out of a RRIF (see 2.1.6.3), or the income portion of a regular annuity.

1.3.8 CPP/QPP CONTRIBUTIONS AND UI PREMIUMS

A federal credit of 17% of all Canada (or Québec) Pension Plan contributions and Unemployment Insurance premiums is available, effectively giving you back about 27% of these amounts when provincial tax and surtax are factored in. If you are employed, these amounts are normally taken off your paycheque at source by your employer. If you are self-employed, you will normally have to calculate and remit CPP/QPP (but not unemployment insurance) contributions on your net self-employment income.

1.3.9 OTHER CREDITS

There are a number of other credits available when computing "basic federal tax". One of them is the dividend tax credit, explained in 5.1.2.

1.4 NON-REFUNDABLE CREDITS—FEDERAL ONLY

1.4.1 POLITICAL CONTRIBUTIONS

Contributions to federal political parties and to candidates in federal election campaigns entitle you to a credit, which is federal only. Many of the provinces also have their own credits for contributions to *provincial* parties and candidates.

Note that contributions to a candidate in a federal leadership campaign are not eligible for the credit. However, political parties sometimes set up funds that allow you to contribute to the party itself and direct that your contribution be used to support a particular leadership candidate.

To encourage small political donations by many people, the credit is most generous at the lowest levels. The credit is 75% for the first $100 of donation; 50% for the next $450; and 33.33% for the next $600. There is no additional credit for donations beyond $1,150.

EXAMPLE

Mark contributes $200 to the federal Liberal party in 1995.

Mark's political contribution credit for 1995 will be 75% on the first $100 ($75) plus 50% on the next $100 ($50), for a total of $125. There is no reduction in provincial tax resulting from this credit.

1.4.2 OTHER CREDITS

Other federal credits include the investment tax credit, which is an incentive for those carrying on business to invest in particular regions or sectors of the economy (see 7.2.9); the labour-sponsored funds tax credit (see 5.4.9); and the foreign tax credit, which offsets the impact of foreign tax paid on one's income from a foreign source, to reduce double taxation.

1.5 REFUNDABLE CREDITS—FEDERAL ONLY

A "refundable" credit is one that is paid to you even if you have no tax to pay for the year.

1.5.1 CHILD TAX BENEFIT

The Child Tax Credit was a refundable credit before 1993. It has been eliminated and replaced with a monthly non-taxable "Child Tax Benefit" payment, which combines the benefits of the former family allowance, Child Tax Credit and dependent child credit. Thus, these items no longer appear on your income tax return.

The Child Tax Benefit is aimed at low and moderate income families. It begins to be phased out once family income exceeds $25,921. Depending on the number of children you have and whether you claim child-care expenses, you can still receive a portion of the Child Tax Benefit even when your family income is quite high.

1.5.2 Goods and Services Tax Credit

The GST Credit is aimed at low-income families. It is designed to offset the GST paid by consumers on most goods and services (see Chapter 17). This credit is normally $198 per adult (but up to $303 in some cases) and $105 per child in the family, reduced by 5 cents for each dollar that the parents' income exceeds $25,921. The credit is prepaid in quarterly instalments to qualifying families, based on their previous year's income.

Many provinces also have sales tax credits for low-income taxpayers. For the Québec credit, which parallels the GST credit, see 14.2.15.

EXAMPLE

Jeffrey and Margaret are married and have two dependent children. Their combined income is $25,000.

For 1995, their combined GST credit will be $606 ($198 for each parent and $105 for each child). Since their combined income is below $25,921, the credit is not reduced. The $606 effectively offsets the GST paid on $8,657 of taxable goods and services purchased during the year. Thus, although the credit is paid through the income tax system, it operates to alleviate the effects of GST on low-income families.

1.5.3 GST Rebate

In addition to the GST credit described in 1.5.2, certain employees and members of partnerships can claim a GST rebate on their income tax returns. The rebate is available to employees who claim income tax deductions relating to their employment expenses, and partners who claim deductions on expenses they incur outside the partnership to earn partnership income. (See 6.9.1 and 17.4 for more details.)

1.6 Old Age Security and UI Benefits Clawback

Old Age Security is paid monthly to most Canadian residents who are 65 or over. For high-income taxpayers, these payments are completely taxed back through a special tax, known informally as the "clawback", paid through your income tax return.

The tax applies to taxpayers whose net income (after most deductions such as RRSP contributions) is over $53,215. Spouses' incomes are not pooled; each taxpayer's income is considered separately.

For each dollar of income over $53,215, 15¢ of Old Age Security is taxed, until all of it is taxed back. This means that the benefit is fully taxed back once your net income exceeds about $83,500.

The amount of tax paid back will be a deduction for tax purposes, so you are not taxed a second time on the payments as income.

EXAMPLE

Brian is a senior citizen. He receives $4,500 in old age security payments in 1995. Brian's net income, including the old age security, is $63,215.

The excess of Brian's income over $53,215 is $10,000; 15% of that is $1,500. The clawback is therefore $1,500. Since this amount has been repaid due to the clawback, Brian then deducts $1,500 from net income in computing taxable income (his taxable income is reduced to $61,715), to offset the fact that the $1,500 was originally included in his income. In effect, he repays $1,500 of his $4,500 due to the clawback, and pays tax on the remaining $3,000 at his normal marginal rate.

A different clawback applies to unemployment insurance benefits. If your net income exceeds $63,570, you will be required to pay back, through your income tax return, a portion of any UI benefits you received during the year. However, the total amount you pay back will never exceed 30% of the benefits. The remaining 70% remains taxable in the normal way.

1.7 PLANNING OPPORTUNITIES

1.7.1 CLAIM MARRIED-EQUIVALENT CREDIT

If you are unmarried, widowed, divorced or separated from your spouse, and you support another family member (such as a child) in your home, make sure you claim the "equivalent to married" credit for that person. The credit will be worth about $1,459.

Remember that you can no longer make such a claim for a child if you are in a common-law relationship that meets the definition outlined in 1.3.1.

1.7.2 FAMILY PLANNING

Tax considerations should hardly be paramount when planning to have (or adopt) children, but note that if you do so, you may become eligible for the federal Child Tax Benefit (see 1.5.1). Also, if you live in Québec, note that the Québec government pays families cash allowances for new-born or adopted children (see 14.2.8).

If you have children who work part-time (e.g., summer employment, paper route, etc.) and their income is below the basic amount of $6,456 that can be earned tax-free, you might consider filing a tax return for them to report their earned income for RRSP purposes and allow them to build up an unused contribution limit, which they may be able to use in a later year when they become taxable (see 2.1.3). This can be especially useful when your children are in their teenage years and can expect to earn much more income within the next seven years.

1.7.3 Claim moving expenses

When considering a move, ensure if possible that your move coincides with a new employment location or a new place of business, and that you move 40 km closer to your new work location than your old home is (to the new work location). Substantial deductions may then be available to the extent that you are not reimbursed by your employer (see 1.2.2).

1.7.4 Higher-income spouse claim credits to reduce high-income surtax

Where you have a choice as to which spouse will claim certain credits, such as charitable donations, note that credits are worth slightly more to very high-income individuals. That is because of the additional surtax that applies to individuals with high "basic federal tax". This additional surtax is an extra 5% of basic federal tax in excess of $12,500. Almost all provinces also have surtaxes on high levels of provincial tax, which can boost the effect of credits still further.

If you are paying any of these surtaxes and your spouse is not, it is better for you to claim most of the credits that can be allocated between the two of you.

1.7.5 Medical expense credit—spouse and year-end options

As we have seen, either you or your spouse may claim all medical expenses incurred for the two of you. Because of the threshold of 3% of net income (see 1.3.5), you should combine all of the family's medical expenses on one return. It is normally better for the lower-income spouse to make the claim, provided that spouse has enough tax to pay to use up the credit, since the 3% threshold will be smaller. On the other hand, the credit can be slightly more valuable to a high-income spouse because it will reduce the application of high-income federal and provincial surtaxes (see 1.7.4).

When claiming medical expenses, you can pick any 12-month period ending in the year. If, for example, you made no claim for 1994, and you have large medical expense bills in February 1994, January 1995 and November 1995, you might be better off to use January 1995 as the end of your 12-month period, claim the February 1994 and January 1995 expenses for 1995, and leave the November 1995 expenses to be claimed on your 1996 return.

You can also plan for the timing of medical expenses, since they are based on when they are *paid*. If you are using a December end for the 12-month period, and you have pending expenses (perhaps for medical equipment purchases or large dental bills) that are due early in the new year, consider prepaying them so that you can claim them one year earlier.

1.7.6 MEDICAL EXPENSES—CLAIM FOR DEPENDANTS

As discussed in 1.7.5 above, you should combine all of the family's medical expenses on one return to minimize the effect of the "3% or $1,614" threshold. You can claim the expenses of any of the following persons, if they are dependent on you for support: your child, grandchild, parent, grandparent, brother, sister, uncle, aunt, niece or nephew; or any of those relatives of your spouse (including a qualifying common-law spouse as outlined in 1.3.1). Except for your or your spouse's child or grandchild, the person must be resident in Canada.

If the dependant has net income under $6,456, you can claim the medical expenses without restriction. To the extent the dependant has net income exceeding $6,456, the medical expenses you can claim are reduced by 68% of that excess. If a dependant has sufficiently high income, you will not be able to claim that person's expenses at all, since the reduction will exceed the total value of that dependant's medical expenses. (Note that it doesn't matter who *paid* the expenses; what matters is who the "patient" was.)

1.7.7 IF YOU ARE SEPARATING

While marriage breakdown is often an occasion for bitter disputes, you and your spouse (through your lawyers, if necessary) should co-operate to minimize your joint tax bill and share the resulting savings. If you will be paying support either for your spouse or for the children, and you are in a higher tax bracket than your spouse, it is to the benefit of both that you reach a written separation agreement that meets the *Income Tax Act*'s requirements to allow support payments to be deductible to you and taxable to your spouse (see

1.2.1). The tax your spouse will have to pay will be more than offset by your own savings.

For example, if you are in the 41% bracket (taxable income from $29,590 to $59,180) and your spouse is in the 27% bracket (income under $29,590), then for each $1,000 that you pay in support payments, you save $410 and your spouse will pay $270.

The same rules apply when a common-law couple separates, if they meet the criteria for common-law spouses outlined in 1.3.1.

1.7.8 Investigate whether you can claim the disability credit

If you or a member of your family is seriously ill or disabled, investigate whether you can claim the disability credit (see 1.3.3). Revenue Canada's view as to whether the credit is available is not always correct, as can be seen from the many cases where the Tax Court has decided in the taxpayer's favour. Therefore, if you believe you fit within the legal definition of disabled under the Income Tax Act, you should pursue your claim even if it is denied.

The credit can be transferred to another family member in many cases where the disabled person does not have any income.

1.7.9 Plan for at least $1,000 of pension income per person

Because of the pension income credit (see 1.3.7), you should aim to have at least $1,000 of qualifying "pension income" plus another $1,000 for your spouse, if possible.

Once you are over 65 (or at any age if such payments have been received as a result of the death of your spouse), annuity payments out of an RRSP and the income portion of a regular annuity also qualify for the pension income credit.

1.7.10 Political contributions

If you are interested in the greatest "bang for your buck", consider a contribution to your favourite federal political party or election candidate. A donation of $100 will cost you only $25 (see 1.4.1).

1.7.11 Charitable donations

If you donate only small amounts over a year, consider combining two or more years' donations into one year to put yourself over the $200 threshold. A $100 donation above the $200 level for the year costs you only about $50 instead of about $73 below that level.

If you and your spouse donate separately, you should combine your receipts and claim them all on one return (Revenue Canada's administrative practice is to permit this), to avoid having to get the low-rate credit on $200 twice. Due to the operation of the federal and provincial high-income surtaxes, the higher-income spouse should claim all the donations.

Once you are over the $200 level, consider making extra contributions in December rather than early in the new year. Your tax saving through the donations credit will come one year earlier.

If you have valuable works of art or other "cultural property" that you are considering donating to a museum or gallery, consult your tax adviser about how to maximize your charitable donation claim without having to pay tax on a capital gain in respect of your gift.

If you wish to donate a large sum to a university or hospital, and it will exceed 20% of your net income for the year, contact the university to determine whether the donation can be structured as a "Crown gift" (technically, a donation to the provincial government that is redirected to the university). See 12.7.2.

Other, more esoteric tax planning steps you can undertake with charities are discussed in 12.7.

1.8 REFERENCES

The following publications can be obtained (in person or by telephone request) from your nearest Revenue Canada District Taxation Office:

Interpretation Bulletin IT-99R4, "Legal and accounting fees"

Interpretation Bulletin IT-110R2, "Deductible gifts and official donation receipts"

Interpretation Bulletin IT-118R3, "Alimony and maintenance"

Interpretation Bulletin IT-178R3, "Moving expenses"

Interpretation Bulletin IT-495R, "Child care expenses"

Interpretation Bulletin IT-513, "Personal tax credits"

Interpretation Bulletin IT-515R, "Education tax credit"

Interpretation Bulletin IT-516R, "Tuition tax credit"

Interpretation Bulletin IT-517, "Pension tax credit"

Interpretation Bulletin IT-519, "Medical expense and disability tax credits"

Interpretation Bulletin IT-523, "Order of provisions applicable in computing an individual's taxable income and tax payable"

Information Circular 75-2R4, "Contributions to a registered political party or to a candidate at a federal election"

Brochure, Alimony or Maintenance

Brochure, "Are You Moving?"

Brochure, "Students and Income Tax"
Brochure, "Tax Information for People with Disabilities"
Form T1-M, "Claim for moving expenses"
Form T778, "Calculation of child care expenses deduction"
Form T929, "Attendant care expenses"
Form T2201, "Disability credit certificate"
Form T2202A, "Tuition and education credit certificate"
Form T2222, "Calculation of Northern Residents Deductions"
Form T1GSTC, T1 General income tax return, "Federal goods and services tax credit"

2 RRSPS AND OTHER TAX DEFERRAL PLANS

PLANNING TIPS

- Contribute as much as you can to an RRSP
- Contribute early in the year instead of the following February
- Consider a self-directed RRSP for greater flexibility
- Consider shares of a labour-sponsored venture capital corporation for your RRSP
- Consider RRSP rather than additional RPP contributions
- Contribute to spouse's (or common-law spouse's) RRSP, if your projected income on retirement will be higher
- Transfer retiring allowances or severance pay to your RRSP
- Consider making an over-contribution of up to $2,000 to your RRSP
- Consider Home Buyer's Plan withdrawals to buy or build your first home
- Withdraw funds from RRSP in low-income years
- Convert RRSP to annuity or RRIF when you turn 71
- Consider an individual pension plan
- Find out when your pension plan contributions are vested
- Consider RESP for your children

Deferred income plans, particularly RRSPs and registered pension plans, are the most widely-used tax shelters in Canada. Put simply, almost everyone should have one.

The concept of deferred income plans is quite simple, although the particular rules can get rather complex. In this chapter, we'll take you through the basic rules, so you understand the system in general, and then discuss the options you have and steps you can take for tax planning.

Québec residents should also review Chapter 14, which deals with Québec taxation.

2.1 REGISTERED RETIREMENT SAVINGS PLANS—RRSPS

2.1.1 WHAT IS AN RRSP?

You hear a lot about RRSPs every February, when the annual contribution deadline approaches. Although the acronym stands for

Registered *Retirement* Savings Plan, an RRSP does not necessarily have anything to do with retirement. It can be used simply as a tax deferral tool.

The concept behind an RRSP is quite simple. If you agree to put some of your salary away and not have immediate access to it, the tax system will tax that income—along with all the interest and other income it earns—when it is *received* rather than when it is *earned.*

EXAMPLE

If you earn $60,000, you pay tax on $60,000.

Suppose you earn $60,000 but you put $2,000 of that into an RRSP. You will be taxed on only $58,000—the amount you have ***received.***

If, some years later, the $2,000 you put away has grown (in a tax-free environment) to $3,000, you can take the $3,000 out of your RRSP, and it will be taxed (added to your income) at that point. Again, the original $2,000, now grown to $3,000, is being taxed in the year it is ***received*** *rather than when it was* ***earned.***

The rules governing RRSPs are more complex than the above example indicates, of course. The amount you can contribute to an RRSP is limited in various ways.

2.1.2 HOW DO YOU SET UP AN RRSP?

An RRSP can be set up easily at almost any bank or trust company or through a stockbroker or life insurance agent. Basically, you just fill out a form and contribute money to the plan. Some institutions will give you your official tax receipt immediately; others will mail it to you some weeks later, in time for you to file it with your tax return.

2.1.3 HOW MUCH CAN YOU CONTRIBUTE?

Contributions to an RRSP are deductible for any given year if they are contributed *in the year* or within *60 days after the end of the year.* So if you contribute by February 29, 1996, you can get a deduction for your 1995 tax return (and any resulting refund will come sometime in the spring of 1996). The deadline is usually March 1, but 1996 is a leap year—so make sure you don't wait until March 1 this year!

There are three factors that limit the amount you can contribute to an RRSP: a dollar limit, which is $14,500 for 1995 and $13,500 for 1996-97; a percentage (18%) of the previous year's "earned income"; and your "pension adjustment". We'll look at each of these in turn.

Dollar limit

The RRSP contribution limit is being raised to $15,500, but the increase has been delayed over several years:

Year	RRSP limit
1991	$11,500
1992	$12,500
1993	$12,500
1994	$13,500
1995	$14,500
1996	$13,500
1997	$13,500
1998	$14,500
1999	$15,500

Percentage of previous year's earned income

The annual deduction is limited to **18%** of the **previous** year's earned income. That is, 18% of your 1994 earned income is the dollar limit for your 1995 contribution (made by February 29, 1996).

"Earned income" is the same as "salary" for most employees—the gross amount of salary, before deductions for income tax, UI, CPP, etc., which are withheld at source. "Earned income" includes business income, if you are self-employed or are an active partner in a business. It also includes:

- research grants, net of deductible related expenses
- royalties from works or inventions that you authored or invented
- taxable alimony, maintenance and child support received (see 1.2.1)
- net rental income from real estate
- disability pension income received under the CPP/QPP

Earned income is *reduced* by

- deductible alimony, maintenance and child support you pay
- most deductible employment-related expenses, such as union dues and travelling expenses (but not pension plan contributions)

Earned income does not include most investment income, such as interest or dividends, or capital gains. Nor does it include pension benefits, retiring allowances, severance pay, death benefits or amounts received from an RRSP, RRIF or deferred profit-sharing plan.

If your 1994 earned income was $80,555 or more, your 1995 contribution will be limited to $14,500 (minus the pension adjustment as discussed below). Otherwise, you will be limited by the 18% factor.

Similarly, if your 1995 earned income is $75,000 or more, your 1996 contribution will be limited to $13,500 (minus the pension adjustment as discussed below). Otherwise, you will be limited by the 18% factor for 1996.

Pension adjustment

Once you have calculated your maximum contribution limit as 18% of your previous year's earned income, subject to the dollar limits shown in the table above, you must subtract your **pension adjustment**, if any. This figure represents the deemed value of your pension earned for the previous year. In other words, the more that has been put aside (by you and your employer combined) towards your retirement pension, the less the *Income Tax Act* allows you to contribute to an RRSP.

If you are *not* a member of an employer's pension plan or deferred profit-sharing plan, your pension adjustment is zero, and you can contribute the full 18% of previous year's earned income (subject to the annual dollar limits).

Otherwise, your pension adjustment for 1995 should appear on your 1994 T4 slip, as well as on your Notice of Assessment received in the spring of 1995 following filing of your 1994 return.

For "money-purchase" pension plans (see 2.2.1), the pension adjustment is the total contributions made towards your pension by you and your employer combined. The same applies to deferred profit sharing plans (see 2.3), except that the contributions are made only by your employer. For "defined benefit" pension plans (the type of pension plan most employees belong to), the pension adjustment is based on a calculation that takes into account the benefit you may receive down the road based on the past year's employment.

In some situations, the calculation of your RRSP limit may also be reduced by a **past service pension adjustment** ("PSPA"). In general terms, a PSPA can arise when your pension benefits under a defined benefit pension plan are improved on a retroactive basis.

EXAMPLE

Melanie is a chemical engineer who belongs to her employer's pension plan. Her 1994 earned income was $60,000. Her pension adjustment for 1995, as reported to her on her 1994 T4 slip and her 1994 assessment received from Revenue Canada in mid-1995, is $3,200.

Before accounting for her pension adjustment, Melanie's contribution limit for 1995 is 18% of her 1994 earned income, to a maximum of $14,500. 18% of her 1994 earned income is $10,800. From this amount she must deduct her pension adjustment of $3,200. Melanie may therefore contribute up to $7,600 to an RRSP by February 29, 1996 for a deduction on her 1995 tax return.

Carry forward of unused deduction room and undeducted contributions

If in any year you contribute less than the maximum to an RRSP, you can "carry forward" the extra deduction room and make that much more contribution in any of the following seven years. In many cases the effective carry-forward period can actually work out to be much more than seven years, since the unused deductions can be used against new earned income, which creates its own new deduction room.

As well, if you contribute an amount for a year but choose not to deduct the amount for that year, you can claim the deduction in any subsequent year (provided you still have contribution room).

EXAMPLE

Melanie, from the example above, has $7,600 of contribution room for 1995. She chooses to contribute only $5,000 to an RRSP for the year.

Melanie has unused RRSP contribution room of $2,600 to carry forward. She may make that much more of contribution for any of the following seven years (1996-2002) and likely even beyond that, if she continues to have earned income. If Melanie's contribution limit for 1996 is again $7,600, she can contribute up to $10,200 for deduction in 1996.

You should carefully review your assessment from Revenue Canada to make sure that the contribution limit reported is correct, before relying on it. A wrong statement from Revenue Canada will not entitle you to deduct a contribution that you cannot otherwise deduct.

In some cases you might contribute more than you can actually deduct. We discuss overcontributions in 2.1.7.4.

2.1.4 WHAT IS YOUR CONTRIBUTION WORTH?

What is your contribution worth in tax savings? It depends on your marginal tax rate. The rates vary among the provinces due to different provincial tax rates (see Appendix II), but they are *approximately*:

27% on income up to $29,590

41% on income from $29,590 to $59,180

50% on income over $59,180

In the example above, if Melanie's taxable income, after other deductions, would be between $34,590 and $59,180 anyway, her contribution of $5,000 to an RRSP will save her about 41% of that, or $2,050, in tax for 1995. For someone whose taxable income stays over $59,180 even after making the RRSP contribution, the same $5,000 contribution would be worth about $2,500. Clearly, RRSPs are more tax-effective to those with higher incomes.

You should keep the value of your deduction in mind and try to take maximum advantage of the carry-forward mechanism in claiming your RRSP deductions. In a low-income year, for example, it may be advantageous to make your maximum RRSP *contribution*, but to defer claiming the *deduction* until a later year when your income is taxed at a higher marginal rate. However, beware of any potential exposure to minimum tax (see Chapter 11) if you are claiming a very large RRSP deduction in any single year.

2.1.5 WHAT HAPPENS TO THE FUNDS IN THE RRSP?

While your funds are in the RRSP, they are not subject to tax at all. No matter what amounts of interest, dividends, capital gains—or losses—result, there will be no tax effect until you withdraw the funds. (As we shall see, you must close out the RRSP by the end of the year in which you turn 71, but even then the tax effects can be partially deferred.)

The effects of having income compound without tax are quite dramatic. Compare the following two situations: A, where you invest $5,000 of your salary in an RRSP for 10 or 20 years at 10%, and B, where you earn the same 10% but it is subject to tax. The example assumes a 50% marginal tax rate.

	1995	2005	2015
A. Invest $5,000 in an RRSP	$5,000	$12,969	$33,637
After withdrawal		$ 6,484	$16,818
B. Do not put the $5,000 in an RRSP, so you are taxed on it immediately as salary	$2,500	$ 4,072	$ 6,633

In case A, you pay 50% in tax when you withdraw the funds, but they have grown substantially in the meantime. After 20 years, your $5,000 is worth $16,818 *after* tax. In case B, since the annual 10% interest is taxed, you have only 5% to reinvest for compounding purposes. The fact you can use the $6,633 (after 20 years) directly in case B, without having to pay 50% tax on it as in case A, doesn't come close to making up for the tax-free compounding of interest.

Of course, if you are paying non-deductible interest such as mortgage interest, that interest also effectively compounds on a pre-tax basis, and you might be better off to pay down your mortgage rather than contribute to an RRSP. In such a case, you can generally use all your unused RRSP contribution room by making and deducting a "catch-up" RRSP contribution in a later year, when you have the funds to contribute.

As we mentioned earlier, your RRSP can be invested in a number of different forms. The simplest, and usually lowest-paying, is a deposit account that pays interest monthly or twice a year. Many people invest instead in longer-term Guaranteed Investment Certificates (GICs) or term deposits. If you are dealing with a bank, trust company or life insurance company, these will be your normal options, and the only issue will be what interest rate you can earn on, say, a one-year versus a five-year certificate. Of course, you will not want to tie your money up for five years if you think you may want to withdraw it sooner, such as for use in the Home Buyer's Plan (see 2.1.8).

If you are ambitious and willing to take a little more risk with your funds by investing in stocks or bonds of your own choosing, you can set up a **self-directed** RRSP. This is normally done through a stockbroker or financial institution, subject to an annual fee in the $100-150 range (plus normal commissions on any stock trades). You then decide what your RRSP invests in. There are restrictions—the system tries to ensure that your money, while not necessarily "safe", is at least invested in reasonable places. "Qualified investments" for an RRSP include:

- cash
- government, Crown corporation or municipal bonds
- GICs, term deposits and treasury bills ("T-Bills")
- certain government-insured mortgages
- shares or bonds of corporations listed on Canadian stock exchanges
- mutual funds
- shares listed on certain foreign stock exchanges and bonds of certain foreign governments (however, as discussed below, no more than 20% of an RRSP may be invested in foreign assets)
- certain small business shares

The rules governing the details (e.g., which mortgages and small business shares are qualified investments) are extremely complex, and you should consult a professional adviser if you wish to do more with your self-directed RRSP than simply buy, say, T-Bills and Hydro bonds (which are generally regarded as good safe investments, incidentally). However, if you have the time to give it the attention it needs and are willing to take a little more risk, a self-directed RRSP can prove to be much more rewarding in the long run. The control you will gain over invesment decisions will diversify your risk and give you the flexibility to pursue a different range of investment opportunities—including some that are generally only possible through self-directed RRSPs, like stripped bonds, mortgage-backed securities and other less commmon RRSP investments. With a self-directed RRSP, you may be able to achieve greater integration of your RRSP assets with your overall financial plan including the ability to invest in shares listed on certain foreign stock exchanges as well as certain foreign government bonds and other foreign properties.

Generally, only 20% of the cost amount of all property held by your RRSP can be invested in foreign property. The calculation is performed at the end of each month. Foreign property values over the 20% threshold are subject to a special tax of 1% per month payable by the RRSP. The 20% limit is generally based on the property's cost at the time of purchase, not its current market value. Your RRSP's administrator should monitor your RRSP's foreign content holdings and warn you if it is in danger of going off-side.

With the right investment mix, you can boose your self-directed RRSP's foreign content to a maximum of 40% of the cost amount of property held by it. To assist small businesses in obtaining equity financing, a special rule permits you to increase your RRSP's holdings of qualifying foreign property without penalty by $3 for every $1 that you invest in a certain Canadian small business corporation. That means a 6.67% holding of a qualifying small business property will enable you to increase your foreign property holdings by 20% (3 x 6.67%), up to the 40% maximum.

However, if you own more than 10% of the shares of a small business, your RRSP's ability to invest in that business may be restricted or denied. Since these restrictions and the rules governing the types of small businesses that qualify are quite complex, you should consult your tax advisor if you are considering increasing your self-directed RRSP's foreign content through small business investments.

It is even possible for you to arrange for your RRSP to hold your own mortgage—in other words, you put funds into your RRSP, receive a tax deduction, and lend the funds to yourself. This is not easy to do, however; the mortgage must be federally insured, and various other restrictions apply.

Investing in your own mortgage may make you feel good, but does not always make sense financially. Since the investment must be at the market rate, you may be no better off depending on the size of the mortgage, once all fees (legal, appraisal, etc.) are taken into account.

If you and your spouse have not owned a home in the past five years, you can borrow funds from your RRSP to purchase or build a home. This program, called the "Home Buyers' Plan", is discussed in 2.1.8 below.

2.1.6 How do you get money out of an RRSP?

There are basically four routes for getting your money out of an RRSP. You must make use of one of them by the **end of the year in which you turn 71**. We discuss these options below.

2.1.6.1 WITHDRAW THE FUNDS

The first, and easiest, is simply to **withdraw the funds**. The amount withdrawn from the RRSP is included in your income for the year in which you do so. It is taxed as ordinary income, just as if it were salary, even if some of the value of the RRSP represents capital gains (which outside an RRSP are normally only partially taxed and could be entirely exempt). A percentage to cover tax will be withheld at source by the financial institution and remitted to Revenue Canada on your behalf (see 2.5.9). You will then report the income and amount of tax withheld on your annual income tax return and either receive a refund or, if not enough was withheld, make up the difference.

2.1.6.2 PURCHASE AN ANNUITY

The second method is to purchase an **annuity**. None of the RRSP proceeds will be taxed immediately, but the annuity payments will be taxed as you receive them. (As discussed in 1.3.7, up to $1,000 per year of the income may effectively be exempted through the pension income tax credit.)

There are three general kinds of annuities: "term-certain", payable to you or your estate for a fixed number of years; "single life", payable to you as long as you are alive; and "joint and last survivor life", payable as long as either you or your spouse is alive. Numerous additional options are available, such as a guaranteed term as part of a life annuity, indexing for inflation, reduction of payment on death of your spouse, reduction of payment when Old Age Security payments begin, and so on. You should discuss the available possibilities, and their effect on the monthly annuity payment you receive, with your life insurance agent. (A life annuity may only be acquired from a life insurance company. Term-certain annuities are available from trust companies as well.)

2.1.6.3 CONVERT RRSP TO RRIF

The third thing you can do with your RRSP is to convert it into a **Registered Retirement Income Fund**, or RRIF (pronounced "riff"). A RRIF is somewhat like an RRSP, in that you can have it invested in various kinds of securities. However, you must withdraw at least a "minimum amount" from the RRIF each year, and report what you withdraw for tax purposes. (Again, up to $1,000 per year of such income may effectively be exempted through the pension income tax credit, as explained in 1.3.7.)

For RRIFs set up before 1993, the amount that must be withdrawn from the RRIF each year up to age 78 is 1/N of the value of the RRIF at the beginning of the year, where N is the number of years left until you (or your spouse) turn 90. After age 78, and for all ages for RRIFs set up in 1993 or later, the amount is a fraction that increases gradually each year, levelling out at 20% once you turn 94.

2.1.6.4 Convert locked-in RRSP to Life Income Fund (LIF)

A life income fund provides an alternative to a life annuity when certain individuals, who were formerly members of a registered pension plan, terminate employment or plan membership. The LIF is also an option for individuals who have transferred pension funds to a **locked-in RRSP** (see 2.1.7.2).

A LIF is a RRIF for tax purposes (see 2.1.6.3) with additional restrictions. Like any other RRIF, a minimum amount must be withdrawn each year. As well, under a LIF there is a *maximum* amount that can be withdrawn each year until age 80. (Thus, the funds remain "locked in", just like a pension or locked-in RRSP.) The remaining balance of funds in the LIF must be used to purchase a life annuity by December 31 of the year in which the individual turns 80.

A LIF can offer an attractive income alternative to a life annuity option. LIFs are now available in all provinces except Newfoundland and Prince Edward Island; however, they can not (yet) be purchased with funds governed by federal (as opposed to provincial) pension regulations. You should consult your professional adviser to determine whether this option is available for you.

2.1.7 Special RRSP rules

A number of rules deal with special situations with respect to RRSPs. We will refer to them only briefly; you should consult your professional adviser if you are in these situations.

2.1.7.1 Spousal plans

The RRSP rules allow you to contribute to an RRSP for your spouse, and claim the deduction yourself. Your total contributions (to your own and your spouse's plans) are still subject to your normal limits (18% of previous year's net income or (for 1995) $14,500, minus any pension adjustment). The advantage is that your spouse will ultimately be the one who reports the income for tax purposes, when the funds are withdrawn on retirement or otherwise. If your spouse has less income than you, this can result in significantly less tax on the income.

To prevent spousal RRSPs from being used for "income splitting" (see Chapter 3), the amount you contribute will be taxed back to you (rather than your spouse) to the extent any amount is withdrawn by your spouse in the year *in which* you contribute *or in the next two calendar years*. See 3.3.12.

EXAMPLE

Janet and Zito are married. Zito contributes $5,000 to Janet's RRSP in February 1996, and claims the deduction on his 1995 tax return.

If Janet withdraws the funds at any time up to the end of 1998, $5,000 of the amount withdrawn will be treated as Zito's income, not Janet's. (If, however, Zito's contribution had been made in December 1995, this would only be the case until the end of 1997.)

This rule does not apply if the spouses are separated or divorced.

Note that, in general, there will be little effect on the real ownership of the funds under provincial law if you and your spouse separate or divorce. The rule in most provinces is that such funds will be pooled and shared between the spouses. There are rules in place to allow a tax-free split up of RRSP funds in such situations.

2.1.7.2 TRANSFERS TO AND FROM RRSPS

RRSPs can generally be transferred, with no tax consequences, to other RRSPs or to RRIFs, by simply filling out a form.

Under pension legislation you may be prevented from immediately withdrawing pension benefits from your employer's plan on your departure from the company. This legislation is commonly referred to as "locking-in" legislation. Pension benefits subject to this legislation may be transferred to a locked-in RRSP. Locked-in RRSPs are essentially subject to the same restrictions on withdrawal of funds as was the original pension plan. For example, you can not usually access the locked-in plan funds until you are within ten years of your normal retirement date. On the other hand, you do have more flexibility in deciding how to invest the funds. A locked-in RRSP may be convertible to a life income fund, or LIF (see 2.1.6.4).

Where the pension legislation permits a transfer from a registered pension plan to a locked-in RRSP or LIF, there are generally no tax consequences to such transfers, though the *Income Tax Act* may restrict the amounts that can be transferred from a "defined-benefit" pension plan.

Special rules allow a "retiring allowance" (which, as defined in the *Income Tax Act*, includes severance pay and amounts received for wrongful dismissal) to be transferred tax-free to an RRSP, rather than taxed as income when received. The amount that can be transferred is normally limited to $2,000 for each calendar year (or part year) of employment before 1996, plus $1,500 for years of employment before 1989 for which employer pension contributions have not vested. (If the amount you transfer this way is large, you could trigger the minimum tax. See Chapter 11.)

2.1.7.3 DEATH

On death, a taxpayer is normally taxed on the entire amount of any RRSPs or RRIFs, except where the funds are left to the taxpayer's spouse, in which case they are included in the spouse's income (see 12.7.1). To the extent the funds come from an RRSP, they can be transferred to the spouse's own RRSP or RRIF for a deduction that offsets the income inclusion. These funds may also be used to acquire an annuity. If there is no surviving spouse, and the RRSP or RRIF funds are left to a financially-dependent child or grandchild, the RRSP or RRIF funds can either be taxed in the hands of the child or grandchild or used to buy an annuity until age 18. The executor of the deceased's estate should obtain professional advice on these matters.

See Chapter 12 for a general discussion of the tax effects of death.

2.1.7.4 OVERCONTRIBUTIONS

The RRSP contribution limits were discussed in 2.1.3. What happens if you contribute more than the maximum?

First, understand that your financial institution will not prevent you from overcontributing. Your tax affairs are your business, and it is not for the financial institution to tell you whether you may or may not contribute.

Second, any contributions over the maximum are **non-deductible**. However, once the funds are in your RRSP, they are taxable when withdrawn (whether on retirement or earlier), just like the funds that were deductible when you contributed them. Therefore, there is double taxation—once when you earn the income (and receive no deduction despite putting the funds into the RRSP), and once when you withdraw the funds from the RRSP.

Third, overcontributing can be valuable despite the double taxation, because of the huge beneficial effect of tax-free compounding (as illustrated in the table in 2.1.5). Also, you can often deduct an overcontribution in a later year as new contribution room is created. There is therefore a rule preventing excessive overcontributions. Up to **$2,000** can be contributed without penalty. Above the $2,000 level, the excess is subject to a penalty tax of **1% per month**.

The $2,000 figure is designed to catch those cases where you might have miscalculated your pension adjustment (see 2.1.3) and contributed a little too much. However, as long as you are certain about your pension adjustment, you can use the $2,000 deliberately if you wish.

Until February 27, 1995, the overcontribution limit was **$8,000.** If you overcontributed before that date, you must use up the excess over $2,000 by deducting it against your RRSP contribution room in 1996 and on as new room becomes available.

2.1.8 THE HOME BUYERS' PLAN

Under the Home Buyer's Plan, if you qualify, you are allowed to withdraw up to **$20,000** as a **loan from your RRSP** to buy or build a home, without counting the withdrawal as income. You must then repay the loan, without interest, over the next 16 years.

Who may use the Home Buyer's Plan?

The Plan may only be used by what the government calls a **"first-time buyer"**. You are not a "first-time buyer" if you have owned and lived in a home as a principal place of residence at any time during the **five calendar years** up to and including the current year. (For the current year, you can use the Plan up to 30 days after you acquire a home.) If your spouse has owned and lived in a home during that period, and you have inhabited that home during the marriage, you also do not qualify. (Remember that "spouse" includes a common-law spouse as outlined in 1.3.1.) Furthermore, you generally cannot use the Plan if you have used it before.

How does the Plan work?

You can borrow (withdraw) up to $20,000 from your RRSP under the Plan. If you and your spouse each have RRSPs, you can thus borrow up to $40,000 between the two of you if you are taking joint ownership in the property. A qualifying home must be acquired **before October 1** of the year **following** the year of the withdrawal. You must also begin or intend, not later than one year after its acquisition, to use the home as a principal place of residence. No tax will apply to the withdrawal.

When you withdraw the funds, you fill out Form T1036, certifying that you have entered into a written agreement to purchase a home, and stating its address. Once you have done this, the financial institution will not withhold tax when it pays the funds to you.

Note that the Home Buyer's Plan does not give you any right to withdraw funds from your RRSP if you didn't already have that right. If your RRSP funds are invested in term deposits or other long-term obligations, you will still need to negotiate with the financial institution to have the funds released as cash. Similarly, if your RRSP funds are in your employer's group RRSP or a "locked-in RRSP", you may not be able to get them out.

Once you borrow the funds, you must normally complete the purchase by September 30 of the *following* year. (A one-year extension may be available if the deal falls through and you buy a replacement property.) If you withdraw less than the $20,000 maximum, you can in many cases withdraw a further amount up to the following January 31 and treat the total as one withdrawal.

The requirement to repay the funds begins in the second year following the withdrawal. You can opt to make any year's repayment up to 60 days after the end of the year.

If you do not make repayments as required, you must include the shortfall in income for tax purposes. In effect, it's treated as a permanent withdrawal from your RRSP and you're taxed on it.

EXAMPLE

Harry has $30,000 in his RRSP. He signs an agreement in September 1995 to purchase a new home. In November 1995 he completes Form T1036 and withdraws $15,000 from his RRSP. The purchase closes in January 1996.

No tax will be withheld from the $15,000 that Harry withdraws, so he can use the full amount towards the home purchase. Since he withdrew the funds in 1995, Harry must repay $1,000 (1/15 of the total) to his RRSP during 1997 or by March 1, 1998. If he repays only $600, he will have to include $400 in income for 1997 and pay tax on that amount.

If Harry repays no more than $1,000 in 1997 (or by March 1, 1998), he will be required to repay 1/14 of the balance, another $1,000, in 1998 (or by March 1, 1999). Suppose he repays $8,000 in 1997, leaving a balance owing of $7,000? For 1998, he will still be required to repay 1/14 of the balance, or $500. The fact he has prepaid more than required will reduce but not eliminate his obligation to continue paying the balance in subsequent years.

Contributions in the year you use the plan

If you contribute to an RRSP and withdraw the same funds within 90 days under the Home Buyer's Plan, you cannot deduct your contribution. For purposes of this rule, any balance that was already in your RRSP can be considered as withdrawn first. Thus, it is only to the extent the amount of your new contribution is needed for the withdrawal (within the 90-day period) that a deduction will be disallowed.

Home Buyers' Plan—some special situations

The Home Buyers' Plan may be used for building a new home on an existing lot that you own. Instead of an agreement to purchase the home, you must have an agreement in place to construct it.

If you withdraw the funds but your home purchase does not close, you can generally cancel your participation in the Plan and return the funds to your RRSP with no adverse tax consequences. Alternatively, if you buy another qualifying home as a replacement, you can remain in the Plan.

If you have contributed to a spousal RRSP, your spouse must normally wait two to three years before withdrawing the funds or they will be taxed back to you (see 2.1.7.1). However, with the Home Buyers' Plan, your spouse can borrow the funds to purchase a qualifying home, and to the extent they are not repaid over the 16 years, it is your spouse that must include the difference in income, not you. (Note, however, that if your spouse withdraws the funds and does not purchase a qualifying home, so that the full amount withdrawn is taxed in the current year, the attribution rule *will* apply and you, not your spouse, will be taxed on the withdrawal.)

If you become a non-resident of Canada, you must repay the entire outstanding balance to the RRSP within 90 days. Otherwise, the balance will be included in your income for the year that you became non-resident.

If you should die while you have an outstanding balance to repay, that balance will be included in your income for the year of death and tax will be payable by your estate (see 12.1.1). However, if you leave a surviving spouse, your executor and your spouse may make a special election to have your spouse take over the obligation to repay the funds over the remainder of the 15-year period, and the balance will not be included in your income for the year of death.

Should you use the Home Buyers' Plan?

At first glance, the Plan seems attractive, since it gives you ready access to a potentially large chunk of cash. However, there are three costs to consider.

First, you lose the **tax-free compounding** in your RRSP (see the example in 2.1.5). Balanced against this is the fact that you have probably reduced the mortgage interest expense you would otherwise have to pay out of after-tax dollars. Nevertheless, the value of the RRSP may be significantly less, at your retirement, than it otherwise would have been. If you are depending on your RRSP for your retirement income, you will want to forecast the reduction in income that will result from withdrawing a large chunk of the funds now and repaying it to the RRSP over 15 years.

Second, you have to be able to sustain the **cash flow** to repay the RRSP; if you cannot, you will end up being taxed on the funds you have withdrawn. When figuring out the cash you need to handle your mortgage and property tax payments, don't forget the $^{1}/_{15}$ minimum repayment to the RRSP in each year beginning with the second year after the withdrawal (due by 60 days after the end of the year). Of course, since you are repaying borrowed funds and not contributing new money to the RRSP, no deduction is available for the amounts you repay.

Third, you might not be able to make a contribution to your RRSP for the current year. This will depend on the balance in your RRSP. If your withdrawal does not exceed the value you had in the RRSP 90 days before the withdrawal, you have no problem. Otherwise, you may have to postpone the current year's contribution, and save it up for a later year. The result would be one less year for those funds to have earned tax-free interest, and higher tax to pay in the current year since you will not have a contribution to deduct.

Nevertheless, if you need the funds to help you purchase your first home, the Home Buyers' Plan may be a significant help.

2.2 Registered Pension Plans—RPPs

2.2.1 Ordinary RPPs

A registered pension plan is set up by an employer for its employees. Virtually all large companies, and many smaller ones, have such plans. These are quite different from the Canada Pension Plan (or, in Québec, the Québec Pension Plan), to which all employed and self-employed taxpayers must contribute.

The employer contributes (and deducts for tax purposes) an annual amount on behalf of each employee. Unlike most other employment benefits, these amounts are not taxed as benefits from employment in the year they are contributed. Instead, employees are taxed on the income from the pension when they *receive* it, which is normally after retirement.

In some cases, employees may be required or permitted to make additional contributions to the plan, which they can deduct for tax purposes in the year contributed.

Once an employee retires, or becomes otherwise eligible for the pension (e.g., on leaving for other employment after a certain number of years of being in the pension plan), all of the pension income is taxed as regular income as it is received. Up to $1,000 per year may effectively be exempted through the pension income tax credit (see 1.3.7).

There are two general kinds of pension plans: money-purchase and defined benefit. **Money-purchase** plans are analogous to RRSPs, in the sense that whatever the funds earn determines the amount of the pension payments. The pension plans of most employees are **defined benefit** plans. With such plans, you know from the beginning how much your pension will be, usually based on a percentage of your actual salary over a specified number of years. It is up to the employer to contribute enough, and to the pension fund management to invest wisely, to make sure that the plan remains sufficiently well funded to make those payments.

2.2.2 Individual Pension Plans—IPPs

An individual pension plan ("IPP") is exactly what the name implies—a registered pension plan designed and structured for one individual member. It is possible for owner-managers to meet the qualifications to have this type of pension plan registered with Revenue Canada.

The IPP concept is a two-pronged retirement saving strategy. First, your employer (or your own company, if you are an owner-manager) sets up a personalized, defined benefit, registered pension plan for you. Second, you also make the maximum allowable contribution to your RRSP (or your spouse's RRSP), although the fact that you belong to an IPP means that your RRSP limit is significantly lowered. The IPP concept is an alternative to the basic retirement saving strategy. whch would be simply to make the maximum possible RRSP contributions (the "RRSP route".)

Generally speaking, the IPP concept will be suitable for you if you are

- a key executive and/or owner-manager of a corporation
- over 40 years old; and
- earning a base salary of more than about $100,000

An IPP may also be worth considering if you are already in your employer's group RPP but the benefits from that RPP are not as generous as you would like them to be.

The main advantage of the IPP is that, if you are over 40, you and your employer will be allowed to make higher annual contributions than you would otherwise be entitled to under the RRSP route. In addition to maximizing tax savings, the higher allowable contributions under the IPP concept can be looked on as a form of forced savings. As well, an RPP is generally creditor-proof, while most RRSPs are not.

At termination or retirement, any surplus in the IPP can be returned to the member after paying personal tax. The surplus is the excess of IPP assets over the actual cost of the defined benefit pension to be provided under the terms of the plan. Alternatively, the tax sheltering may be allowed to continue if your IPP is able to opt, upon your retirement, to "self-annuitize" (i.e., have the IPP administer and pay you, the beneficiary of the plan, a life annuity rather than purchase one from a life insurance company). This can have the effect of stretching out the additional tax sheltering represented by any accumulated IPP surplus well into the years beyond retirement and quite possibly until your and your spouse's death.

Depending on your particular circumstances, an IPP could also provide some scope for making past service pension contributions. This can further enhance the tax sheltering value of an IPP.

The rules regarding IPPs are quite complex. You should consult your professional tax adviser for more information.

2.3 DEFERRED PROFIT-SHARING PLANS—DPSPs

Deferred profit-sharing plans are less common than registered pension plans. They operate the same way in that contributions are made by the employer and are only taxed in the employee's hands when received, normally on retirement.

Employer contributions to DPSPs are based on profits and are not usually expressed as a fixed dollar amount per employee each year. Such plans may be used, for example, by smaller companies which are not sure of profits and do not wish to commit themselves to large pension contributions, especially if they end up losing money for the year.

Employer contributions to DPSPs are generally limited to $7,750 for 1995 ($6,750 for 1996) per employee. They also cannot exceed 18% of the employee's salary from the employer for the year. Your employer's contributions to a DPSP add to your pension adjustment, and they therefore reduce the amount you can contribute to an RRSP (see 2.1.3).

Employee contributions to a DPSP are not permitted.

DPSPs cannot be set up for employees who are also major shareholders (over 10% of any class of shares) in the employer corporation, or for members of their families. They therefore cannot be used for owner-managers of small businesses.

2.4 Registered Education Savings Plans—RESPs

The RESP is a rather different animal from the other plans we have seen. Contributions to a RESP are *not* deductible. However, the income in the plan grows tax-free, so RESPs enjoy the effect of tax-free compounding of interest, which we illustrated in 2.1.5 above.

There are two basic ways of investing in a RESP. You may enroll in an existing group plan; there are two or three major ones which advertise heavily in baby magazines and pediatricians' offices. Or, if you prefer, you can set up an individual plan, in which case you will have control over the investment of the funds as well as choosing the beneficiaries of the plan.

One normally enrolls one's children or grandchildren (or a friend or relative's children) while they are young. If the child goes to college or university, the RESP provides an income to help cover the child's expenses. The income will be taxable to the child, who normally will not have much other income and so will pay little or no tax.

If the child does not go on to post-secondary education, the amounts contributed to the RESP, but not the income earned from it over the years, will be repaid to the contributor. The surplus investment income earned is available to other beneficiaries as scholarships, or can be donated to educational institutions.

The maximum contribution to RESPs by all taxpayers is limited to $1,500 per year and $31,500 lifetime in respect of any one beneficiary. In addition, the maximum period over which income generated in an RESP may be sheltered from tax is 26 years. RESPs set up after February 20, 1990 may make payments only to individuals who are *full-time* students.

2.5 Planning opportunities

Having covered the basics of deferred income plans, let us look at some planning techniques available.

2.5.1 RRSP: CONTRIBUTE EARLY AND OFTEN

If you have cash in the bank earning interest, even if you are young and not yet concerned about retirement, you should contribute as much as possible to an RRSP. The example we saw in 2.1.5 above shows how valuable it is to have your funds earning tax-free income.

If possible, you should contribute early, rather than waiting till the deadline. Your 1996 contribution, for example, may be made any time until March 1, 1997 if you intend to deduct it on your 1996 tax return. If you contribute at the beginning of 1996, all of the income earned for that extra year will accumulate tax-free. The effect of early contributions over several years will be dramatic. Do ensure, however, that you have enough contribution room before you commit your contribution for the year, and remember that each year's contribution will be limited to 18% of your *previous year's* earned income.

You can store up any unused RRSP contribution room if you can't afford to make a contribution now, and make your contribution and claim the deduction in later years within the carry-forward period.

If you have the cash and the contribution room, but do not want to claim a deduction in the current year because you are already in a low tax bracket, make the contribution but delay the deduction. As discussed in 2.1.3, you can claim the deduction in any later year. If you are confident of being in a higher tax bracket within the next year or so, this strategy can maximize the tax-free growth of funds while also maximizing your tax savings.

For cash-flow purposes, you may wish to set up a monthly transfer of a few hundred dollars from your regular bank account to your RRSP account. That will ensure steady contributions to the RRSP over the course of the year.

When considering investments within your RRSP, bear in mind the one major drawback of long-term investments such as five-year GICs. If you decide to withdraw the funds sooner for tax purposes (see 2.5.7 below), or to use the Home Buyer's Plan (see 2.1.8), you may have a problem.

2.5.2 CONSIDER A SELF-DIRECTED RRSP

Despite the annual administration fee, a self-directed RRSP provides you with the opportunity to realize a better return and will certainly give you much more flexibility. You don't have to be a financial expert to profit from your self-directed RRSP; its portfolio can be as simple or complicated as you wish. Unlike the array of fixed income and other "blue chip" type RRSPs offered by banks and brokerage houses, a self-directed RRSP allows you to direct how the funds are invested and enables you to consider some less common, potentially more profitable RRSP investment strategies.

However, the broader range of investment options you may acquire with a self-directed RRSP comes with a higher level of risk. That level of risk depends on your investment choices but, of course, in some cases, higher risks can mean higher rewards. Nevertheless, it is usually prudent to spread your investments over a wide range of options and to ensure that at least a portion of your investments have fixed rates of return, such as GICs.

Consider contributing shares (or interest-bearing investments) that you already own to your self-directed RRSP in lieu of cash contributions. Shares in small businesses can be contributed in limited circumstances (for example, you must not be a controlling shareholder of the corporation). However, most shares and bonds of Canadian public corporations are fair game. If you have shares that you intend to hold for a long time, you can contribute them to your RRSP and get a tax deduction without any cash outlay.

Note that capital gains and dividends are effectively fully-taxed when withdrawn from an RRSP, since you're taxed on the total amount withdrawn. So if you contribute shares (or buy shares inside your RRSP), any capital gains and dividends will eventually be taxed at a higher rate than if you earned them directly (see 4.2 and 5.1.2). If you leave the funds in the RRSP for long enough, the deferral of tax and tax-free compounding of interest should more than make up for the tax rate differential, however.

A transfer of investments to your RRSP can trigger a capital gain, since the transfer will be deemed to take place at fair market value. However, you are prohibited from claiming a capital loss (see 4.3) on the transfer of investments to your RRSP.

If you have a self-directed RRSP, make sure to pay the administration fee *outside the RRSP* rather than from the RRSP account. (Your broker or financial institution should give you this option.) If you pay the fee from your RRSP funds, you reduce the pool of funds available to grow tax-free. If you pay it from another account, Revenue Canada permits you to deduct the fee as "Carrying charges" at line 221 of your tax return. This deduction will not affect your contribution limit, so if the fee is $125 you can effectively get a maximum tax deduction of $14,625 in respect of your RRSP for 1995.

Consider using your self-directed RRSP to hold or refinance a mortgage on property owned by you or by other family members at prevailing mortgage rates. Whether this makes financial sense will depend on your particular circumstances. If your house is unencumbered by a mortgage, you can take out a new mortgage from your RRSP — if you use those funds to invest in securities and other business opportunities, your interest payments and set-up costs paid outside your RRSP may be tax-deductible. As a general rule of thumb, to be a worthwhile investment, the mortgage's principal should be in the $50,000 to $100,000 range with a term of at least five years. Alternatively if you don't have that much cash in your RRSP, some financial institutions offer a program through which the mortgage is "shared" between your RRSP and your institution.

To expand and diversify your investments in a self-directed RRSP, take advantage of the ability to invest up to 20% of the cost amount of your RRSP's holdings in foreign property. Also consider increasing your RRSP's foreign content up to 40% by investing in qualifying small Canadian businesses (see 2.1.5). Another indirect way of further increasing your self-directed RRSP's foreign property content is to invest in a qualifying mutual fund trust. As long as the trust meets certain conditions, the mutual fund trust in which you invest can also invest up to 20% of the cost amount of its holdings in foreign property.

2.5.3 CONSIDER A LABOUR-SPONSORED VENTURE CAPITAL CORPORATION

If you live in Ontario, Québec, British Columbia, New Brunswick, Saskatchewan, Manitoba, Nova Scotia or Prince Edward Island, a 40% credit is available for an investment of up to $5,000 per year in a "labour-sponsored venture capital corporation", or LSVCC (see 5.4.9 and 14.3.4). In Newfoundland, Alberta and the territories, only the 20% federal credit is available.

You can buy LSVCC shares and contribute them to your RRSP. You can also generally have the shares bought directly by your self-directed RRSP, provided the RRSP uses "new" or previous contribution funds (but not earnings). Either way, you claim the credit on your personal income tax return.

When combined with the deduction for the RRSP contribution, a $5,000 investment in an LSVCC may cost you as little as $350 after tax. Particularly if you are not otherwise making the maximum possible RRSP contribution, an investment in an LSVCC for your RRSP may be worth considering. Before taking the plunge and investing in a LSVCC, make sure you evaluate the relative merits from an investment perspective, as they are generally a higher risk and probably illiquid investment. (See also 5.4.9 and 5.7.6.)

2.5.4 CONSIDER RRSP RATHER THAN ADDITIONAL RPP CONTRIBUTIONS

If you have been making voluntary contributions to your registered pension plan under a money purchase provision, consider contributing to an RRSP instead. The amount you can contribute will normally be the same, but the RRSP will give you much greater flexibility in the future. If you want to make sure you never have access to the funds before retirement, then by all means continue to contribute to your pension plan.

2.5.5 CONTRIBUTE TO SPOUSE'S RRSP

If your spouse's income is expected to be lower than yours, either on retirement or at some earlier time (including, for example, due to expected maternity leave), you should consider contributing funds to your spouse's RRSP rather than your own, and make the contribution no later than December rather than the following February. Your spouse may then be able to withdraw the funds in the future (after waiting until the third year after the year in which you last contributed to any of your spouse's plans) and pay less tax than you would have on the same income. We explore this technique in more detail in 3.3.11, in the chapter on Income Splitting.

If you are over 71 and have "earned income" in the previous year, note that this will create new RRSP room for you in the current year. As long as your spouse is under 72, you can still claim a deduction for a spousal RRSP contribution.

2.5.6 Transfer retiring allowance or severance pay to RRSP

As noted in 2.1.7.2, retiring allowances and severance pay can be transferred to your RRSP, to a limit of $2,000 per year of employment before 1996, plus $1,500 for any years of employment before 1989 for which your employer's pension contributions have not vested. If you are making such a transfer, make sure you review the minimum tax implications (see Chapter 11).

2.5.7 Consider non-deductible contribution of $2,000 to RRSP

A penalty tax of 1% per month applies to RRSP contributions above the level permitted (see 2.1.7.4). However, a cumulative margin of $2,000 is allowed before the penalty tax kicks in, to account for cases where an individual inadvertently contributes too much.

If you are already contributing the maximum for both 1995 and 1996, consider making an additional contribution of up to $2,000 to further benefit from the compounding effect of tax-free growth. As long as your total excess contributions from January 1, 1991 through the rest of your lifetime do not exceed $2,000, the penalty tax will not apply. As a practical matter, you should be able to claim the entire $2,000 as a deduction in the next year, as new RRSP deduction room is created.

As discussed above (see 2.5.5), new RRSP room continues to be created after age 71 if you have earned income. Thus, you may be able to claim a deduction for your undeducted $2,000 overcontribution after reaching age 72 if you have sufficient earned income in the previous year.

If you overcontributed $8,000 before February 27, 1995, you must use up $6,000 of that overcontribution against your current RRSP deduction room before deducting any other contributions for 1996 or later years. See 2.1.7.4.

2.5.8 Planning for the Home Buyers' Plan

If you are in the market for a first home, look at the Home Buyers' Plan (see 2.1.8) as a possible source of cash flow. Be aware, however, of two factors. First, you must plan to have enough cash flow to pay back the amount borrowed over the 15-year period required, so as not to have the RRSP withdrawals taxed as income. Second, your retirement income will be reduced by the tax-free growth that is lost by having a lower balance in the RRSP for a number of years. See the discussion in 2.1.8 under the heading "Should you use the Home Buyer's Plan?".

If you are about to be married and your future spouse owns a home that you will be living in, consider borrowing funds under the Home Buyer's Plan before your wedding. Once you are married, you will not be able to do so. However, you are not restricted by a previous home owned by your spouse, as long as you do not live in it while married. Therefore, if you plan on buying a new home after your wedding, you should not (romantic considerations aside) move into your spouse's current home until you have made your withdrawal under the Plan.

The same applies if you have been living common-law for less than 12 months (and have not had a child together). Once you reach 12 months of living together, you are considered "married" for income tax purposes (see 1.3.1). If your mate owns your present home, but you are planning on "moving up" to a larger home, you should consider withdrawing funds under the Home Buyer's Plan before you have lived together for 12 months. However, you will have to take ownership (or at least part ownership) of the new home in your own name.

If you are planning to buy a new home and you are close to the four-year cutoff that will requalify you as a "first-time buyer", consider waiting and making your purchase at a time when you can use the Home Buyer's Plan. For example, if you sold your last home in 1991, you can use the Plan as of January 1, 1996.

If your RRSP balance is not yet at $20,000 and you intend to use the Home Buyer's Plan to its fullest, make your contribution early enough that it can sit in the RRSP for 90 days before you withdraw the funds. Then the amount you contributed can be withdrawn as well without affecting your deduction for the contribution.

If you live in Québec and are buying a home before 1996, you may also be eligible for the "Premier Toit" credit (see 14.2.14).

2.5.9 RRSP WITHDRAWALS IN LOW-INCOME YEARS

RRSPs can be considered as a tax averaging tool rather than just a mechanism for retirement saving. If you are still fairly young and not too worried about retirement income, you can withdraw funds from your RRSP whenever there is a tax advantage to doing so.

Suppose you plan to take some time off to care for your young children, for example, or to go on an extended vacation or take up some other activity. During such years, where your employment income will be low, you can withdraw funds from your RRSP and perhaps pay tax at the 27% rate instead of 41% or 50%. The advantage of low-rate taxation will have to be balanced against the advantage of tax-free growth available by leaving the funds in the RRSP.

In an anticipated low-income year following a high-income year, you can even consider contributing in February, claiming a deduction (say at 41%) for the previous year, and withdrawing the funds, to be taxed at the low (27%) rate.

You will need to plan around the withholding tax on RRSP withdrawals, however. Under the Income Tax Regulations, a withdrawal of up to $5,000 is subject to 10% withholding; over $5,000 and up to $15,000, 20%; and over $15,000, 30%. You may be able to arrange withdrawals so that they incur the least possible withholding tax, leaving you with the use of the funds until you file your tax return the following April. Bear in mind, however, that you may have a tax liability to settle up on April 30 to the extent that your tax rate on the income exceeds the withholding tax rate.

2.5.10 When you turn 71

By the end of the year in which you turn 71, you will have to decide what to do with your RRSP. A straight withdrawal will rarely be the best option, since you will be taxed on the total income—and none of it will be eligible for the pension tax credit (see 1.3.7). Instead, if you wish to have some control over the investments, you should purchase a RRIF (see 2.1.6.3). If you prefer simply to have a steady monthly income that you don't have to worry about, contact your life insurance agent and purchase an annuity (see 2.1.6.2).

If you are setting up an annuity, consider the effect of the tax brackets on your income. Your main goal, of course, is to ensure that you have enough income each month to meet your needs. If you can satisfy those needs with a longer-term annuity that keeps your income below the high-tax brackets, you may be better off.

2.5.11 Consider an Individual Pension Plan

If you are an executive earning over $100,000 and your employer does not have a registered pension plan (or your employer does have one, but it is not as generous as you would like), consider approaching your employer to discuss establishing an IPP (see 2.2.2 above) on your behalf as part of your compensation package. If you are an owner-manager of a corporation, there is nothing to stop you from setting up an IPP.

There are many complex factors and issues you will need to consider before concluding whether or not an IPP is right for you. Professional assistance in this regard is a must.

In general, some of the advantages an IPP can offer you include: permitting you and your employer to maximize tax deductible contributions; maximizing tax sheltering on your retirement savings (and potentially the value of your estate); and providing better protection from creditors. In addition, your employer will be required to top up the funds in the IPP if investment performance is poor and there will be insufficient funds (as determined by an actuary) to pay you the defined benefit pension promised under the plan. This last "advantage" will no doubt be a point of concern to your employer.

There are also significant potential disadvantages of an IPP which you should carefully consider. For example, you will lose the flexibility to split income on retirement, since contributions cannot be made to the IPP for your spouse, as can be done with RRSPs. In contrast to RRSPs, which can be cashed in any time, contributions made to the IPP will be locked in under pension benefits legislation until retirement, at which time they must be used to provide retirement benefits (usually in the form of a life annuity or life income fund). An RRSP, on the other hand, provides a variety of options, on termination or retirement (see 2.1.6). In addition, start-up and ongoing costs of administration of an IPP will be higher than those of your RRSP. This is due to the complex regulatory environment governing pension plans. For example, an actuarial valuation will be required at startup and every three years thereafter; and certain forms must be filed annually.

2.5.12 VESTING OF RPP BENEFITS

If you are a member of a company pension plan, find out how long it takes for your contributions to be "vested". Once they are vested, the pension you have earned becomes yours, and almost all employers will allow you to take the full pension benefits with you if you change jobs. On the other hand, if they are not vested, you get your own contributions back in cash when you leave—but no pension down the road. The vesting of your pension benefits can be a major factor in career change decisions.

2.5.13 CONSIDER AN RESP

If you have children who you expect will attend college or university, and you expect to be financing their education anyway, consider investing in an RESP. You might also want to do this for grandchildren, nieces and nephews, or other children whose education you would like to support.

2.6 REFERENCES

The following publications can be obtained (in person or by telephone request) from your nearest Revenue Canada District Taxation Office:

Interpretation Bulletin IT-124R6, "Contributions to registered retirement savings plans"

Interpretation Bulletin IT-167R5, "Registered pension funds or plans—Employee's contributions"

Interpretation Bulletin IT-307R3, "Registered retirement savings plan for taxpayer's spouse"

Interpretation Bulletin IT-320R2, "Registered retirement savings plan—Qualified investments"

Interpretation Bulletin IT-337R2, "Retiring allowances"

Interpretation Bulletin IT-363R2, "Deferred profit sharing plans—Deductibility of employer contributions and taxation of amounts received by a beneficiary"

Information Circular 72-22R8, "Registered retirement savings plans"

Information Circular 77-1R4, "Deferred profit sharing plans"

Information Circular 78-18R4, "Registered retirement income funds"

Information Circular 79-8R3, "Forms to be used to directly transfer funds to or between plans or to purchase an annuity"

Information Circular 93-3, "Registered education savings plans"

"RRSPs and Other Registered Plans for Retirement — Tax Guide"

Brochure, "Calculating your 19__ RRSP Deduction Limit"

Brochure, "Home Buyers' Plan for 19__ Participants"

Form TIE-OVP, "Individual return for RESP overpayments"

Form T1023, "Calculation of earned income for 19__"

Form T1036, "Home buyers' plan—application for withdrawal after March 1, 1993"

Form T1037, "Home buyers' plan—RRSP repayment"

Form T2097, "Identification of amounts transferred to an RRSP for 19__"

Form T2205, "Calculation of amounts from a spousal RRSP or RRIF to be included in income for 19__"

3 INCOME SPLITTING

PLANNING TIPS

- Higher-income spouse should pay household expenses
- Pay a salary or consulting fee to spouse and/or children
- Lend business assets, to generate income from business rather than property
- Lend funds and charge the minimum rate of interest, where the funds can be invested for a higher yield
- Pay the interest on your spouse's investment loans
- Transfer property at fair market value, for future appreciation
- Lend or transfer funds so spouse or child can earn secondary income (on the reinvested attributed income)
- Deposit child tax benefit payments directly into bank accounts for children
- Transfer future capital gains to children
- Pay lower-income spouse's taxes and instalments
- Transfer shares that will pay capital dividends
- Contribute to spousal RRSP
- Give funds to child who will be 17 by the end of the year
- Allow children to invest funds they earn
- Assign CPP benefits to spouse, if both are over 60 and one has higher benefits than the other
- Transfer unused tax credits to spouse
- Pay children over 18 for child-care

3.1 WHY INCOME SPLITTING?

The Canadian tax system uses *progressive* tax rates, whereby the marginal rate of tax (tax on additional income) increases as taxable income increases.

The marginal rate of tax varies from province to province, but is *approximately*:

27% on income up to $29,590

41% on income from $29,590 to $59,180

50% on income over $59,180

As can be seen, the tax payable on two $30,000 incomes will be significantly less than that on one $60,000 income—about $4,500 less, in fact. Taxpayers, therefore, have an incentive to "split" income between, for example, a high-income earner and a non-working spouse or children.

The *Income Tax Act* contains a number of measures to prevent the most obvious kinds of income splitting. However, some opportunities are available. We shall look first at the rules, so you understand the context in which to plan, and then at the planning opportunities that remain.

Note that most of this chapter will be irrelevant to you if you do not have funds invested and earning income that is subject to tax. The very best tax planning technique is usually to channel all extra cash into paying off any non-deductible interest such as your mortgage or credit-card balances.

3.2 RULES THAT PREVENT INCOME SPLITTING

3.2.1 INDIRECT PAYMENTS

The *Income Tax Act* provides that a payment or transfer made "pursuant to the direction of, or with the concurrence of" a taxpayer to some other person is to be included in the taxpayer's income to the extent it would have been if paid to the taxpayer. So, for example, if you arrange for your employer to pay part of your salary to your spouse, the income will still be taxed in your hands and you will not have accomplished anything.

3.2.2 ATTRIBUTION BETWEEN SPOUSES

Suppose you earn $90,000 per year and your spouse earns $10,000. Your marginal tax rate (tax on any additional income) is 50% and your spouse's is 27%. Assume you have $10,000 in bonds that generate $1,000 per year in interest and decide to give, or lend, the bonds to your spouse. As a result you hope to pay only $270 tax on the income instead of $500.

This is the kind of transaction that the **attribution rules** cover. These rules attribute income from property (in our example, the $1,000 of investment income each year) back to the person who transferred or loaned the property.

The attribution rules with respect to spouses provide that where *property* (including money) is *transferred or loaned, directly or indirectly* by you to your spouse (or a person who has since become your spouse), then all *income* or loss *from the property*, and any *capital gain or loss* on the disposition of the property will be *attributed back* to you. So, in our example, the $1,000 income on the $10,000 investment that you gave to your spouse must be reported on your tax return, not your spouse's—and so will be subject to tax of about $500 rather than about $270. This will be true year after year—as long as you and your spouse remain together, any income from the bonds will be taxed in your hands. If you transfer shares, for example, and your spouse sells the shares at some later time, any capital gain or capital loss relative to *your* original cost must be reported as *your* capital gain or loss, subject to the usual rules for capital gains (see Chapter 4).

Note that common-law spouses who meet the criteria outlined in 1.3.1 are considered spouses for tax purposes, and are therefore subject to these attribution rules as well.

There is an exception to this attribution rule; an exception that applies to the rules we will see later as well. If you transfer for fair market value consideration (e.g., sell the bonds to your spouse for $10,000 cash) and report the resulting gain, the rule will not apply. (If you realize a loss on the transfer, a special rule deems the loss to be zero. However the denied loss can be added to your spouse's cost for tax purposes.) If the consideration includes indebtedness (e.g., you sell the bonds for a $10,000 promissory note), or if you simply lend funds or property to your spouse, then to avoid the attribution rule you must charge (and, of course, report!) interest on the loan. The interest rate must be at least equal to Revenue Canada's prescribed interest rate at that time or a commercial rate of interest. For this exception to apply, the interest must actually be *paid* in each year, or by the following January 30. If the January 30 deadline ever passes without the interest being paid, that year's income and *all* future income from the loaned property will be attributed back to the lender.

EXAMPLE

On January 1, 1995 you lend $10,000 cash to your spouse, who puts the money in the bank and earns $500 interest over the course of the year.

If you do not charge interest, then the $500 will be attributed back to you and taxed in your hands. Suppose you do wish to charge interest. The minimum rate would have to be either:

- *the rate that would apply between two arm's-length parties (assume 8% for this example); or*
- *Revenue Canada's rate at the time the loan was granted (assume 7%).*

If your spouse is required to pay interest on the anniversary date of the loan and actually pays you at least $700 in interest by January 30, 1997, then the $500 interest will not be attributed back to you. But then, of course, you have to report the $700 in interest income from your spouse, so you are no further ahead. In fact, your spouse is technically only allowed to deduct $500 of the interest paid to you, on the basis the additional $200 was not paid for the purpose of earning income.

Revenue Canada's prescribed rate, which is set quarterly, is for this purpose 4% lower than the rate that applies to late payments of tax (see 13.3).

3.2.3 ATTRIBUTION WITH RESPECT TO MINOR CHILDREN

Suppose you lend $10,000 in bonds to your daughter, who is in high school and can earn $1,000 in interest without paying any tax at all.

The attribution rules apply to children under 18. Where property is transferred or loaned, there will be attribution of income (or loss), but *not* of capital gains or losses. The attribution applies only for years in which the child is still under 18 *at the end of* the year.

Not all children under 18 are caught by the rule. It depends on the child's relationship with the taxpayer who transfers or lends the property. Attribution applies where the taxpayer and the child "do not deal at arm's length", a phrase that is defined to include all persons who are "related" as defined in the *Income Tax Act*. Generally, this will cover one's child, grandchild, great-grandchild (including one's spouse's child, one's child's spouse, etc., where "spouse" includes a common-law spouse as outlined in 1.3.1) or brother or sister (including brother-in-[common]-law and sister-in-[common]-law). This rule also specifically applies to nieces and nephews. For other relationships, it is a "question of fact" whether two taxpayers deal at arm's length.

The attribution rule for minors does not apply to income earned from investing the Child Tax Benefit that has replaced family allowances (see 1.5.1).

Although the attribution rule with respect to minors does not apply to capital gains and losses, the transfer of the property to the minor itself will generally be deemed to take place at fair market value. So any capital gain or loss accruing up to the time of the transfer will be triggered immediately in the transferor's hands, and it is only the gain or loss accruing *after* the transfer that when realized will be taxed in the child's hands.

The exceptions that we saw in 3.2.2, where the transferred property is acquired for fair market value or where interest is paid on any indebtedness or loan, also apply to this attribution rule.

3.2.4 ATTRIBUTION ON LOANS TO ADULT FAMILY MEMBERS

One further rule applies to loans (but not transfers) of property to other persons with whom the taxpayer does not deal at arm's length—such as, for example, one's children who are over 18, or one's in-laws or grandparents. If one of the main reasons for the loan was to achieve income-splitting and thereby reduce taxes, the income will be attributed back to the lender. So if you lend $10,000 to your adult son who is in university, and the purpose is to allow him to earn the $1,000 interest and pay little or no tax on it (rather than, say, to allow him to use the $10,000 to pay for his tuition), the $1,000 of interest will be attributed back to you. The exception where interest is charged and paid, as outlined in 3.2.2, applies in this case.

3.2.5 SPECIAL ANTI-AVOIDANCE RULES

If you are creative and devious enough, you may have thought of some possible ways around the rules we have just described. Don't bother. The *Income Tax Act* provides a number of special rules designed to thwart the loopholes that creative tax planners exploited in years past. We will summarize them only briefly; basically, anything you can think of has probably been thought of before.

(1) *Substituted property.* If property is substituted for transferred or loaned property, the attribution rules will apply to income or capital gains from the substituted property, and so on *ad infinitum* (to the extent that attribution would have applied to income from the original property). So if you give $10,000 in bonds to your spouse, who then sells them and buys $10,000 in stocks, any dividends and capital gains on the stocks will be attributed back to you.

(2) *Transfers to a trust or corporation.* In general, transfers to a trust will result in the same application of the attribution rules as if the transfer were made directly to the beneficiaries of the trust. Transfers to a corporation which result in a benefit to a "designated person" (spouse or related minor children, using the same definition we saw in 3.2.3) are also caught in most cases. So, for example, if you and your spouse each own half the shares in a corporation, and you give $10,000 to the corporation so that your spouse will benefit, you will be taxed as though you had received interest from the corporation. This attribution rule does not apply where the corporation is a "small business corporation" (see 4.3.2).

(3) *Back-to-back loans and transfers.* If you lend or transfer property to a third party, who then lends or transfers it to a "designated person" (your spouse or related minor children), it will be treated as though you had lent or transferred the property directly.

(4) *Guarantees.* If you arrange for a third party (e.g., a bank) to lend funds to a "designated person" on the strength of your guarantee, it will be treated as though you had lent the funds directly.

(5) *Repayment of existing loan.* If you lend funds to a "designated person", and they use the funds to pay off another loan that they used to buy property, your loan will effectively be treated as if it had been used to buy that property. (This is the flip side of the "substituted property" case covered in (1) above.) So, for example, if your spouse borrows $10,000 to invest in bonds, and you then lend your spouse $10,000 which is used to pay off that loan, the interest from the bonds will be attributed back to you.

(6) *Reverse attribution.* The attribution rules can be ignored if you try to use them to turn the tables on Revenue Canada and have them apply in the opposite direction from that intended.

(7) *General anti-avoidance rule.* The Act provides a general anti-avoidance rule (GAAR), applicable to all transactions. If you come up with a way of avoiding the attribution rules that is not caught by the existing rules but is a misuse or abuse of the *Income Tax Act*, it may be caught by GAAR.

3.3 Planning opportunities

In this section we discuss the planning opportunities available to achieve income splitting. For many of these to work, you need to keep careful documentation. Separate bank accounts for spouses will allow you to trace each one's funds properly. (Under provincial family law, this will not normally affect either spouse's rights to the family's funds on marriage breakdown.)

3.3.1 Higher-income spouse should pay expenses

The simplest technique is to make sure that daily living expenses (groceries, mortgage or rent payments, credit-card bills, etc.) are paid by the higher-income spouse. This will allow the lower-income spouse to maintain a larger investment base for earning future income that is taxed at a low rate.

3.3.2 Salary or consulting fee to spouse and children

If you carry on a business, either personally or through a corporation, rather than having purely employment income, consider paying a salary to your spouse and/or children. The salary must be "reasonable" in light of the services they perform for the business. Such services might include bookkeeping, filing, other administrative work, business development planning and acting as a director of the corporation. Revenue Canada auditors are usually fairly flexible in interpreting what constitutes a "reasonable" salary, provided services are genuinely being provided.

The impact of payroll taxes, Canada Pension Plan contributions and unemployment insurance premiums should be weighed against any potential tax savings expected from implementing this strategy.

Consider also whether your spouse can provide services on a contract (consulting) basis rather than as an employee. This would allow your spouse the advantages of self-employment income (see Chapter 7), including writing off expenses and deferral of taxation by picking an appropriate year-end. This is an aggressive tactic and should only be implemented with appropriate professional advice.

Another possibility is to bring your spouse into partnership with you. Taxation of partnerships is discussed in 7.3.

3.3.3 Loans of business assets

The attribution rules, as we have noted, apply to income from *property*—such as interest, dividends, rent and royalties. They do not, however, apply to income earned from a *business*. So if you can transfer or lend business assets in such a way that your spouse or child carries on business on a regular and continuous basis to earn income from business rather than from property, there will be no attribution. Such a step should only be undertaken with proper professional advice, to ensure that the legal steps required to effect the transfer are properly completed and that the possibility of the general anti-avoidance rule applying is minimized.

Note that this generally cannot be done for a passive interest in a partnership (including an interest in a limited partnership). Income from the partnership's business is technically business income, but it is deemed to be property income for purposes of the attribution rules unless the taxpayer is actively engaged in the partnership's business or is carrying on a similar business.

3.3.4 Loans on which interest is charged

As we saw in 3.2.2, the attribution rules do not apply where property or funds are loaned and interest is charged at a minimum rate, provided the interest is actually paid. Where assets are expected to produce a return that is well in excess of the minimum rate (the lower of a reasonable commercial rate and the Revenue Canada prescribed rate), it may make sense to lend the funds or assets and charge a rate of interest sufficient to avoid the application of the attribution rules. The excess yield from the assets over the amount of interest charged will then effectively be transferred to the lower-income taxpayer and not attributed back to the lender.

If interest rates are rising, the current Revenue Canada prescribed rate may be relatively low, since there is a time lag before it is set each quarter. Where such an opportunity arises, consider making a loan to your spouse on which interest is charged, "locking in" at the low prescribed rate, and having your spouse use the funds to invest at current market rates.

3.3.5 Pay interest on spousal loans

If your spouse has taken out an investment loan, consider paying the interest. There will be no attribution provided you do not pay any principal on account of the spousal loan. (Since the amount you pay is not actually invested by your spouse, there is no property from which income can be attributed.) This technique will preserve your spouse's assets and thereby increase his or her investment income.

3.3.6 Transfers for fair market value

As we have seen, the attribution rules also do not apply where property is transferred in exchange for consideration equal to the property's fair market value. (Where the consideration includes indebtedness, such as a promissory note, interest must be charged as outlined above.) A transfer at fair market value may be beneficial where the assets are expected to produce a high yield or to increase in value in the future.

3.3.7 Reinvestment of attributed income

We have seen that attribution applies to the income from property that is transferred or loaned. But what about the income from that income (secondary income)? Suppose you give $10,000 to your spouse, who earns $1,000 in interest in the first year, and the $1,000 is attributed back to you. In the second year, your spouse invests the $1,000 as well as the $10,000, and the $1,000 generates a further $100 in interest.

This "secondary income" is not attributed back to you, as it is not income from the property that was transferred. It is thus taxed in your spouse's hands. Over time, a significant stream of such secondary income can be built up. However, accurate records must be maintained. You may wish to have your spouse keep two bank accounts, one for the income that is attributed back to you and one into which all income from the first account is deposited. Only the income from the first account would be reported on your return.

3.3.8 Child Tax Benefit payments

Child Tax Benefit payments, which are non-taxable, have replaced the pre-1993 family allowance, Child Tax Credit and dependent child credit (see 1.5.1).

The attribution rules do not apply to Child Tax Benefit payments. If you deposit them to an account in the child's name, the investment income earned on the account will not be attributed back to you. Over time, a significant investment can be built up, the income from which is taxed in your children's hands. You may wish to withdraw the balance from the account annually and purchase higher-yielding bonds or term deposits.

3.3.9 Transferring future capital gains to children

As we saw in 3.2.3, the attribution rules with respect to minor children do not apply to capital gains. If you have assets that are expected to increase substantially in value (such as shares of a corporation), consider transferring them to your children or to a trust for your children. Any dividends will be attributed back to you as long as your children are under 18 at the end of the year in which the dividend is paid, but capital gains on sale of the assets will not be.

For example, suppose you own shares in your private business corporation. You invested $10,000 originally, and they are now worth $20,000. But you expect the corporation to do well over the coming years. If you give the shares to your children, you will be deemed to have disposed of them at $20,000, but the capital gain may be shielded by the capital gains exemption (see 4.4.1). If, a few years later, your children sell the shares for $100,000, the $80,000 capital gain will be taxed in their hands, not yours, and possibly taxed at a lower marginal rate, even if the capital gains exemption is no longer available at that point.

Other assets that might be appropriate for transfer to children are those which will normally generate capital gains but not income. Examples include jewellery, art and shares in speculative public companies.

Transfers to children should be done with proper professional advice. In some provinces there is a question as to whether minors can legally own property such as shares. You may need to set up a trust for this purpose.

3.3.10 PAYMENT OF SPOUSE'S TAXES

One way to effectively transfer funds is for you to directly pay your spouse's income tax liability—both in April and any instalments that are due during the year. Simply make sure that the cheque paying your spouse's taxes is drawn on your own account. Since the amount you pay goes directly to the government and is not invested by your spouse, there is no property from which income can be attributed. The result is that any funds your spouse would otherwise use to pay income taxes can be invested without the income being attributed back to you.

3.3.11 PAYMENT OF CAPITAL DIVIDENDS

Normally, dividends that are paid on shares you transfer to your spouse or minor children will be attributed back to you, as we have seen. However, the tax system provides for "capital dividends", which are always tax-free. Such dividends represent a distribution of the untaxed 1/4 of a corporation's capital gains. (For an example, see 8.2.4.)

If you transfer shares of a corporation, and the shares subsequently pay capital dividends, there will be no attribution of the income because it is not taxed in anyone's hands in the first place. As well, any income earned from reinvesting the dividends will not be attributed. This technique can work well for shares of private holding companies, but must be undertaken with proper professional advice to minimize the application of various anti-avoidance rules which could turn the dividends into taxable dividends.

3.3.12 SPOUSAL RRSP

A contribution to your spouse's RRSP, as we saw in 2.1.7.1, is specifically allowed by the *Income Tax Act*. When the funds are turned into an annuity or RRIF on retirement, there will be no attribution of the income back to you.

A further technique can be used at any time before retirement. Contributions to your spouse's RRSP, if withdrawn by your spouse, are taxed back in your hands to the extent you have made any spousal contributions in the year of withdrawal or in the two previous years. This means that you can split income, provided you can wait 24-36 months and not make spousal contributions in the meantime. It also means foregoing the benefits of leaving the funds to grow tax-free in the RRSP (see 2.1.5).

EXAMPLE

On December 31, 1995 you contribute $14,500 to an RRSP for your spouse.

This entitles you to a deduction of $14,500 for 1995 (assuming you have adequate contribution room—see 2.1.3— and have made no contributions to your own RRSP for 1995). Any withdrawals of up to $14,500 from your spouse's RRSPs in 1996 or 1997 will be attributed back to you; but on January 1, 1998, your spouse can withdraw the full $14,500, which will be taxed to your spouse as recipient provided you make no further spousal RRSP contributions in 1996, 1997 or 1998.

Of course, when you contribute to a spousal RRSP you lose your own RRSP contribution room, so the tax advantages of this technique are somewhat limited in scope, but it does achieve income splitting over the long term. You must also consider, however, whether your spouse having a higher income at retirement will affect eligibility for the old age credit (see 1.3.2) and will trigger the old age security clawback (see 1.6)—if those programs are even still around!

Note also that in this example, if you contributed for 1995 on January 1, 1996 rather than December 31, 1995, your spouse would have to wait until January 1, 1999 to withdraw the funds without attribution back to you. Contributions to spousal plans should thus not be put off to January or February, as is often done with one's own contributions.

3.3.13 CHILDREN 17 AND OLDER

Consider giving your children funds that they can invest. If your child turns 17 in the year you make the gift, the funds can be invested in a one-year (or longer) term deposit or certificate, which will not require interest to be reported until the year in which the child turns 18, and thus no attribution will follow. (If the investment is for more than one year, interest must still be reported annually; see 5.2.2.) Do not simply loan the funds without considering the special attribution rule discussed in 3.2.4.

You might also consider a gift of enough funds so that the income earned on the funds will cover the child's university tuition and residence over four (or more) years. Of course, you must be prepared to lose the funds, since they will legally belong to your child and not to you. Consider the use of a trust (with proper legal advice) if this is a concern.

3.3.14 ALLOW CHILDREN TO INVEST THE FUNDS THEY EARN

Consider lending your child, interest-free, an amount equal to what he or she earns over the summer and would otherwise spend. This will allow the child to earn investment income on his or her own earnings, and the investment income will not be attributed back to you.

Suppose you have a daughter who attends university and who earns $10,000 over the summer, and your normal arrangement with her is that she uses her income to pay for her tuition and basic expenses. If you lend her $10,000 interest-free, she can use the funds you lend her to pay her tuition and living expenses, and invest her summer earnings. Since the $10,000 invested represents her own funds, the income earned on that amount will not be attributed back to you and will be taxed at her marginal rate (or not taxed at all if her income is low enough). You could then repeat this process through several years of university, and have your daughter pay back the entire amount of the loan when she graduates, using the funds she has invested from her own earnings. Alternatively, you could lend her less money each year, as she will have her investment income available as an additional source of funds.

3.3.15 ASSIGNMENT OF CPP BENEFIT PAYMENTS

You may direct that up to 50% of your Canada Pension Plan benefits be paid to your spouse, provided both of you are over 60. If either of you does this, a portion of the other spouse's CPP is assigned automatically back to the first spouse.

If both spouses are eligible for maximum CPP benefits, assignment will not change anything, since each will assign half of the maximum to the other. But if one has high CPP benefits and the other has low benefits or none, the assignment can effectively transfer up to half of the CPP income.

The attribution rules specifically do not apply to an assignment of CPP benefits. If you and your spouse are both over 60, and you have higher CPP benefits and are in a higher tax bracket, you should consider such an assignment, which is done by completing a form available from Health and Welfare Canada. This assignment might not be advantageous, however, if it affects your spousal tax credit claim (see 1.3.1).

Benefits from the Québec Pension Plan (QPP) can be assigned to your spouse by completing a form available from Régie des rentes du Québec.

3.3.16 Transfer of tax credits to spouse

The transfer of tax credits is not really an income splitting measure, but it should be part of a couple's tax planning (see 1.3 and 5.1.3.5).

3.3.17 Pay children over 18 for child care

The deduction for child-care expenses was discussed in 1.2.3. No deduction is allowed for payments you make to a person related to you who is under 18. Once your older children turn 18, if you are the lower-income spouse you can pay them for child-care or baby-sitting services that permit you to earn employment or business income. Your adult child will need to give you a receipt and report the income for tax purposes.

3.4 References

The following publications can be obtained (in person or by telephone request) from your nearest Revenue Canada District Taxation Office:

Interpretation Bulletin IT-295R4, "Taxable dividends received after 1987 by a spouse"

Interpretation Bulletin IT-307R3, "RRSP for taxpayer's spouse"

Interpretation Bulletin IT-335R, "Indirect payments"

Interpretation Bulletin IT-369R, "Attribution of trust income to settlor"

Interpretation Bulletin IT-510, "Transfer and loans of property made after May 22, 1985 to a related minor"

Interpretation Bulletin IT-511R, "Interspousal and certain other transfers and loans of property"

Form T2205, "Calculation of amounts from a spousal RRSP or RRIF to be included in 19__ income"

4 CAPITAL GAINS AND LOSSES

PLANNING TIPS

- Carefully review whether your gains and losses are on income or capital account
- Make Canadian securities election if you wish to ensure capital treatment
- Use capital loss carryforward and carryback where available
- Consider filing late election to use capital gains exemption
- Consider delaying the sale of all or part of an asset until after the year end
- Consider transferring securities to RRSP, instead of contributing cash
- Claim capital gains reserve where not all of sale price received
- "Purify" corporation to create qualified small business corporation shares
- Make election to treat rented-out property as principal residence
- Plan around your CNIL balance when using capital gains exemption
- Keep at least 1 unit of mutual funds or other investments that have an exempt capital gains balance

As you may know, capital gains and losses are given special treatment in the income tax system. Capital gains are taxed at a lower rate than regular income; and individuals are entitled to an exemption for capital gains on certain kinds of property. In this chapter we'll describe the rules in general, and then look at some of the planning opportunities.

4.1 WHAT IS CAPITAL?

Before we get into the rules that apply to capital gains and losses, it helps to understand what we mean by "capital". Capital property is property that, if sold, will lead to a capital gain (or capital loss). The alternative is property that, when sold, leads to full income inclusion of any gain as income from business. For example, if you speculate on real estate, and you buy and sell a number of properties, your gains on the sales will probably be business income rather than capital gains.

There are no clear rules defining capital property. The *Income Tax Act*'s only comment is to define a "business" as including "an adventure or concern in the nature of trade". The courts have developed guidelines over the years, from which a general picture emerges. If you buy property with the intention of reselling it, and particularly if you sell it quickly and engage in many such transactions, your profit is likely to be considered income from business. If you buy property with the intention of earning income (e.g., rent or dividends) from it, and particularly if this is an isolated transaction and you hold the property for a long time, any gain on a sale is likely to be a capital gain.

If you wish to ensure that your trades on the stock market will always result in capital gains rather than business income, you may file an "Election on Disposition of Canadian Securities" form (Form T123) with any year's tax return. Once you do so, *all* "Canadian securities" you ever own will be considered to be capital property for the rest of your life. This includes, generally, shares in Canadian corporations, investments in mutual funds, and bonds, debentures or other debt issued by individuals or corporations resident in Canada (except a corporation related to you). Certain taxpayers, such as traders and dealers, are not allowed to make this election.

If you are unsure as to whether property you own is capital property or not, you should consult your professional advisers.

4.2 Capital gains

Capital gains occur only when property is sold (or deemed to have been disposed of under special rules, which we'll see in 4.5.4 and 4.5.5). So if you own, say, a rental property that has increased in value tenfold, you do not pay any tax on the increase until you actually sell the property. The capital gain is taxed only in the year of the sale.

The basic calculation of a capital gain is easy to understand: proceeds of disposition (normally the sale price), minus any selling expenses (e.g., real estate commissions), minus the **"adjusted cost base"**, equals the capital gain. In most cases the adjusted cost base is simply your cost of the property, but this figure is "adjusted" in various ways. (For the adjusted cost base of an interest in a partnership, see 7.3.5.). Where you have used the election to trigger part of your capital gains exemption (see 4.4), your "cost" will be higher than the actual cost.

Capital gains are, in effect, taxed at a lower rate than regular income. This is done by including in income only the **taxable capital gain,** which is three-quarters of the capital gain. (For sales from 1972 to 1988, the fraction was one-half, meaning that capital gains were half-taxed; for 1988 and 1989 the fraction was two-thirds.)

EXAMPLE

Jennifer paid $5,000 (including commission) for shares of the TD Bank in 1990. In 1995, she sells the shares for $6,100, of which her broker keeps $100 as commission.

For 1995, Jennifer has a capital gain of $1,000. The taxable capital gain is three-quarters, or $750, and this amount is included in her income for tax purposes.

We have mentioned in earlier chapters the marginal rates of tax on ordinary income. With three-quarters taxation of capital gains, the effective rates of tax are *approximately*:

Income level	Salary income	Capital gain (3/4)
$0-$29,590	27%	20%
$29,591-$59,180	41%	31%
$59,181 and up	50%	37%

The exact rates vary by province.

If you have very large capital gains, minimum tax may apply. See Chapter 11.

4.3 CAPITAL LOSSES

4.3.1 ORDINARY CAPITAL LOSSES

A capital loss occurs when the capital gain calculation produces a negative amount; that is, the adjusted cost base is greater than the proceeds of disposition minus the selling expenses. Just as capital gains are less heavily taxed than regular income, capital losses are less useful to you than regular (business) losses.

An **allowable capital loss** is *three-quarters* of a capital loss. This amount can be offset against taxable capital gains. In normal circumstances, if you have no taxable capital gains, the loss *cannot* be used against other income, however.

EXAMPLE

Brent earns an annual salary of $40,000. In October 1995, Brent sells some shares of a mining company, which cost him $2,000 several years before, for $6,000 after commission. In November 1995, he sells some bars of gold he bought in 1982 for $18,000, and receives only $10,000 since the price of gold has come down.

Brent has a $4,000 capital gain on the shares, which is a $3,000 taxable capital gain. He also has a $8,000 capital loss on the gold, which is a $6,000 allowable capital loss. This completely wipes out the taxable capital gain, but the extra

$3,000 of allowable capital loss cannot be used to reduce his salary income of $40,000. It can only be used against taxable capital gains of other years, as outlined below.

Allowable capital losses that can't be used in any given year, as in this example, can be **carried back** and applied against taxable capital gains of any of the previous three years, subject to whether the capital gains exemption was used in that prior year. This can be done even though your previous year's return has already been assessed. They can also be **carried forward** indefinitely; this balance is known as "net capital losses" and can be used against taxable capital gains in any future year.

Before May 23, 1985, up to $2,000 per year of allowable capital losses was allowed to be used against other income (such as employment income). If you disposed of any capital property at a loss before that date, you may still use this $2,000 deduction per year. Your unused pre-May 23, 1985 net capital losses less any capital gains exemption claimed since then is called your "pre-1986 capital loss balance".

4.3.2 ALLOWABLE BUSINESS INVESTMENT LOSSES

There is an exception to the general rule that allowable capital losses cannot be used against ordinary income. It applies to **allowable business investment losses**. These arise when there is a loss on shares of, or debt owing by, a **small business corporation**.

The term "small business corporation" has a very specific meaning in the *Income Tax Act*. It need not, in fact, be small. The corporation must meet a number of tests, which are that it be resident in Canada, a private corporation, not controlled in any manner by non-residents or public corporations, not listed on a Canadian or any of 26 foreign stock exchanges, and, most importantly, that substantially all (taken by Revenue Canada to mean 90% or more of the value) of its assets be used in an active business carried on primarily in Canada. Shares and debts in other small business corporations can qualify as such assets.

A capital loss on the shares or debt of a small business corporation (including, in some cases, simply determining that the debt has gone bad and will not be repaid) is called a "**business investment loss**". Three-quarters of this amount, the "allowable business investment loss" (ABIL), can be deducted against any other income such as employment income or investment income. However the amount of the ABIL that can be deducted against other income must be reduced by any capital gains exemption claimed in prior years. In addition, if an ABIL is deducted against other income, an equal amount of taxable capital gains must be realized in later years before commencing to use the capital gains exemption again. The availability of an ABIL is an extra incentive to investment in private Canadian businesses.

EXAMPLE

Janet carries on business as the proprietor of a clothing store, from which she nets $50,000 per year in business income. In 1985, Janet invests $10,000 in shares in XYZ Jewellery Inc., a corporation run by her brother which meets the definition of "small business corporation". In December 1995, the corporation goes bankrupt and Janet's shares become worthless.

Janet has a $10,000 business investment loss in 1995, resulting in a $7,500 allowable business investment loss. She can use this against her $50,000 business income, and so will be taxed in 1995 as if she had earned only $42,500.

Allowable business investment losses that can't be fully used (because you have already wiped out all of your income) are given the same treatment as business losses (see 7.4). That is, they can be carried back and used to offset income in any of the three previous years (even though you have already filed returns and paid tax for those years), or they can be carried forward and used to offset income in any of the next seven years. Any unused balance remaining after the seventh year is reclassified as an allowable capital loss.

4.4 THE CAPITAL GAINS EXEMPTION

Every individual (but not a trust or corporation) is entitled to a lifetime **$500,000 "capital gains exemption"** on certain small business shares and farm property.

The **general $100,000 capital gains exemption, which applied to all kinds of property, was eliminated** effective February 22, 1994. However, an election is available to use up your exemption for gains accrued to that date, and this election can be filed until April 30, 1997, as we shall see below in 4.4.4. If you did make the election (or if you make a late one), you have until the end of 1997 to change or revoke it.

Technically, under the *Income Tax Act* and on Revenue Canada's forms, the exemption is called the capital gains *deduction.* Where it applies, the taxable capital gain is still included in income for tax purposes (see 4.2), but an offsetting **deduction from net income** is allowed when computing "taxable income", the last step on the tax return before calculating tax and tax credits (see 1.1.1).

4.4.1 QUALIFIED SMALL BUSINESS CORPORATION SHARES

Up to $500,000 of capital gain on "qualified small business corporation shares" can be exempt.

The meaning of "small business corporation" was discussed in 4.3.2 above. The definition of "qualified small business corporation share" is very complex. In very general terms:

- the business must use substantially all (considered by Revenue Canada to mean 90% or more of the value) of its assets in carrying on an active business in Canada, except for shares and debt in other small business corporations
- nobody but you or a person "related" to you can have owned the shares for the two years before you sell them
- throughout the two-year period, more than 50% of the corporation's assets must have been used principally in an active business, or invested in other small business corporations.

Consult your tax adviser for the specific details as they apply to any shares you own.

EXAMPLE

Arnold has not used any of his capital gains exemption in the past. He owns all the shares of a corporation. The shares, which are "qualified small business corporation shares", originally cost him $30,000. In 1995, Arnold sells the shares for $230,000.

Arnold's capital gain is $200,000. Three-quarters of the gain, or $150,000, goes into Arnold's income for 1995, but an offsetting capital gains deduction of $150,000 is allowed in computing his "taxable income"—so he pays no extra tax, except possibly for minimum tax (see Chapter 11). Of his $500,000, Arnold still has $300,000 of capital gains ($225,000 of taxable capital gains) that can be exempt in the future.

As can be seen from the example, it doesn't matter whether you think of the exemption as covering **$500,000** (in the example, $200,000 plus $300,000) of **capital gains**, or **$375,000** ($150,000 plus $225,000) of **taxable capital gains**. It comes to the same thing.

There is a special election that lets you take advantage of the exemption for qualified small business corporation shares if the corporation goes public, without having to actually sell the shares. (Once the corporation becomes a public corporation, the shares will no longer qualify for the exemption.)

4.4.2 QUALIFIED FARM PROPERTY

The $500,000 exemption generally applies to **family farms** and **farm quotas** that meet certain conditions. In general terms, if you acquired the property before June 18, 1987 and it was used in the business of farming by you or a member of your family either in the year you sell it or in any five previous years, it will be qualified farm property. If you acquired it after June 17, 1987, you normally have to have owned it for at least two years, been engaged in farming on a regular and continuous basis, and have earned more gross income from farming than from other sources. Similar rules also apply to allow the exemption to be claimed for gains realized on the sale of shares of a **family farm corporation** or an interest in a **family farm partnership**.

If you own farm property that you are considering selling, you should obtain professional advice to determine whether you are eligible for the $500,000 exemption.

Note that your $500,000 exemption is limited to the *total* gains on both small business shares and family farms (plus any other exemption claimed up to February 22, 1994, as discussed in 4.4.4 below) over your lifetime. If, for example, you have already claimed an exemption in respect of $420,000 of gain on small business shares, the maximum exemption available to you for farm property would be $80,000.

4.4.3 RESTRICTIONS ON USE OF THE EXEMPTION

The *Income Tax Act* provides rules to prevent people from taking what is considered unfair advantage of the capital gains exemption. The exemption is supposed to exempt capital gains from being taxed. If, however, you are able to use the system of capital gains taxation to claim capital-related losses against other income, the rules prevent you from getting the exemption as well. We'll look at the details in this section.

4.4.3.1 CAPITAL LOSSES DEDUCTED AGAINST REGULAR INCOME

There are two kinds of allowable capital losses that can be written off against ordinary income. These are allowable business investment losses (see 4.3.2) and a much rarer bird, pre-1986 capital losses, which can still be used up at $2,000 per year (see 4.3.1).

If you have either of these kinds of losses, you will lose your capital gains exemption to the extent that the losses are or can be written off against your ordinary income. The idea is that such losses should effectively be netted against your taxable capital gains first. In other words, you cannot both have a gain that is sheltered by the capital gains exemption, and also use certain capital losses against your other income.

4.4.3.2 CUMULATIVE NET INVESTMENT LOSS (CNIL)

As is discussed in 5.3, interest paid on a loan is deductible if you use the loan to invest in shares. Even though your real reason for buying the shares may be to obtain capital gains, the fact that the shares *could* pay dividends (which are income from property) is generally considered enough to make the interest on the loan deductible as interest on funds borrowed to earn income from property.

Tax policy-makers considered it unfair for people to be able to take out large loans, write off the interest, and use the funds to buy shares which would increase in value, giving them a capital gain which was tax-free due to the capital gains exemption. This kind of "double-dipping" was stopped beginning in 1988.

Your capital gains deduction (normally taken, as we have seen, when calculating your "taxable income") is therefore *reduced* by the amount of your **cumulative net investment loss**, or CNIL (pronounced "senile"). The basic idea is that if you borrow money, buy an investment and the investment goes up in value, you shouldn't be able to get both the capital gains exemption and your interest writeoff.

The actual calculation is rather more complicated. Your CNIL is the total of your **investment expenses** minus all your **investment income**, cumulative since January 1, 1988. "Investment expenses" includes interest you have deducted, investment counsel fees, partnership losses (except where you are an active partner), losses from rental property, and most tax shelter writeoffs. Investment income includes interest, dividends ("grossed-up" by one-quarter as explained in 5.1.2), rental income and income from a partnership where you are not an active partner.

EXAMPLE

Arnold has not used any of his capital gains exemption in the past, but has claimed a total of $10,000 in net investment expenses since 1988, so his CNIL balance is $10,000. He owns all the shares of a corporation. The shares, which are "qualified small business corporation shares", originally cost him $30,000. In 1995, Arnold sells the shares for $230,000.

Arnold's capital gain is $200,000. Three-quarters of the gain, or $150,000, goes into Arnold's income for 1995. Because of his $10,000 CNIL balance, the offsetting capital gains deduction is only $140,000, not $150,000.

In effect, Arnold must "eat through" his CNIL balance and pay tax on the $10,000 before he can start to use his capital gains exemption.

Note that the CNIL limitation applies even though the investment expenses and the capital gain are unrelated. However, taxable capital gains that are actually taxed, because you cannot or do not offset them with your capital gains exemption, effectively reduce the impact of the CNIL balance.

Note also that the calculation of the exemption (and CNIL) is done at the *end* of the year. It is therefore possible to realize a capital gain that you think is exempt, but for which you cannot claim the exemption because you create a CNIL balance later on in the same year.

4.4.4 THE $100,000 EXEMPTION AND THE ELECTION AS OF FEBRUARY 22, 1994

Until February 22, 1994, there was a general $100,000 exemption for capital gains on any property. The $100,000 was included in the total $500,000 allowed over an individual's lifetime for all property (including farms and small business shares). However, it did not apply to investment real estate (including certain shares or partnership interests whose value was based on real estate) acquired after February 1992. For investment real estate acquired earlier, the exemption was prorated based on the number of months you owned the property before and after March 1, 1992.

The federal budget of February 22, 1994 eliminated the regular exemption for gains after that date. However, the budget also introduced an **election** for gains accrued to February 22, 1994. To the extent you would otherwise have been able to claim the exemption (see 4.4.3), you can *elect* to treat any property as if you had sold it on budget day at a particular price and **immediately reacquired** it at the same price. The price should not be higher than the fair market value of the property on February 22, 1994. (The exemption was also eliminated for Québec tax purposes and a virtually identical election was introduced.)

The election was generally due by May 1, 1995, the due date for filing your 1994 tax return. If for some reason you did not make the election on time, you have until **April 30, 1997** to file a late election, provided you pay a penalty at the time you file the election. The penalty is 0.33% (i.e., $1/3$ of 1% = 0.33%, or 0.00333) of the taxable capital gain that results from the election, for each month or part month that the election is late.

Since the penalty increases for every month or part month that goes by after May, 1995, the longer you wait to make the election, the higher the penalty. If you elect a deemed gain of $100,000, the late-filing penalty per month will be $250 ($100,000 × $3/4$ × 0.00333).

The amount of the late filing penalty will rise in proportion with the amount of your elected gain. You will have to weigh the penalty—which you must pay at the time you file the election—against the potential tax savings that will result sometime later when you sell the property. If you are also making the election for Québec tax purposes, you'll have to pay the same penalty when you file your Québec election.

If you made the election on time (or if you make a late one), you have until **December 31, 1997** to amend or revoke it. If you file an amended election to report a larger taxable capital gain for a particular property, you'll have to pay a penalty of 0.33% of any additional taxable capital gain that results from increasing your election, for each month or part month that the amended election is filed past the original May 1, 1995 deadline. No penalty will result if you cancel your election or amend it to reduce the elected capital gain.

You can only file an amended election in respect of the same property upon which you originally elected. This rule stops you from transferring the bumped-up portion of the adjusted cost base of one asset to another asset. If you've used up your exemption and you want to elect in respect of a different property, you must cancel your original election and file a new one. Before you do, be sure to factor in the increased penalty that will probably result.

Making the election will in most cases have no immediate tax effect, but will give you a higher cost base for the property (see 4.2). Thus, when you eventually sell the property, the tax on the capital gain will be lower or eliminated entirely. You may even have a capital loss down the road (see 4.3) as a result of making the election if the property declines in value.

Flow-through entities—mutual funds and others

Certain investments can have capital gains calculated at the investment level and then flowed through to you so that you report the capital gain on your personal income tax return. These are called "**flow-through entities**". They include mutual funds (see 5.1.3.4), segregated funds (similar to mutual funds, but offered through life insurers), partnerships (see 7.3.3), investment corporations, mortgage investment corporations, employee profit sharing plans and certain other special trusts.

You can have capital gains on flow-through entities in two ways. First, gains incurred in the entity are flowed through to you. Second, you can sell your interest in the entity.

You can make the election to trigger your capital gains exemption in respect of holdings in flow-through entities. The same late penalty applies as above, if you make the election late. However, the effect of the election is very different than for other property. Rather than increasing your cost base in the investment (as in the example above), your election creates an "**exempt capital gains balance**" that you can use until the year 2004 to reduce any capital gain resulting from either the sale of the property or capital gains flowed through to you. Thus, you can shield "flow-through" gains in future years, even though you may not have sold the investment. This balance will only apply **until the year 2004**, after which the effect of the election will be lost (subject to any future changes in the rules). Furthermore, the exempt capital gains balance can only shield you against tax on capital gains; it cannot create or increase a capital loss, as can happen with the increased cost base on other property. However, if you still have an exempt capital gains balance with respect to a property at the end of the year 2004 and you still own at least 1 unit or share of that property, the remaining balance will be added to the adjusted cost base of the remaining property in 2005.

You will have to track the "exempt capital gains balance" for **each** mutual fund or other investment on which you make the election. You cannot use the balance from one fund to shield capital gains distributions from another fund. Once you sell **all** of your interest in any given investment, your exempt capital gains balance for that investment goes to zero (even if you reacquire it later). See 4.6.13.

4.5 SPECIAL CASES

4.5.1 PRE-1972 PROPERTY

If you have property that you have owned since before 1972, when capital gains were not taxed at all, only the gain accruing since the end of 1971 will be taxed. For publicly-traded shares, valuation is easy; for real estate and shares in private businesses, valuation as of December 31, 1971 may be difficult to do. When you report such a gain, you will need to estimate the value of the property on that date, and use that as the cost of the property (assuming it is higher than your actual cost).

4.5.2 RESERVES

If you sell a property for a capital gain but do not receive all of the proceeds right away, you may be able to claim a **reserve**, to defer recognition of the gain for tax purposes.

Suppose, for example, you sell a house you have been renting out. The house cost you $100,000 and you sell it for $300,000. But you take back a mortgage for $150,000. You can normally claim a reserve on the capital gain, reflecting the fraction of the purchase price that you haven't yet received. In this case, since you haven't received half of the purchase price, you would only have to recognize half of the gain in the year of sale.

Under the reserve rules, you must recognize at least 1/5 of the gain each year (cumulatively), so that the entire capital gain must be accounted for by the fourth year after the year of sale.

4.5.3 PRINCIPAL RESIDENCE

As you probably know, a gain on selling your home is normally completely exempt from taxation. This is completely separate from the capital gains exemption discussed in 4.4. In this case, you don't even include the gain into income in the first place.

The exemption is based on the definition of "principal residence". This term includes, among other things, a house, a condominium and a share in a cooperative housing corporation (co-op). It also includes the land around the house, but normally only up to 1/2 hectare (about 1.2 acres). You, or your spouse or child, must have "ordinarily inhabited" the residence for it to qualify, so you can't use the exemption on property you rent out without ever having lived in it, or for vacant land. However, it need not have been your "principal" residence in a literal sense. (It can be a cottage, for example.)

Since 1982, each family unit is limited to one "principal residence" at a time. For this purpose, the family unit means you, your spouse (including a common-law spouse as outlined in 1.3.1), and any unmarried children under 18. So if you designate your house as your principal residence for a period of several years, your spouse cannot also designate your cottage as a principal residence over the same period. (The designation is only made when you file your tax return for the year in which you sell the property, so you can decide at that point which property to claim the exemption on.)

If a member of your family unit has owned a second residence (say, a cottage) since before 1982, a partial exemption may still be available. That is because each taxpayer was entitled to a principal residence exemption before 1982—the "family unit" concept wasn't yet in place. In such a case, the gain accruing to December 31, 1981 may continue to be exempt.

An exemption is also available in some cases where you rent the property out, either before or after you use it as your own residence. If you move out of your home and rent it out, you can continue to designate it as your residence for up to four years (provided you do not claim any other property as your principal residence and you file a special election with your tax return for the year in which you begin to rent the property). If you move due to relocation of your or your spouse's employment, the four-year period can normally be extended indefinitely, provided you move back to the home upon leaving that employment.

If you acquire property and rent it out, and then move in at some later date, you can file a special election with your tax return for the year in which you move in, to defer the capital gain that would normally apply when you change the property from income-earning to personal-use. If you do this, you may be able to get an exemption for four years during which you rented the property.

4.5.4 Death

When you die, you are generally deemed for tax purposes to have sold your capital property for its current fair market value, thus triggering a capital gain on all of the increase in value that has accrued since you purchased it. This prevents gains from accruing indefinitely without ever being taxed. In fact, although there are no estate taxes or succession duties in Canada, the taxation of accrued capital gains on death is thought by some to be a close equivalent.

EXAMPLE

Morris bought shares in Bell Canada in 1975. When he dies in November 1995, the shares are worth $20,000 more than he paid for them (after all commissions). Assume he used up his capital gains exemption on other properties.

Morris will be deemed to have sold the shares before his death for a capital gain of $20,000, three-quarters of which ($15,000) will be included in his income for the year of death.

Where property is left to your spouse, the gain will be put off until your spouse's death, at which point the entire capital gain will be taxed in your spouse's hands. A trust set up for your spouse can also be used to defer the gain, if certain conditions are met. However, your executor in both situations may elect to have this rule not apply to one or more of your properties, so as to use up your unused net capital losses and give your spouse a higher cost base for the assets.

Any net capital losses carried forward from previous years, which as we saw in 4.3.1 can normally only be used only against capital gains, can be used against all other income for the year of death and for the immediately preceding year, except to the extent the capital gains exemption has been claimed.

For further details on the treatment of capital gains on death, see 12.1.2.

4.5.5 OTHER RULES

Non arm's length transfers—When you give or sell property to a member of your family, you are normally deemed to have received fair market value for it, triggering recognition of any accrued capital gain (or loss) for tax purposes. However, if you transfer property to your spouse, it is normally deemed to have been sold at your cost unless you elect to realize a gain. This rule also applies to common-law spouses who meet the criteria outlined in 1.3.1.

Personal-use property—No capital loss is available on personal-use property, except for "listed personal property" (jewellery, works of art, stamps, coins and rare books), losses on which can be used only against listed personal property gains. As well, capital gains on personal-use property only apply to the extent the sale price exceeds $1,000.

If you change a property from personal use to income-earning use, you are normally deemed to have sold it at its fair market value, requiring you to recognize for tax purposes any accrued capital gain.

Options—Special rules apply to determine capital gains where you purchase or grant options (e.g., on the stock market).

Superficial loss—If you sell property (e.g., shares) to trigger a capital loss, and you or your spouse or a corporation which you control acquire identical property within 30 days before or after your sale, the capital loss will be called a "superficial loss" and ignored for tax purposes. The denied loss will be added to the cost of the identical property.

Insurance or expropriation proceeds—If property of yours is lost or destroyed, or expropriated, any insurance settlement or expropriation payment is considered to be proceeds of disposition, for purposes of the calculation described in 4.2.

Emigration—If you leave Canada and become non-resident, you are deemed to have sold most of your assets at fair market value, and will have to recognize any resulting capital gains. This will not apply to some assets (unless you elect otherwise), such as land and shares in private corporations, any capital gains on which will be taxed by Canada even when you are non-resident. However, for such assets (technically known as "taxable Canadian property"), a tax treaty between Canada and the country in which you live may be able to prevent Canada from taxing the gain when you do sell the property (see 14.4.8).

Note that while there are some "national" **LSVCCs**, in some provinces you can only obtain the provincial credit if you invest in an LSVCC based in the province. In Québec, for example, there are only two eligible LSVCCs (see 14.3.4).

4.6 PLANNING OPPORTUNITIES

4.6.1 GAINS AND LOSSES—INCOME OR CAPITAL

As we have seen, capital gains are only three-quarters taxed, and gains to February 22, 1994 may be eligible for the capital gains exemption. It is therefore much better to have capital gains than regular income.

On the other hand, capital losses are of limited use, while business losses can be deducted against other income.

To the extent possible within the law, therefore, you should try to classify your gains as capital gains and your losses as business losses. For example, if you buy and sell a commodity on the stock market, how you classify the transaction may depend on whether you have a gain or a loss. Where you are near the borderline between income and capital (see 4.1), you have some leeway to classify the transaction as either. Of course, you should be consistent; you could not take two essentially identical trades and call one a capital gain and the other a business loss.

If you are buying and selling real estate and doing well at it, try to gather data for your files that will support your claim to be engaging in capital transactions. For example, you will want to show that you are purchasing properties purely for their investment value as rental properties, and that any sales were not originally planned but were required by a change in circumstances.

Revenue Canada may well reassess you on these classifications, if you are audited. At that point you would have to decide whether to fight the assessment via a Notice of Objection (see 13.5.1), or to accept it and pay the tax that you would have paid in the first place, plus interest.

4.6.2 Canadian securities election

If you are active in the stock market, or if you are buying and selling private corporation shares or debt, you may wish to make the Canadian securities election (see 4.1) to ensure that all of your current year and future transactions will be on account of capital. This will prevent Revenue Canada from claiming that you are buying securities for the purpose of selling them and therefore earning business income rather than capital gains.

The downside of making the election is that you will never be able to claim losses on Canadian securities as business losses in the future. Since this is generally hard to do in respect of shares anyway, this may not be a problem for you. You should consider your entire financial position and possibly obtain professional advice to determine the likely effects of the election.

4.6.3 Use loss carryforward and carryback

If you have any net capital losses or allowable business investment losses that cannot be used in the current year, look into whether you can carry them back to any of your three prior years' returns. Revenue Canada is required to reopen and reassess your return when you make such a claim.

Make sure as well that you keep track of any such losses that you can't carry back, and carry them forward to use in future years.

4.6.4 Consider filing late election to use capital gains exemption

As discussed in 4.4.4, the election to "crystallize" accrued capital gains to February 22, 1994 should normally have been filed by May 1, 1995 to avoid a penalty. If you did not file it, however, consider whether you still should. You will have to balance the penalty against the advantages of the higher cost base in the property, which will give you a lower capital gain when you sell it (or even a capital loss if the property declines in value). Since the penalty increases each month, file the election as soon as possible once you decide to do so. Note that the election will make retroactive changes to your 1994 return, not your current year's return.

Be very careful not to elect more than 10% over the fair market value of the property as of February 22, 1994—in other words, be fairly conservative in your valuation. If your election is for more than 10% of the amount eventually determined to be correct (by Revenue Canada or the courts), the excess will actually *reduce* your adjusted cost base. In some cases, this means that filing an overstated election can be worse than filing no election at all!

In some cases, you might want to consider cancelling your election and filing a late one before April 30, 1997. For instance, you might have made the election on one property (A) and, for unforeseen reasons, end up selling a second property (B) on which you didn't make the election sooner than you thought. In that case, you can revoke the election on Property A and file a late election on Property B. You should calculate the costs and benefits of filing a new election versus leaving your original election intact, especially if you think you might also sell off Property A sometime soon.

If you have not filed an election yet and you are not sure whether you should file an election at all, consider filing a late election on a qualifying property that you own for a nominal amount. That will buy you an extra eight months to amend or revoke your election (that is, by December 31, 1997, instead of by the April 30, 1997 late filing deadline). The late filing penalty on such a low amount will be "small change" and the other tax effects of your increased 1994 net income will be minimal. If you later sell that property before 1998 and realize a capital gain, you can then conduct a precise cost/benefit analysis to compare the costs of amending your 1994 tax return versus your current year savings.

Be aware that the election can have some side effects. It will increase your 1994 "net income", which can result in a reduced old age credit (see 1.3.2), medical expense credit (see 1.3.5), Child Tax Benefit (see 1.5.1) and GST Credit (see 1.5.2). You could also find yourself required to repay Old Age Security or unemployment insurance benefits (see 1.6), and possibly liable for minimum tax (see Chapter 11). If you live in Manitoba or Saskatchewan, a 2% provincial "flat tax" on 1994 net income will apply to the taxable capital gain. On the other hand, if you make large charitable donations, a higher net income will give you a higher threshold for claiming such donations (see 1.3.4).

Remember also that the election might not work as anticipated for various reasons. For example, any CNIL balance as of the end of 1994 (see 4.4.3.2) will effectively become subject to tax. You may also have a problem if you had capital losses during 1994. All capital gains and capital losses for that year must be netted together (see 4.3.1) before any remaining gains can be shielded with the capital gains exemption.

4.6.5 Delay all or part of an asset sale until after year-end

If you sell an asset after the end of the year, any tax on the capital gain will apply one year later, giving you the use of the funds for an extra year except to the extent you are required to make quarterly tax instalments (see 13.2.2). A sale on December 31, 1995 will require tax to be paid by April 30, 1996; a sale on January 1, 1996 will require tax to be paid by April 30, 1997.

Note that most stock and bond market transactions normally settle three business days after the trade is entered. (This is standard practice in the brokerage industry and is recognized by Revenue Canada. It changed from five days to three in June 1995.) Because of weekends and public holidays, a stock market sale after **December 22, 1995** will normally result in the disposition counting as taking place in 1996 for income tax purposes.

In some circumstances, you may wish to sell half of an asset at the end of December and the other half at the beginning of January. Doing this will split your capital gain across the two years. This can be beneficial for two reasons. First, you may be able to reduce the marginal rate which applies in both years, by keeping your total taxable income below about $59,000 for each year. Second, you may be able to avoid minimum tax (see Chapter 11), due to the $40,000 minimum tax exemption available for each year.

4.6.6 Transfer securities to RRSP

If you have a self-directed RRSP, transferring shares to it may be a way to get your annual RRSP contribution writeoff without actually laying out any cash. Alternatively, if the RRSP has cash in it, you can sell shares to the RRSP for cash, which would let you get some cash out (though it would not count as a contribution to the plan, of course). In either case, you may have to pay tax on any accrued gain on the shares (or on gains accrued since February 22, 1994, if you made an election in respect of them; see 4.4.4).

There are some limitations and drawbacks to holding shares in an RRSP. See 2.1.5 and 2.5.2.

4.6.7 Claim capital gains reserve

If you are selling capital property but not receiving all of the proceeds, consider claiming a reserve in respect of the portion of the gain that has not yet been received in any given year. This would apply, for example, where you take back a mortgage on property you sell, or where you sell property for a series of payments spread over time. See 4.5.2 above for details. However, this might not be beneficial where you may be in a higher tax bracket in later years.

4.6.8 CHANGE PRINCIPAL RESIDENCE OWNERSHIP

Where you and your spouse have owned two residences (such as a regular home and a summer cottage) since before 1982, it may be possible to structure your holdings so that the pre-1982 portion of the capital gain on the second residence will be exempt. Consult a professional adviser on this matter.

If you have adult children, consider giving them the ownership of a second residence. If you own your house and your 19-year-old son owns the cottage, he can designate it as his principal residence when he sells it. However, at the time you transfer it to him you will have to recognize any increase in value since you purchased it (subject to a reduction if you made an election to use your capital gains exemption on it). You should also be sure you are satisfied with the *legal* effect of what you are doing (giving away your cottage!) before you embark on such a transaction for tax purposes.

4.6.9 USE EXEMPTION FOR QUALIFIED SMALL BUSINESS CORPORATION SHARES

If you own shares in a small business, and are considering selling them, or transferring them to your children, you should investigate whether the corporation's shares qualify for the $500,000 capital gains exemption. There may be steps you can take to "purify" the corporation so that it meets the criteria discussed in 4.4.1.

It is also possible to transfer the assets of a business which you carry on personally (as a proprietor) into a corporation on a tax-free basis in order to take advantage of the $500,000 exemption. This procedure, known as a "section 85 rollover", requires professional advice, as do other mechanisms for "crystallizing" the exemption (see 8.8.6).

The federal government re-examined the $500,000 exemption for small business shares in 1994, and announced in the February 1995 budget speech that it remains a "valuable measure" and that no changes are being made. However, it is still possible that the exemption will be repealed or restructured in the February 1996 budget or at some other time. You may wish to take advantage of it now in case it is eliminated.

4.6.10 MAKE ELECTION TO TREAT RENTED-OUT PROPERTY AS PRINCIPAL RESIDENCE

If you are moving out of your home and renting it out, or if you have acquired a rental property which you are planning to occupy at some point, you can make an election in your tax return to treat the property as your principal residence even during the period when it is rented out. See 4.5.3.

4.6.11 Emigration—Elect to Trigger Exemption

If you are becoming a non-resident of Canada, you will normally be deemed to have sold any capital property at its fair market value on the day you emigrate. This will not apply to "taxable Canadian property" on which the capital gain will be taxed anyway when you eventually sell it (see 4.5.5 above), subject to any override in the tax treaty between your new country of residence and Canada.

Once you are non-resident, however, you cannot use the capital gains exemption. So if you still have room in your $500,000 exemption, and you own taxable Canadian property (i.e. farm property or shares in a qualified small business corporation) that qualifies for exemption, you may wish to elect, in the return of the year in which you emigrate, to have such properties included in the deemed disposition at fair market value. That way, you will trigger a gain that is absorbed by the $500,000 exemption, and only the increase from the current fair market value will be taxed in Canada when you, as a non-resident, eventually dispose of the property.

If you are becoming non-resident, you need to obtain professional advice. The effects of Canadian tax law, the foreign tax law, and any tax treaty between Canada and the country you are moving to must all be considered.

4.6.12 Plan Around Your CNIL Balance

If you are claiming the capital gains exemption for small business shares or farm property (see 4.4.1 and 4.4.2), any cumulative net investment loss (CNIL) balance will prevent you from using the exemption, as discussed in 4.4.3.2. The CNIL is calculated at the **end** of the year, on December 31. If you have a CNIL balance, consider reducing or eliminating it before the end of the year. This can be done by increasing your investment income. For example, if you are the owner-manager of an incorporated business (see Chapter 8), you may be able to reduce your salary and increase your dividends from the corporation to use up your CNIL balance. There may also be situations where you can advance interest receipts to before the end of the year, or defer deductible interest payments until after December 31, to reduce your CNIL.

4.6.13 Keep at Least 1 Unit of Investments with Exempt Capital Gains Balance

This planning tip applies if you own any mutual funds, partnership interests or other investments that qualify as "flow-through entities", and you made the election to trigger the capital gains exemption in respect of them (see 4.4.4). Making the election created an "exempt capital gains balance" for **each investment**, which you can use to offset capital gains from the investment, both gains from selling it and gains flowed through to you from it until the year 2004.

If you are selling the investment and some exempt capital gains balance will remain, consider retaining one unit or share. That way, if you either invest in the same fund again, you can continue to use the remaining balance or if you own at least one unit or share at the end of the year 2004, any remaining balance can be added to the adjusted cost base of the property.

EXAMPLE

David owns 10,000 units of a mutual fund, which as of February 22, 1994 was worth $1 more per unit than he paid for it. He filed the capital gains election with his 1994 return with respect to that fund, creating a $10,000 "exempt capital gains balance".

In January 1996, the mutual fund has dropped in price so that the gain is only 40¢ per unit from its February 1994 value, and David decides to sell his investment.

If David sells all the units, he will have a $4,000 (40¢ per unit) capital gain against which he can use $4,000 of his exempt capital gains balance. The remaining $6,000 will be lost forever.

*David should instead sell only 9,900 units, **keeping say 100 units**. His capital gain will still be 40¢ per unit ($3,960), against which he can use $3,960 of his exempt capital gains balance. Since he still owns at least one unit, however, David's exempt capital gains balance for this mutual fund remains at $6,040. If he later repurchases some units of this fund, he can shelter up to $6,040 of future gains, up to the year 2004, with this balance.*

If David still owns the units at the end of the year 2004, he can add any balance remaining to the adjusted cost base of the units and thereby reduce a future capital gain or increase a future capital loss.

4.7 REFERENCES

The following publications can be obtained (in person or by telephone request) from your nearest Revenue Canada District Taxation Office:

Interpretation Bulletin IT-78, "Capital property owned on December 31, 1971—Identical properties"

Interpretation Bulletin IT-84, "Capital property owned on December 31, 1971—Median rule (Tax-free zone)"

Interpretation Bulletin IT-107, "Costs of disposition of capital property affected by the median rule"

Interpretation Bulletin IT-120R4, "Principal residence"

Interpretation Bulletin IT-133, "Stock exchange transactions—Date of disposition of shares"

Interpretation Bulletin IT-170R, "Sale of property—When included in income computation"

Interpretation Bulletin IT-218R, "Profits, capital gains and losses from the sale of real estate"

Interpretation Bulletin IT-232R2, "Non-capital losses, net capital losses, restricted farm losses, farm losses and limited partnership losses"

Interpretation Bulletin IT-236R3, "Reserves—Disposition of capital property"

Interpretation Bulletin IT-387R2, "Meaning of identical properties"

Interpretation Bulletin IT-456R, "Capital property—Some adjustments to cost base"

Interpretation Bulletin IT-459, "Adventure or concern in the nature of trade"

Interpretation Bulletin IT-479R, "Transactions in securities"

Interpretation Bulletin IT-484R, "Business investment losses"

"Capital Gains Election Package"

"Capital Gains Tax Guide"

Form T123, "Election on disposition of Canadian securities"

Form T664, "Election to report a capital gain on property owned at the end of February 22, 1994"

Form T657, "Calculation of capital gains deduction"

Form T936, "Calculation of cumulative net investment loss"

Form T2091, "Designation of principal residence"

5 Investments and Tax Shelters

Planning Tips

- Structure investments to make interest deductible
- Acquire investments to mature after year-end
- Consider acquiring preferred shares to enhance after-tax yield
- Consider setting up a trust for children
- Consider investments in tax shelters
- Look into investing in a labour-sponsored venture capital corporation
- Consider the merits of acquiring an exempt life insurance contract
- Make sure you use or preserve your exempt capital gains balance for mutual fund investments

In this chapter we look at how investment income is taxed, how interest expense can be written off, and the various tax shelters that are available. After discussing the rules, we present a number of tax planning ideas at the end of the chapter.

5.1 Dividends

5.1.1 What is a dividend?

A dividend is a distribution of profits to the shareholders (owners) of a corporation. A corporation may have many classes of shares. **Preferred shares** are shares on which dividends must generally be paid first, before dividends can be paid on a corporation's **common shares**.

Preferred shares typically pay a fixed annual or quarterly dividend. In some ways, they are similar to bonds or other debt, since the return is a fixed percentage. However, a corporation is not *required* to pay dividends on its preferred shares as long as it does not pay dividends on its common shares. If the corporation suffers losses, its board of directors may well decide not to pay dividends on preferred shares.

From a tax point of view, for individuals, preferred shares are identical to common shares (which typically pay dividends that bear some relationship to the corporation's profits).

5.1.2 How is a dividend taxed?

Dividends received by individuals from Canadian corporations are taxed in a rather peculiar manner, designed to reflect the fact that the corporation paying the dividend has already paid tax on its profits. The amount included in the individual's income is "grossed-up" to reflect the total amount of *pre-tax* income that the corporation is presumed to have earned. The individual then receives a credit to offset the tax the corporation is presumed to have paid (at about 20%). In no case, however, is the *actual* income earned or tax paid by the corporation taken into account.

Canadian dividends received are **grossed-up** by one-quarter. That is, you add 25% to the amount received, and show the total as income from dividends on your tax return. The offsetting federal dividend tax credit is then two-thirds of the amount of the gross-up—two-thirds of that 25%, or, if you like, 13.33% of the total you showed as dividend income. This dividend tax credit is then augmented by about half as much again, since the provincial tax is calculated on a reduced federal tax. (In the example below, we use 58%, the Ontario rate, as the provincial tax rate for illustrative purposes.)

EXAMPLE

*Melissa earns $35,000 per year. She also owns shares in Canadian Inc., which pay her a dividend of **$1,000** in 1995.*

*Melissa's income for 1995 will be $35,000, plus the $1,000 dividend, plus a gross-up of one-quarter of the dividend, or $250. Her tax will be calculated on this income of **$36,250**. From the tax, she will deduct her regular credits (see Chapter 1) and a dividend tax credit of **$166.67** (two-thirds of the $250 gross-up). When her provincial tax and federal surtax are calculated, at 58% and 3% of the federal tax respectively, her tax will be reduced by a further **$101.67**, since the federal tax has been reduced by the credit. Melissa's $1,000 dividend is therefore taxed at about 41% of $1,250, but then reduced by a total of about **$268** in dividend tax credit and reduced provincial tax and surtax. The net result is that the dividend is taxed at about 25% instead of 41%.*

(See 8.2.1 for more detail on the dividend tax credit from the perspective of the corporation.) The effect of the dividend tax credit is to tax dividends at *approximately* the following rates:

Income level	Salary income	Dividend income
$0-$29,590	27%	7%
$29,590-$59,180	41%	25%
$59,180 and up	50%	33%

The exact numbers vary by province. Remember that these numbers apply only to dividends from **Canadian** corporations. Dividends on foreign corporations are taxed as ordinary income.

5.1.3 SPECIAL CASES

5.1.3.1 STOCK DIVIDENDS

A corporation will sometimes pay a **stock dividend** by issuing new shares to pay the dividend rather than giving you cash. In such a case, the gross-up and dividend tax credit still apply, and you must pay tax on the stock dividend even though you have received no cash. The amount of the dividend on which the gross-up is calculated is the increase in the paid-up capital resulting from the issue of new shares.

5.1.3.2 Capital dividends

You may also receive **capital dividends** from private corporations. They are completely tax-free (see 3.3.11). A capital dividend is generally a distribution of the untaxed one-quarter of capital gains. As we saw in 4.2, that fraction of the capital gain is not taxed at all. The capital dividend mechanism is used to distribute the untaxed portion without any tax consequences to the shareholder. (For an example, see 8.2.4.)

5.1.3.3 Dividends received by a corporation

Intercorporate dividends are normally tax-free. The assumption is that once a corporation has paid tax on its income, its profits can be distributed through a chain of holding corporations with no further tax consequences until an individual receives a dividend at the end of the chain. However, a special refundable tax ("Part IV tax") can apply to intercorporate dividends in some circumstances, including most dividends received on investments in public corporations. The Part IV tax is 25% until June 1995 and rises to 33 1/3% as of July 1995.

5.1.3.4 Mutual funds

Mutual funds are pools of assets that are invested by professional managers, either in general investments or in a particular sector (such as real estate or natural resources). A mutual fund corporation will pay dividends, but may designate all or a portion of the dividends as "capital gains dividends", to reflect capital gains earned by the mutual fund. From the taxpayer's point of view, such dividends are treated as capital gains rather than dividends, and subject to the usual capital gains treatment (including eligibility for the capital gains exemption) discussed in Chapter 4.

5.1.3.5 Election to transfer dividends from spouse

Since the dividend tax credit is a credit against tax owing, it is worthless if there is no tax to pay. If your spouse's income is very low, and you claim a credit for your spouse as a dependant (see 1.3.1), a relatively small amount of dividend income, when grossed-up by 25%, can take your spouse over the $538 income threshold and thereby reduce your spousal tax credit. At the same time, since your spouse does not pay any tax, the dividend tax credit is of no use.

In such a case, you may elect to report all of your spouse's dividend income on your own tax return. While this may result in the income being taxed at a higher rate, it will avoid the erosion of the spousal tax credit. You will have to calculate tax both ways to see which is better. This election is done by including the dividends directly on Schedule 5 (Investment income) on your tax return, not Schedule 2 (Amounts transferred from spouse).

5.2 Interest income

5.2.1 General rule

Interest income is taxed at the same rates as employment or business income.

5.2.2 Accruing interest

Suppose you acquire a seven-year term deposit for $1,000 which will return $1,700 after seven years. When do you report the $700 in interest?

The answer depends on when you acquired the investment. If you bought it in 1990 or later, you must declare, **each year**, the interest accrued to the anniversary date of when you acquired it. Your financial institution should issue you a T5 slip showing the interest accruing on all such long-term investments.

If you acquired the investment before 1990, you must report the accruing interest at least **every three years**, though you have the option of reporting it annually if you wish.

The accrual rules apply to almost all kinds of investments, including stripped bonds (see 5.2.3 below), Canada Savings Bonds, and mortgages or loans to relatives on which interest is allowed to accrue.

EXAMPLE

In 1990, Christine lent $10,000 to her cousin, who is attending university and needed the funds for tuition and residence. Her cousin agreed in writing to pay 10% annual interest (not compounded) on the loan, but that he will not pay back the loan or the interest until after he has graduated and secures a job.

Christine is required to report and pay tax on $1,000 of accrued interest income each year beginning in 1991. If in 1995 *her cousin pays her $15,000 to cover the loan and all interest, she will only report $1,000 as income in 1995, since she will have already reported $4,000 over the previous four years.*

5.2.3 STRIPPED BONDS AND CLIPPED COUPONS

Stripped bonds are long-term government or government-backed (e.g., provincial hydro) bonds which pay interest when their coupons are cashed in. A typical bond might have a 20-year term, have a face value of $100,000 and come with coupons paying $5,000 in interest, cashable every six months. At the end of the 20 years one simply redeems the bond for $100,000.

Brokerage firms often acquire such bonds and split up the bond and its coupons, selling them separately. The $100,000 bond maturing in 20 years, in our example, might be sold for $15,000, while the forty $5,000 coupons would be sold at prices reflecting the length of time until their maturity.

For tax purposes, the difference between the discounted price of the bond (or coupon) and the amount you receive when it is redeemed is considered to be interest. Because of the annual (or three-year, if bought before 1990) accrual rule, such bonds generally are unattractive to many taxpayers—you have to pay tax annually on interest that you will not receive for some time. However, they can be excellent investments for RRSPs and other tax-free plans (see 2.1.5).

One should be cautious when acquiring stripped bonds or clipped coupons—or, for that matter, any long-term bond. If you need to sell them before they mature, you will find that their value fluctuates considerably due to trends in interest rates. If interest rates in general have gone up, the resale value of your bond or coupon will likely have gone down.

5.3 DEDUCTIBILITY OF INTEREST EXPENSE

As a general principle, interest is deductible for tax purposes as long as the loan was used **for the purpose of earning income** from a business or property. So, if you borrow money to buy shares on the stock market, or to invest in a business, the interest you pay is generally deductible. Such expenses are also called **carrying charges**.

On the other hand, if you buy an investment with a fixed interest rate, you cannot deduct interest on your loan beyond the rate that your investment pays. For example, if you borrow at 15% and lend the funds to a relative at 10%, you can only deduct 10% interest on your loan. Where the investment is in preferred shares, it is the grossed-up amount of the dividend (see 5.1.2) which determines the amount of interest that can be deducted. If the dividend rate is

8%, being effectively 10% when grossed-up by 25%, then once again only the first 10% of interest on the loan can be deducted.

Interest is not deductible where the loan was taken out for some purpose other than to earn income subject to tax. Examples include:

- home mortgage, except to the extent you use a home office for business purposes (see 7.2.7)
- car loan, where the car is used solely for personal use
- credit cards, except to the extent the charges are for business expenses
- loan to contribute to an RRSP
- interest on late income tax or instalment payments

If you dispose of the property that you borrowed money to acquire, you can continue to deduct the interest in certain cases even though the underlying source of income has been lost. The rules in this respect are complex, and professional advice may be required if you are in this situation.

Interest on a car loan, where the car is used for your employment or business purposes, is limited to the employment or business portion of $250 or $300 per month: see 6.9.1 and 7.2.5.

Revenue Canada often pays special attention to deductions for interest expenses. It is wise to keep on file, along with your tax return, accurate records showing the amount of the loan, the purpose of the loan and the interest paid during the year, along with the relevant financial statements and possibly a confirming letter from your financial institution. It may be appropriate to file this information with your tax return if you have done so in previous years.

For minimum tax purposes, interest expense must be added back to your income if it relates to tax shelters or other "tainted" deductions. See 11.2.

5.4 Tax shelters

Tax shelters are no longer as important to tax planning as they were some years ago. For a variety of reasons, there are now relatively few publicly-offered vehicles for sheltering your ordinary income from tax.

Contrary to popular perception, tax shelters are generally not "loopholes" in the system. Preferences are given to certain types of investment as a deliberate move by the government to stimulate economic activity in a particular area. Whether it is investment in Cape Breton Island, creation of Canadian films, scientific research or exploration for oil and gas, the specific writeoffs and credits in the *Income Tax Act* are put there to encourage you, the taxpayer, to invest funds in a particular sphere.

One should only invest in a tax shelter if, after taking the tax benefits into account, there is a reasonable expectation of profit from the shelter. The tax benefits alone should rarely control your investment decision.

There are relatively few tax shelters around, even compared to a year ago. A press release issued by the Minister of Finance on December 1, 1994 announced a number of new rules that make many tax shelters unattractive. Draft legislation released on April 26, 1995 made some of these rules, which are highly technical, even tighter. Although these changes had not been enacted at time of writing, they almost certainly will be.

When investing in tax shelters, one must be aware of the possible application of the **minimum tax** (see Chapter 11). Québec residents should also read Chapter 14. Finally, you must always be aware of the possible application of the general anti-avoidance rule, mentioned in the Introduction.

We do not discuss RRSPs and other tax deferral plans in this section. They were dealt with in detail in Chapter 2.

5.4.1 TAX SHELTER IDENTIFICATION NUMBER

Anyone selling an interest in a tax shelter is required to obtain an identification number from Revenue Canada and provide that number on all documents and financial statements relating to the shelter. *If you do not have the identification number, or if any penalties relating to the identification number are payable by the promoter and have not been paid, you will not be able to claim the benefits of the shelter.*

For the purposes of this rule, a tax shelter is defined, generally, as an investment that is advertised or represented as entitling you to writeoffs or deductions over four years that will exceed your investment (net of any tax credits or other benefits you obtain). Flow-through shares (see 5.4.4) and the deferred income plans we saw in Chapter 2 (RRSPs, etc.) are excluded from the definition.

Because of this rule, caution is required when considering investments in tax shelters. Note, however, that the identification number does **not** indicate approval by Revenue Canada of the proposed benefits. It merely ensures that the shelter has been registered for administrative purposes, making audit and reassessment easier for Revenue Canada if it eventually decides to disallow some or all of the tax benefits.

Any deduction relating to an investment that requires a tax shelter identification number must be added back into income for minimum tax purposes. See 11.2.

5.4.2 LIMITED PARTNERSHIPS

A number of shelters involve the purchase of an interest in a limited partnership. A limited partnership is a **partnership**, in that you share the profits of the business with the other partners, and report a percentage of the partnership's income (or loss) directly as your income—whether or not you have received any of the profits. This is in contrast to corporate profits, which are reported only when distributed as dividends, as we saw in 5.1.2 above. However, a limited partnership is similar to a corporation in that you have **limited liability**—you cannot be sued for the partnership's debts. In general, you can only lose your original investment.

Because you can report partnership losses directly on your own tax return, limited partnerships are an attractive investment where the partnership business is expected to have losses in its initial years (either real losses due to startup costs, or tax-created losses due to high writeoffs available on certain kinds of investments).

However, you may not write off more than the original cost of your investment. The *Income Tax Act*'s "at-risk" rules provide that you cannot deduct more than the amount you have at risk in a limited partnership. As well, draft legislation released on April 26, 1995 severely restricts the use of limited partnerships to create losses where there is "non-recourse" debt (i.e., you are required to contribute amounts to the partnership, but cannot be forced to do so from your own funds, only from the profits from your partnership interest).

EXAMPLE

Kevin invests $6,000 for 1/100 of a limited partnership undertaking bona fide business activities. In its first year, due to high expenses and special writeoffs available, the partnership records a $1 million loss for tax purposes.

Although 1/100 of the loss is $10,000, Kevin may only deduct $6,000, being his "at-risk amount", on his tax return. The remaining $4,000 will be usable against Kevin's income from the partnership at any time in the future.

Losses from limited partnerships must be added back into income for minimum tax purposes. See 11.2.

5.4.3 LIMITED PARTNERSHIPS USED TO FINANCE MUTUAL FUND COMMISSIONS

Limited partnerships as an investment vehicle were discussed in 5.4.2 above. Mutual funds were described in 5.1.3.4.

Many mutual funds are "no-load" funds, meaning that the investor pays no fee to buy into the fund, and pays no fee to have the units redeemed by the fund, provided the investor holds the units for some period of time (typically five to eight years).

When a stockbroker (investment dealer) sells a unit of a mutual fund, the broker receives a commission of about 3% of the investment. Where the fund is a "no-load" fund, the investor is not supplying the cash to pay the broker's commission. This cash has to come from somewhere.

A "mutual fund limited partnership" (MFLP) is a limited partnership set up to fund these commissions. When you invest in an MFLP, your investment is used to pay commissions to brokers who sell units in a specific mutual fund. You then receive income from the mutual fund over several years in the form of "distribution fees", which are a portion of the mutual fund company's annual management fee. Such a management fee is a reflection of the market value of the fund, so you are in effect indirectly investing in the mutual fund itself. To the extent the mutual fund investors redeem their units before the point at which they can do so without fees, you also share in the "redemption fees" paid by those investors.

For tax purposes, Revenue Canada permits you to claim your share of the limited partnership's selling commissions incurred before July 1995 as a deductible expense over three years: 50% in the first year, 25% in the second and 25% in the third year. However, effective July 1995, Revenue Canada's position is that selling commissions should be amortized over three years on a straight-line basis. Your income from the distribution fees and redemption fees is taxable in the years you receive it.

MFLPs can be an attractive investment, particularly if you are currently in a high tax bracket and expect to be in a lower bracket in a few years (e.g., if you plan to retire). Of course, as with any investment, you should carefully study the prospectus to determine the risks and benefits. Although MFLPs may be attractive, they may prove to be illiquid, and your anticipated profit will depend on the investment return of the fund.

5.4.4 FILMS AND TELEVISION PRODUCTIONS

Certified Canadian films and TV productions used to be a popular shelter because of the possibility of writing off one's entire investment over two years. However, this is no longer possible and films are no longer attractive investments for purely tax reasons. The tax benefits can still be substantial, but they are no longer "shelters" in the sense of being usable to shelter one's other income.

The tax benefits depend on whether the particular production is **certified** or not. For certification the production must meet a number of Canadian content requirements, and your investment must be at least 5% paid initially and be completely paid within four years.

Certified productions entitle you to a deduction for capital cost allowance (depreciation) of 30% on the balance of your investment each year. That is, on a $1,000 investment you can deduct $300 in the first year, leaving a balance of $700. In the second year, you can deduct 30% of the $700, or $210, and so on. As well, to the extent your film investments actually earn income, you can deduct the entire cost against such income (netted among all your film investments).

Until the end of 1995, certified productions were exempt from the "at-risk" rules for limited partnerships described in 5.4.2. This exemption has been eliminated for new investments as of 1996, with the effect of eliminating most film tax shelters. (A direct credit to film producers is now available instead, as an alternate way of supporting the Canadian film industry.)

The deduction available for **non-certified** productions is quite limited: 15% in the first year and 30% in subsequent years, on a declining balance basis, but *only against your net film revenues for each year.*

5.4.5 RESOURCE ACTIVITIES

Two areas that receive special incentives from the tax system are mining, and oil and gas exploration. Tax shelters in these areas usually involve either limited partnerships (see 5.4.2 above) or **flow-through shares**. However, their appeal over the last few years has diminished greatly.

Flow-through shares are special shares issued by a corporation involved in resource exploration. Under the *Income Tax Act*, the corporation can "renounce" some of its resource expenses, and will not be able to claim them for tax purposes. In exchange, it passes the rights to these claims to the owners of the flow-through shares. If the corporation is in its early years and not making a profit anyway, the flowing-through of the deductions allows the shareholders to use writeoffs which otherwise could not currently be used by the corporation.

Whether you invest in a limited partnership or flow-through shares, the particular deductions you get will depend on the classification of the partnership or corporation's income and expenses. You will receive a statement and/or an information slip indicating your share of some or all of: business income or loss (partnership only); investment income and dividends (partnership only); Canadian exploration expenses (fully deductible); Canadian development expenses (30% deductible); Canadian oil and gas property expenses (10% deductible); and resource allowance (25% of certain production and processing income).

At the time of investment in the shelter you can usually obtain a forecast of the expected expenses and their classification, along with the implications for your tax return.

5.4.6 BUSINESS VENTURES

Some tax shelters involve investing in ongoing business ventures, either through limited partnerships or through a direct purchase of property. These are cases where the property is eligible for a high rate of capital cost allowance (depreciation), thus giving you a substantial writeoff relative to your cash investment.

The tax system restricts capital cost allowance claims available in respect of certain "leasing properties", such as nursing homes, recreational vehicles, hotels and yachts, in cases where you are not personally active in the day-to-day operation of the business. In general, the restrictions limit your claim to your income from that business, so you cannot use the capital cost allowance to shelter other income. Consult a professional adviser for details on the restrictions regarding any particular kind of asset.

5.4.7 COMMODITY STRADDLES

If you are very aggressive and willing to risk the possible application by Revenue Canada of the *Income Tax Act*'s general anti-avoidance rule, you can consider commodity straddles and similar transactions.

In a commodity straddle, you would take both "buy" and "sell" futures positions on a particular commodity, where the positions are not exactly offsetting. By year-end, the commodity can be expected to have fluctuated in value, and you will have a loss on one of the contracts but a gain on the other. You then get out of the contract which has lost value before year-end, and either get out of the other contract in the new year or buy a new contract as a hedge at the time you get out of your loss position. The result will be a loss in the current year, offset by a gain in the next year—or, in other words, deferral of tax.

For the above technique to work, you have to consider yourself a speculator, so that the transactions result in business loss and income rather than capital losses and capital gains (as we saw in 4.3.1, capital losses are not very useful). Revenue Canada's position is that once you have treated such transactions as being on income account, you cannot revert to calling them capital transactions in the future. Note also that the general anti-avoidance rule might be applied to your transactions; see the Introduction.

5.4.8 REAL ESTATE INVESTMENTS

In past years, MURBs (multiple unit residential buildings) were a popular tax shelter, allowing extra writeoffs not normally available on real estate properties. They were phased out beginning several years ago, however, and 1993 was the last year for which owners of MURBs could claim any tax benefits.

Real estate can still be a good investment, when the tax benefits are combined with rental income and capital appreciation. Mortgage interest expense, property taxes and maintenance costs can all be written off. Capital cost allowance (depreciation) for buildings is normally 4% per year on a declining balance basis, but cannot normally be used to create or increase a loss used against other income. (No capital cost allowance is available for land.)

5.4.9 LABOUR-SPONSORED VENTURE CAPITAL CORPORATIONS

A "labour-sponsored venture capital corporation", or LSVCC, is a fund sponsored by organized labour that provides venture capital to start-up businesses.

An investment in an LSVCC of up to $5,000 entitles you to a special federal tax credit of 20% of your investment. In addition, all provinces except Alberta, New Brunswick and Newfoundland provide a further 20% credit against your provincial income tax which you claim on your provincial T1C form when filing your tax return (see 14.3.4 if you live in Québec). Like an RRSP contribution, the investment can be made up to 60 days after the end of a year and still qualify for the credit for that year. An LSVCC investment can be made through your RRSP (see 2.5.3).

Generally, you may redeem your investment whenever you wish, but certain restrictions and charges may apply depending on which fund you invest in. If you do not keep the investment for at least five years (two years if you reach age 65, retire or cease to be resident in Canada), the special credits must be repaid.

5.5 Trusts

A trust is an arrangement whereby a trustee holds property for the benefit of one or more beneficiaries. A trust can be set up at any time, or on death by one's will.

Trusts are taxed as separate taxpayers. A trust created on death will be taxed at the same rates as an individual. All other trusts are taxed at a flat rate, which is the top rate of tax (about 50%, depending on the province).

Trusts can be a useful way of directing income to children and other relatives. To the extent a trust distributes its income to its beneficiaries, the beneficiaries rather than the trust pay tax on that amount.

Any arrangements involving trusts should be set up with proper professional advice, particularly taking into account the attribution rules discussed in Chapter 3.

Trusts are discussed in more detail at 12.3.

5.6 Exempt life insurance contracts

The life insurance industry has developed attractive products that allow you to build up cash in a tax-sheltered environment. There are many issues to look at when considering whether to acquire such a contract, such as the underlying mortality costs and administrative expenses, a guaranteed minimum rate of return, comparison to a similar return in a non-tax sheltered environment, your required life insurance coverage, your income objectives and so on.

Life insurance is discussed in more detail at 12.6.

5.7 Planning opportunities

5.7.1 Structure investments to make interest deductible

As we have seen (5.3 above), interest on consumer loans and home mortgages is normally not deductible, while interest on loans taken out to purchase income-generating investments is deductible. You should therefore try to ensure that all loans you take out are for a deductible purpose.

If you have a home mortgage as well as investments that can be easily sold, consider whether you can sell the investments, pay off the mortgage, and borrow new funds (secured by the same mortgage, if necessary) for the purpose of purchasing new investments. You will of course be required to recognize any capital gains on the sale of the investments, beyond the level you may have elected for capital gains exemption purposes effective February 22, 1994 (see 4.4.4).

There is a possible danger of this plan being in contravention of the general anti-avoidance rule. Consult a tax professional to minimize the chances of the rule applying.

5.7.2 ACQUIRE INVESTMENTS TO MATURE AFTER YEAR-END

As a general deferral technique, acquire investments that mature after year-end rather than before. For example, if you are investing in T-Bills on July 15, and you can choose between maturity dates of December 29 and January 2, then you should choose January 2 if all else is equal. That way you will defer reporting and paying tax on the income by one year.

Of course, tax considerations should not override normal investment considerations, such as the available rates of return and the question of when you will need access to the funds.

5.7.3 BUY PREFERRED SHARES

Since they pay dividends rather than interest, preferred shares may offer a better after-tax rate of return while still coming close to a guaranteed yield. (The yield is never completely guaranteed, but many major public companies will continue to meet preferred share dividend expectations even when they suffer losses.)

The yields on preferred shares usually reflect the fact that dividends are less heavily taxed than interest (as well as the fact that dividend payments are not deductible to the corporation). If current interest rates are around 8%, preferred share yields may well be around 6%. You will have to monitor preferred share prices on the market to find the best yields. See Appendix V, which contains a dividend/interest yield comparison.

5.7.4 SET UP TRUST FOR CHILDREN

Consider setting up a trust for your children's education or to provide them with financial support. This will have to be done with adequate legal and tax advice, taking the attribution rules into account. See Chapter 3 for a discussion of the attribution rules.

5.7.5 Consider investments in tax shelters

A number of the tax shelters discussed in 5.4 can be good investments. From a purely tax point of view, resource funds and limited partnerships used to finance mutual fund commissions may offer the best benefits. You should always ensure that any investment is sound from a financial point of view, rather than just for tax write-offs.

For films: evaluate, among other things, the past performance record of the people involved in the production, the production's advertising and promotion budget, the sales potential via conventional distribution, pay-TV and video sales, the distribution mechanism, and the structure of remittances to investors.

For resource funds: look at the track record of the promoters, the geological and engineering expertise available, the type of exploration to be undertaken and the expected tax effects of the various types of expenditures.

For limited partnerships used to finance mutual fund commissions, look at the performance of prior limited partnerships used to finance the same family of mutual funds, the investment return of mutual funds administered by the same mutual fund manager, and the history of early redemption of units in that group of mutual funds.

For any investment, make sure that you have a tax shelter identification number if the investment meets the definition of a tax shelter, and that there are no unpaid penalties in respect of the shelter (see 5.4.1).

Always be aware of the possible application of the general anti-avoidance rule, where tax shelters are being promoted without a favourable advance tax ruling from Revenue Canada.

Be aware of the possible application of the minimum tax (see Chapter 11).

5.7.6 Look into investing in a labour-sponsored venture capital corporation

The LSVCC was outlined in 5.4.8. An investment in an LSVCC can be transferred to your RRSP or bought by your RRSP with "new" funds you have contributed for that purpose (see 2.5.3).

If you live in a province that matches the federal credit, you receive 40% of your investment back in credits on your tax return. If you invest the maximum $5,000 by February 29, 1996 for your 1995 taxation year, your actual cost is $3,000. If you then transfer the investment to your RRSP (or have the RRSP make the investment with "new" funds), you can deduct the full $5,000; if you are in a 53% tax bracket, this will save you a further $2,650.

The result is that the cash cost of a $5,000 investment can be as low as $350, if you have contribution room in your RRSP that you are not otherwise using. However, as previously noted (see 2.5.3), you should carefully evaluate the relative investment merits of these funds before taking the plunge.

5.7.7 ACQUIRE AN EXEMPT LIFE INSURANCE CONTRACT

An exempt life insurance contract (see 5.6) can help you meet two planning objectives at once: having insurance coverage, and providing retirement income from tax-sheltered growth. Professional advice is a must when assessing the merits of this type of "investment".

5.7.8 USE EXEMPT CAPITAL GAINS BALANCE FOR MUTUAL FUNDS

This tip applies if you own any mutual funds that qualify as **"flow-through entities"**, and you made the election to trigger the capital gains exemption in respect of them (see 4.4.4). Making the election has created an **"exempt capital gains balance"** for each mutual fund, which you can use to offset capital gains from that fund, both gains from selling it and gains flowed through to you from it.

Where a mutual fund (or any other flow-through entity) has **allocated** capital gains to you for the year, make sure to use the exempt capital gains balance to claim a deduction on your return to offset the taxable capital gain that you have reported. It is up to you to remember that this balance is available to offset such gains until 2004. After that time any remaining exempt capital gains balance is added to the adjusted cost base of the mutual fund. If you are thinking of selling a mutual fund and the gain to be realized on the sale is not large enough to use all of the exempt capital gains balance, consider selling all but a few of the units. You could continue owning the few units until say 2005. Then they could be sold with any resulting capital gain or loss taking into account the remainder of the exempt gains balance, since this remaining balance will be added to the adjusted cost base of the remaining units at the end of 2004.

5.8 REFERENCES

The following publications can be obtained (in person or by telephone request) from your nearest Revenue Canada District Taxation Office:

Interpretation Bulletin IT-66R6, "Capital dividends"

Interpretation Bulletin IT-67R3, "Taxable dividends from corporations resident in Canada"

Interpretation Bulletin IT-148R2, "Recreational properties and club dues"

Interpretation Bulletin IT-195R4, "Rental property—Capital cost allowance restrictions"

Interpretation Bulletin IT-232R2, "Non-capital losses, net capital losses, restricted farm losses, farm losses and limited partnership losses"

Interpretation Bulletin IT-274R, "Rental properties—Capital cost of $50,000 or more"

Interpretation Bulletin IT-295R4, "Taxable dividends received after 1987 by a spouse"

Interpretation Bulletin IT-367R3, "Capital Cost Allowance—Multiple-unit residential buildings"

Interpretation Bulletin IT-381R2, "Trusts—Deduction of amounts paid or payable to beneficiaries and flow-through of taxable capital gains to beneficiaries"

Interpretation Bulletin IT-394R, "Preferred beneficiary election"

Interpretation Bulletin IT-396R, "Interest income"

Interpretation Bulletin IT-445, "The deduction of interest on funds borrowed either to be loaned at less than a reasonable rate of interest or to honour a guarantee given for inadequate consideration in non-arm's length circumstances"

Interpretation Bulletin IT-503, "Exploration and development shares"

Interpretation Bulletin IT-524, "Trusts—Flow-through of taxable dividends to a beneficiary—After 1987"

"Rental Income Tax Guide"

Form T776, "Statement of real estate rentals"

6 If You Are Employed

Planning Tips

- Arrange to get non-taxable benefits
- Where possible, request reduction of source withholdings
- Pay interest owing on loan from employer within 30 days of end of year
- Consider employees' profit-sharing plan for cash-flow purposes
- Transfer retiring allowances to an RRSP
- Consider a stock option plan, stock purchase plan or phantom stock plan
- Keep track of, and maximize, business use of car
- Take steps to minimize the taxable benefit from car operating costs
- Avoid employer-owned vehicles costing over $24,000
- Reduce time company car is available for personal use

As a general principle, all ***income*** *(including tips) and* ***benefits*** *from or related to your employment are taxed, except where the* Income Tax Act *specifically provides otherwise. Also as a general principle, you cannot claim any deductions against employment income, except for those that are specifically allowed by the system. There are, however, many special rules, and we examine some of them in this chapter.*

6.1 Employment benefits

6.1.1 Non-taxable employment benefits

Certain employment benefits are not taxable, even though many of them are deductible expenses to the employer. The government is therefore providing an incentive to employers to provide these benefits, since the after-tax returns are greater than straight salary.

Non-taxable benefits include:

1. Contributions to a registered pension plan (the pension is taxable when received: see 2.2).
2. Contributions to a group sickness or accident insurance plan.
3. Contributions to a "private health services plan", such as those covering drugs, medical expenses and hospital charges not covered by public health insurance, and dental fees.

4. Free or subsidized school services for your children.
5. Contributions to a supplementary unemployment benefit plan.
6. Contributions to a deferred profit-sharing plan.
7. Reimbursement of certain moving expenses on relocation.
8. Payment of club dues if your membership in the club may potentially benefit the employer's business (however, these dues are normally not deductible to the employer).
9. Employee discounts, where such discounts are commonly available to other employees (but not below the employer's cost).
10. One Christmas gift, wedding gift or similar gift of up to $100, where the employer does not deduct the cost for tax purposes.
11. Counselling services related to mental or physical health, employment termination, or retirement.
12. Subsidized meals, where you are required to pay a reasonable charge covering the cost of the food.
13. Uniforms or special clothing you need for your job.
14. Transportation to the job, if provided directly by the employer.
15. Board and lodging at, and transportation to, a "special work site" where you work temporarily or a "remote work site" that is remote from any established community.
16. Use of your employer's recreational facilities.
17. Transportation passes given to bus, rail and airline employees, except for airline employees travelling on a space-confirmed basis.
18. Transportation and parking costs, whether paid directly by the employer or reimbursed to you, if you are blind or are disabled due to a mobility impairment.
19. The cost of an attendant to assist you at work if you are disabled.

Note that where your employer contributes to a sickness or accident insurance plan, a disability insurance plan or an income maintenance insurance plan, any benefits you receive from the insurance will be taxable (but reduced by your own (previously non-deductible) premium payments to the plan.)

6.1.2 Taxable employment benefits

In general, employment benefits other than those listed above are taxed as though you had received an equivalent amount of income. Examples include:

1. Tips (gratuities) that you receive from customers.
2. Board, lodging, and rent-free or low-rent housing (with some exceptions for remote or special work sites).
3. Travelling expenses for personal travel, including expenses for your spouse to travel on a business trip of yours, unless your spouse was engaged primarily in business activities on behalf of the employer during the trip.
4. Personal use of employer's automobile (see 6.4 below).
5. Gifts, except for $100 per year as noted above.
6. Allowing you and/or your family to use a vacation property.
7. Holiday trips, prizes and incentive awards.
8. Use of frequent-flyer credits that you earn through employer-paid trips but use for personal trips (this is Revenue Canada's view; the valuation of this benefit has not yet been tested in the courts).
9. Payment of provincial (public) health insurance premiums (note that many provinces no longer charge such premiums)
10. Life insurance premiums.
11. Reimbursement for the cost of tools used in employment duties.
12. Most tuition fees, except where you are given time off with pay during working hours to attend the classes, in which case it's assumed the tuition is for the employer's benefit.
13. Loans to employees (see 6.2 below).
14. Stock option plans (taxed only when you exercise the option: see 6.3 below).
15. Income tax return preparation and financial counselling (but not retirement or re-employment counselling)

In general, where the employer pays GST on goods or services (see 17.1), and then provides those goods or services to you as a taxable benefit, the calculation of the taxable benefit will require an additional 7% to account for the GST. This applies, for example, to automobiles.

6.2 Loans to employees

If you receive a low-interest or interest-free loan from your employer (or past or future employer), you are considered to have received a benefit from employment. The benefit is set at Revenue Canada's current prescribed rate of interest, which varies quarterly, minus any interest you actually pay during the year or within 30 days after the end of the year. The prescribed rate is now 4% lower than the rate charged on late payments of tax; see 13.3. (There may be an offsetting deemed interest deduction, as we shall see.)

EXAMPLE

Rebecca receives a loan of $10,000 from her employer on January 1. She is required to pay it back one year later, without interest. Assume the prescribed rate throughout the entire year is 6%.

Rebecca is considered to have an employment benefit of $600, and will be required to include this amount in her employment income.

Exceptions

A **home purchase loan** is taxed on the same basis as other employee loans, but the rate applied in calculating the imputed interest for the first five years of the loan will not be greater than the prescribed rate in effect at the time the loan was made. At the end of the five-year period, it is considered a new loan, and the prescribed rate at that time will be the maximum for the next five years.

EXAMPLE

Keith receives an interest-free loan from his employer to help him buy a house. (He is not relocating, just moving from an apartment to a house.) At the time, the prescribed interest rate is 6%. Two years later, interest rates have gone up, and the prescribed rate increases to 10%.

Keith will still pay tax on the interest benefit calculated at only 6% of the amount of the loan. If the prescribed rate had gone below 6%, he would, however, pay tax on imputed interest at the lower rate as long as it stayed below 6%.

If you **relocate**, and receive a home purchase loan to acquire a residence at least 40 km closer to your new work location, then a special deduction in computing your taxable income is available to you for the first five years of the loan equal to the interest imputed on $25,000. Note that you must still report the entire interest amount as a taxable benefit, and claim this special deduction as a separate item on your tax return.

Where you use funds borrowed from your employer to purchase **investments** or to purchase an **automobile** (or aircraft) to be used for your employment, you can obtain an offsetting deduction. The amount of imputed interest that you include in your income as a taxable benefit is deemed to have been *interest paid by you*. As a result, if such interest would otherwise have been deductible, you can deduct it. (As we saw in 5.3, interest paid on loans to acquire investments is deductible, and as we shall see in 6.9.1, interest paid on loans to acquire a car is deductible if the car is required by your terms of employment.) The effect is to eliminate the tax cost of the taxable benefit.

If you are a **shareholder** of the company as well as an employee, or if a member of your family is a shareholder, you must be especially cautious. It is possible for the *entire* amount of the loan, rather than the imputed interest, to be included in your income for tax purposes, unless stringent conditions are met. In general, you can avoid this rule if the loan is made for certain specific purposes and with arrangements for repayment within a reasonable time. Alternatively, the entire loan must be repaid within one year, and not be part of a series of loans and repayments (see 8.2.6).

6.3 STOCK OPTION PLANS

A stock option plan is an arrangement whereby a corporation gives an employee the right (an option) to invest in its shares at a given price. The price may or may not be less than the market price at the time the option is granted. For example, suppose you work for a corporation whose stock trades at $20. In 1995, you are given an option to buy up to 1,000 shares at $20, good until 1997. If, in 1996, the stock is trading at $30, you can exercise the option, buy 1,000 shares for $20,000, and then, if you wish, turn around and sell the shares on the market for $30,000.

The general rule is that you are considered to receive a benefit from employment, not when the option is granted (1995 in the above example), but when you exercise it (1996). The taxable benefit is the difference between the price you pay ($20,000) and the value of the shares when you exercise the option ($30,000). You would, therefore, report a taxable benefit of $10,000 in your employment income for 1996. (The adjusted cost base of the shares to you will be $30,000, so you will not be doubly taxed when you subsequently sell them.)

An offsetting partial deduction is available if certain requirements are met. The first requirement is that the shares be normal common shares (not preferred shares). Second, the exercise price must be no less than the fair market value of the shares at the time the option was granted. (Otherwise you could simply exercise the option the day you received it, so the benefit would be just like cash.) Third, you must deal at arm's length with the corporation (meaning essentially that you or members of your family do not control it). If these conditions are met, you can claim a deduction from income of one-quarter of the amount of the taxable benefit. The effect of this deduction is to make the taxable benefit taxed at the same three-quarters rate as a capital gain.

Another exception to the system of taxing stock options applies where your employer is a **Canadian-controlled private corporation** with which you deal at arm's length. In such a case, you do not record the taxable benefit until you *sell* the shares, rather than when you exercise the option and acquire them. And, if you have held them for at least two years at the date of sale, you can claim the deduction when computing your taxable income for one-quarter of the benefit without having to meet the first two requirements outlined in the previous paragraph. This exception is designed to stimulate employee participation in ownership of small businesses. It also recognizes that valuation of shares in a private company at the time you exercise the option may be difficult.

6.4 Company automobiles

Special rules apply for determining the taxable benefit when your employer provides you with an automobile.

There are two elements to the benefit that must be reported for tax purposes: a **standby charge**, and the benefit in respect of **operating costs**. These will normally be reported together on your T4 statement from your employer as a single amount, and included in your total "income from employment" for tax purposes.

The standby charge is, essentially, 2% of the original cost of the car for each month that it is available to you—i.e., 24% per year. (For automobile sales persons, it can instead be 1.5% per month of the average cost of the dealer's cars acquired in the year.) You can have this amount reduced *only* if you can show both (a) that your business use of the car is 90% or more of the kilometres driven, and (b) that your personal use of the car is less than 12,000 km in the year.

Note that driving between your home and your place of employment is normally *not* considered business use. It can thus be very difficult to satisfy the above tests for a reduction in the standby charge.

Where the car is leased, the standby charge is two-thirds of the monthly leasing cost instead of 2% of the purchase price.

An extra 7% must be added to the employee's taxable benefit to reflect the GST embedded in the value of the automobile to you. (Your employer may also be required to remit an amount of GST on the taxable benefit to Revenue Canada; see 17.3.3).

The taxable benefit for **operating costs** is 12¢/km of personal use. If your employer pays *any* operating costs during the year in respect of your personal use of an employer-provided car (and you don't fully reimburse your employer by the following February 14), the 12¢ rate applies. If you are employed principally in selling or leasing automobiles this rate is 9¢. (Again, your employer must remit part of this amount as though it were GST collected; see 17.3.3.)

An alternative calculation is available for the operating expenses where your business use of the car exceeds 50%. If you notify your employer in writing *by December 31* that you wish this option, the operating costs benefit will be a flat **50% of the standby charge**.

If you receive a reasonable **allowance** for automobile expenses, the allowance will not be included in your income if it is based *solely* on the number of kilometres driven in the performance of your employment duties. If it is a flat amount not calculated in terms of your employment-related driving, it will be taxable (though you may be able to claim offsetting automobile expenses: see 6.9.1). Revenue Canada accepts as a "reasonable allowance" 31¢/km for the first 5,000 km and 25¢/km thereafter (4¢ more in the Yukon and Northwest Territories); in some cases you may be able to justify a higher amount as "reasonable".

6.5 Deferred compensation

Various techniques have been tried over the years to avoid paying tax on employment income by having some of it held back in one way or another. (In general, employment income is taxed when received.)

Registered pension plans and **deferred profit-sharing plans** were discussed in 2.2 and 2.3. They are accepted mechanisms for deferring employment income.

Employee profit-sharing plans are not widely used. They do not defer the taxation of employment income. Contributions are made by the employer, based on profits for the year. Although the contributions are paid to the plan, the amounts contributed are treated as income of the employees for tax purposes. Such plans can therefore operate as forced savings plans for bonuses. Income (such as interest income) earned within the plan must be allocated to specific employees, who pay tax on it as it is allocated (even if it is not paid to them.)

The rules for **salary deferral arrangements** catch most arrangements for deferred compensation. For example, if you agree with your employer that your salary for 1995 will be $50,000, plus a further $10,000 to be paid in 1999, you will be taxed on the whole $60,000 in 1995. You can generally only escape this taxation if there is a substantial risk of forfeiting the future income.

The salary deferral arrangement rules allow certain exceptions. One is a self-funded leave of absence program, sometimes used by teachers, academics and others to fund sabbatical leaves. Provided you meet all of the conditions, you can arrange for your employer or a trustee to hold back a portion of your salary every year for up to six years, not recognize that portion as employment income each year, and receive it in the sabbatical year, paying tax on it then. Another exception is an arrangement whereby you have a right to receive a bonus to be paid within three years.

Retirement compensation arrangements are arrangements made outside the registered pension plan system, whereby a custodian will receive funds from an employer and make payments after the employee's retirement or termination. Such plans are discouraged, with a 50% refundable tax that applies to the payments made by the employer to the custodian (and which is refunded when the payments are made to the employee, at which point the employee reports the income for tax purposes).

6.6 Retiring allowances and severance pay

A "retiring allowance", as defined in the *Income Tax Act*, includes what one would normally call severance pay or termination pay, as well as a court award or settlement for wrongful dismissal. It also includes, of course, a payment by an employer for long service on retirement.

A retiring allowance, like ordinary employment income, is included in your income. However, as we saw in 2.1.7.2, part or all of it can be transferred to an RRSP and thus sheltered from immediate tax.

The amount that can be transferred is $2,000 for each calendar year (or part year) of service before 1996, plus $1,500 for each year (or part year) before 1989 for which employer contributions to your pension plan have not "vested". ("Vested" pension rights are those that you can take with you on retirement or termination; see 2.5.12.)

Legal fees incurred in establishing your retiring allowance are deductible against the retiring allowance. See 6.9.6 below.

6.7 Death benefits

A death benefit is an amount paid in recognition of a deceased employee's service. It is usually paid to the deceased's spouse or children. Subject to the $10,000 exemption outlined below, it is taxable.

The first $10,000 of death benefits paid in respect of any one employee is exempt from tax. The employee's spouse gets the exemption; to the extent there is no spouse or the spouse receives less than $10,000 and other taxpayers receive such funds, any remaining amount of exemption can be split among the other recipients. Note that "spouse" includes a common-law spouse who meets the criteria outlined in 1.3.1.

Note that life insurance proceeds are completely different from death benefits, and are not taxed at all when received.

6.8 Overseas employment tax credit

If you are resident in Canada but you work outside Canada for a period of six months or more, a special tax credit may be available. To be eligible, you must be working for a Canadian employer (or its foreign affiliate) on certain kinds of projects, such as mining, oil and gas exploration or production, agriculture, construction or engineering. If you are self-employed, you may be able to get this credit by incorporating your business and working as its employee.

The credit effectively allows you to offset the tax payable on up to $100,000 of overseas employment income per year, but is limited to 80% of that income. The details are very complicated; see the reference information in 6.11 below.

6.9 Deductions from employment income

The only deductions allowed against employment income are those specifically provided for in the *Income Tax Act*. We look at some of them below.

Note that, in general, where you can deduct expenses from your employment income, you can also receive a rebate of GST paid on those expenses (see 17.4). That rebate will itself be considered income from employment in the year in which you receive it, except where it relates to capital cost allowance (see 6.9.1).

6.9.1 Using your own automobile for employment

If you are required by the terms of your employment to use your own automobile and are not receiving a (non-taxable) reasonable allowance based on the number of kilometres you drive for employment purposes (see 6.4), you can deduct a portion of your automobile expenses from your employment income. (You must file with your tax return Form T2200 on which your employer certifies that you were required to use your own vehicle.)

First, you can deduct **operating costs**, such as gas, repairs and car washes, to the extent they relate to your employment. You will need to keep a detailed log of your driving, to track your employment-related use as opposed to your personal use. Note that driving between home and work is normally considered personal use (however, see 6.10.13).

Second, you can deduct **capital cost allowance** (depreciation), or your monthly lease payments for the proportion of employment-related use. The allowable rate of capital cost allowance is 15% in the year of acquisition of the car, followed by 30% *on the remaining balance* in each subsequent year. However, there is a cap on the cost of the car for this purpose:

Date car purchased	Limit
Before June 18, 1987	none
June 18, 1987-August 31, 1989	$20,000
September 1, 1989 to December 31, 1990	$24,000
January 1, 1991 or later	$24,000*

*plus GST and PST on $24,000

EXAMPLE

Michelle buys a new car in January 1995 for $30,000 plus 7% GST and 10% provincial sales tax. She is required to drive 10,000 km for employment-related purposes during the year. She also drives 10,000 km on personal trips.

Since half of her driving is employment-related, Michelle can claim half of the capital cost allowance normally allowed for a car. Although she spent $30,000, the cost is capped at $24,000, plus $2,400 provincial sales tax and 7% GST (total of **$28,080***), for tax purposes. The maximum capital cost allowance for the year of acquisition is 15%. Fifteen per cent of $28,080 is $4,212. Michelle can therefore claim* **$2,106** *as a deduction against her employment income for 1995.*

Further, because she uses her car partly for business, Michelle can claim a GST rebate in 1995 from Revenue Canada equal to 7/107 of her capital cost allowance claim. That is, 7/107 of the $2,106 Michelle can deduct as capital cost allowance, or $137.78, is refunded to her. This $137.78 is deducted from the undepreciated capital cost of the car at the beginning of 1996. See 17.4.

In the above example, we have assumed that Michelle's employer is a GST registrant. If, instead, she was employed by a financial institution or by a non-GST registrant, she would not be entitled to the employee GST rebate which, as shown, amounts to $137.78 in the first year.

If you **lease** the car, your deduction in respect of the lease payments is restricted to parallel the dollar limit on purchases:

Date lease entered into	Limit
Before June 18, 1987	none
June 18, 1987-August 31, 1989	$600
September 1, 1989 to December 31, 1990	$650
January 1, 1991 or later	$650*

*plus GST and PST

Third, you can deduct **interest** on any loan you have taken out to purchase the car (including financing on the purchase itself, where you make monthly payments that combine interest and capital). Your monthly interest is limited to:

Date car purchased	Deductible interest limit
Before June 18, 1987	none
June 18, 1987-August 31, 1989	$250
September 1, 1989 or later	$300

EXAMPLE

Michelle, who bought a new car in January 1995 for $30,000, is paying $700 per month on her car loan. She paid $2,000 down and the loan interest rate is 15%.

Calculations show that Michelle pays $350 per month in interest for the first month, and slightly less over the following months. Her interest for tax purposes over the year will be limited to $300 per month, or $3,600. Of this, she can deduct half, or $1,800, to reflect the proportion of her driving which was employment-related.

If you are **reimbursed** by your employer for employment-related use of your automobile, the reimbursement payments are not taxed. Of course, you cannot deduct your own expenses to the extent you have been reimbursed for them.

As noted in the example above, if you pay GST on a car and you are entitled to deduct capital cost allowance (on the proportion of your employment-related use), you can receive a rebate of GST related to the amount of your deduction. See 17.4 and the example above. The rebate claim is filed with your income tax return. The amount of this rebate will reduce the capital cost of the car (and your base for further depreciation) in the year you receive it.

6.9.2 TRAVELLING EXPENSES

If you are required by your employment to spend funds on employment-related travel, as outlined in the case of automobile expenses above, the amounts you pay will normally be deductible. Examples might include parking, taxis and train fares.

If you travel for a transportation company (e.g., as a bus or truck driver or a flight attendant), you can also deduct costs of meals and lodging to the extent you are not entitled to be reimbursed. The deduction for meals will be further restricted to 50% of your cost (see 7.2.6).

6.9.3 COMMISSION SALES PERSON'S EXPENSES

If you are employed as a sales person under a contract that requires you to pay your own expenses, and you earn commissions, you may be able to deduct the costs of your employment-related expenditures—the same kinds of costs as could be claimed if you were self-employed (see 7.2). To do so, you must be required by your contract of employment to pay your own expenses, and you must be ordinarily required to carry on your duties of employment away from your employer's place of business. The total expenses you claim this way cannot exceed your total commission income.

6.9.4 SUPPLIES, ASSISTANT'S SALARY AND HOME OFFICE

If you are required by your contract of employment to pay for any supplies or to pay for an assistant or substitute, you can deduct the cost of the supplies or the assistant's salary.

You can also deduct expenses relating to a home office, in limited circumstances. First, you must be required by your employment contract to maintain the office, and your employer must sign a certificate (Form T2200) that you file with your return. Second, either the home office must be the place where you "principally perform the duties of employment", or you must use it on a regular and continuous basis for *meeting* people (such as your employer's customers) in the ordinary course of your employment. The second restriction is parallel to that which applies to self-employed people, as outlined in more detail in 7.2.7. The effect is that the deduction is rarely available to employed individuals. You will normally only be able to claim it if you spend more of your time working at home than at your employer's premises.

6.9.5 UNION AND PROFESSIONAL DUES

Union dues are deductible for tax purposes. These are normally withheld at source and reported on the T4 you receive from your employer.

Dues required to maintain a legally recognized professional status are deductible, even if you do not need to maintain that status for your current job. Your status as a lawyer, engineer, accountant, physician, architect, nurse, dentist, etc., will qualify for this purpose. Dues to voluntary associations are not deductible, unless you are self-employed (see 7.2.2).

6.9.6 LEGAL FEES

If you spend money on a lawyer to recover unpaid wages, you can deduct the legal fees.

Legal fees you incur to establish your right to a "retiring allowance" (which includes severance pay), or to private pension plan benefits, are deductible. However, you can only deduct the legal fees against the *income from the retiring allowance or pension benefits in that year*. To the extent you have not yet received that income, you can "carry forward" the expenses for up to seven years and claim them against such income in those later years. (See 6.10.5 if you transfer your retiring allowance to an RRSP.)

EXAMPLE

Lewis was fired from his job in 1993. He retained a lawyer and sued for wrongful dismissal, spending $3,000 in 1993 and $5,000 in 1994 in legal fees. In 1995, the case is settled and his former employer pays him $50,000.

Lewis can deduct his $8,000 in legal fees only in 1995 against his $50,000 "retiring allowance" income, thus recognizing only $42,000 as income in that year.

See also 1.2.5 regarding the deductibility of legal fees that are not related to employment.

6.9.7 Musicians' instruments

If you are employed as a musician and required to supply your own instrument, you may deduct any maintenance, rental and insurance costs. If you have purchased the instrument, you may claim capital cost allowance (depreciation), at a rate of 10% for the first year, and 20% of the remaining balance in each subsequent year. All of these deductions can only be used to offset your income from employment as a musician, not against other income.

6.9.8 Artists' expenses

If you are employed as an artist (including, for example, a painter, sculptor, playwright, literary author, composer, actor, dancer, singer or musician), you may deduct up to $1,000 of your actual expenses incurred in order to earn income from such activities. This deduction is limited to 20% of your income from artistic employment, and the $1,000 limit is reduced by any amounts you claim as automobile expenses (see 6.9.1) and musical instrument costs (6.9.7).

Of course, if you earn income from your artistic activities that is not employment income, you are self-employed, in which cases *all* your expenses are normally deductible (see 7.2.2).

6.9.9 Northern employees

If your employer pays for you to take a vacation trip, with or without your family, the value of the taxable benefit is included in your income (see 6.1.2).

If you live in northern Canada, a deduction is available to offset all or part of this benefit. Provided you meet certain residency requirements, the deduction can eliminate the taxable benefit associated with up to two trips per year, based on the cost of airfare to the nearest large Canadian city. (There is no limit to the number of such trips if they are taken to obtain medical services not available locally.)

See also 1.2.6, regarding the special deduction for residents of northern Canada, and 6.1.1 and 6.10.1, regarding the non-taxability of benefits relating to a remote work site.

6.10 PLANNING OPPORTUNITIES

6.10.1 ARRANGE TO GET NON-TAXABLE BENEFITS

Ask your employer to make use of the non-taxable benefits outlined in 6.1.1 as much as possible.

If you have an employment benefit package where you and the employer share the costs, try to have the cost-sharing reallocated so that your employer pays for all the non-taxable benefits and you pay for the benefits that are taxable if your employer pays them. In many cases, without changing the cost to your employer, you can reduce your tax burden this way.

One non-taxable benefit that is sometimes overlooked is that of board and lodging at a "special work site" or "remote work site". A special work site need not be remote in the sense of isolated; as long as the duties you perform at that location are of a temporary nature, and you maintain another residence, the board (i.e., food) and lodging paid by your employer are a non-taxable benefit. This could apply, for example, if you spend several months in another city working on a project for your employer.

6.10.2 WHERE POSSIBLE, REQUEST REDUCTION OF SOURCE WITHHOLDINGS

If you have a loan from your employer on which imputed interest is assessed as a taxable benefit, your source deductions of income tax will reflect that taxable benefit. If, however, you are using the funds for a purpose that allows you an offsetting deduction (see 6.2), you may write to Revenue Canada, setting out that fact, and request that your employer be permitted to reduce the source withholding. An example of this is where you use the loan proceeds for investment purposes.

As well, in any other situation where you expect to receive a refund after filing your return (e.g., due to personal tax credits, RRSP contributions, medical expenses or charitable donations, alimony and maintenance payments), you should review the TD1 form you file with your employer and seek to have source withholdings reduced. You can ask your local Revenue Canada district office to permit your employer to reduce your source withholdings for deductions not normally provided for on the TD1 form, such as RRSP contributions and alimony and maintenance.

However, if your employer withholds from your remuneration RRSP contributions, union and professional dues and alimony and maintenance payments for direct remittance to the intended recipient, the employer can take these withholdings into account in calculating your tax withheld at source without requesting permission from Revenue Canada.

Although many taxpayers look forward to receiving a tax refund, it is not good tax planning to get one. If you get a refund, that means Revenue Canada has been holding your money and not paying you interest on it for many months. Although fiscal responsibility is needed to make sure you can pay your tax when it is due, it is better to be required to send a cheque to Revenue Canada at filing time, since it means that you have had use of the funds (for investment or other purposes) in the meantime. However, you must pay instalments if the difference between your tax payable and amounts withheld at source is more than $2,000 in both the current year and either of the two preceding years. (See 13.2.2.)

Note that interest is not paid on refunds for the first 45 days of processing after the filing deadline—i.e., until after June 14 for most employees. If you have a June 15 filing deadline because you have self-employment income (see 7.2.1), interest will not be paid until 45 days after April 30 or 45 days after the date that the return is actually filed, whichever is later. (see 13.1.1).

6.10.3 Pay interest owing on loan from employer within 30 days of end of year

If you have received an interest-bearing loan from your employer, consider deferring the payment of interest on the loan until January 30 of the next calendar year (see beginning of 6.2). This will provide you with a cash flow advantage. Make sure you do pay the interest by that date, however.

6.10.4 Consider employees' profit-sharing plan

Employees' profit-sharing plans, described in 6.5, have one tax advantage. There is no source withholding on the amounts paid into the plan, or on the amounts paid by the plan to you. Careful timing of the employer's contributions and the plan's disbursements can give you better cash flow than would a straight bonus payment.

6.10.5 Transfer retiring allowances to an RRSP

If you have received a retiring allowance (including any payment for accumulated sick leave credits, but not including vacation pay), you can transfer it into an RRSP, subject to the limits noted in 6.6.

This applies to a retiring employee as well as an award of severance pay or a payment for wrongful dismissal (which is also a "retiring allowance" in tax terminology). See 6.6 above.

Note that you should probably not transfer the maximum amount to an RRSP if you have incurred legal fees in obtaining your award (even if the case was settled without going to court). Legal fees can be carried forward for up to seven years and deducted against the "retiring allowance" income (see 6.9.6). If you transfer the entire retiring allowance into an RRSP, the legal fees will never become deductible. (When you take payments *out* of the RRSP, they are no longer considered a "retiring allowance".) However, if you intend to leave the funds to grow tax-free in the RRSP for many years, you may want to consider transferring the maximum anyway.

6.10.6 Set up stock option plan

Encourage your employer to set up a stock option plan as an employment benefit. It may cost your employer very little, and can even bring investment funds into the corporation to some extent. (The cost is the dilution of the existing shareholders' interests.)

If your employer is a Canadian-controlled private corporation, stock options are particularly attractive because you will not need to pay any tax until you dispose of the shares, and even then you will often be eligible for a favourable tax treatment (see 6.3). Be cautious about relying on such shares too much for your future, however; shares in private corporations are not liquid, and can become worthless very easily if the corporation runs into trouble.

If you receive shares in a Canadian-controlled private corporation through a stock option plan, consider contributing some of them to your RRSP if the shares qualify for that purpose (see 2.1.5 and 2.5.2).

6.10.7 Consider a stock purchase plan

A stock purchase plan is a possible alternative to a stock option plan. With a stock purchase plan, you would acquire the shares right away, rather than options. The acquisition might be assisted by a loan from your employer (see 6.2). Any increase in value of the shares will be a capital gain and only $^{3}/_{4}$ taxed (see 4.2).

Needless to say, a stock purchase plan is not a good idea unless you are quite confident in the future prospects for the company's shares.

6.10.8 Consider a phantom stock plan

A phantom stock plan avoids the requirement that you acquire shares in the corporation, and thus may be more attractive to your employer's controlling shareholders. Under such a plan, you receive bonuses based on the increase in value of your employer's shares. Such bonuses are simply taxed as employment income. If they are not paid to you on an ongoing basis, you will need to determine whether they constitute a salary deferral arrangement (see 6.5), in which case they will be taxed in your hands even if not received.

6.10.9 KEEP TRACK OF BUSINESS USE OF CAR

Whether you drive your employer's car or your own, keep careful track of the distance you drive for purposes related to your employment (see 6.4 and 6.9.1). You may wish to keep a log book on the dashboard, or record your business driving in your daily appointment calendar.

6.10.10 TAKE STEPS TO MINIMIZE TAXABLE BENEFIT FROM CAR OPERATING COSTS

If your employer pays only part of the operating costs of an employer-owned car that you use, the taxable benefit from operating costs (see 6.4) can cost you more than the amount the employer pays. Sometimes the employer pays only the insurance and the employee pays for all gas and repairs, or the employer does not pay most operating expenses but might cover an occasional major repair bill.

For example, suppose you put 20,000 km on your company car over the year, all of which is personal use (including driving to work and back). Your employer pays the insurance ($500 per year) and you pay the rest of the operating expenses. Your taxable benefit for operating costs will be 12¢ per personal-use kilometre, or $2,400, which will typically cost you some $1,000 to $1,200 in tax. So having the employer pay for the insurance is very disadvantageous.

In such a case you should *repay* the $500 to the employer *by February 14* of the following year, so that the "12¢ per kilometre" rule will not apply. Of course, your employer can pay you additional salary of $500 which will simply be taxable as income, to offset your repayment of the insurance costs.

Also, if your employment-related use is more than 50%, you must decide (and notify your employer in writing) *by December 31* if you want to use the special calculation for the operating expenses benefit rather than the fixed rate of 12¢ per personal kilometre. A benefit of one-half of the standby charge will be to your advantage where the cost of the car is relatively low (for a small car, or a car that was purchased used), and the number of personal kilometres is relatively high even though it is less than 50% of the total use.

6.10.11 AVOID EXPENSIVE EMPLOYER-OWNED VEHICLES

If you drive a company car that was purchased after June 17, 1987 and cost more than $20,000 or $24,000 (see 6.9.1), there is an element of double taxation. Your taxable "standby charge" benefit will be 2% per month of the *actual* cost of the car. However, only $20,000 or $24,000 can be written off (over time) as capital cost allowance by your employer. For cars purchased after 1990, the $24,000 cap is increased by both the GST and PST paid on the first $24,000.

It may be more economical for you to purchase the car yourself and arrange for an appropriate increase in remuneration from your employer.

6.10.12 Reduce time company car is available for personal use

The standby charge is based on the number of 30-day periods in the year that a company car is "made available" to you or a member of your family. The actual calculation is based on the number of *days* during which the car is available. This number is divided by 30 and rounded to the nearest whole number, and rounded down if it is exactly in the middle.

If you can get the number of "available days" down to 345, which is 11.5 30-day periods, the standby charge will therefore be reduced to only 11 times 2% of the automobile cost instead of 12 times 2%.

If you take three weeks or more of vacations or business trips during the year, leave the car at the company's premises during those times. If the car cost $20,000 new, you can thus reduce your taxable income for the year by $400 (and save $160-$200 in tax) by getting the number of "available days" down to 345. Note, however, that Revenue Canada holds the view that the car is still made available to you during this time unless you are *required* to return the car and control over its use to your employer. You might wish to arrange for your employer to impose this requirement on you.

6.10.13 Maximize employment-related use of car

As noted, driving to and from work is considered personal use rather than business use. If, however, you travel from your home to a business call (to visit a client or supplier, for example), that will constitute business use.

You can maximize your employment-related travel by making all of your business calls at the beginning and end of your day, before you go to work and after you leave work. You can thus make your entire trip from home to work count as travel for employment purposes.

6.11 References

The following publications can be obtained (in person or by telephone request) from your nearest Revenue Canada District Taxation Office:

Interpretation Bulletin IT-63R4, "Benefits, including standby charge for an automobile, from the personal use of a motor vehicle supplied by an employer"

Interpretation Bulletin IT-113R3, "Benefits to employees—stock options"

Interpretation Bulletin IT-148R2, "Recreational properties and club dues"

Interpretation Bulletin IT-158R2, "Employees' professional membership dues"

Interpretation Bulletin IT-196R2, "Payments by Employer to employee"

Interpretation Bulletin IT-222R, "Advances to employees".

Interpretation Bulletin IT-337R2, "Retiring allowances"

Interpretation Bulletin IT-352R, "Employees' expenses incurred in performing duties of office or employment"

Interpretation Bulletin IT-421R2, "Benefits to individuals, corporations and shareholders from loans or debt"

Interpretation Bulletin IT-470R, "Employees' fringe benefits"

Interpretation Bulletin IT-497R2, "Overseas employment tax credit"

Interpretation Bulletin IT-508, "Death benefits—calculation"

Interpretation Bulletin IT-522, "Vehicle and other travelling expenses—employees"

Information Circular 73-21R7, "Away from home expenses"

Information Circular 77-1R4, "Deferred profit sharing plans"

"Employment Expenses Tax Guide"

Form TD1, "199_ Personal Tax Credit Return"

Form T626, "Overseas employment tax credit"

Form T777, "Statement of employment expenses"

Form T2200, "Declaration of conditions of employment"

Form GST 370, "Employee and partner GST rebate"

7 If You Are Self-Employed

Planning Tips

- Arrange to be a consultant rather than employed
- Maximize income for "stub period" ending December 31, 1995
- Deduct transportation expenses
- Keep track of and maximize the business use of your car
- Claim business meals and entertainment expenses
- Write off home office expenses
- Pay salary or consulting fees to spouse or children
- Use loss carryovers
- Acquire depreciable assets before year-end
- Consider claiming less CCA than the maximum

In this chapter we highlight some of the major topics in the taxation of business income. If you are in a partnership, see also 10.2; if you are in Québec, see also Chapter 14. It goes without saying that anyone with a substantial amount of business income should obtain proper professional advice.

7.1 Employee or Independent Contractor?

As you will see in this chapter, people who are self-employed, carrying on business for themselves, generally have wider scope for tax planning than do employees.

It is important to understand that carrying on a business has nothing to do with setting up a corporation (which is discussed in Chapter 8). Any taxpayer can carry on business. If you set up a second-hand-clothing-for-cash exchange in your basement, you are carrying on business. If you decide to put a name to your business (say, "XYZ Second-Hand Clothing"), that is just you carrying on business under that name. You have not created a new entity. You simply have a **proprietorship**, which means you are the proprietor of a business.

The distinction between employee and independent contractor (i.e., self-employed) is not always clear in cases where you receive most or all of your "work" income from one source. If you provide services to an organization, you can be classed in either group, depending on the facts.

EXAMPLE

Lisa is a computer programmer. She develops software for ABC Corporation, and is paid for each hour she works. She does a lot of her work at home, though she goes to ABC's offices for regular meetings.

Is Lisa an employee of ABC, or an independent consultant who carries on business and whose major (or only) client is ABC?

In cases like this, one must look at all the facts to determine the person's status. There are no hard and fast rules. *In general*, you are more likely to be considered an employee if you:

- work a set number of hours per day
- have to account for your time to the company
- are told what to do each step of the way
- are a member of the company's group life, drug, dental and pension plans and receive other "benefits"
- use the company's computer equipment and supplies and have an office at the company.

At the other extreme, you would likely be considered an independent contractor carrying on your own business as a proprietor if you:

- agree to get the job done, but you don't make a commitment for any particular number of hours on any particular day
- work on your own with no supervision, and simply report back to the company periodically on progress
- issue invoices and receive cheques (with no source deductions for income tax, UIC or CPP) and receive no employee benefits
- use your own equipment and work at home, going to the company for planning meetings only
- provide services to more than one company.

These examples are fairly extreme. Between them is a large fuzzy area, where each case will depend on its facts. Note that it doesn't matter very much what you and the company *call* your relationship; more specifically, calling it independent contracting doesn't make it independent contracting unless the facts support such a claim.

One case where Revenue Canada has a clear administrative policy is that of real estate agents. You will be considered self-employed if you are entitled to the full amount of commissions, and either (a) you pay only a fixed amount to your broker for administrative operating costs, or (b) you pay a percentage of your gross commissions to your broker to cover such costs, and you set your own commission rate for sales on your listings.

Revenue Canada has a questionnaire, Form CPT-1, through which your employer can supply the details of its relationship with you and ask for a ruling as to whether you are an employee or not for CPP purposes (and, by extension, for income tax purposes). However, there is no requirement to apply for such a ruling, and you and your employer/client are not bound by Revenue Canada's administrative decisions. If, after receiving professional advice, you believe that you are legally an independent contractor, then you are quite entitled to proceed on that basis. (Of course, your employer/ client may not be willing to risk not withholding tax at source, if Revenue Canada has expressed the view that you are an employee.)

7.2 TAXATION OF THE BUSINESS

In this section we review how your business income is taxed. If you are a professional, see also Chapter 10.

7.2.1 BUSINESS YEAR-END

Until 1995, you could pick a year-end for any business when you started the business. The income was then taxed only in the taxation year in which the business year *ended.*

For example, if you started a profitable consulting business in mid-1994, you might choose to have the business year end on January 31. Then you would not report any of the income on your 1994 return. Instead, *all* of the income for the year ending January 31, 1995 would go onto your 1995 return (filed in the spring of 1996).

This rule allowed individuals and partnerships carrying on business to defer paying tax by up to a year. This option has been eliminated by the February 1995 federal budget. Effective 1995, all individuals, and all partnerships which have any individuals as members, **must use a calendar year** for reporting their income. Your year-end is now December 31.

A special transitional rule applies if you have been in business since before January 1, 1995 and were not already using a calendar year-end. You must now report two business "years" on your 1995 return: one ending on your normal year-end and the other ending on December 31. Since the result may be much higher income for 1995, you may spread the "extra" income (for the period ending December 31) over 10 years, reporting at least 5% in 1995, 10% more by each of the next 8 years, and the final 15% by 2004.

EXAMPLE

Andy is a lawyer who earns $120,000 per year. His business year-end has always been January 31.

For the 12-month year ending January 31, 1995, Andy's income is $120,000. As well, he must recognize the income for the 11 months running from February 1 to December 31, 1995 **($110,000)**. *For this "stub period", he must report 5% of the income, or $5,500, in 1995.*

For each year from 1996 through 2003, Andy must include a further 10% ($11,000) of his 1995 "stub period" income. The final 15% ($16,500) must be included by 2004.

The income inclusion is done by reporting the full amount of the stub period income in 1995, and claiming a **"reserve"** (deduction) against that income of up to **95% in 1995**. The amount of the reserve is then included in 1996 income, and a new reserve can be taken for 1996 of up to 85% of the original stub-period income. As a result, you may choose to report (and pay tax on) more than the minimum in any given year. The real requirement is to pay tax cumulatively on 5% of the income in 1995, 15% by 1996, 25% by 1997, 35% by 1998, and so on.

If you are a proprietor or an individual who is a member of a partnership composed of individuals, you or your partnership can elect to keep the off-calendar year-end by using an "**alternative method**" of eliminating the tax deferral announced in July, 1995. Under the alternative method, you or the partnership must add to the business income for the actual off-calendar fiscal period an estimate of income earned between the end of the 1995 fiscal period and December 31, 1995. The adjustment is determined by prorating the actual off-calendar fiscal period. For example, if your traditional fiscal year-end is January 31, 1995, the additional amount taxable in 1995 under the alternative method would be $^{11}/_{12}$ of your actual income for the fiscal period ended January 31, 1995. Similar adjustments will be made in future years. You will be able to claim a reserve for the 1995 adjustment amount similar to the reserve described above.

If you have a non-calendar fiscal period and initially adopt the alternative method, you may later change to a December 31 year-end, but once you do, you will not be able to go back to an off-calendar year-end. The election to use this alternative method must be made by June 15, the tax return due date for individuals reporting business income.

7.2.2 BUSINESS INCOME AND EXPENSES

As a general principle, business income for tax purposes is based on generally accepted accounting principles. (Among other things, this means operating on the **accrual** basis: you record your income when you have billed your clients, whether or not you have been paid.) However, there are many adjustments required for tax purposes. Some of them are discussed in the sections below.

When you earn business income, there is normally no withholding of tax at source. If you are providing services to a single organization, and are able to classify your relationship as one of independent consultant rather than employee (see 7.1), you can submit invoices that will be paid in full, without tax (or UIC premiums or CPP contributions) being taken off and remitted to

Revenue Canada. You may, however, be required to pay instalments of income tax. Instalments are discussed in 13.2.2.

In general, expenses are deductible if they are laid out to earn income from the business and are in reasonable amounts. There are certainly exceptions, as we shall see in the following sections. However, the underlying principle is the reverse of that for employees. **Employees can only deduct expenses that are specifically permitted under the *Income Tax Act*. Someone carrying on business can deduct any expenses that are not specifically prohibited by the *Income Tax Act*, provided such expenses relate to the earning of business income.**

GST paid by your business is normally not considered an expense. As long as the goods and services you provide are themselves subject to GST, or are zero-rated (completely free of GST), any GST you pay is fully recoverable as an input tax credit. See 17.1. However, if you are using the "Quick Method" of GST reporting, whereby you remit a percentage of your gross sales, most GST you pay will be treated as part of the deductible expense to which it relates. See 17.2.3.

7.2.3 UI, CPP AND OTHER PAYROLL TAXES

Unemployment insurance is available only to those who are employed. If you carry on business for yourself, you are neither required nor permitted to pay UI premiums. This will save you over $3,050 in 1995 when taking into account both the employee and employer's portions; on the other hand, it means that if your consulting contracts terminate and you are left without work, you cannot benefit from UI.

Canada Pension Plan contributions are split equally between employees and their employers. If you are self-employed, you are required to pay the "employer's share" to make up what is not being paid for you, as well as your own share. Since you are not employed, no CPP contributions are withheld from your income. As a result, you will find yourself required to pay up to $1,701 for 1995 in mandatory CPP contributions when you file your return, offset by a tax credit worth about $460. (If it's any consolation, you'll get it back in the form of a pension after you turn 65, or optionally as early as age 60.)

Many provinces also have payroll taxes that apply to employment income. In some cases, they apply to self-employed income as well. For example, Ontario's "Employer Health Tax" (EHT) applies to individuals with self-employment income over $40,000 per year. For self-employed individuals with incomes under $200,000, this tax is about 0.78% of self-employment income over the $40,000 threshold. The top rate applicable to self-employed individuals, when income exceeds $400,000, is about 1.52%. This will not be considered a deductible expense for income tax purposes, but to compensate, the rate has been set lower than the rate for employers on salary and wages paid to employees. (Technically the rate is the same as for employers, but the tax is reduced by a 22% credit.)

7.2.4 CAPITAL COST ALLOWANCE

The treatment of capital expenses is one of the major differences between business income based on accounting principles and income calculated for income tax purposes. In both cases, you cannot simply write off the cost of purchasing major capital assets (furniture, buildings, computers, automobiles, etc.). You must spread the cost over several years.

For accounting (not tax) purposes, a professional will make a judgment call as to the appropriate depreciation to claim. Various methods of depreciation can be used.

For tax purposes, depreciation is subject to strict rules and limitations, since it reduces your income (and thus the tax you pay). The income tax system of depreciation is called **capital cost allowance** (CCA); the rules are numerous and complex.

In very general terms, your capital assets are grouped into **classes**, and capital cost allowance can be claimed annually against each class. The "declining balance" method is used for most classes; the maximum you can claim against each class is a fixed percentage of the **"undepreciated capital cost"**. What you claim then reduces that balance for next year's claim.

For most acquisitions, only one-half of the CCA you could otherwise claim for the asset will be allowed in the year of acquisition.

Some common CCA rates	
Buildings acquired after 1987 (class 1)	4%
Buildings acquired 1979-1987 (class 3)	5%
Furniture and fixtures (class 8)	20%
Computer hardware (class 10)	30%
Automobiles (class 10 or 10.1)	30%
Most computer software (class 12)	100%
Tools costing less than $200 (class 12)	100%

Note that you are never required to claim the maximum CCA. You may in any year choose to claim less than the maximum, or nothing at all, for any given class of assets. The undepreciated capital cost for that class will remain intact, so you can make claims in later years based on that carried forward balance.

7.2.5 AUTOMOBILES

As a general principle, you can deduct the proportion of your automobile expenses that represents your business use of the vehicle, normally based on kilometres driven. So if half of your driving is done for your business (excluding driving from your home to your own place of business) and half is personal use, you can deduct one-half of the expenses of the car for that year. The expenses would include gas, washes, repairs, insurance, interest on financing the vehicle, leasing costs if the car is leased, and capital cost allowance if you own it.

However, there are limits to how expensive a vehicle you can write off. Your claims for CCA and leasing costs will be based on a maximum cost:

Date car acquired	Purchase Limit	Lease Limit
Before June 18, 1987	none	none
June 18, 1987-August 31, 1989	$20,000	$600
September 1, 1989 to December 31, 1990	$24,000	$650
January 1, 1991 or later	$24,000*	$650*

*before GST and PST

(For most businesses, since you get back all GST paid as an input tax credit (see 17.1), "before GST and PST" effectively means "plus PST".)

In addition, where you have financed the purchase of a car, your monthly interest expense before determining the business portion will be limited to:

Date car purchased	Deductible interest limit
Before June 18, 1987	none
June 18, 1987-August 31, 1989	$250
September 1, 1989 or later	$300

These rules are identical to those for employees' use of a vehicle for employment purposes; (see 6.9.1).

The $24,000 limit also applies for purposes of calculating your GST input tax credit (see 17.1).

7.2.6 Meals and entertainment

If you take a client or potential client (or a group of such people) to lunch or dinner, you can normally consider the cost of the meal as a business expense. The *Income Tax Act* restricts the amount you can claim to **50%** of the amount paid; the restriction is designed to deny a deduction for some of the personal benefit you receive (since you would need to eat anyway). The same 50% limitation applies to entertainment expenses, such as taking a client to a sports event.

7.2.7 Home office expenses

If you have an office in your home, you can claim a portion of your ongoing home expenses as business expenses, subject to the restrictions discussed below. The portion will normally be based on the fraction of the home that is used for your office (you can usually exclude common areas, such as hallways, kitchen and washrooms, when making the calculation). The expenses you can claim include:

- rent, if you are a tenant
- mortgage interest (but not the principal portion of blended mortgage payments)
- property taxes
- utilities: electricity, heat, water, gas
- telephone (if you have a separate business telephone which is fully deductible, consider whether you also use your personal phone for business calls)
- outside maintenance: lawn care, snowplowing
- minor repairs and supplies
- home insurance

EXAMPLE

Mary is a computer programmer and works as a consultant to various companies. She works in her home, where her office is a room that is 200 square feet. The total area of the rooms in her house (bedrooms, living room, dining room and the office) is 2,000 square feet.

Provided her home office qualifies (see below), Mary can claim 10% of her mortgage interest, property taxes, house insurance, utilities, etc., as expenses for tax purposes.

You may also claim capital cost allowance on the appropriate fraction of your home, but this is often not advisable. If you claim CCA, Revenue Canada will take the position that that fraction of your home is not part of your principal residence, and will disallow your claim for the principal residence exemption (see 4.5.3) in respect of that portion of the home. Any CCA you claimed can also be "recaptured" into income when you sell your home. (If you bought your home at the top of the housing market and do not expect to recover your costs when you sell, claiming CCA may be a good idea, however.)

The home office expenses are subject to restrictions. First, you can only claim the expenses **against your income** from the business. You therefore cannot use home office expenses to produce an overall business loss that is applied against other income. However, losses disallowed because of this rule can be carried forward and used in any later year against income generated from the same business.

Second, the home office will only be allowed if you fall into one of these two categories:

(a) your home is your **principal place of business**—that is, you do not have an office elsewhere. Note that if you have one major client and that client provides you with an office on its premises, it is still the client's premises and it will not disentitle you to your claim for a home office;

or

(b) the home office is used exclusively for your business, and is used "on a **regular and continuous basis** for meeting clients, customers or patients".

EXAMPLE

Les is a chiropractor and has an office outside his home. He also has an office in his basement, where he does a lot of his business's paperwork and occasionally sees patients (usually neighbours who come over for treatment in the evening).

Les will not be able to claim any expenses in respect of his home office unless he can show that he uses it "on a regular and continuous basis" to see patients.

Of course, *supplies* that relate exclusively to your home office are fully deductible and not subject to the above restrictions. Fully deductible expenses would normally include a separate business phone line; fax and printer paper; laser printer or photocopier toner cartridges; computer repairs (assuming your computer is used only for your business); and so on.

7.2.8 Capital gains

Any capital gains that you realize are accounted for directly, through the capital gains system discussed in Chapter 4. They are not counted within the business's income. This means that capital gains are taxed in the *calendar year* in which they are realized, even if your business year-end will occur after the end of the calendar year. Thus, capital gains realized in 1995 will not go into your "stub period" income for purposes of the reserve described in 7.2.1.

7.2.9 Investment tax credits

Federal investment tax credits (ITCs) are available for investment in certain regions of the country (e.g., the Maritimes) and for investment in scientific research and experimental development.

Like capital gains, ITCs fall outside your business income calculation and therefore can be claimed in the return for the calendar year in which they are generated, even if your business income will not be taxed until the next year.

Unused ITCs can be carried back three years or carried forward for up to ten years.

7.3 Partnership

If you join together to carry on business with one or more other people—which could include your spouse—you will be in **partnership**. You are still, for tax purposes, carrying on business. (As well as the discussion below, see 10.2, where some special rules applying to partnerships are discussed.)

7.3.1 How partnership income is taxed

Partnerships do not pay tax. Partnerships with more than five partners are required to file "information returns" with Revenue Canada, reporting partnership income, but these are not tax returns. (Partnerships do account for GST directly: see 17.3.3.)

The individual partners must each report their share of the partnership's income (or loss) as their own, *whether or not they have taken any of the profits out of the partnership*. Effective 1995, the partnership is required to report income as of December 31 (see 7.2.1). Resource allowances and various other resource-related expenses (see 5.4.4) are claimed by the individual partner rather than at the partnership level.

Note that a partnership cannot pay a "salary" to a partner. Even if you, as a partner, receive something called a "salary", it is really partnership drawings (withdrawal of profits or capital from the partnership). You are *not* taxed on your partnership drawings, but on your **share of the partnership's income**, which may be very different.

If the partnership suffers losses, you can normally claim your share of those losses against your other sources of income. (This may not be the case where the partnership is a limited partnership: see 5.4.2.)

7.3.2 Adjustment of partnership allocation

The allocation of partnership income (or losses) among the partners is normally left up to the partners to resolve. If you set up an unreasonable allocation for income-splitting purposes, however, Revenue Canada may disallow your allocation and substitute a reasonable one.

For example, if you supply all of the capital and do almost all of the work in your business, and your spouse does almost nothing, Revenue Canada could be expected to disallow a 50/50 allocation of the business's income between the two of you.

7.3.3 CAPITAL GAINS

Capital gains or losses realized by a partnership are allocated to the individual partners at the end of the partnership's taxation year. This will continue to be the case where the partnership has elected to follow the alternative method and keeps its off-calendar year-end (see 7.2.1). However, effective 1995, partnerships which must use a December 31 year-end, such gains or losses will always be reported by the individual partners in the calendar year in which they are realized.

7.3.4 ALLOCATION OF INVESTMENT TAX CREDITS

Investment tax credits (see 7.2.9 above) earned by a partnership are allocated to the individual partners and claimed in the year in which the partnership's year ends.

7.3.5 GAIN OR LOSS ON PARTNERSHIP INTEREST

When you are a member of a partnership you own a "partnership interest", which has an adjusted cost base for capital gains calculation purposes (see 4.2). If you sell your interest in the partnership (or are deemed to dispose of it at fair market value on death or emigration; see 4.5.4 and 4.5.5), the adjusted cost base will determine whether you have a capital gain or capital loss.

Your initial cost base is the capital you put into the partnership. Each year, when you report your share of the partnership's **income**, that amount is **added** to your cost base (since you have already been taxed on it, it should not be taxed again if you sell your interest without withdrawing the profits). When you **withdraw** profits from the partnership (see 7.3.1 above), the amount you withdraw **reduces** your adjusted cost base. Thus, in simplified terms, your adjusted cost base is your contributions, plus all partnership profits, minus all partnership losses and your withdrawals. (The details are much more complicated and there are many special rules, but that is the essence of it.)

A partnership is a "flow-through entity" for purposes of the 1994 capital gain election, so you may have an "exempt capital gain balance" that you can use against the capital gain until the year 2004 (see 4.4.4).

7.3.6 Assessment of partnership

Under new rules introduced on April 26, 1995, Revenue Canada will be able to issue a "**determination**" of a **partnership's income or loss**. This "determination" will be much like an assessment of a taxpayer's tax (see 13.4.1), in that it will be binding on the partners unless a Notice of Objection is filed. One partner will have to be designated by the partnership to file any such Notice of Objection, and the other partners will not be able to object directly to the determination. These new rules will take effect only after the legislation implementing them is passed (which is likely to happen in 1996).

7.4 Business losses

If your business expenses claimed for tax purposes exceed the revenues from the business, you have a loss. You also have a loss for tax purposes if you share in a portion of a partnership's loss.

You can only claim a business loss against other income if your business has a **"reasonable expectation of profit".** As well, if your loss arises from a limited partnership, you may not be able to claim it; see 5.4.2.

A business loss must first be used in the year in which it arises, to offset income from other businesses and other types of income, such as employment income, interest, (grossed-up) dividends and taxable capital gains. You do not have any choice in this matter; even if, for example, the tax on your dividend income could be offset by the dividend tax credit anyway, you must apply your business losses against any income you have in that year.

Business losses not deductible in the year they arise are called **non-capital losses**. They can be applied to other years' income. They can be carried **back for up to three years** and **forward for up to seven years**. They can be applied against any source of income in those years. All such claims are optional.

EXAMPLE

Judy earned $40,000 in 1993 and $50,000 in 1994 as an employee. In 1995 she goes into business for herself. Her business year-end is December 31, and for her 1995 business year she suffers a loss for tax purposes of $100,000.

Judy can file a form requesting that her non-capital loss from 1995 be applied against any amount of her 1993 and 1994 income. She will then receive a refund for the tax she paid in those years. If she wipes out all of her 1993 and 1994 income, she will still have a $10,000 non-capital loss, which can be carried forward to future years.

Judy should not, however, use up $90,000 of her loss. She only needs to use enough to bring her 1993 and 1994 income so low that she pays no tax at all ($6,000 or so). If she wishes, she *may choose to use even less, and leave some of the 1993 and 1994 income taxed at relatively low rates.*

7.5 Planning opportunities

Self-employed taxpayers should almost always obtain professional advice, due to the large potential for planning legitimate deductions for business income purposes. Below we set out some of the most common planning ideas. If you are a professional, see also Chapter 10 for additional tax planning possibilities.

7.5.1 Arrange to be a consultant rather than employed

If you are currently employed in a position where you maintain a fair amount of independence from your employer, investigate whether you can change your relationship so that you become an independent consultant rather than an employee (see 7.1). You will need to document the details of your relationship carefully, in case Revenue Canada challenges you in the future.

If you succeed in becoming independent, you will be able to take advantage of all of the planning tips mentioned below. You will lose certain advantages, however, including the right to unemployment insurance benefits, the employer's contribution to the Canada Pension Plan for you, and possibly all of the employment benefits you now have (pension plan, drug plan, etc.). You may wish to negotiate to have your cash compensation increased in exchange for any employment benefits you are giving up.

7.5.2 Maximize income for "stub period" ending December 31, 1995

As discussed in 7.2.1, effective 1995 you must report business and partnership income on a calendar-year basis.

If you were already in business before January 1995 and not using a calendar year, your business income for the second part of 1995 (the "stub period" from the end of your business year to December 31) can be spread over 10 years. See the example in 7.2.1.

As a general rule, you should therefore seek to **maximize** your income for the 1995 "stub period". Suppose, for example, your marginal tax rate is 50% and you can find a way to accelerate $20,000 of income from January 1996 back to December 1995. Instead of paying the $10,000 of tax on your 1996 return (tax due by April 30, 1997), you can spread the burden over 10 years, paying $500 in tax by April 30, 1996, a further $1,000 by each of April 30, 1997 to 2004, and the final $1,500 by April 30, 2005.

Depending on the nature of your business, there may be various ways to "advance" your income to December 1995 for this purpose. For example, you might issue invoices earlier than you otherwise would, or defer expenses from late 1995 to early 1996.

For purposes of calculating your "stub period" income, you must claim the maximum capital cost allowance (see 7.2.4) and other reserves. You will not be allowed to include taxable dividends received in "stub period" income. Professionals' work-in-progress must also be excluded.

Once you have maximized your "stub period" income, you can choose how quickly to report it over the 10 years 1995-2004, subject to the cumulative minimums outlined in 7.2.1. If, for example, you find that you have very low income in 1998, you might choose to recognize much more than the minimum required, so as to have that income taxed at a low rate. Of course, it is impossible to predict now what your income levels, and tax rates, will be over the next 10 years.

If you are a proprietor or an individual who is a member of a partnership and your business is cyclical or growing, consider making the election to keep your off-calendar year-end under the "alternative method" (see 7.2.1). Since this method requires you to add to your income an amount based on your prior fiscal year's actual income to arrive at an estimate of your calendar-year income for tax purposes, you may be able to defer taxes on a portion of your current year's income if you expect your income to rise from one year to the next.

If you're starting a business in 1995, you may be able to use the alternative method to defer the tax on your 1995 income until 1996 and to reduce or eliminate your 1996 tax instalments. Bear in mind, however, that you will not be able to claim the reserve for 1995 and you will have more tax to pay in 1996.

7.5.3 Deduct transportation expenses

You cannot consider transportation from your home to your own office as a business expense. However, if you have an office in your home, and you travel from there to your major client (who might happen to provide you with an office on its premises), you are engaging in business travel.

Keep records of all such business trips, and deduct the appropriate costs of parking, public transit, taxicabs, etc. Where you are using your own car, make sure to log the business distance travelled as well as gas purchases and repairs.

7.5.4 Automobile planning tips

See the planning tips suggested for employees in 6.10.9 and 6.10.13. The same considerations apply to business use of your own car.

7.5.5 Claim business meals and entertainment expenses

As noted in 7.2.6, 50% of business meals and entertainment expenses are deductible. Make sure you claim all lunches and dinners that you can justifiably relate to your business. For audit purposes, you should make a notation on your receipt of the individual(s) treated and the reason for the meeting.

7.5.6 Write off home office expenses

If you meet the tests outlined in 7.2.7, write off all home expenses for which you are eligible. Make sure to claim your business portion of some of the less obvious expenses, such as garden service, driveway snowplowing, lightbulbs and minor repairs. You will need to keep receipts on file; do not simply estimate your expenses.

7.5.7 Pay salary or consulting fee to spouse or children, or bring spouse into partnership

See 3.3.2 for comments on this income-splitting tip.

7.5.8 Use loss carryovers

Use any non-capital losses (business losses) carefully. As noted in 7.4, when carrying such losses back or forward to other years, the amount you claim is optional.

When using non-capital losses against income for any given year, consider whether you want to keep some of the income taxed at a low rate. For example, if you have a loss in 1995 and are carrying it back to 1994, any taxable income below $29,590 was taxed at only about 27%. If you (confidently) expect to have a large income within the next few years, so that you can apply the loss against income which will otherwise be taxed at approximately 50%, you are probably better off *not* to bring your 1994 taxable income below the $29,590 level.

Of course, you should never use loss carryovers to reduce your taxable income below the level (about $6,500, or more depending on the credits you can claim; see 1.3) where no tax is payable anyway.

7.5.9 Acquire capital assets before year-end

One-half of the normal capital cost allowance for an asset is allowed for the year in which you acquire it. Acquiring an asset just before your year-end will accelerate the timing of your tax writeoff.

Note that assets are normally required to be **available for use** and not simply "on the books" to be eligible for CCA, unless you have owned them for at least two years. The term "available for use" has a specific and complex definition, and professional advice should be sought if you are unsure as to how it applies in your case.

7.5.10 Consider claiming less CCA than the maximum

In some circumstances you may wish to claim less CCA than you are entitled to (see 7.2.4). For example, if you have old non-capital losses or investment tax credits that will otherwise expire, you are better off to not claim CCA, use up the losses or credits, and save your "undepreciated capital cost" balances for CCA claims in future years.

You might also choose not to claim CCA if you are in a low-income year and expect your income to be much higher (and thus taxed at higher marginal rates) in subsequent years. Such a decision should only be made after careful analysis of the present value of the future tax savings, including the impact on your ability to make an RRSP contribution in the subsequent year.

As noted in 7.5.2, you cannot claim less CCA than the maximum for the "stub period" income for 1995 that can be spread over 10 years.

7.6 References

The following publications can be obtained (in person or by telephone request) from your nearest Revenue Canada District Taxation Office:

- Interpretation Bulletin IT-50R, "Capital cost allowance—Date of acquisition of depreciable property"
- Interpretation Bulletin IT-79R3, "Capital cost allowance—Buildings or other Structures"
- Interpretation Bulletin IT-131R2, "Convention expenses"
- Interpretation Bulletin IT-232R2, "Non-capital losses, net capital losses, restricted farm losses, farm losses and limited partnership losses"
- Interpretation Bulletin IT-514, "Work space in home expenses"
- Interpretation Bulletin IT-518, "Food, beverages and entertainment expenses"
- Interpretation Bulletin IT-521, "Motor vehicle expenses claimed by self-employed individuals"
- Interpretation Bulletin IT-525, "Performing artists"
- "Business and Professional Income Tax Guide"
- "Guide to the Partnership Information Return"

Brochure, "Paying Your Tax by Instalments"
Brochure, "Canada Pension Plan—Information for the Self-employed"
Form CPT1, "Request for a Ruling as to the Status of a Worker"
Form T1A, "Request for Loss Carry-Back"
Form T2038, "Investment tax credit (Individuals)"

8 If You Have Your Own Corporation

Planning Tips

- Pay salary to spouse and children
- Defer income to the next calendar year by accruing bonuses
- Calculate optimum salary/dividend mix
- Maximize capital dividend payments
- Consider repayment of capital
- Keep the corporation a small business corporation at all times
- Consider crystallizing your capital gains exemption
- Consider a holding corporation
- Consider a corporate partnership
- Multiply capital gains exemption
- Consider an individual pension plan
- Be cautious about having investment income in your corporation

In this chapter we suggest some tax planning techniques that are available if you are an owner/manager—that is, you carry on your business through a corporation. We will not discuss tax planning for the corporation itself, except in relation to how to most effectively get its profits into your hands.

8.1 Taxation of the Corporation

A corporation is a distinct legal entity, and if you have an incorporated business, the corporation's profits are not yours simply to take. You, as a director of the corporation (even if you are the sole director), act in a different capacity from yourself as a shareholder of the corporation. Legally, as a shareholder your only right is to elect the board of directors, who then cause the corporation to take specific actions.

To extract funds from the corporation you must follow one of the "correct" methods we discuss in 8.2 below. If you do not, the tax system will penalize you.

For tax purposes, the corporation's business and investment income will be calculated in much the same way as your own. (See 7.2 regarding the calculation of business income.) As with individuals, certain deductions (such as loss carryforwards) are available in computing taxable income. The corporation then pays federal tax and provincial tax on its taxable income.

The federal corporate tax rate effective February 28, 1995 (including federal surtax) is **29.12%**, and **22.12%** for income from manufacturing and processing. However, for small "Canadian-controlled private corporations", the federal rate on the **first $200,000** of "active business income" is **13.12%**. (A Canadian-controlled private corporation is a corporation that is resident in Canada and is not controlled in any manner by any combination of non-residents or public corporations.) The small business rate is not available for large corporations. It begins to be phased out once the corporation's capital exceeds $10 million.

Provincial tax varies, but is typically around 16% of taxable income. All provinces have reduced rates for the first $200,000 of business income; they range from 5-10%. The combined tax burden is thus about **23%** on the first $200,000 of a small business corporation's income, and about **45%** on the remainder.

8.2 WAYS OF EXTRACTING FUNDS FROM THE CORPORATION

Since the corporation is legally a separate "person", you must follow one of the methods described below to get your hands on the corporation's income.

8.2.1 DIVIDENDS

Dividends are the distribution of a corporation's profits to its shareholders. They are **not deductible** to the corporation. In your hands, dividends will be grossed up by one-quarter and eligible for a dividend tax credit worth approximately the same amount (one-quarter of the actual dividend). See 5.1.2 for details.

If the corporation earns income, pays tax on it and pays what is left to you as a dividend, the combined effect of the corporation's tax and your personal tax will be about the same as if you had earned the income directly, if the corporation's tax rate is 20%. This is called "integration".

Where the corporate rate (federal plus provincial) is more than 20%, the combined effect of the two levels of tax will normally be that more tax is paid than if you had earned the same income directly. Conversely, where the corporate tax rate is less than 20%, paying dividends results in less tax than if you were to pay tax directly on the business income.

EXAMPLE

Ken owns all the shares of Ken Ltd. Ken Ltd. earns $100,000 in small business income, which is taxed at a combined federal/

provincial rate of 20%. Ken Ltd. then pays the remaining $80,000 as a dividend to Ken.

Ken will "gross up" the $80,000 dividend by one-quarter, or $20,000, and will pay tax on $100,000, which conceptually represents the corporation's original income. He will then receive a combined federal/provincial dividend tax credit worth about $20,000, equal to the amount of tax the corporation paid. So Ken and the corporation will together be taxed as if Ken had earned the $100,000 on his own.

Note that Ken's gross-up and dividend tax credit will be 25% of the dividend regardless of the rate of tax that Ken Ltd. *actually* paid.

8.2.2 Salary

Where the corporation pays you a salary, the amount paid is deductible to the corporation and taxable to you as employment income. If the corporation pays all of its profits to you as salary, you are therefore in much the same position as you would be if you earned the income directly, without having a corporation.

Although your salary may become quite high in such situations, Revenue Canada's general policy is not to consider it an unreasonable deduction (for the corporation) where you are the owner/manager of the corporation. It is usually acceptable to consider the corporation's income is due to your efforts, and therefore that a salary equal to that income is a reasonable one. Of course, you are paying tax on the salary anyway.

You may decide on a base salary followed by a bonus, to be paid to you after the corporation has calculated its income at the end of the year. In general, you are taxed on employment income only when you receive it, while the corporation can accrue salary or bonus, counting it as deductible in the year even though it is paid after year-end.

However, any salary or bonus that is deducted by the corporation must actually be *paid* to you no later than 179 days after the end of the year. (As an administrative concession, Revenue Canada actually allows you 180 days instead of 179.) Otherwise, it is not deductible by the corporation until the year in which is it actually paid.

8.2.3 Payments on loans from shareholders

If you lend funds to the corporation (or if you did so when originally setting up the business), the corporation can **repay any amount of the loan** without tax consequences. Such a repayment of capital is neither deductible to the corporation nor taxable to you.

You could arrange to have the corporation pay you interest on your loan. The interest paid will normally be taxable to you as investment income. The tax effect would be about the same as if the corporation paid you that amount in salary. However, if your loan to the corporation does not *require* that interest be paid or there is no formal loan document, there is a danger that the interest will not be deductible to the corporation since it has not been paid pursuant to a legal obligation to pay interest. (Conversely, if you arrange for documentation requiring that interest be paid, the annual interest accrual rule discussed in 5.2.2 may require you to include interest in your income even in years when it is not paid!)

8.2.4 CAPITAL DIVIDENDS

We mentioned capital dividends in 3.3.11 and 5.1.3.2. As you will recall from Chapter 4, only three-quarters of capital gains are taxed. When a "private" (i.e., non-public) corporation realizes a capital gain, the untaxed portion is added to its "capital dividend account". Similarly, one-quarter of capital losses reduce the capital dividend account.

Any amount in the corporation's capital dividend account may be paid out entirely tax-free to its shareholders. This preserves the non-taxability of the appropriate fraction of the capital gain.

EXAMPLE

Kathryn owns all the shares of Kathcorp Inc. In 1995, Kathcorp Inc. sells some land for a capital gain of $120,000, three-quarters of which is brought into Kathcorp's income and taxed as a taxable capital gain.

Kathcorp can pay a dividend of up to $30,000 (one-quarter of the capital gain) to Kathryn in 1995 or any later year, provided an election under the Income Tax Act to make the dividend a "capital dividend" is made beforehand. The capital dividend will then be completely tax-free to Kathryn. (Of course, because it is a dividend, it is not deductible to Kathcorp.)

8.2.5 REPAYMENT OF CAPITAL

Any amount that is less than the corporation's "paid-up capital" may be paid out to the shareholders as a repayment of capital, with no tax consequences, if the paid-up capital is reduced by that amount.

Paid-up capital is essentially the amount of capital contributed to the corporation in exchange for its shares. However, the figure can be adjusted in various ways for tax purposes, as a result of transactions involving the corporation.

EXAMPLE

ABC Corp. was capitalized with $50,000, the amount that the original shareholders contributed when subscribing for 1,000 common shares.

If the directors of ABC approve a reduction in paid-up capital to $20,000 and a simultaneous repayment of $30,000 in capital to the shareholders, there will be no tax consequences for either ABC or its shareholders. The $30,000 simply comes out tax-free. ABC then has 1,000 common shares issued with a paid-up capital of $20,000.

Similarly, if shares are redeemed or cancelled by the corporation, any amount paid on the redemption or cancellation, as long as it does not exceed the paid-up capital of the shares, will come out free of tax.

8.2.6 Loan to shareholder

All of the mechanisms we have looked at so far—dividend, salary, repayment of a shareholder loan, capital dividend and repayment of capital—are legitimate ways to get your hands on the corporation's income or funds. We now turn to some of the rules designed to prevent you from doing so without following the normal routes.

Suppose the corporation simply lends you its funds? If you do not fit within certain exceptions, the *entire* amount of the loan will simply be included in your income. This is a very serious penalty, because the corporation receives no deduction for the amount of the loan, and you do not benefit from the dividend tax credit. The same rule applies if you become indebted to the corporation in some other way (e.g., you buy property from it, but pay for the property with a promissory note rather than cash.) However, where a loan has been included in your income and you subsequently repay it, you will be allowed a deduction from your income.

To avoid this provision, the loan must fall into one of the following exceptions:

- a loan made in the course of the lender's ordinary business, with bona fide arrangements made at the time the loan was made for repayment within a reasonable time
- a loan to an employee who (along with family members) does not own 10% of the shares of any class of the corporation, where the reason for the loan is the individual's employment rather than the shareholding (this exception was introduced in draft legislation released on April 26, 1995, but will be retroactive to 1991)
- a loan to an employee, where the reason for the loan is the individual's employment rather than the shareholding, to help the employee purchase (a) a home, (b) shares in the employer or a related corporation, or (c) a car to be used in employment duties
- a loan that is repaid within one year of the end of the corporation's taxation year in which the loan was made, and which is not part of a series of loans and repayments.

If the loan falls into one of the above exceptions, but is made at no interest or at a low rate of interest, you will be considered to be receiving a taxable benefit from the corporation based on the difference between Revenue Canada's current "low rate" prescribed rate of interest (see 13.3) and the rate that you are paying. This rule is exactly the same as for loans to employees, which we saw in 6.2. As in the case of employees, you may be allowed an offsetting deduction as a notional interest expense (which affects your entitlement to the capital gains exemption: see 4.4.3.2) if such expense would otherwise meet the rules concerning the deductibility of interest.

8.2.7 DEEMED DIVIDENDS

Certain types of actions that involve changes to a corporation's capital structure will deem you to have received a dividend from the corporation. Generally, this happens when the corporation takes actions that would otherwise allow you to extract profits as a repayment of capital.

For example, if the corporation redeems shares that you own, any amount paid by the corporation in excess of the paid-up capital of the shares is deemed to be a dividend (and not part of your proceeds of disposition for capital gains purposes).

8.2.8 SHAREHOLDER APPROPRIATIONS

We have covered all of the "proper" mechanisms for extracting funds from a corporation. Suppose you don't follow any of the legalities and you simply take the corporation's funds or property, and use them as your own? If you are the sole shareholder, there will be no one to object to you doing this.

In such cases, the *Income Tax Act* deems that any benefit the corporation confers on you will be brought into your income for tax purposes. So, for example, if you simply take $10,000 out of the corporation's bank account without declaring a dividend, that $10,000 will be added to your income (without you benefitting from the dividend tax credit).

Clearly, it is to your advantage to follow the more conventional mechanisms for extracting funds. In 8.8.3 we shall explore some of the considerations that will affect your decision as to the appropriate mix between salary, dividend and other forms of remuneration for yourself.

8.3 EFFECT OF HAVING A HOLDING COMPANY

You may choose to interpose a holding company between yourself and your corporation for various reasons, one of which may be to hold excess funds in the holding company secure from the creditors of the operating company. For example, you own 100% of the shares of Yourname Holdings Ltd., which owns 100% of the shares of Yourname Manufacturing Ltd. In general, dividends can be paid from the manufacturing company to the holding company without any tax effects.

Having a holding company can cause other problems, however. In particular, it could make it more difficult to realize the $500,000 exemption in respect of capital gains on the value of the operating company (see 4.4.1).

8.4 Shareholders' agreements

Where you share the ownership of a private corporation, it is usually wise to have a shareholders' agreement. Such an agreement can set out rights and obligations of the shareholders that go beyond the basic ownership of shares.

Typically, a shareholders' agreement will provide for the orderly termination of the relationship between the shareholders if there is a future disagreement, or death or disability of one of the key shareholders.

EXAMPLE

George and Alan start a small manufacturing business together. Each owns 50% of the shares of the corporation. Over the years, the business becomes very successful, but George and Alan cannot get along and decide that one of them must leave.

George and Alan signed a shareholders' agreement that contains a "shotgun" clause. George now offers Alan $500,000 for Alan's shares in the corporation. If Alan refuses to sell, the agreement provides that Alan must buy George's shares for the price George is offering ($500,000).

The "shotgun" clause is just one example of a provision that can resolve (or prevent) major disputes between key shareholders. Typical provisions in a shareholders' agreement deal with:

- desire of a shareholder to sell his or her shares
- dissension among shareholders
- death or disability of a shareholder
- agreement as to who the directors and/or officers of the corporation will be
- agreement to vote the shares in a particular way on certain issues
- what will happen if the corporation's shares are awarded to a key shareholder's spouse on separation or divorce

Tax considerations play a major part of planning for shareholder agreements. The tax treatment of life insurance payments, the availability of the $500,000 capital gains exemption, the valuation of shares, and many other issues must be considered. Clearly, shareholder agreements should always be drafted with proper professional advice as to both the legal and the tax issues.

8.5 Pension plans for small business owners

Registered pension plans were discussed in 2.2. Both "money-purchase" and "defined-benefit" pension plans can be used to accrue benefits for major shareholders (see also 2.2.1, re individual pension plans). However, this is a complex area and professional advice is essential.

If you are a small business owner and you don't want the trouble of administering a pension plan, you may simply want to set up an RRSP for yourself and ensure that you have sufficient "earned income" (i.e., salary from the corporation) to be able to make adequate contributions (see 2.1.3).

8.6 Investment income earned in a corporation

Until June 1995, it was generally advantageous to have investment income earned in a corporation, if you did not need to extract the funds. Although investment income (such as interest) is not eligible for the low "small business" rate of corporate tax, the regular corporate tax rate (combined federal/provincial) is about 44%, which is substantially lower than the rate that applies to high levels of personal income. Therefore, if you were able to leave the funds in the corporation, incorporating your investment portfolio was often a good idea.

Effective July 1995, a new 6 2/3% refundable tax applies to interest and other investment income in a Canadian-controlled private corporation. Most dividends received by a private corporation from public companies are also subject to a refundable tax (Part IV tax), which effective July 1995 increases from 25% to 33 1/3%. These refundable taxes are paid back to the corporation only when it has paid out sufficient dividends (resulting in tax being paid by the shareholders).

As a result of these changes, there is generally no tax advantage to earning investment income in a corporation. In some cases there is a definite disadvantage. The precise calculation depends on your province of residence, your level of personal income, the extent to which you need to extract the funds from the corporation, and the way in which you extract those funds.

8.7 Selling the business

If you decide to sell your incorporated business, there are two general approaches that can be taken. One is for the corporation to sell the **assets** of the business. The other is for you to sell the **shares** of the corporation.

If your shares are "qualified small business corporation shares" (see 4.4.1), you may be able to claim an exemption for up to $500,000 of your gain on the sale. Even if they are not, you may have elected with respect to the accrued gain on the shares to February 22, 1994 (see 4.4.4), so that you can now sell the shares with a reduced or no tax cost. No capital gains exemption is available to the corporation if it sells the assets. From your point of view, it may therefore be preferable to sell the shares.

The buyer of your business, however, will often prefer to purchase the assets. One reason is that this will normally allow the buyer to claim higher capital cost allowance on the cost of depreciable assets (see 7.2.4).

No goods and services tax (GST) applies on a sale of shares. On a sale of assets, GST will usually apply, but can almost always be recovered by the purchaser in the form of an input tax credit (see 17.3.1). Also, in many cases on the sale of part or all of a business an election can be made to have no GST apply to the sale.

Needless to say, any purchase and sale of a business must be done with detailed professional advice.

If your business goes public without you selling the shares, you can make a special election to "crystallize" part or all of your accrued capital gain, and get the $500,000 exemption as if you had sold the shares.

8.8 Planning opportunities

The planning opportunities discussed below relate only to how best to get funds out of the corporation. For the corporation's own tax planning, professional advice is essential.

8.8.1 Pay salary to spouse and children

Consider whether you can accomplish income-splitting by having the corporation pay a salary to your spouse and/or your children. See 3.3.2 for comments on this tip.

8.8.2 Defer income to the next calendar year by accruing bonuses

If the corporation's year-end occurs after early July, it can declare a bonus to you as of its year-end, but pay the bonus after December 31. (The bonus must be paid within 180 days after year-end to be deductible in the year: see 8.2.2.) The corporation can thus get a deduction from its income, but you do not have to recognize the income personally for tax purposes until a year later.

8.8.3 Calculate optimum salary/dividend mix

Careful analysis will be needed to calculate the best mix of salary and dividends for your case. It will depend on your cash flow needs, your income level, the corporation's income level, the corporation's status for tax purposes, and many other factors. Computer spreadsheets and planning tools are available to assist in this task.

In many cases, the best strategy for a small business corporation is to pay enough salary to reduce the corporation's income to $200,000. This maximizes the amount of income that is taxed at the low small business rate, without having corporate income taxed at the high rate that applies to income beyond $200,000.

However, you will usually want to pay yourself (and any employed family members) enough salary to allow the maximum possible contribution to an RRSP (see 2.1.3).

Note also that if you are in a business that can suffer a downturn, paying out a large salary can prevent you from carrying back a later year's losses. Suppose, for example, your business earns $1 million in 1995, and you pay out $800,000 to yourself as a salary, leaving $200,000 as the business's income. If in 1996 the business loses $1 million, you will have no way of carrying back the loss against your personal income. If you had left the funds as business income and paid out dividends, you would be able to carry back the 1996 loss to 1995, retroactively wiping out the business's 1995 corporate tax, and obtain a refund of that tax from Revenue Canada.

8.8.4 Maximize capital dividend payments

If the corporation has realized any capital gains, you should cause it to pay out capital dividends as your first choice for extracting funds. Capital dividends, as we saw in 8.2.4, are entirely tax-free.

If you allow a capital dividend account to build up in the corporation without paying capital dividends, the account can be reduced or wiped out by future capital losses. Once you have paid out capital dividends, however, they are safely out of the corporation, and subsequent capital losses will have no effect on them.

8.8.5 Consider repayment of capital

If the corporation was originally funded with a substantial amount of capital, consider extracting funds by a reduction of the paid-up capital of the corporation (see 8.2.5). Make sure the corporation remains sufficiently capitalized to satisfy any requirements of its creditors or bankers.

8.8.6 Keep the corporation a small business corporation, or crystallize your capital gains exemption

If possible, ensure that your corporation remains a "small business corporation" (see 4.3.2) and that your shares are "qualified small business corporation shares" (see 4.4.1) at all times. This will preserve, respectively, your ability to claim allowable business investment losses in respect of any loss on the corporation's shares, and the $500,000 capital gains exemption on any gain.

Note that you cannot always predict when the sale of the shares will be triggered for tax purposes. On the death of any shareholder, there will be a deemed disposition of that shareholder's shares at their fair market value unless the shares are transferred to a spouse or a qualifying "spousal trust" (see 12.3.2).

As an alternative, you may wish to *crystallize* your capital gains exemption. Crystallizing means triggering a capital gain on your shares of a qualified small business corporation, while continuing to own (or at least control) the corporation. This will permanently increase your adjusted cost base of the shares and possibly eliminate the need for the corporation to retain its qualified small business corporation status. Several techniques (such as selling shares to a family member) can be used to crystallize an exemption; professional advice should be sought. Crystallization may be a good idea given that the federal government could eliminate the $500,000 exemption at some point in the future.

8.8.7 Consider a holding corporation

Consider interposing a **holding corporation** between yourself and the operating company. One reason for doing this is to pay out dividends from the operating business to make the funds harder for creditors to reach, while keeping the income subject to a lower level of taxation than would apply if it were paid out to you personally.

If your children do not have any ownership in the business, you can consider bringing them in as shareholders at the time you set up the holding corporation. (See the estate planning example in 12.5.2 for one way of doing this.) This may be desirable for several reasons including income splitting as well as planning for your succession. However, if your children are under 18 you must be particularly careful about the attribution rules (see 3.2.3).

A holding company is often appropriate where you have family members involved in ownership of your share of the business (perhaps for income-splitting purposes), and there are other shareholders not related to you. If you and your family members own shares in the holding corporation, and the holding corporation owns all of your family's interest in the operating company, the other shareholders of the operating company need not be concerned with your internal family arrangements.

You should be cautious about accumulating funds in a holding company, however. If you intend to treat the holding corporation as qualifying for the $500,000 capital gains exemption, you can run into trouble if the corporation begins to have a substantial amount of funds that are used for generating investment income, rather than owning only the shares in the operating corporation. You may also be caught by the attribution rules (see Chapter 3), depending on when and how you introduced family members as shareholders of the corporation. Note also that investment income in a corporation is subject to an extra refundable tax that makes the up-front cost of earning the income very high (see 8.6).

8.8.8 Consider corporate partnerships

An alternative to the use of holding companies is a corporate partnership. This is a partnership between your corporation and one or more other corporations (owned by other people). There are a number of advantages to this form of corporate structure, including the deferral of tax in the initial years and increased flexibility concerning remuneration. Professional advice should be obtained to determine whether this structure is appropriate.

8.8.9 Multiply capital gains exemption

As we saw in 4.4.1, the $500,000 capital gains exemption is available for "qualified small business corporation shares". If you arrange for your spouse to invest in common shares of your corporation, you can effectively double the available exemption by each claiming $500,000. Your spouse's own funds must be used for the investment, to avoid the attribution rules discussed in 3.2.2. You may also be able to multiply the exemption by transferring shares to your children.

On death, it is possible to double the available capital gains exemption by leaving shares to your spouse or to a trust for your spouse. See 12.1.2 and 12.3.2.

8.8.10 Consider an individual pension plan

As an alternative to saving for retirement exclusively through an RRSP, consider having your company establish an individual pension plan. See 2.1.1 and 2.5.9.

8.8.11 Be cautious about keeping investments in a corporation

As noted in 8.6, a special refundable tax applies to interest income earned by a Canadian-controlled private corporation. This may make it unattractive to have interest-paying investments in a corporation. It may well be cheaper to hold them personally.

Be particularly wary of moving investments into a corporation carrying on active business. You will likely jeopardize the status of the corporation's shares from being eligible for the $500,000 capital gains exemption (see 4.4.1). In addition, the creditors of the active business will have access to the investments.

8.9 References

The following publications can be obtained (in person or by telephone request) from your nearest Revenue Canada District Taxation Office:

Interpretation Bulletin IT-66R6, "Capital dividends"

Interpretation Bulletin IT-67R3, "Taxable dividends from corporations resident in Canada"

Interpretation Bulletin IT-109R2, "Unpaid amounts"

Interpretation Bulletin IT-119R3, "Debts of shareholders, certain persons connected with shareholders, etc."

Interpretation Bulletin IT-432R2, "Appropriation of property to shareholders"

9 FARMING

PLANNING TIPS

- Establish that your farming business has a reasonable expectation of profit
- Classify farming as a chief source of income
- Claim deductions available for the self-employed
- Take advantage of the special rules for computing farm income
- Use the $500,000 capital gains exemption
- Take advantage of intergenerational transfer rules
- Claim alternative principal residence exemption where appropriate

The income tax system has a number of special rules to deal with farming. We outline them in this chapter.

9.1 FARMING—A BUSINESS OR NOT?

No matter what kind of activity you undertake, you are only allowed to write off losses for tax purposes if you are engaged in a business "with a reasonable expectation of profit" (see 7.4). This issue comes up repeatedly in the case of part-time farmers.

"Farming", for tax purposes, includes a number of activities ranging from growing crops to raising poultry, fur farming, fruit growing, keeping bees and training horses for racing. The *Income Tax Act* classifies people engaged in farming into three groups. The principal difference among the groups is the extent to which they can deduct expenses relating to their farming activities.

At one extreme are the full-time farmers, for whom farming is **a chief source of income**. Such people are allowed to treat their farming business like any other business, and can therefore claim losses against other income for tax purposes if they suffer losses in any given year (see 9.3.1 below).

At the other extreme are people who do not have a "**reasonable expectation of profit**" from their farming activity. Such people are sometimes called "hobby farmers", as farming is considered to be their hobby rather than something they are doing in order to make money. Hobby farmers may not deduct any losses from their farming activity.

In the middle are the people who *do* have a reasonable expectation of profit, but whose "chief source of income is neither farming nor a combination of farming and some other source of income", to quote the *Income Tax Act*. Such people are allowed only "**restricted farm losses**", limited to certain dollar amounts (see 9.3.2).

EXAMPLE 1

Darryl lives on his farm and raises dairy cattle. Almost all his income comes from selling the cows' milk. In 1995, Darryl's cows have a bad year and he loses $30,000.

Darryl will be able to deduct his $30,000 against any other income he has (such as investment income) and carry it over to be used in other years (see 9.3.1). His farming loss is very much like a loss from any other kind of business, such as manufacturing or retailing.

EXAMPLE 2

Bob is a jeweller who lives and works in Toronto. He spends his weekends on his ranch, where he keeps a stable of race-horses. In past years, Bob's horses have won a fair amount of prize money. In 1995, Bob has a bad year and spends $30,000 on maintaining his horses without winning any prize money at all.

Bob's loss will likely be considered a "restricted farm loss", and only a portion of it (see 9.3.2) will be deductible against his jewellery business income. Although his horse-racing business (which for income tax purposes is considered farming) does have a reasonable expectation of profit, it is not a chief source of income to him and therefore falls into the "restricted" category.

9.2 COMPUTING FARMING INCOME

If you are engaged in a farming business—whether or not your losses will be "restricted" as we saw in 9.1—you may take advantage of a number of special rules when calculating income for tax purposes.

9.2.1 THE CASH METHOD

Businesses are generally required to follow the accrual method of accounting for income. That is, you take your sales for the year into income, even though you may not have been paid for some of those sales until after your business year-end. You claim expenses the same way (see 7.2.2).

For a farming business, you may choose to use the "cash method" instead. In general, this means you will count payments received, rather than your sales—and only deduct amounts that you have paid, but not still-unpaid expenses that you have incurred.

This usually provides a certain amount of deferral of income, and may result in lower tax payable. Once you have chosen the cash method, you are normally required to continue to use that method for the farming business for all subsequent years.

When you are using the cash method, you may, if you wish, include into income any amount up to the fair market value of your inventories on hand at year-end. The amount you include will then be deductible in the following year. You might wish to do this for 1995, for example, if you had very low income in 1995 and can see by April 1996 (when you file your return) that your 1996 income will be substantially higher, enough to put you into a higher tax bracket.

9.2.2 Purchases of inventory

If you are using the cash method of accounting, it is clearly possible to generate a loss for tax purposes by purchasing large amounts of inventory. Special rules have been introduced to deal with this possibility and to limit the loss you can claim.

In general, you will be denied a loss that is attributable to purchases of inventory. However, for horses and certain registered bovine animals, you can deduct a portion of the loss. Professional advice should be obtained when dealing with these complex rules.

9.2.3 Cost of improving land for farming

Normally, when calculating income from a business, the cost of work done to improve land is considered a capital expense and is not deductible. However, for a farming business, amounts paid for clearing land, levelling land or installing a land drainage system are deductible.

9.2.4 Sales of livestock in a drought region

If you are farming in a region designated for the year as a "drought region", special relief is available if you sold a significant portion of your breeding herd. This rule is designed to allow you to defer paying tax where you are forced to sell off part or all of your herd because of drought. The list of regions designated for the year is determined by Agriculture Canada's Prairie Farm Rehabilitation Administration in Saskatoon each September.

The rule only applies where, by the end of the year, you have sold off (and not replaced) at least 15% of your "breeding herd". When it applies, some or all of your sales of the breeding animals are not counted into your income, but are deferred until a later year when your area is no longer designated as a drought region.

9.2.5 Forced destruction of livestock

If you have livestock that is diseased, you can be forced by the government to destroy the livestock under the *Animal Contagious Diseases Act* or similar legislation. If you receive compensation for the destruction, the compensation is included in your income. However, a special rule allows you to deduct all or part of this compensation and include it in your income in the next year. This allows you to defer paying tax on the compensation by one year.

9.2.6 Net income stabilization account (NISA)

The NISA program has created a number of tax issues including certain planning opportunities. You should consult your tax advisor to ensure that you are taking maximum advantage of the program from an income tax perspective.

9.3 Farming losses

9.3.1 Ordinary farm losses

As we saw in 9.1, if your **chief source of income** is farming, or your chief source of income is "a combination of farming and some other source of income", you may deduct your farm losses as though they were ordinary business losses.

The carryover available for such losses is somewhat more generous than that for normal business losses (non-capital losses), which we saw in 7.4. Like normal losses, farm losses can be carried back and used against income of the past **three years**. They can also be carried forward, and used against income in any of the next **ten years** (rather than seven).

9.3.2 Restricted farm losses

As noted in 9.1, a loss from farming cannot all be used if you do not meet the "chief source of income" test. In such a case, the loss you claim is limited to the first $2,500, plus one-half of the next $12,500 (that is, up to an additional $6,250).

EXAMPLE

Bob the jeweller, whom we met in 9.1 above, loses $30,000 on his racehorses in 1995.

Bob's "restricted farm loss" will be $2,500, plus one-half of the next $12,500. Since his total loss is more than $15,000, he reaches the maximum, and he can only deduct $8,750 against the income from his jewellery business for 1995.

Any amount of loss that cannot be used because of the "restricted farm loss" rules can be carried back for three years and forward for ten years, but can be used only against farming income. So, in our example, Bob has $21,250 that can be used to offset income from his horse operations during the years 1992-1994 and 1996-2005.

9.4 INVESTMENT TAX CREDITS

Investment tax credits (see 7.2.9) are available for investment in agricultural equipment in the Maritimes and the Gaspé region of Québec. The amount of the credit is generally 10%. Unused credits may be carried back three years and forward for ten.

9.5 TRANSFERS OF FARMING ASSETS

A number of special rules, as outlined below, are available to alleviate the tax burden of selling or transferring a farm and the assets of a farming business.

9.5.1 CAPITAL GAINS EXEMPTION

As discussed in 4.4.2, a $500,000 exemption from capital gains is available on the disposition of "qualified farm property".

9.5.2 TRANSFER TO CHILDREN OR GRANDCHILDREN

Normally, if you sell or give property to members of your family other than your spouse, you are deemed to have sold the property for its "fair market value", and will thus have to recognize as a capital gain the difference between your original cost (or the value on February 22, 1994 if you elected to use your capital gains exemption on the farm property) and the property's current value. (See 4.5.5 and 4.4.4.)

If you transfer property used in a farming business to a child, grandchild or great-grandchild (including a spouse of your child, a child of your spouse, etc., where "spouse" includes a common-law spouse as outlined in 1.3.1), you can avoid this rule. If you simply give the property, it will be deemed to be transferred at your cost (adjusted cost base (see 4.2) for capital property, or undepreciated capital cost (see 7.2.4) for depreciable property). If you sell it for something in between your cost and the current market value, that amount will be accepted for tax purposes. Any gain on the property will thus be deferred.

For this "rollover" rule to apply, you or your spouse or one of your children must have used the property "principally" in a farming business in which you, your spouse or children were actively engaged on a regular and continuous basis.

When the rollover applies, the recipient (your child, grandchild, etc.) will be deemed to have acquired the farm property for the amount at which you are deemed to have sold it. This means that the gain will eventually be taxed, if the child sells the property at some later time.

EXAMPLE

Florence operates a wheat farm in Saskatchewan. In 1995, Florence decides to retire and gives the farm to her grandson Daniel. The farmland cost her $10,000 in 1975 and is now worth $150,000.

Florence is deemed to receive $10,000 for the land, and so has no capital gain. Daniel is deemed to have acquired the land for $10,000; if he ever sells the land, the $10,000 figure will be used as his cost for capital gains calculation purposes. (Of course, if Daniel transfers the farm one day to his *child, a further rollover will be available, assuming the rules have not changed.)*

9.5.3 Principal residence exemption

As we saw in 4.5.3, the exemption in respect of the gain on the sale of a principal residence normally applies to the house itself plus one-half hectare of surrounding land. The gain on any land beyond one-half hectare is subject to the normal rules for capital gains.

For land used in a farming business, another option is available. That is to claim, instead of the ordinary principal residence exemption, a special exemption of $1,000 plus $1,000 for each year since 1972 during which the house was your principal residence. You subtract this amount from your total gain on both house and land.

9.5.4 Capital gains reserve on sale of farm to child

We discussed capital gains reserves briefly in 4.5.2. It was noted there that the capital gain must be recognized at a cumulative rate of one-fifth each year, so that no reserve can last for more than four years after the year of sale.

Where you sell property used in a farming business (including land) to your child, grandchild or great-grandchild, the allowable reserve is **10 years** rather than five. As with the rules discussed in 9.5.2, a spouse of your child, grandchild or great-grandchild, and a child, grandchild or great-grandchild of your spouse also qualify. (For this purposes, "spouse" includes a common-law spouse as outlined in 1.3.1.)

9.6 PLANNING OPPORTUNITIES

9.6.1 ESTABLISH THAT YOUR BUSINESS HAS A REASONABLE EXPECTATION OF PROFIT

For you to be able to claim any losses at all (even restricted farm losses), you must establish that your farming business is carried on with a "reasonable expectation of profit" (see 7.4). You will need to keep records that establish this claim on an objective basis. If your activities never actually turn a profit over many years, a claim that you had a reasonable expectation of profit will be hard to sustain in court.

9.6.2 CLASSIFY FARMING AS CHIEF SOURCE OF INCOME

A large number of reported court cases have considered the question of whether farming, or farming in combination with some other source, constitutes a taxpayer's "chief source of income". You may wish to consult a tax professional to determine what facts will best establish a claim that will entitle you to a full deduction for farm losses, rather than the more limited deduction for "restricted farm losses" (see 9.1).

9.6.3 CLAIM DEDUCTIONS AVAILABLE FOR THE SELF-EMPLOYED

See 7.2 and 7.5 for ideas as to deductions that can be claimed by the self-employed. If you successfully establish that you are carrying on a farming business with a reasonable expectation of profit, such deductions will be available to you.

9.6.4 MAKE USE OF SPECIAL RULES FOR CALCULATING FARM INCOME

A number of the special rules available for farmers were discussed in 9.2. You should review your situation, consider obtaining professional advice and consider to what extent you can make use of these rules. For example, you might well find it advantageous to use the cash method of recording income (9.2.1).

9.6.5 USE THE $500,000 CAPITAL GAINS EXEMPTION

If you are disposing of farm property, investigate whether it qualifies for the $500,000 capital gains exemption (see 4.4.2). In some circumstances you may be able to take action, such as delaying the sale, so as to gain time to reorganize your affairs in order to take advantage of the exemption.

9.6.6 Take advantage of intergenerational transfer rules

If you are transferring farm property to a child, grandchild, etc., be aware of the rollover described in 9.5.2. (It applies automatically; no special election is needed.) Note that you may wish to realize a partial capital gain, in order to use up your $500,000 capital gains exemption and give your child a higher cost base in the property. In such a case, you will need to sell the property to your child for an amount greater than your cost. (Where land is being transferred, don't forget to consider the possible cost of provincial land transfer tax. GST may apply as well, depending on the circumstances.)

9.6.7 Claim alternative principal residence exemption where appropriate

Consider making the special election (see 9.5.3) to exempt $1,000 per year on your entire farm rather than just the house and one-half hectare. This election can be useful where you have occupied the property for many years and the value of the house is small relative to the land. Alternatively, consider whether you might claim more than the one-half hectare under the principal residence exemption if you can substantiate that such additional land was necessary for your personal use and enjoyment of the property.

9.7 References

The following publications can be obtained (in person or by telephone request) from your nearest Revenue Canada District Taxation Office:

- Interpretation Bulletin IT-156R, "Feedlot operators"
- Interpretation Bulletin IT-232R2, "Non-capital losses, net capital losses, restricted farm losses, farm losses and limited partnership losses"
- Interpretation Bulletin IT-268R3, "Inter vivos transfer of farm property to a child"
- Interpretation Bulletin IT-322R, "Farm losses"
- Interpretation Bulletin IT-349R2, "Intergenerational transfer of farm property on death"
- Interpretation Bulletin IT-373R, "Farm woodlots and tree farms"
- Interpretation Bulletin IT-425, "Miscellaneous farm income"
- Interpretation Bulletin IT-427R, "Livestock of farmers"
- Interpretation Bulletin IT-433R, "Farming or fishing—Use of cash method"
- Interpretation Bulletin IT-485, "Cost of clearing or levelling land"

Interpretation Bulletin IT-526, "Farming—Cash method inventory adjustments"

Information Circular 86-5R, "Part XVII—Capital cost allowance, farming and fishing"

Information Circular 86-6, "Basic herds"

Form T2042, "Statement of farming income and expenses"

"Farming Income Tax Guide"

10 PROFESSIONALS

PLANNING TIPS

- Elect the modified accrual method for computing income
- Adjust billings and drawings to maximize 1971 receivables
- Maximize interest deductibility
- Pay retiring partners income or capital as appropriate
- Consider paying club dues at partnership level
- Incorporate your business if you work on certain overseas projects

Most of income tax planning for professionals is the same as that for other self-employed people (see Chapter 7). Self-employed professionals are, after all, carrying on business. However, a number of special rules exist. We consider them in 10.1. As well, many professionals carry on their practice in partnership; we look at some rules that apply to partnerships in 10.2. In 10.3 we offer some planning tips that are particularly relevant for professionals.

10.1 SPECIFIC RULES THAT APPLY TO PROFESSIONALS

10.1.1 THE MODIFIED ACCRUAL METHOD OF ACCOUNTING FOR INCOME

As we noted in 7.2.2 and 9.2.1, businesses other than farming businesses are generally required to report income on the accrual basis. That is, you take your sales into income even though you may not be paid until after your year-end.

Most businesses must also account for **work in progress**—work that has been done but not yet billed. However, there is an exception for the professional practice of an **accountant, dentist, lawyer, medical doctor, veterinarian** or **chiropractor**. If you are practising one of these professions, you may elect to *exclude* work in progress from your income.

EXAMPLE

Dianne is a lawyer who is in sole practice. Her business year-end is December 31. She spends almost the entire month of December 1995 preparing for a major trial, which takes place in January. She does not bill the client until the conclusion of the trial, in January 1996.

If Dianne elects to exclude work in progress from her income for 1995, she will not have to recognize as income any amount in respect of her work in preparing for the trial until her business year ending December 31, 1996.

This method of accounting is sometimes called the "modified accrual" method. It is not the cash method, since once an amount has been billed, it must be reported as income even if not yet paid. But excluding work in progress is a step away from the full accrual method.

Once you choose to exclude work in progress, you must normally continue to do so for all future years.

Upon retirement or withdrawal from the business, the remaining work in progress is brought into your income. Such income is considered to be "earned income" for RRSP contribution limit purposes (see 2.1.3).

10.1.2 1971 RECEIVABLES

If you have been in practice continuously since before 1972, you may still have a "1971 receivables" balance.

Before 1972, professionals were allowed to use the cash method of accounting, much as farmers still are. In your 1971 taxation year, therefore, you would exclude from income your billings which had not yet been paid.

With the change to the accrual (or modified accrual) method, a special allowance was provided as a transitional rule, to preserve the deferral of taxation of these receivables and avoid taxing the professional too heavily in any one year. The allowance takes the form of a deduction for "1971 receivables".

Each year, you can deduct your original 1971 receivables, up to a limit of your receivables at the end of the current year. (For a partnership, however, the limit is the adjusted cost base of your interest in the partnership.) However, whenever the amount you claim goes down in any year, that lower amount will be your maximum for future years. As your receivables fluctuate from year to year, therefore, your 1971 receivables deduction may eventually become very small.

EXAMPLE

Norm is an architect who has been in practice since 1964. At the end of 1971, his receivables totalled $10,000. Since then, he has claimed a deduction for his 1971 receivables of $10,000 every year. Most years he has had substantial amounts outstanding at the end of the year, but in 1980 he was ill in November and December, and his year-end receivables were only $3,000. In 1995 Norm earns $200,000 from his practice, and his year-end receivables are $30,000.

The maximum deduction Norm can claim in 1995 is $3,000. That has been the limit for his 1971 receivables deduction since 1980 (when he had to bring $7,000 of his 1971 receivables into income).

10.1.3 PROFESSIONAL CORPORATIONS

Some provinces allow certain professionals to incorporate their professional practices. For example, lawyers in Alberta and physicians in Nova Scotia can be incorporated.

For tax purposes, a professional corporation is generally treated like any other small business corporation. See Chapter 8.

Effective 1995, professional corporations which are members of partnerships must use a December 31 business year-end. This is the same rule as applies to individuals carrying on business (see 7.2.1). A professional corporporation which is not a member of a partnership, however, retains its normal year-end.

10.2 SPECIFIC RULES THAT APPLY TO PARTNERSHIPS

In 7.3 we discussed the taxation of partnerships in general. In this section we shall look at two rules applicable to partnerships that are of particular relevance to professionals.

10.2.1 DEDUCTIBILITY OF INTEREST PAID BY THE PARTNERSHIP

As we saw in 5.3, interest paid is normally deductible as long as the funds borrowed are used to earn income from business or property. Where a partnership borrows funds for working capital, the interest is therefore clearly deductible.

What if the partnership borrows funds in order to make a distribution of profits and/or capital to the partners? The tax treatment of the interest paid on such borrowings is in flux. Draft legislation was released by the Department of Finance in December 1991, but the rules have not been enacted and may yet be changed further. At the moment, it is proposed that interest paid on such borrowings will normally be deductible, up to the amount of the partnership's "tax equity" or "adjusted equity" (depending on when the distribution is made and when the legislation is passed). You should obtain professional advice to determine how these rules will apply to your partnership, if they do come into force.

10.2.2 INCOME PAYMENTS TO RETIRED PARTNERS

Normally, if you withdraw from a partnership, and you receive a payment to compensate for your interest in the partnership, the payment will be considered capital. That is, any excess over your adjusted cost base in the partnership will be a capital gain, and taxed as discussed in Chapter 4. (Your adjusted cost base is essentially the amount you contributed to the partnership, plus your share of the profits on which you have been taxed, minus your drawings. See 7.3.5.)

Another option is available under the *Income Tax Act*, however. If your partners agree to pay you a share of the income from the partnership, and to treat it explicitly as an income payment, you will be considered as still being a partner for tax purposes. You will therefore be taxed on that income, but your former partners will effectively pay less tax, since their partnership income will in part be allocated to you.

EXAMPLE

Joel, an accountant, retires from his firm at the beginning of 1995. There are three other partners, who share equally in profits. The firm's income for 1995 is $300,000. The partners agree to pay Joel $60,000 upon his retirement, and declare the $60,000 to be a share of the income from the partnership (rather than as a repayment of his capital interest).

Joel will be required to report the $60,000 as income. However, each of the partners will effectively get a deduction of $20,000, since after Joel's allocation, there is only $240,000 to be divided three ways. Each partner will thus report $80,000 in income instead of $100,000.

Note that the continuing income payments to a retired partner are not included in "earned income" for purposes of calculating the retired partner's RRSP contribution limit.

10.3 PLANNING OPPORTUNITIES

For planning tips relating to professional and business income generally, see 7.5. In particular, if you are affected by the new requirement to report business and professional income on a calendar-year basis for 1995, see 7.5.2.

10.3.1 ELECT THE MODIFIED ACCRUAL METHOD

If you are practising one of the eligible professions (see 10.1.1), you will almost certainly want to elect to exclude work in progress from your income. This can create a substantial deferral of tax. The only reason not to do so might be if you are in your first year or two of practice, with relatively low income, and you wish to recognize income earlier while it can be taxed at relatively low rates.

10.3.2 ADJUST BILLINGS AND DRAWINGS TO MAXIMIZE 1971 RECEIVABLES

If you have been in sole practice since before 1972, and you still have an untaxed "1971 receivables" balance, you will want to make sure your receivables are high enough at the end of each year that your deduction is not reduced at all. This can be done by issuing billings towards the end of the year.

If you are a member of a partnership and you have a 1971 receivables balance, you need to keep the adjusted cost base of your interest in the partnership at a high enough level to preserve the 1971 receivables. This can be done by delaying drawings towards the end of the year, or even by investing additional capital in the partnership before the year-end.

10.3.3 MAXIMIZE INTEREST DEDUCTIBILITY

General techniques for making all of your interest deductible were discussed in 5.7.1. As a member of a partnership, consider whether you can accelerate your drawings or have the partnership repay a portion of your capital contribution. You could then use the funds to pay off non-deductible debt (such as a home mortgage), while the partnership can borrow funds to replace the lost working capital. The interest would then become deductible. (Alternatively, you yourself could borrow funds to inject back into the partnership. However, Revenue Canada could challenge such an arrangement under the general anti-avoidance rule if it considers this type of refinancing technique to be a misuse or abuse of the *Income Tax Act.*)

10.3.4 PAY RETIRING PARTNER INCOME OR CAPITAL AS APPROPRIATE

If you (or a partner of yours) are withdrawing from a partnership, you will need to calculate the best way of paying out the retiring partner's interest.

On the one hand, if you are retiring and have a high cost base in your partnership (perhaps as a result of electing to apply your capital gains exemption to your partnership interest as of February 22, 1994—see 4.4.4), it may be best to receive a capital payment. This amount could be entirely exempted from tax. However, it will effectively be paid in after-tax dollars by the other partners.

On the other hand, if your partners choose the option of an income payment (see 10.2.2), you will be fully taxed on it (possibly at lower rates than the continuing partners, if your income is going down substantially). However, your partners will effectively receive a deduction for the amount paid to you.

10.3.5 CONSIDER PAYING CLUB DUES AT PARTNERSHIP LEVEL

As you may know, most club dues are not allowed as business expenses. Many professional partnership agreements therefore provide that such dues should be paid by the partners personally (since they are not deductible in computing the partnership's income anyway).

You should consider having the partnership pay such dues even though they are not deductible. The reason is that the individual partners' adjusted cost bases in the partnership are not reduced by such disallowed expenses, even though the assets of the partnership are reduced by making the payments. The result can be that, on an eventual sale of the partnership interest, there will be less capital gain (or more capital loss) as a result of having had the partnership pay the club dues.

10.3.6 INCORPORATE YOUR BUSINESS IF YOU WORK ON CERTAIN OVERSEAS PROJECTS

If you work outside Canada for six months or more in a field such as engineering, construction, mining, oil and gas or agriculture, you may be able to use the overseas employment tax credit (see 6.8) to eliminate much or all of your Canadian tax. To do this you will need to incorporate your business, so that you do the work as an employee of the corporation. The corporation, rather than you personally, would contract to do the work (e.g., provide your engineering services). You should obtain professional advice if you are in this situation since, among other things, the "personal services business" rules must be considered.

10.4 REFERENCES

The following publications can be obtained (in person or by telephone request) from your nearest Revenue Canada District Taxation Office:

- Interpretation Bulletin IT-90, "What is a partnership?"
- Interpretation Bulletin IT-135R, "Investment interest in a professional business" [for 1971 receivables]
- Interpretation Bulletin IT-138R, "Computation and flow-through of partnership income"
- Interpretation Bulletin IT-242R, "Retired partners"
- Interpretation Bulletin IT-358, "Partnerships—Deferment of fiscal year-end"
- Interpretation Bulletin IT-457R, "Election by professionals to exclude work in progress from income"
- Information Circular 89-5R, "Partnership information return"
- "Business and Professional Income Tax Guide"
- "Guide to the Partnership Information Return"
- Form T2032, "Statement of income and expenses from a professional practice"
- Form GST 370, "Employee and partner GST rebate"
- Form T5013, "Partnership Information Return"

11 Minimum Tax

Planning Tips

- Have 35 cents regular income for each $1 in exempt capital gains
- Continue generating interest expense and business losses
- Watch out for RRSP deductions
- Limit "tainted" tax shelter deductions

11.1 Outline

The minimum tax was enacted as a political solution to the perception that many high-income taxpayers were paying little tax through the use of tax shelters and other so-called tax preferences. It is relatively narrow in focus, concentrating on specific shelters and credits.

The minimum tax is an *alternative* tax calculation. You must calculate your tax both normally and under the minimum tax rules, and pay the higher of the two.

In simplest terms, you calculate minimum tax by taking your taxable income, adding back "tainted shelter" deductions (such as resource writeoffs, tax shelters and RRSP/RPP contributions) and the untaxed one-quarter of capital gains, taking a $40,000 exemption and then calculating federal tax at 17%. Most personal credits, but not the dividend tax credit or investment tax credits, are then allowed as with regular tax. Once federal surtax and provincial tax are added in, the minimum tax rate comes to about 27%, varying slightly depending on the province. If you live in Québec, see 14.2.22 regarding the Québec minimum tax.

Minimum tax paid can be recovered in later years to the extent your regular tax exceeds your minimum tax. Minimum tax does not apply to the year of death.

11.2 Calculating the Tax

Somewhat simplified, the calculation is as follows:

1. Start with your **taxable income** (after all deductions allowed for regular tax purposes).
2. **Add back the deductions** that you are not allowed to claim for minimum tax purposes:
   - losses from any investment that requires a tax shelter identification number (see 5.4.1; this is new as of 1995)

- losses from a partnership where you are a limited partner or passive partner (see 5.4.2; this is new as of 1995)
- CCA on Canadian films (see 5.4.4)
- resource writeoffs (see 5.4.5)
- carrying charges, such as interest expense, relating to any of the above (see 5.3; this is new as of 1995)
- RRSP contributions and transfers of retiring allowances (see 2.1.3 and 6.6)
- RPP contributions (see 2.2.1)
- employee home relocation deduction (see 6.2)
- employee stock option deduction (see 6.3)

(These are sometimes called "tainted" deductions, since you cannot claim them for minimum tax purposes.)

3. Add **one-quarter of all capital gains**, whether the other three-quarters was eligible for the capital gains exemption or not. (Note that you don't add back the exemption; that is still allowed for minimum tax purposes. It's the one-quarter which is *never* taxed that you add back no matter what.)
4. **Deduct the gross-up** on dividends (see 5.1.2). Since the dividend tax credit will not be allowed for minimum tax purposes, you are only taxed on the actual dividend received, rather than on the grossed-up amount.
5. **Deduct $40,000** as your basic minimum tax exemption. This gives you your "adjusted taxable income".
6. Calculate federal tax at **17%**.
7. Deduct **personal credits** (see 1.3), such as your basic credit, other dependants, old age, disability (for self or spouse only), CPP contributions, UI premiums, tuition, education, medical and charitable. Do not deduct investment tax credits (7.2.9), political contribution credits (1.4.1), pension tax credits (1.3.7), transfer of unused tax credits from spouse (3.3.15), tuition and education credits transferred from a child (1.3.6), dividend tax credits (5.1.2) or labour-sponsored venture capital credits (5.4.8).
8. If the resulting tax is higher than your federal tax calculated normally, you must pay the minimum tax. **Federal surtax and provincial tax** will be calculated on this figure rather than your regular federal tax figure.

11.3 Minimum tax carryover

If you find that you have to pay minimum tax in any given year, the excess of your minimum tax over your regular tax becomes a "minimum tax carryover", which can be used in any of the next **seven years**.

In a future year, you can use the carryover to the extent your regular tax exceeds your minimum tax.

EXAMPLE

Your 1995 regular federal tax is $30,000. Your 1995 minimum tax (federal) is $35,000.

You must pay the $35,000 tax, plus surtax and provincial taxes (total about $56,000). However, you have a $5,000 federal minimum tax carryover. If, in 1996, your regular federal tax is $32,000 and your minimum (federal) tax is $22,000, you can deduct the carryover from your regular federal tax and pay only $27,000 basic federal tax (before calculating provincial tax and surtaxes).

11.4 Planning considerations

11.4.1 Have 35 cents regular income for each $1 in exempt capital gains

The minimum tax can have a serious impact on capital gains, particularly where the capital gains exemption would otherwise enable you to avoid regular tax entirely.

EXAMPLE

Max sells the shares of his small business corporation for a $480,000 capital gain, which is fully exempt under the enhanced capital gains exemption (see 4.4.1). Max has no other income in 1995.

Max will pay no regular tax. For minimum tax purposes, however, his adjusted taxable income will be $120,000 (one-quarter of the gain), minus the basic $40,000 exemption. His federal minimum tax will therefore be 17% of $80,000, or $13,600, minus personal credits. Max's total tax for 1995, including surtax and provincial tax, will be about $20,000. This federal minimum tax of $13,600 (net of personal credits) may be carried forward for seven years and applied against regular federal tax payable in those years.

As a general rule of thumb, minimum tax will not apply if you have at least 35 cents of "regular" income for each $1 in capital gains which are fully exempt due to the capital gains exemption. If your gains are relatively small, they may be shielded by the $40,000 exemption anyway.

11.4.2 Continue generating interest expense and business losses

There are two important deductions that are not affected by the minimum tax. The first is deductible interest paid (see 5.3) on loans not used for tax shelter purposes. The second is business losses and loss carryforwards (see 7.4) other than loss carryforwards that are attributable to "tainted" shelters (see 11.4.4). Where it otherwise makes sense from a business perspective, you can generate such deductions without triggering any minimum tax liability. Keep in mind, however, that high interest expense may give you a high cumulative net investment loss (see 4.4.3.2) and thus make the capital gains exemption unavailable to you, to the extent you would otherwise want to use it (see 4.4.1 and 4.4.2).

11.4.3 Watch out for RRSP deductions

As noted in 11.2, contributions to an RRSP are normally added back for minimum tax purposes. The $14,500 for 1995 or $13,500 for 1996 maximum normal RRSP contribution (see 2.1.3) will not normally create much of a problem in this respect. However, if you are transferring a large retiring allowance (see 2.1.7.2) to an RRSP, you may inadvertently trigger a minimum tax liability.

11.4.4 Limit "tainted" tax shelter deductions

Be aware of possible minimum tax implications when planning for large tax shelter claims, particularly on resource funds (see 5.4.4) such as drilling funds and flow-through shares. Resource expenses that exceed your total income from such funds (and are therefore claimed as losses) must be added back for minimum tax purposes.

To the extent you have loss carryforwards from previous years that are attributable to "tainted" shelters, they must also be added back to your taxable income for minimum tax purposes.

As a general rule of thumb, you can have "tainted" tax shelter losses equal to about 41% of your other income without being affected by minimum tax.

11.5 References

The following form can be obtained (in person or by telephone request) from your nearest Revenue Canada District Taxation Office:

Form T691, "Calculation of minimum tax"

12 Estate Planning

Planning Tips

- Make a will (or review your existing will)
- Consider an estate freeze
- Consider setting up a family trust
- Take steps to minimize probate fees
- Make sure you have sufficient insurance
- Consider planned charitable gifts and bequests
- Plan for the succession of your business
- Consider effects of foreign estate taxes

In this chapter we provide an overview of the rules that apply on death. We then survey some estate planning strategies you can use to minimize the taxes arising on death and to leave as much as possible to your beneficiaries. Estate planning can be extremely complicated, and depends very much on your personal situation and goals. Professional advice is highly recommended.

12.1 Taxes on Death

12.1.1 Tax payable by the estate

When a person dies, the executor or administrator of the estate must file a "**terminal return**" for the deceased to report income up to the date of death. Although the regular T1 return form is used, there are a number of special rules for this return. For example:

- charitable donations, which can normally be claimed for the year of donation or carried forward to future years (see 1.3.4), can be carried back and claimed in the previous year
- medical expenses, which can normally be claimed for a 12-month period ending in the year (see 1.3.5), can be pooled for any 24-month period that includes the day of death
- the full amount of the deceased's RRSP (see 2.1) is brought into income for the year of death, unless the beneficiary of the RRSP is the deceased's spouse or certain dependants (see 2.1.7.3); if the RRSP funds are not transferred to the spouse's own RRSP, the spouse must report the funds as income for tax purposes
- any balance borrowed by the deceased from an RRSP under the Home Buyer's Plan (see 2.1.8) and not yet repaid may be included in income

- minimum tax (see 11.1) does not apply to the year of death
- capital property is generally deemed disposed of at its fair market value (see 12.1.2 below)
- certain kinds of income earned but not received by the deceased before death can be reported on a separate return (against which the deceased's personal credits can be claimed a second time)

The terminal return for the deceased, along with any tax payable, is due by the usual deadline (see 13.1) or six months after death, whichever is later. Thus, for example, if someone dies on March 10, 1996, that person's 1995 return is due by September 10, 1996.

Any income earned after death will be subject to tax as part of the estate. The estate is treated as a separate person which must file a return as a **trust** each year until all of the assets are distributed. (Sometimes this can take several years, but normally an estate can be wound up within one year.) Any income paid to beneficiaries of the estate may be taxed in their hands directly, instead of in the estate.

Note that life insurance proceeds received as a result of an individual's death are not subject to income tax. Life insurance is discussed in more detail in 12.6 below.

12.1.2 DEEMED DISPOSITION OF CAPITAL PROPERTY

Canada has no estate tax or inheritance tax, nor do any of the provinces. To the extent you simply have cash in the bank and you leave it to your family, there will be no tax to pay at all (other than probate fees, discussed in 12.1.3 below).

Many people, however, have capital assets (stocks, real estate, jewellery, etc.). As a general rule, capital assets are deemed for tax purposes to have been sold at their fair market value immediately before death. This results in the realization of any accrued capital gains or losses at that time. This rule was discussed in 4.5.4 as well. If you own depreciable property, recaptured depreciation or a terminal loss may also be triggered.

EXAMPLE

Agnes dies in 1995. Her only capital assets are her house, which has a cost base of $50,000 and is now worth $600,000; a diamond ring, which has a cost base of $5,000 and is now worth $10,000; and a stock portfolio, which has a cost base of $10,000 and is now worth $17,000.

The house will be deemed sold at fair market value just before Agnes' death, but there will be no capital gain because it is Agnes' principal residence (see 4.5.3). The ring and the stocks will also be deemed sold at their current values, for a total gain of $12,000. Three-quarters of the capital gain, or $9,000, will be taxed as a taxable capital gain on Agnes' final return.

As can be seen, the normal capital gains rules apply, including the availability of any exemptions.

The major exception to the "deemed disposition" rule is where you leave assets to your **spouse**, or to a **spousal trust** (a trust that meets certain requirements, as outlined in 12.3.2 below). In such a case, you are deemed to have sold your assets at their cost, so no capital gain results. Your spouse (or the trust) then inherits that cost for tax purposes along with the assets. When your spouse (or the trust) sells the assets, or on your spouse's death, the full capital gain or loss from your original purchase price will be taxed.

There is, however, a special rule under which your executor may elect to realize a capital gain or loss on a property-by-property basis when assets are left to your spouse on your death. This election may be beneficial if your executor elects to trigger a capital gain in order to use loss carryforwards or a capital gains exemption. Alternatively, triggering a capital loss may recover tax in the year prior to death, since capital losses in the year of death may be carried back to the immediately preceding year and used against any income, except to the extent that the deceased previously claimed the capital gains exemption (see 4.4).

12.1.3 PROBATE FEES

Probate fees are charged by the courts in each province except Quebec for granting "probate" on a will, or for approving the administration of an estate where there is no will. In theory they are administrative fees, but in most provinces they are really disguised taxes.

In some cases, the assets of the deceased can be distributed and the estate wound up without going to the court for probate. Generally, however, probate is required before third parties (e.g., banks) will release property to the executor.

Probate fees are highest in Ontario, where they are 0.5% of the estate for the first $50,000 and 1.5% of the excess. In other provinces they are typically 0.3% to 0.6% of the value of the estate. Alberta has progressive flat rates to a maximum of $6,000; the probate fees for large estates in other provinces can be substantial as there is no maximun.

The fee generally applies to the total value of the assets of the estate, without any deduction for debts other than those encumbering real property. Property held by two people as "joint tenants" with right of survivorship (rather than as "tenants in common") is not subject to probate, since on the death of one joint tenant the property does not form part of the estate but simply is wholly owned by the other.

EXAMPLE

Jonah, who lives in Ontario, dies in 1995. His estate consists of a house worth $500,000, with a $200,000 mortgage on it,

$100,000 in personal effects, and the shares of his business, worth $1 million. He also owes $80,000 on a personal line of credit to the bank at the time of his death.

The value of Jonah's estate for probate purposes is $1,400,000. The house is counted as $300,000 (i.e., minus the mortgage), and his other assets are $1,100,000. The $80,000 debt is not deducted. The fee for probating Jonah's will is $20,500.

12.1.4 Death benefits

Death benefits may be paid by the deceased's employer to the surviving spouse or other family members. Up to $10,000 of such benefits are tax-free (see 6.7).

12.2 The will

12.2.1 Purpose of a will

The will is a key element of estate planning. It allows you to provide for an orderly distribution of your assets in accordance with your desires and in a way that minimizes the tax burden on your estate and on your beneficiaries.

If you do not make a will, the provincial law will determine how your assets are distributed. In Ontario, for example, the *Succession Law Reform Act* provides that the surviving spouse gets the first $200,000 of the estate and divides any additional amounts with the deceased's children in accordance with a formula.

In 12.7.1 below we discuss some of the provisions you can consider including in your will.

12.2.2 The executor

In your will, you should designate one or more persons as your **executor**. The executor should be someone you can trust to take charge of your affairs and distribute your assets in accordance with your desires as set out in your will. The executor will normally apply to the court for letters probate (see 12.1.3), which will give the executor the right to take over your property, manage it and distribute it to your beneficiaries.

The responsibilities of the executor include determining the assets and liabilities of the estate, filing all income tax returns for the deceased and the estate (including any foreign succession duty or tax returns) and paying the debts (including all taxes) of the deceased.

Ideally, you should choose an executor who is familiar with your personal situation. Often the executor will be your principal beneficiary (such as your spouse). Sometimes this may not be appropriate, however, because of a possible conflict of interest with other beneficiaries.

You should consider naming an alternate executor should your executor not be alive. Otherwise your estate may be handled by the executor of your executor's estate. Naming an alternate executor is also important in case the named executor is either unable to or chooses not to act. This can avoid costly court proceedings.

If you do not make a will or if your will is invalid, the process of obtaining court approval for distribution of your assets may be more cumbersome and expensive. Your representative or heirs must apply to the court to appoint an **administrator** to administer and distribute the estate in accordance with a formula set out in legislation.

12.3 TRUSTS

12.3.1 WHAT IS A TRUST?

A trust is an arrangement whereby one or more persons (the **trustees**) hold legal title to property (the **trust property**) for the benefit of other persons (the **beneficiaries**). The person who creates the trust and puts ("settles") property into it is called the **settlor**.

EXAMPLE

Brian is leaving the country to work in Africa for several years. He gives Paul $80,000 to hold in trust for Brian's two teenagers, Dianne and Darryl. Brian draws up a trust agreement that allows Paul to use the trust funds to pay for Brian's children's education, to invest the funds not yet used, and to pay half of the capital of the trust to each child when he or she turns 23.

In this example, Brian is the settlor, Paul is the trustee and Dianne and Darryl are the beneficiaries. Paul will have legal ownership of the $80,000, but he is required to use it only for Dianne and Darryl's benefit and not for his personal use. If the trust document permits, he can pay himself a fee for his services as trustee.

There is no requirement that the settlor and the trustee be different people. (In the example above, Brian could simply declare and document that he is holding funds in trust for his children, and a trust would be created.) Similarly, the settlor and the beneficiary can be the same person. (This is what happens when you put funds into a self-directed RRSP, for example. You are the settlor and beneficiary, and a trust company is the trustee of your assets (see 2.1.5).). However, the choice of settlor, trustee and beneficiaries will affect the taxation of the trust and its beneficiaries. For example, there are a number of attribution rules that apply to trusts, including those outlined in Chapter 3. Careful planning is required.

Note that the mechanics and terminology of trusts are different in Quebec, which is governed by the province's *Civil Code* rather than by the common law which governs the rest of Canada. A new *Civil Code* came into effect in Quebec on January 1, 1994.

12.3.2 WHAT KINDS OF TRUSTS ARE THERE?

A trust can be set up during the settlor's lifetime (as in the example above). Such a trust is called an ***inter vivos*** (Latin for "among the living") **trust**.

A trust can also be created by the settlor's will, in which case it is called a **testamentary trust**.

A trust for the settlor's spouse that meets certain conditions is a **spousal trust**. The principal conditions are, first, that **all of the income** of the trust must be paid to the spouse during the spouse's lifetime, and second, that **none of the capital** can be distributed to anyone other than the spouse during the spouse's lifetime. (After the spouse's death, however, the capital can be distributed to someone else, such as the settlor's children.) Such a trust can be either testamentary or *inter vivos*. Transfer of property from the settlor to a spousal trust does not trigger tax on any accrued capital gain; instead the property passes at the settlor's cost, and any capital gain is taxed only when the trust eventually disposes of the property or the spouse dies (see 4.5.4 and 12.1.2).

Note that if your will creates a trust, that trust will be separate from your estate. The estate is taxed as a trust for as long as it takes to wind up your affairs and distribute your assets. A trust set up in your will, on the other hand, can be designed to continue for many years beyond your death.

12.3.3 WHY WOULD I USE A TRUST?

A trust offers tremendous flexibility in structuring your affairs and controlling the future use of your property. The powers of the trustees can be strictly limited and defined; or they can be given full discretion as to when and whether to pay income or distribute capital to the beneficiaries, how to manage the trust property and when to wind up the trust.

12.3.4 HOW IS A TRUST TAXED?

A trust is a **separate person** for income tax purposes. The trustee must file a "T3" trust tax return and pay tax on the trust's income.

A trust is generally taxed as an individual, but is not eligible for the personal credits (see 1.3.1). A testamentary trust pays tax at the same rates as individuals (see 3.1), but an *inter vivos* trust pays tax at a flat rate — the top rate of tax for individuals (about 50% when provincial tax is factored in).

The trust's income includes its income from carrying on business (see Chapter 7), from taxable capital gains (see Chapter 4) and from investments (interest, dividends, rent, etc. — see Chapter 5). Amounts payable or paid out to beneficiaries are deducted, and the beneficiaries report such income on their tax returns.

Certain kinds of income, such as capital gains and dividends, preserve their character when flowed through to a beneficiary. Thus, such income can be treated as capital gains (see Chapter 4) or as dividends (see 5.1.2) on the beneficiary's tax return.

Until the end of 1995, a family trust that meets certain conditions may use a special rule under the *Income Tax Act* to treat amounts as paid to beneficiaries even though they are not actually payable or paid to specific beneficiaries. This is called a **preferred beneficiary election**. Provided the trust and the beneficiary agree, the income will be taxed in the beneficiary's hands, and in a later year can be paid out by the trust to any beneficiary free of tax. This can be useful where a beneficiary (such as a young child) has no other income, and so can receive a certain amount of income tax-free. Effective January 1, 1996, the preferred beneficiary election is only available where the beneficiary is disabled (as defined in 1.3.3). However, income can still be allocated to a beneficiary for tax purposes by making it payable to the beneficiary.

Every 21 years a trust is deemed to dispose of all of its property, so that accrued capital gains are taxed. This deemed disposition can be deferred by family trusts by making an election in many cases. However, the February 1995 federal budget proposes to eliminate this election effective 1999, so that the 21-year rule will apply to all family trusts. If you are considering a family trust, current advice from a qualified tax professional will be essential.

12.4 FAMILY LAW

Provincial family law can have a significant impact on your estate planning. Every province has legislation to protect the interests of spouses on marriage breakdown. This legislation may apply on death as well. We shall use Ontario law for purposes of this description. The laws of each of the ten provinces are different, however, and professional advice should be obtained.

On marriage breakdown, Ontario's *Family Law Act* provides for a division of "net family property", which includes almost all property acquired (or increase in value in property) during the marriage. Business assets, shares in a small business corporation and investments are typically all included in "net family property".

Each spouse's assets are totalled up and an equalizing payment is required, so that each spouse ends up with half of the property acquired during the marriage.

The above provisions apply on death as well. The surviving spouse may elect to take one-half of the difference in net family property rather than whatever has been left under the deceased's will. Clearly, such rules can interfere with one's estate planning, and should be considered when making a will.

Spouses can agree to have these provisions of the *Family Law Act* not apply by signing a "domestic contract". Separate independent legal advice for each spouse is required before signing such a contract.

12.5 Estate freezing

12.5.1 What is an estate freeze?

Estate freezing is the term used to describe steps taken to fix the value of your estate (or some particular asset) at its present value, so that future growth will go to your children and not be taxed on your death. It is a field of tax planning that is generally accepted as legitimate by Revenue Canada, and several provisions of the *Income Tax Act* are designed to facilitate it.

Estate freezing is most often used when you own a business that you expect will grow in future years. Your children may be involved in running the business. Even if they are not, you may want them to own it after your death.

12.5.2 How does one freeze an estate?

There are many different forms of estate freeze, some of them very complex. The following example is one of the simplest forms:

EXAMPLE

You own all of the common shares of X Corp. (your business). Your original share investment in X Corp. was $100, and it is now worth $400,000. You expect it to increase in value significantly over the next several years. You have two children, both in their early 20s, who work in the business.

First, you exchange your common shares of X Corp. for 400 new preferred shares (a step that can be taken without triggering any income tax). The preferred shares are voting shares. They are also retractable at any time, at your option, for $1,000 per share. In other words, you can demand that the corporation pay you $400,000 for your shares at any time.

Each of your children then subscribes for 50 new common shares in X Corp., paying $1 per share. Since X Corp. is worth

$400,000, and your preferred shares are retractable for $400,000, the common shares have negligible value at the moment.

Over the next few years, the value of X Corp. rises to $900,000. Now your preferred shares are still worth only $400,000, but the common shares are worth $500,000. You have thus transferred the "growth" in the corporation to your children at no tax cost to you.

Note also that since your preferred shares are voting shares, you have kept control of the corporation. You have 400 votes and your children together have only 100.

The mechanics of an estate freeze are complex, and there are numerous income tax rules that have to be considered. The basic concept, however, is generally as outlined above. Often you will set up a holding company or a family trust as part of the freeze, rather than having your children subscribe directly for shares in the operating company.

12.5.3 BENEFITS OF AN ESTATE FREEZE

An estate freeze can significantly reduce the tax payable on your death, if the value of your business is "frozen" sufficiently early. The lower cost base will effectively be transferred to your children, and so the tax on the subsequent capital gain will be deferred until they sell the business (or until their deaths). You can also multiply the availability of the capital gains exemption for small business shares (see 4.4.1), if it is still available when your children eventually dispose of the shares. At the same time, you do not need to give up control of the business.

You can also continue to receive income from the corporation, either by declaring dividends on the preferred shares, or by drawing a salary if you continue to work in the business..

If you use a trust to invest in the common shares, you can retain flexibility with respect to allocating the shares of the business among your children later.

At the time you set up the freeze, you can trigger part or all of the accrued capital gain on your shares to date. This may allow you to use your capital gains exemption (see 4.4.1), for example. Be aware of the various restrictions on claiming the exemption (see 4.4.3).

Depending on how the freeze is structured, you can achieve income splitting (see Chapter 3) by directing income into the hands of your children for tax purposes. Note that certain attribution rules do not apply if your corporation qualifies as a "small business corporation" (see 4.3.2) or your children have reached the age of 18 (see 3.2.5).

Whether an estate freeze is useful to you will depend very much on your business, your financial position, your future plans and your goals. Qualified professional advice should be obtained before this type of planning is undertaken.

12.6 Life insurance

Life insurance plays many roles in estate planning. For example, it can:

- allow you to accumulate funds on a tax-sheltered basis to supplement retirement income
- provide replacement income for your dependants
- provide a fund for emergency expenses or children's education in future years
- pay for final expenses such as funeral costs
- assist in funding the succession of a business in a closely-held corporation
- fund capital gains tax liability that arises on death (see 12.1.2); in certain situations, it may even be possible to eliminate this liability

Insurance proceeds received on the death of the life insured are not taxable. By the same token, the premiums you pay for your life insurance are generally not tax deductible.

If your corporation is the beneficiary of a policy on your life, the corporation may be able to transfer the life insurance proceeds to other shareholders without any tax applying.

Your need for insurance will change as factors such as your income, investment portfolio and dependants change. Therefore, a regular review of your coverage is important.

There are many different life insurance products available. These products can generally be divided into two types: term insurance and permanent insurance.

Term (or "pure") insurance policies usually have lower premiums at younger ages. You are paying for the risk of your death in the current year, and nothing more. As long as you continue to pay the premiums, your coverage will continue; many policies guarantee renewal without additional medical evidence as long as you remain in the plan. However, the cost of premiums can increase dramatically in later years. Most term policies terminate at age 70 to 75.

A **permanent insurance** policy (often called **"whole life"** or "universal life") combines the pure insurance coverage with an investment fund. As a result, the cost of premiums when you are young is often much higher than term insurance. However, many permanent insurance policies offer fixed premiums for guaranteed maximum terms (say, 10 or 20 years); at the end of the term, the policy is fully paid for. The policy can be designed so that the investment fund or cash surrender value accumulates tax-free. Such a fund can be borrowed against or "cashed out" in later years. However, there may be a tax cost.

Permanent insurance products are usually desirable for the following three purposes:

- capital gains tax funding
- estate equalization (to allow for an even distribution of your estate, such as where you wish to leave business assets to beneficiaries active in a family business and non-business assets to those family members not active in the business)
- business succession planning
- tax-sheltered, long-term investment strategies

When buying insurance, consider who should be the beneficiary. If your estate is the beneficiary, the insurance proceeds will form part of your estate on your death, and will be subject to any claims that creditors have on your estate. The proceeds will also be subject to probate fees (see 12.1.3 above). You may therefore want to have the insurance proceeds payable directly to your spouse or another beneficiary, so that they bypass the estate. The investment fund or cash surrender value of a policy can also be protected from creditors during your lifetime where certain beneficiaries are named.

12.7 CHARITABLE GIFTS AND BEQUESTS

In this section we look at some ways you can structure charitable gifts, both during your life and through your will, to maximize your estate planning goals and take best advantage of the available tax credits. The options are much broader than simply leaving a sum of money to a charity in your will.

12.7.1 THE TAX CREDIT FOR CHARITABLE DONATIONS

The tax credit for charitable donations was discussed in 1.3.4. To the extent your total donations exceed $200 per year, you receive a credit worth about 50% of the donation in most cases. The limit of donations you can claim each year is **20% of your "net income"** (see 1.1.1). Any donations you do not claim can be carried forward for up to five years and used in a future year.

Charitable gifts can be made through your will. A bequest in your will is treated as if the gift was made in your final year and is claimed for credit on your final tax return. To the extent the donations are not used on your final return (because they exceed 20% of net income or for any other reason), they can be carried back and claimed for credit in the previous year (subject to the 20% limitation for that year).

As you can see, large bequests in your will (or large donations during your lifetime) may become unusable for tax purposes, if they far exceed the threshold of 20% of your net income. You may therefore want to consider other options, so as to maximize the tax credits and maximize the funds available to your beneficiaries—both family members and charities.

12.7.2 GIFTS TO THE CROWN

Gifts to the federal or a provincial government (**"Crown gifts"**) are not subject to the 20% limitation. Several provinces have laws that allow the creation of Crown agency foundations that benefit universities, colleges, hospitals and museums. Some of these institutions have taken advantage of this rule and made arrangements with their provincial governments to be supported by "Crown foundations". As a result a donation to a Crown foundation can go to support a particular university, hospital or museum. Since it is a gift to the province, it is not subject to the limitation of 20% of your income, and the entire amount is available for tax credit. (Of course, you have to be paying enough tax for the year for the credit to be fully usable.)

12.7.3 GIFTS IN KIND

Both during your lifetime and on your death, you can donate property to a charity as an alternative to money. A gift of property is called a **gift in kind**. Examples include artwork, shares and real estate, as well as some more esoteric gifts we discuss below, such as life insurance or a residual interest in real property. (You cannot "give" services, however—only property.)

A gift in kind is normally valued at its **fair market value**. For purposes of determining the tax credit for your donation, it will be the same as a gift of cash. Thus, the tax credit will generally be worth about 50% of the value of the property. However, at the same time you are deemed to have disposed of the property at its fair market value—meaning that you must recognize any capital gain or income that would apply had you sold the property for that price.

EXAMPLE

David owns shares in a mining company that have a cost base to him of $10,000. In 1995, the shares are worth $50,000, and he donates them to a hospital foundation (that is not a Crown foundation). David's employment income in 1995 is $70,000.

*David is deemed to have disposed of the shares for $50,000, and so must recognize a $40,000 capital gain, 3/4 of which is brought into his income as a $30,000 taxable capital gain (see 4.2). His total income for tax purposes is thus $70,000 + $30,000, or **$100,000**.*

David gets a receipt from the hospital foundation for $50,000. Since his income (including the taxable capital gain) *is only $100,000, the maximum charitable donation he can claim for 1995 is $20,000 (20% of $100,000). This will entitle him to a credit worth about **$10,000**. The remaining $30,000 can be carried forward and used in one of the next five years, if David has sufficient net income.*

Where you make a gift of capital property, you can file an election with your tax return to use a **lower amount** than the fair market value, for purposes of determining both your proceeds of disposition of the property and the value of your donation. You can elect any amount between the adjusted cost base (see 4.2) and the actual fair market value.

EXAMPLE

*Using the above example, David decides instead to elect in his tax return to treat the shares as valued at **$18,000** rather than $50,000. Thus, he is deemed to have disposed of them for $18,000, and so must recognize an $8,000 capital gain, $^3/_4$ of which is brought into his income as a $6,000 taxable capital gain (see 4.2). His total income for tax purposes is thus $70,000 + $6,000, or **$76,000**.*

*As a result of having filed an election at $18,000, David receives a receipt from the hospital foundation for that amount. Since his income (including the taxable capital gain) is only $76,000, the maximum charitable donation he can claim for 1995 is $15,200 (20% of $76,000). This will entitle him to a credit worth about **$7,600**. The remaining $2,800 of his deemed $18,000 donation can be carried forward and used in one of the next five years, if David has sufficient net income.*

Whether the election is useful depends on a number of factors, including David's tax bracket, his other sources of income and deductions, and his prospects for income in future years against which to use up the charitable donation carryforward. In this example, the current year's tax is substantially reduced, since David's income is $24,000 lower due to the lower capital gain while his tax credit is only $2,400 lower.

12.7.4 Gifts of Cultural Property

Gifts of "cultural property" to certain public authorities or institutions (such as museums) are not subject to the 20% limitation. In addition, if the cultural property is certified by the government as a national treasure with cultural significance to Canada, the donation will be equal to the property's fair market value for purposes of the credit but no taxable capital gain will result.

The election described above in 12.7.3 can also be used by artists for gifts of work they have created (which is inventory rather than capital property).

12.7.5 Gifts of Life Insurance

If you have a "whole life" insurance policy (see 12.6), you can donate it to a charity by transferring the ownership of the policy to the charity and having the charity become the registered beneficiary of the policy. The value of your donation for tax purposes will be the value of the policy—that is, the cash surrender value, plus any accumulated dividends and interest that are also assigned, minus any policy loan outstanding. However, to the extent that value exceeds the cost of the policy to you, you must recognize the excess as income, as if you had cashed in the policy.

Once you have donated the policy to the charity, if you continue to pay the premiums on the policy, each such payment will be considered to be an additional charitable donation entitling you to a tax credit.

Note that if you simply make the charity a beneficiary of a life insurance policy that you continue to own, there will be no tax benefits available to you or your estate.

12.7.6 Purchasing an annuity from a charity

You can purchase an annuity from a charity, whereby you give the charity a sum of money up front and receive a fixed annual payment through the rest of your life.

While the "cost" of this type of annuity is usually more than the market price to purchase an annuity from a life insurance company offering the same annual income, the annuity purchased from a charity may actually provide you with more annual disposable income and allow you to make a sizable gift to the charity at the same time. Here's how. If the total payments that you expect to receive from the charity during your lifetime are less than the original sum you gave to the charity, the annual payments to you will be tax-free. You will also be entitled to a tax credit on the difference according to the usual rules as outlined above.

Revenue Canada has published a table outlining the number of annual payments that donors can expect to receive based on their age at the time the annuity is purchased.

If the total payments that you expect to receive are more than the original sum given to the charity, the excess amount will be taxable on an annualized basis.

12.7.7 Charitable insured annuity

Another twist is to set up a "charitable insured annuity". You buy an annuity from a life insurance company, and use part of the monthly payments to pay the premiums on a life insurance policy with a charity as the owner and beneficiary. Thus, you receive an income stream over your lifetime (from the annuity), and tax credits for the insurance premiums you pay. On your death, the charity receives the insurance proceeds.

12.7.8 CHARITABLE REMAINDER TRUSTS

If you have property that you would like to donate to a charity, but you need the income from the property during your lifetime, consider donating a "residual" interest in the property—that is, the capital that will remain on your death. One way to do this is to set up a "charitable remainder trust". This is a trust (see 12.3) whose conditions are that the *income* be paid to you during your lifetime, while the *capital* will go to the charity on your death. In some cases, you can transfer the residual interest in property (e.g., real estate) directly, without setting up a trust.

The value of a gift of the residual interest in a property is its discounted present value. This value will depend on factors such as the current fair market value of the property, current interest rates, and your life expectancy. The gift entitles you to the normal tax credit for charitable donations. If you arrange to receive less income from the trust (or property) that you might otherwise be entitled to, the value of your donation may be higher.

Such a gift has several attractions. First, the charity gets a vested interest in the property right away, and need not worry about whether you will leave the property to it in your will (or whether your will might be contested). Second, you get an immediate tax credit for the amount of your donation (the residual value). Third, you continue to receive the income from (or use of) the property for the rest of your life.

Aside from the cost of professional fees in structuring a charitable remainder trust, you will be deemed to have disposed of the remainder interest for its fair market value. This may lead to a capital gain and income inclusion for tax purposes, as in the examples in 12.7.2 above. (As with those examples, you can elect to have the value set at a lower amount for both disposition and charitable donation purposes.) In addition, the trust will have to file an annual tax return (see 12.3.4), though it will normally not pay any tax since all of its income will be flowed out to you.

12.8 PLANNING OPPORTUNITIES

You would not want to do extensive estate planning on your own. With the suggestions below, however, you can assemble a general picture of your goals and how they might be met, and be much more informed when obtaining professional advice. You will need to consult a professional tax adviser, as well as a lawyer for purposes of executing a will.

The need for professional advice does not stop with the planning. The tax rules on and after death are complex. If you are an executor, you should seek advice with respect to how to minimize the tax burden on the estate. If you do not, you can be sued by the beneficiaries. The courts have found executors liable for failing to take active steps to structure the estate's affairs to minimize income tax.

12.8.1 Make a will (or review your existing will)

To avoid difficulties and additional costs in administering your estate, it is very important to make a will (see 12.2.1). While in some provinces an entirely handwritten will may be valid, it is strongly advisable to have your will prepared or reviewed with the assistance of a lawyer to ensure it meets your wishes and takes tax and family law considerations into account. If your lawyer is not a tax specialist, you may want to get professional tax advice as well. Consider carefully who will be your executor (see 12.2.2).

The primary function of a will, of course, is to specify where and when your assets are to be distributed. You may want to leave specific properties (e.g., jewellery, furniture or shares in your business) to specific beneficiaries. You may want to leave a stated sum of money to certain people and to named charities (make sure you get the correct legal name of the charity). You will also want to specify a "residual" beneficiary, who will get everything left in the estate after your specific bequests are satisfied.

Quite possibly you will simply leave everything to your spouse, or to a trust that meets the requirements of a "spousal trust" (see 12.3.2). As discussed in 12.1.2, there will be no tax on the accrued capital gains on your property when the property is transferred to your spouse or the spousal trust, provided the assets vest with your spouse or spousal trust within 36 months of your death.

Note also that the instructions in your will can be overridden in some provinces by family law. In Ontario, for example, your spouse can elect to ignore the will and take the amount of money due to him or her under the "net family property" rules (see 12.4). If this is done, your estate may lose the benefit of the capital gains rollover described above.

There are many tax-oriented clauses that can be included in a will to help minimize the tax liability. The will should include a provision granting executors and trustees broad authority to make or join in any election, designation or allocation under tax legislation. This will ensure that your executor can use benefits such as the principal residence designations and capital gains exemptions. The following clauses should also be considered:

- forgiveness of loans made to family members
- a discretionary power permitting trustees to determine which assets are to form the trust property of a spousal trust

- a reminder to your executors that if you have not made your maximum RRSP contribution at the time of your death, one should be made by your estate to your spouse's RRSP before the required deadline

In your will, you can name the beneficiary of your RRSP, deferred profit-sharing plan, death benefits and insurance proceeds. Alternatively, these plans may allow for naming a direct beneficiary within the plan documents. While designating beneficiaries directly in the plan documents may reduce probate costs, there may also be implications for spousal rights under family law.

If you designate someone other than your spouse as the beneficiary of your RRSP, your estate may have to pay tax on the full value of your RRSP on your death (see 2.1.7.3).

If you have particular desires as to who should have custody or guardianship over your children after your death and while they are under 18, you can put these desires into your will. They will be considered by the court but will not be binding. The court will look to the best interests of the children in making its decision.

Periodic **reviews** of your will are necessary to ensure that your estate plan is consistent with changes in the tax law, which occur regularly, as well as any changes in provincial family law and succession law. In addition, your own personal circumstances may change which could necessitate a change to your will.

Note also that in many jurisdictions, a will becomes void if you marry after making the will, unless it was made in contemplation of the marriage.

Consider also executing a **power of attorney** in the event you become unable to act by reason of disability or mental incompetence. If, for example, you become mentally disabled, the power of attorney would enable the named "attorney" to act in your stead. You may wish to give the power of attorney to the same person you name as your executor. If you live in Ontario, the new *Substitute Decisions Act*, which came into effect in April 1995, makes executing a continuing power of attorney strongly advisable.

12.8.2 CONSIDER AN ESTATE FREEZE

If you have substantial assets, and particularly if you have a business that may go up in value, obtain professional advice as to the appropriateness of freezing your estate (see 12.5). You may be able to substantially reduce the tax payable on your death without seriously impairing access to income or assets during your lifetime.

See 12.5.3 above with respect to the benefits of an estate freeze.

12.8.3 CONSIDER SETTING UP A FAMILY TRUST

Consider whether to set up a discretionary family trust (see 12.3), either now (*inter vivos*) or in your will (as a testamentary trust). In your will, you can provide a separate testamentary trust for each beneficiary. This will allow each trust to benefit from lower graduated rates of tax for the income retained in the trust.

Setting up the trust while you are alive can also provide several advantages:

- by making yourself trustee, you can keep control of the trust assets (such as your business)
- by getting the assets out of your estate, you can reduce probate fees (see 12.1.3)
- because the assets will not be in your estate, they will not form part of the public record that anyone can examine in the court office
- income splitting may be possible, depending on the application of the attribution rules (see Chapter 3)

A trust can also be useful as part of an estate freeze plan (see 12.5). In many cases, you may not know at the time you set up the freeze how you will want the growth allocated among your children. You may also not yet want to give them direct ownership in the business. In such an event you should consider setting up a family trust and having the trust subscribe for the "growth" common shares. If you are the trustee and have discretion as to how to allocate the income and capital of the trust, you can decide several years later (or even in your will) which of your children should inherit the business. This may also provide some protection for your children against family law legislation (see 12.4).

12.8.4 Take steps to minimize probate fees

Probate fee structures vary from province to province. Some of the following techniques can reduce the cost of probating your estate. Note, however, that any planning to reduce probate fees must take numerous other issues (such as family law, income tax effects, land transfer tax and GST) into account, and professional advice is strongly recommended.

- If you are leaving property to your spouse (or another person), consider holding the property as joint tenants with your spouse (or that other person). On your death, the property will pass automatically to the other joint tenant and will not form part of your estate (see 12.1.3). Note that there may be immediate adverse effects if you transfer the property to a joint tenant who is someone other than your spouse (for example, your child). Also, there are some situations where a joint tenancy will be severed on death by provincial legislation.
- Try to keep certain assets out of the estate. This is quite practical in the case of life insurance and RRSPs issued by life insurance companies, where beneficiaries (other than the estate) can be designated in the RRSP plan documents or in

the life insurance policy. Also consider transferring property during your lifetime, either directly to your intended beneficiaries or to a trust.

- Change the situs of property to a different jurisdiction where probate fees are low or fixed (for example, Alberta) through the use of a corporation.
- If you own real estate with no mortgage, and you also owe money (perhaps on a personal line of credit or on a debt secured by other assets), consider having the debt converted to a mortgage or charge on the real estate. It may then reduce the value of the real estate for probate purposes.

12.8.5 Make sure you have sufficient insurance

Review your insurance needs with your advisers to determine the appropriate amount and form of your life insurance. Some of the issues to consider were discussed in 12.6 above. This review should also consider your need for disability insurance. If you become disabled, the financial consequences can be even worse than death.

12.8.6 Consider planned charitable gifts or bequests

There are many ways in which gifts may be made to charitable organizations, including gifts of property (securities, artwork, real estate), life insurance and annuities, with significant tax benefits (see 12.7).

These benefits depend on the type of gift, the timing of the donation and the nature of the charitable organization.

A gift made today can provide a current tax saving and, in addition, a charitable gift annuity (see 12.7.6) or a gift of a remainder interest in a trust or property (see 12.7.8) will also allow you the continued use of or income from the property itself.

Proper will planning can help ensure that your bequest will be made as you intend and provide significant tax savings for your estate.

Careful planning together with an informed adviser can ensure your philanthropic goals are met and the tax benefits are available when you need them most.

12.8.7 Plan for the succession of your business

If you own and manage a business, it could well be your family's largest asset. After your death, the business may be crucial for meeting your family's financial needs. Taking steps to ensure your business' ongoing profitability and management can be just as important as consideration of the planning opportunities to minimize taxes on your death discussed throughout this chapter.

One of the first issues you must resolve is what will happen to the business when you die. You could plan to keep the business in the family, sell it to a buyer outside the family, or liquidate it. Which option you choose will depend on things such as the nature of the business, the likelihood of its continued success after your death, and the abilities of your family members and/or key employees to run the business' operations.

If the family is not capable or does not want to run the business, it may be in everyone's best interests to sell or liquidate the business on or before your retirement. If some family members are quite active in managing the business while others are not, dividing ownership equally among your family might seem fair but it could disrupt the business and create tension in the family. Often in these cases, you should use other family assets to ensure fairness for all family members.

If you decide to keep the business in the family, you should seek professional advice to help you decide whether to transfer ownership during your lifetime or on death, who will receive the business' shares and in what proportion, whether the shares will be gifted or sold, and the most tax-effective way to structure the transfer.

If you do not own 100% of your company's shares, the transfer of its legal control may be smoothed by a carefully drafted shareholder's agreement (see 8.4).

12.8.8 Consider Effects of Foreign Estate Taxes

If you are a U.S. citizen, see 15.8.1 and 15.9.11.

If you are not a U.S. citizen but own assets legally located in the U.S., including real estate, debts owed to you by U.S. citizens or shares in U.S. corporations, see 16.4 and the planning techniques discussed in 16.5.4 through 16.5.14.

If you own assets in other countries, investigate the possibility of estate taxes of those countries (or their states or provinces) applying on your death.

Note that estate taxes and succession duties imposed by other jurisdictions (including U.S. states) are not normally eligible for a foreign tax credit in Canada, even though you may have a Canadian income tax liability as a result of the deemed disposition described in 12.1.2. Double taxation can result. You may need to plan for this ahead of time.

12.9 References

There is little published information on estate planning that is easily understood by the lay person. As well, every individual's case is different. Consult a qualified tax professional for advice.

Revenue Canada publishes the following, which are available (in person or by telephone request) from your nearest District Taxation Office:

Interpretation Bulletin IT-111R, "Annuities purchased from charitable organizations

Interpretation Bulletin IT-210R, "Income of deceased persons—periodic payments"

Interpretation Bulletin IT-212R3, "Income of deceased persons—rights or things"

Interpretation Bulletin IT-226R, "Gift to a charity of a residential interest in real property or an equitable interest in a trust"

Interpretation Bulletin IT-234, "Income of deceased persons—farm crops"

Interpretation Bulletin IT-244R3, "Gifts by individuals of life insurance policies as charitable donations"

Interpretation Bulletin IT-288R2, "Gift of tangible capital properties to a charity and others"

Interpretation Bulletin IT-297R2, "Gifts in kind to charity and others"

Interpretation Bulletin IT-407R3, "Disposition after 1987 of Canadian cultural property"

Interpretation Bulletin IT-427R, "Livestock of farmers"

Interpretation Bulletin IT-510, "Transfers and loans of property made after May 22, 1985 to a related minor"

Interpretation Bulletin IT-511R, "Interspousal transfers and loans of property made after May 22, 1985"

Brochure, "When You Retire"

"Your Guide — Preparing Returns for Deceased Persons"

T3 Guide and Trust Return

13 DEALING WITH REVENUE CANADA

PLANNING TIPS

- File return even if you can't pay balance
- Pay balance by April 30 even if filing later
- File with EFILE for quick refund
- Be aware of interest rates and compounding
- Consider prepayments of instalments
- File notice of objection where appropriate
- Claim changes when return reopened on reassessment
- Sign a waiver only to the extent necessary
- Be sure you understand the legal issues when appealing
- Consider paying balance even when objecting or appealing

In this chapter we deal with the administrative side of the tax system—how tax is collected, how your return is assessed, and what you can do if you disagree with Revenue Canada as to the amount of tax you owe.

13.1 TAX RETURNS

13.1.1 GENERAL

Individuals have traditionally been required to file tax returns by **April 30** each year. Effective with the 1995 return, the deadline for individuals who have business income is **June 15**. The deadline has been extended because individuals and partnerships may now be forced to use a calendar year for business purposes (see 7.2.1 and 7.3), and therefore must always calculate business income for a year ending on December 31. Even though the return may not be due until June 15, any balance of tax owing for the year is due on April 30.

If you have no tax to pay for the year (as distinguished from no balance owing in April), no return is required unless Revenue Canada requests one.

In all provinces except Québec, you file a single return with Revenue Canada to cover both federal and provincial tax. Québec residents and taxpayers with business income from operations in Québec must file a Quebec provincial tax return as well (see Chapter 14).

The return must be postmarked (or transmitted electronically) by the due date. If the return is late, an automatic penalty of 5% of any tax still owing applies. This penalty is increased by 1% of the unpaid tax for each full month that the return is late, to a maximum of 12 months. Repeated failures to file returns result in higher penalties.

13.1.2 Electronic filing of tax returns (EFILE)

Revenue Canada permits most taxpayers to file their returns in electronic form using a personal computer. The system, dubbed **EFILE**, is available across the country, and allows authorized tax return preparers or transmitters to file returns directly to Revenue Canada using tax return preparation and transmission software.

Due to the technical requirements and start-up costs involved, most individuals cannot yet file returns on their own using EFILE. However, most professional tax return preparers now offer this service in addition to preparing the actual tax returns.

The main benefit of EFILE to a taxpayer is the ability to have the return assessed and a refund paid in as little as 1-2 weeks, as opposed to a somewhat longer wait using the conventional filing method. Further, no paper returns or receipts need be filed with the return, although receipts and other supporting documentation still must be retained for any subsequent review by Revenue Canada.

The Québec government has also implemented electronic filing for Québec provincial tax returns.

13.2 Payment of tax

13.2.1 Source withholdings

Tax is withheld at source and remitted to Revenue Canada by employers and others. Tax withheld from a payment to you is considered to have been paid by you to Revenue Canada, even if your employer never remits it. It is also considered to have been paid to you in the sense that it forms part of your income.

Source withholding applies to the following kinds of payments, among others:

- employment income
- pension benefits
- unemployment insurance benefits
- withdrawals from an RRSP
- annuity payments
- payments of passive income to non-residents (interest, dividends, rent, royalties, etc.)
- purchase of real estate from a non-resident (unless the non-resident has a certificate from Revenue Canada)

Note that there is *no* withholding of tax on interest, dividends, rent or royalties paid to Canadian residents. Self-employment income such as consulting fees, being business income (see 7.1), is also paid without source deductions.

13.2.2 Instalments

You must pay instalments if the difference between your tax payable (including provincial tax) and amounts withheld at source is more than $2,000 in both the current year and either of the two preceding years. (For Québec residents, since provincial tax is not collected by Revenue Canada, the threshold is $1,200 of federal tax instead of $2,000 total.)

Quarterly instalments are due on the 15th of March, June, September and December.

There are three possible ways to calculate your instalment obligations.

The first method is for your total instalments, paid in four equal payments, to equal the **tax owing for the year** on your sources of income from which tax is not withheld. In other words, your instalments should equal the balance owing at the end of the year.

The second method is for your quarterly instalments to equal the **tax owing on your previous year's** sources of income for which tax was not withheld. In other words, take the balance you had to pay last year after accounting for source withholdings, and pay that amount over the year in instalments.

The first method requires you to estimate your current year's income. If you guess low, you can end up not paying enough instalments. The second method lets you use the previous year's income, but on March 15, when the first instalment is due, you might not yet have calculated your previous year's total tax. For this reason the third method was introduced.

Under the third method, your March and June instalments are each one-quarter of the total tax owing on income from which tax was not withheld for **two years ago**. Your *total* instalments for the year must still equal the total amount for one year ago, as with the second method. Therefore, the September and December instalments must be enough to reach this total. Revenue Canada will mail you a statement twice a year advising you of your quarterly instalment obligations under the third method.

EXAMPLE

Chris is self-employed as a consultant. Her 1994 tax payable (combined federal/provincial) was $20,000. Her 1995 tax payable was $24,000. She expects her total 1996 tax bill to be $27,000.

Chris should pay quarterly instalments on March 15, June 15, September 15 and December 15, 1996, totalling $24,000, *her tax payable for the previous year. If she wishes, she may pay four instalments of $6,000 each.*

Revenue Canada will advise Chris in February 1996, however, that her March and June payments should be $5,000 each—one-quarter of her 1994 tax payable, since her 1995 figures aren't yet available. If she makes these payments, and then pays $7,000 on each of September 15 and December 15, she will have paid the required $24,000 and met her instalment obligations under the "third method".

The $3,000 balance (assuming Chris' estimate of income for 1996 turns out to be correct) will then be due on April 30, 1997, although her return need not be filed until June 15.

If instalments are made on time and in the correct amount as per any of the three methods, no interest is payable. If instalments are not made when required or are deficient, interest is assessed at Revenue Canada's current high "prescribed rate" (see 13.3), compounded daily. You cannot *earn* interest by paying instalments early, but you can earn "contra-interest" at the same rate as applies to late payments, to offset interest that would otherwise be assessed on late instalments.

EXAMPLE

Chris, from the above example, does not make any instalment payments until June 15, 1996. On that day she makes a single payment of $15,000. She then makes a $2,000 payment on September 15, 1996 and a $7,000 payment on December 15, 1996.

Chris should not owe any interest on instalments, assuming the prescribed interest rate stays constant through 1996. Her June 15 payment can be thought of as three parts: $5,000 due in March, paid three months late; $5,000 paid on time; and $5,000 of the $7,000 not due until September, paid three months early. The payment that is early will generate "contra-interest" to offset the interest that Chris would otherwise have to pay due to her being late with her March payment.

If the interest owing on late instalments is greater than $1,000, you may be subject to an additional penalty of up to 50% of the interest.

13.2.3 PAYMENT OF BALANCE

Any balance of tax owing when the return is filed is due by April 30. This applies whether the return is due April 30 or June 15 (see 13.1).

In addition, any unpaid balance is subject to interest, **compounded daily** at Revenue Canada's prescribed rate (see 13.3).

13.2.4 "DIRECT DEPOSIT" OF REFUNDS

The federal government offers a "Direct Deposit" service whereby tax refunds, GST credits and Child Tax Benefit payments can be deposited directly into your account at any financial institution in Canada. To take advantage of this service, which saves the time it takes to print and mail the cheques and avoids the problem of cheques lost in the mail, complete form T1-DD when you file your tax return. For other government payments, such as monthly old age security or Canada Pension Plan payments, contact your financial institution for the appropriate forms.

13.3 INTEREST

Interest that you owe on late payments of federal tax and instalments and on refunds is calculated at a prescribed rate, which varies quarterly based on the Bank of Canada rate.

The are three different "prescribed" interest rates each quarter. The lowest rate, which is roughly the Bank of Canada rate for the previous quarter, applies for purposes of applying the **attribution rules** (see 3.2.2) and the **employee and shareholder loan** rules (see 6.2 and 8.2.6). The middle rate, which is 2 percentage points higher, applies to **refunds** paid by Revenue Canada. The highest rate, which is a further 2 points higher, applies to **late payments of tax and instalments** owing by taxpayers. (Before July 1995, the middle and high rates were the same, at only 2 points higher than the low rate.)

Although the rate is expressed as an annual rate, it is in fact **compounded daily**, so the effective rate is somewhat higher than shown.

Interest that you owe on late payments runs from when the payment was due. Interest on refunds generally runs from 45 days after the due date for the return, or from the day on which you file your return, whichever is later. However, if you have a June 15 filing deadline because you have self-employment income (see 7.2.1), interest will not be paid until 45 days after April 30 or 45 days after the date that the return is actually filed, whichever is later.

Interest paid to you on a refund is taxable in the year in which you receive it. Thus, if you file your 1995 return when it is due in April 1996 and receive a refund in August, the interest from June 14 included in that cheque must be reported on your 1996 return.

Interest that you are required to pay to Revenue Canada, such as on late payments of tax or instalments, is not deductible.

The federal prescribed interest rates for the last few quarters to time of writing are as follows:

Quarter	Low Rate	Mid Rate	High Rate
Oct.-Dec. 1994	7%	9%	9%
Jan.-March 1995	6%	8%	8%
April-June 1995	8%	10%	10%
July-Sept. 1995	9%	11%	13%

As mentioned above, the high rate applies to late tax and instalment payments and refunds. The low rate applies for the purposes of the attribution rules and shareholder and employee loans.

13.4 Assessment, audit and reassessment

13.4.1 "Quick" assessment

When you file a conventional (paper) return, it is processed over a period of typically 3-6 weeks, after which you receive a "Notice of Assessment" and any refund owing to you. The processing includes a review of the numbers on your return to make sure they are consistent (e.g., that your arithmetic is correct and that any numbers that need to be supported by receipts or information slips are consistent with them).

Most EFILE users can expect their returns to be assessed in 1-2 weeks.

The assessment (whether the return is filed on paper or with EFILE) is normally not based on any investigation beyond what is on your return. It is sometimes referred to as a "quick assessment". The fact that a particular claim is allowed at this point does not mean that Revenue Canada is "letting" you claim it; it merely means that Revenue Canada has not addressed the issue in any detail.

For a partnership, Revenue Canada may issue a **determination** of the partnership's income or loss, which is effectively an assessment of each partner's portion of the income or loss. See 7.3.6.

13.4.2 Audit

Some time after the initial assessment, your return may be selected for **audit**. Most audits of individual taxpayers (as opposed to corporations) are "desk audits", in which the auditor will ask you to supply supporting material for claims you have made. Some audits are "field audits", in which the auditor will come to your place of business to look at your records.

If you use EFILE, you will not have to file any receipts with your return. However, Revenue Canada may later "spot-check" your return to verify certain claims, such as donations, RRSP contributions or tuition fees. This is normally just a formality, designed to maintain the integrity of the EFILE system.

You should be aware of your rights on an audit. The auditor is not entitled to go on a "fishing expedition" through your books. He or she may request specific information, and you may ask why that information is needed. You may wish assistance from your professional advisers in dealing with the auditor, if you anticipate problems.

If you have not engaged in tax evasion, an audit should not normally be cause for concern.

13.4.3 Reassessment

If the audit (or an audit of another taxpayer) turns up an indication that your tax payable should be other than what was initially assessed, Revenue Canada will issue a **reassessment**. If the reassessment results in more tax payable by you, this will not normally be done without you first being consulted and given an opportunity to explain your position.

A reassessment cannot normally be issued more than three years after the date of the original assessment. However, in cases of fraud, or misrepresentation attributable to "neglect, carelessness or wilful default", the reassessment may be issued at any time.

There are several other situations where the three-year limitation does not apply. The most important is where you have filed a **waiver**. The waiver, normally directed to a specific issue that is in dispute, will allow Revenue Canada to reassess you on that issue at any time. You can revoke a waiver on six months' notice to Revenue Canada.

13.5 Objections and Appeals

13.5.1 Notice of Objection

If you cannot come to an understanding with the auditor and a reassessment is issued, or if you disagree with the original assessment, you may file a **Notice of Objection**. This is done by writing to the Chief of Appeals of your local district taxation office. It begins the formal administrative appeal process. The notice should set out the specific issue(s) that you are objecting to.

To be valid, a Notice of Objection must be filed either within 90 days of the date of the assessment or reassessment to which you are objecting, or within one year of the original due date for the return. For example, an objection to an assessment of your 1994 return would have to be filed by April 30, 1996 or 90 days after the (re)assessment you are objecting to, whichever is later.

When you file a Notice of Objection, your objection is reviewed by an Appeals Officer within Revenue Canada. The Appeals Officer is independent of the audit branch, and he or she should conduct the review impartially and objectively

If the period for objecting has expired, you may request a reassessment of your return. In this case, you have no legal right to force a reassessment, but in many cases the reassessment will be issued anyway. Revenue Canada will allow a reassessment of a return for any year back to 1985, if the request meets the guidelines issued under the government's "Fairness Package".

In some cases you can also apply to Revenue Canada or the Tax Court of Canada for extension of the time for filing a Notice of Objection.

13.5.2 Appeal to the Tax Court

The Appeals Officer is normally your last level of appeal within Revenue Canada. A further appeal is available to the **Tax Court of Canada**.

You have a choice between the court's "informal" and "general" procedures for making an appeal.

The **"general" procedure** normally requires you to retain a lawyer. It is similar to higher court proceedings in provincial courts. If the amount of tax in dispute for any one taxation year is more than $12,000 of federal tax (about $19,000 including provincial tax), you must follow the general procedure. In certain "test cases", Revenue Canada may also force a case below the threshold into the "general procedure", in which case Revenue Canada will be required to reimburse you for most or all of your legal fees.

The **"informal" procedure**, as its name suggests, is much less complicated. You may appear on your own, or have someone else (such as a lawyer, accountant, consultant or friend) there to assist you. No specific form needs to be filed to launch the appeal. The formal rules of evidence that normally apply to court proceedings will not necessarily apply. Under the informal procedure, your case will normally be heard fairly quickly, and a judgment given within a year of when you first file the appeal. The decision given is not binding as a precedent for future cases, whether yours or another taxpayer's.

13.5.3 Appeal beyond the Tax Court

A decision of the Tax Court of Canada under its "informal" procedure can be appealed, on a question of law only, in the form of a "judicial review" by the **Federal Court of Appeal**. A decision under the "general" procedure can be appealed directly to the Federal Court of Appeal. In either case you would need a lawyer for such an appeal, which would typically take about two years from time of filing until judgment is given.

Once a decision is given by the Federal Court of Appeal, either you or Revenue Canada may seek "leave to appeal" from the Supreme Court of Canada. Only if a panel of three justices of the Supreme Court grant the application for leave to appeal can an appeal be made. The Supreme Court rarely grants leave to appeal in tax cases; typically only three or four tax cases a year reach the Supreme Court.

13.6 Planning opportunities

13.6.1 File return even if you can't pay balance; pay balance by April 30 even if filing late

As noted in 13.1, a penalty of 5% of unpaid tax applies to a return that is even one day late (plus further penalties if your return is a month or more late). It follows that if you are not able to pay your balance owing, you should still file your return on time. Interest will accrue on the unpaid balance, but the penalty will not apply.

Conversely, if you are unable to get your return completed (or your return is not due until June 15—see 3.1), but you do have a rough idea of how much tax you owe, it is a good idea to pay that amount to Revenue Canada by April 30. Make sure to have it credited to the correct taxation year (and not as instalments for the subsequent year, for example). If you have only a small unpaid balance, the 5% penalty and the non-deductible interest will be minimized.

13.6.2 File with EFILE for quick refund

If you are expecting a refund, consider filing your return electronically through an EFILE authorized preparer. EFILE will significantly speed up the processing of your return and the delivery of your refund. Also, choosing to have your refund deposited directly into your bank account will save additional mailing time.

Even if you are not expecting a refund, you may still choose to use EFILE to reduce the paper burden on you, your EFILE preparer and Revenue Canada. If you are concerned about reassessment of your return down the road, filing with EFILE will normally get your return assessed sooner and start the three-year reassessment period (see 13.4.3) running earlier.

If you prepare your own return, most EFILE preparers will charge only a small fee to transmit your return to Revenue Canada.

13.6.3 Be aware of interest rates and compounding

When forecasting the cost of any tax you owe, make sure to factor in any interest that will apply. As noted in 13.3, interest is compounded *daily*. A 10% interest rate, for example, is equivalent to a rate of about 10.52% in simple annual interest.

The prescribed interest rate changes quarterly; the new rate for each quarter is announced by Revenue Canada in a news release about three weeks before the quarter begins.

The tax treatment of interest must be considered as well. Since interest paid by you to Revenue Canada is not deductible, but interest you receive is taxable, the interest you pay costs up to twice as much. For example, if you receive $200 in interest on your 1995 refund, but are assessed $200 in interest owing on your 1996 return, and you are in a 41% tax bracket, you are out of pocket $82 after tax.

If you have tax owing at April 30 and you know interest will be charged because of late or deficient instalment payments, consider paying an estimate of the interest with your April 30 payment to stop any further interest from accruing.

13.6.4 Consider prepayments of instalments

"Offset" or "contra" interest on early instalment payments can accrue for the sole purpose of offsetting interest on late instalment payments for the same year, as discussed in 13.2.2. It applies at the same rate as for late payments (the "high rate" shown in 13.3). If you have fallen behind in your instalments, consider making an extra or early payment to offset the (non-deductible) interest that will otherwise be assessed.

13.6.5 File notice of objection where appropriate

If you have received an assessment or reassessment you disagree with, it is vital that you file a Notice of Objection before the deadline (see 13.5.1). Even if you are in the midst of discussions with Revenue Canada authorities, and even if you have been assured that a reassessment in your favour will be issued, you should file the Notice of Objection. Otherwise your right to appeal vanishes, and any reassessment will be entirely up to Revenue Canada.

13.6.6 Claim changes when return reopened on reassessment

As we have seen (13.5.1), your right to force a reconsideration of your return expires 90 days after an assessment or reassessment is issued or one year after the due date for the return, unless you file a Notice of Objection.

If a routine reassessment is issued during the three-year period during which Revenue Canada can reassess you, your return is then "open" for 90 days. If there is an issue that you want to contest or change, and you are reassessed for some other reason, you may be able to raise this issue and file a Notice of Objection to preserve your rights of appeal. However, you cannot do this where the return was reopened for any of a number of special reasons (such as a carryback of losses from a later year).

13.6.7 Sign a waiver only to the extent necessary

If you are asked by a Revenue Canada auditor to sign a waiver of the three-year reassessment period (see 13.4.3), consider the request carefully and obtain professional advice before agreeing.

First, consider what the auditor's alternative is if you do not sign the waiver. You are under no obligation to file a waiver simply to be "nice". If the three-year reassessment period is about to expire, and the auditor does not yet have enough information to justify a reassessment, it may be to your advantage not to sign the waiver. Bear in mind that a reassessment normally takes some time to work its way through Revenue Canada's internal system, although it can be rushed through in a couple of days in extreme cases.

Second, make sure that the waiver is very specific and waives the three-year period only in respect of the specific issues that are under investigation or dispute. A blanket waiver of all your rights in respect of a given taxation year would not be appropriate.

13.6.8 BE SURE YOU UNDERSTAND THE LEGAL ISSUES WHEN APPEALING

If you are taking an appeal to the Tax Court of Canada, make sure you understand the legal issues involved. Even if you wish to represent yourself or be represented by a friend or relative, consult with a qualified tax professional before the appeal. Many issues in tax law have answers on which all the experts (and the judge!) will agree, yet which will not be obvious to the non-expert.

13.6.9 CONSIDER PAYING BALANCE EVEN WHEN OBJECTING OR APPEALING

Suppose you are contesting an amount of, say, $5,000, but you are not sure whether you will win or not. Although you have filed a Notice of Objection or perhaps an appeal, you are receiving notices from Revenue Canada Collections asking you to pay. Should you?

As long as you have an objection or appeal outstanding, Revenue Canada cannot start collection action, so in practice you need not pay. It may be a good idea to pay, however. The interest rate charged on late payments (see 13.2.2) is likely higher than you would otherwise earn with your money, or higher than the rate at which you must borrow from the bank. If you ultimately succeed in your appeal, you will get back all the funds you paid, plus interest (at the middle rate shown in 13.2.2).

Note also that when you receive a statement from Revenue Canada, you normally have 20 days to pay without further interest charges applying. If you are going to have to pay anyway, you may as well take advantage of this "interest-free" period and pay the balance on the 20th day.

Taxpayers sometimes think that they should not pay an amount in dispute because "that would be an admission of guilt", or because Revenue Canada would then have no incentive to settle the case. Such reasoning is misplaced. You cannot prejudice your case by paying the tax. The determination as to your legal rights is not affected by whether or not the tax has been paid.

The only circumstance where you are better not to have paid your account is where you are applying for a waiver of interest and penalty, at Revenue Canada's discretion, on the grounds of "inability to pay". Once you have paid, it is a little difficult to argue that you cannot find the money to pay your bill and need a waiver of interest to be able to meet the requested payments!

13.7 References

The following publications can be obtained (in person or by telephone request) from your nearest Revenue Canada District Taxation Office:

Interpretation Bulletin IT-241, "Reassessments made after the four-year limit"

Information Circular 75-7R3, "Reassessment of a return of income"

Information Circular 80-7, "Objections and appeals"

Information Circular 92-2, "Guidelines for cancellation and waiver of interest and penalties"

Information Circular 92-3, "Guidelines for refunds beyond the normal three-year period"

Form T1, "General individual income tax return"

Form T1-DD, "Direct deposit request form for individuals"

Form T183, "Authorization and declaration for electronic filing of the individual income tax return"

Form T400A, "Notice of objection"

Form T1013, "Consent Form"

Form T2029, "Waiver in respect of the normal reassessment period"

Brochure, "Electronic Filing (EFILE)—Questions and Answers"

Brochure, "Your Appeal Rights: Under the *Income Tax Act*"

14 Québec Taxation

Planning Tips

- Be aware of differences in the tax systems
- Purchase home furnishings with RHOSP funds
- Invest in FSTQ or the CNTU fund and transfer shares to RRSP
- Claim credit for housing "direct ascendants"
- Claim refundable credit if you adopt a child
- Senior citizens—consider hiring domestic help
- Claim refundable credit for first-time home buyers

Québec is different from all other provinces in that it does not piggy-back on the federal system of personal taxation. Québec residents must file a separate tax return. The Québec Taxation Act (Loi sur les impôts) *is largely modelled on the federal* Income Tax Act, *but there are a number of differences. We review those in 14.2. In 14.3 we discuss the incentive plans that are unique to Québec. These plans — QSSP, QBIC (or SPEQ), CIP (or RIC), FSTQ and others — form a veritable alphabet soup of incentives to investment in various kinds of Québec activities. In 14.4 we discuss the Québec Sales Tax, which is almost identical to the federal GST.*

14.1 Québec income tax rates

Québec provincial income tax rates are listed in Appendix III. There is an **income tax reduction** for low and middle-income taxpayers. This is the reverse of a surtax (discussed in 1.1.1 and 1.7.4). If tax payable after deducting the non-refundable tax credits is less than $10,000, Québec tax is reduced by an amount equal to 2% of the difference. Thus, for someone whose basic Québec tax is $1,000, the reduction is 2% of $9,000, or $180, while for someone with basic Québec tax of $10,000 or more there is no reduction.

Federal tax is reduced by 16.5% of basic federal tax for Québec residents, with the result that the top *federal* marginal tax rate for Québec residents is 26.5% rather than 31.3% (including surtaxes). The combined effect of federal tax, federal surtax and Québec tax rates are provided in Appendix III.

14.2 Differences from federal tax

In this section we highlight the principal differences between Québec and federal tax law that affect personal tax. We present the topics in approximately the same order as the relevant material appears in the rest of the book.

14.2.1 Child-care expenses

There are a number of differences between the federal rules discussed in 1.2.3 and the Québec rules. First, receipts for the child care expenses must be attached to the Québec tax return. For federal tax purposes, Revenue Canada's administrative policy is that they need only be kept on file.

Second, child-care expenses give rise to a refundable **credit** in Québec instead of a deduction. (See 1.1.2 for discussion of refundable credits and the difference between a deduction and a credit.) The credit is on a sliding scale, worth 75% of the expenses for the poorest families, down to 26.4% for families with a household work income of about $48,000 or more. Thus, instead of being more valuable to higher-income families as is the federal deduction, the Québec credit for child-care expenses is more valuable to lower-income families.

Third, the higher-income spouse may claim the credit for Québec tax purposes. (Of course, since it is a credit, there is generally no difference who claims it.) However, the "earned income" limit is still based on the earned income of the *lower*-income spouse. The rules used to calculate the current deduction will apply to determine the amount eligible for the credit.

Finally, the earned income limit is more generous for Québec tax purposes than it is at the federal level. For federal purposes, the limit is two-thirds of the lower-income spouse's earned income; for Québec purposes, the limit is 100% of the lower earned income.

EXAMPLE

Nicole and Daniel have two pre-school children. Daniel earns $70,000 in 1995, and Nicole earns $12,000 working part-time. They pay $8,500 in 1995 in daycare, required to enable them both to work.

For federal purposes, only Nicole can claim a deduction. Her claim is the least of (a) the amount paid—$8,500; (b) $5,000 per child—$10,000; and (c) two-thirds of her earned income—$8,000. She can thus deduct $8,000 from income.

For Québec purposes, either Nicole or Daniel can take the credit, which will be based on the least of (a) the amount paid—$8,500; (b) $5,000 per child—$10,000; and (c) 100% of Nicole's earned income—$12,000. Since their combined work income exceeds $48,000, the credit is thus 26.4% of $8,500, or $2,244.

14.2.2 Legal fees re variance of support payments

Under the federal system, legal fees to enforce payment of alimony or maintenance (support) owing are deductible, but not fees paid to establish a *right* to alimony or maintenance (see 1.2.5). Nor are fees deductible where they are paid in connection with a court application to increase or decrease such payments. Québec taxation is different, in that fees paid in connection with a court application to increase or decrease the level of support are deductible.

14.2.3 SENIOR CITIZENS

As discussed in 1.3.2, the federal credit for persons who are 65 or older is reduced or eliminated for higher-income taxpayers. This restriction has not been copied in Québec. Thus, the Québec old age credit is available no matter how high your income is.

Beginning in 1995, a new refundable credit is available for persons over 65 who hire **domestic employees**. As announced in Québec's 1994 budget, the new credit will be 30% of expenses of up to $10,000 per year (i.e., a maximum credit of $3,000). It will only be available to lower- and middle-income households; it will be reduced by 10¢ for every dollar of family income over $30,000, and so will vanish entirely once family income exceeds $60,000. For senior citizens who hire domestic help, Revenu Québec will remit federal and Québec payroll taxes on behalf of the elderly (including unemployment insurance contributions), so that seniors do not have to handle the paperwork normally associated with hiring an employee. Payroll taxes paid on behalf of the elderly by Revenue Québec reduce the credit. The elderly will not have to withhold the income taxes of the employee. The employee will be required to pay income tax (federal and Québec) when the employee files his or her tax return.

The details of this credit may be adjusted as a result of a pilot project currently underway in Québec. The aims of this pilot study include better identifying the needs of seniors' households and simplifying the administrative burden of hiring an employee.

Also under review is a 1994 Québec budget proposal to permit seniors to delay the payment of municipal property taxes until the property is sold or the senior dies. At time of writing, no further details about this property tax deferral have been announced.

14.2.4 CHARITABLE DONATIONS

Québec provides a 20% credit for charitable donations, in addition to the 17%/29% federal credit discussed in 1.3.4.

However, for Québec purposes there is a special restriction on the credit for gifts of **works of art** made after May 9, 1995. The valuation of the gift is limited to the price the charity receives when it sells the art. Furthermore, the credit can only be claimed (by the donor) in the year the charity sells the art, which must be within five years of the donation. This rule does not apply to donations to certain museums and galleries, recognized artistic organizations, governments or municipalities.

This restriction was designed to curb ongoing abuses where individuals would obtain appraisals entitling them to value their donations at far higher amounts than can actually be obtained by the charity to whom the art is donated. (Typically, the charity in such cases sells the art at an auction, and the entire valuation, donation and auction process is organized for the charity by an art dealer or auctioneer.)

14.2.5 Tuition fees

Tuition fees, which generate non-refundable credits under the federal system (see 1.3.6), are a *deduction* for the student for Québec tax purposes. Thus, they reduce tax at your marginal rate rather than at the same flat rate for everyone.

Unlike the federal government, Québec does not allow the transfer of undeducted tuition fees to the parent. Instead, Québec increases the non-refundable credit for dependent children or other dependants (see 14.2.8) by $1,650 per semester (for up to two semesters) if the dependant is a full-time student at a post-secondary institution.

14.2.6 Person living alone

In addition to credits for oneself and various types of dependants, analogous to those discussed in 1.3.1, Québec allows a credit of $210 for a "person living alone". To qualify, you must be living on your own (i.e., not with a spouse, common-law spouse, roommate, housemate, etc.), or on your own with dependent children whom you claim for tax purposes, and you must attach to your tax return a real estate tax certificate (Relevé 4), a copy of your property tax bills, or Form TP-752.0.1.h.V ("Declaration concerning the maintenance of a self-contained domestic establishment"). If you are separated but you support your spouse, you cannot claim this credit; however, if you pay only child support and no spousal support, you and your spouse can both claim the credit.

14.2.7 Adults housing "direct ascendants"

Québec provides a tax credit of $550 for an adult taxpayer who has a parent, grandparent or great-grandparents living in the same home. The "ascendant" must be 70 or over (or 60 or over and disabled), but there is no requirement that the "ascendant" be financially dependent on the taxpayer or be in a low-income bracket. (In fact, the "ascendant" could be financially supporting the taxpayer who makes the claim! However, the taxpayer making the claim must own or rent the home.) This measure is designed to encourage family support for the elderly. Since the credit is refundable, it will be paid even to a taxpayer who has no Québec tax to pay for the year.

14.2.8 ALLOWANCES FOR CHILDREN

The federal Child Tax Benefit described in 1.5.1 replaced the former dependent child credit and family allowance payments, as well as the former federal Child Tax Credit. Québec has not (yet) harmonized with these changes, so Québec still provides a non-refundable credit for dependent children ($520 for the first child, $480 for subsequent children) as well as provincial family allowance payments.

In an effort to assist families with young children and stimulate population growth in the province, the Québec government also provides a supplementary **monthly allowance** for children under six, as well as an **allowance for newborn children**. These allowances are not taxed for federal or Québec purposes.

The allowance for newborns provides $500 for the first child born or adopted, $1,000 for the second child in the family, and $8,000 for the third and each subsequent child.

The $500 is paid shortly after birth. The $1,000 is paid in two instalments: one when the child is born and one on the child's first birthday. The $8,000 is paid over five years, in 20 quarterly instalments of $400 each following the child's birth.

As well, Québec's "Maternity Benefit Program" offers a $360 supplement to the federal unemployment insurance benefits that are paid to a woman who leaves work temporarily to have a child, provided her gross family income is less than $55,000. This supplement is taxable for both federal and Québec purposes.

These incentives are, strictly speaking, not tax measures at all, but will be of interest to many taxpayers.

14.2.9 ADOPTION EXPENSES

In 1994, a new refundable credit for **adoption expenses** was introduced. For adoptions finalized in 1995 and later years, the credit is 20% of up to $10,000 in expenses paid by you, or by you and your spouse, to a maximum $2,000 credit per child. (For adoptions finalized in 1994, the credit was 20% of up to $5,000 in expenses). Qualifying expenses include court fees, legal fees, travelling and translation expenses (for adoptions from other countries), and fees charged by approved agencies.

14.2.10 MEDICAL EXPENSES

The federal 17% credit for medical expenses was discussed in 1.3.5.

The Québec credit for medical expenses is 20%. The same threshold of $1,614 or 3% of net income applies, before you can claim any expenses. The list of allowable expenses is generally identical to the federal list. In addition, however, if you (or a dependant) require long-term care that can only be provided in a **Québec health establishment located 250 km or more from your residence**, your moving expenses will be allowed as medical expenses by Québec. For this purpose, "moving expenses" are those listed in 1.2.2.

Also, as noted in 14.2.18 below, the taxable benefit for employer-paid private health insurance premiums also qualifies as a medical expense for Québec purposes.

14.2.11 Political contributions

As noted in 1.4.1, many provinces provide credits for contributions to provincial political parties, riding associations and election candidates. In Québec's case, the credit for 1995 is 75% of the first $200 of such contributions and 50% of the next $200, as a credit against Québec tax. The maximum credit is thus $250. (For 1994, the maximum credit was $140).

14.2.12 Real Estate Tax Refund

You may be entitled to a refund of a portion of the property taxes that apply on your dwelling. If you own the property, taxes eligible for the refund include school, water and municipal taxes. If you rent, the eligible amount is that indicated on the Relevé 4 supplied to you by your landlord each year. The credit is claimed on your Québec tax return.

The eligible property tax is reduced by $430 for each spouse, and further reduced to $1,285 if it exceeds that figure. The maximum refund is 40% of this amount, or $514. The refund is then reduced by 3% of you and your spouse's combined net income, subject to various adjustments. Since it is refundable, the real estate tax refund is paid to you even if you have no Québec tax to pay for the year.

14.2.13 Registered Home Ownership Savings Plans (RHOSPs)

RHOSPs were a popular savings plan until 1985, when they were abolished under the federal tax system. Before 1985, contributions to an RHOSP could be deducted (subject to certain dollar limits), and the withdrawals were not taxed at all provided the funds were used to purchase a first home.

When RHOSPs were abolished, the federal rules were changed to allow withdrawals from all existing plans without paying any federal tax. Most Canadians therefore simply withdrew their RHOSP funds. However, Québec did not follow this federal change. For Québec tax purposes, the funds withdrawn must be spent on the purchase of a home or new household furnishings (residential furniture and major appliances). Furnishings are eligible if they are delivered by 60 days after the end of the year. If the funds are not used for one of the above purposes, they are taxed by Québec in the year of withdrawal.

If you withdraw funds from an RHOSP account to make an eligible purchase, you should file form TP-955-V ("Statement of the use of funds from a Registered Home Ownership Savings Plan") with your income tax return for the year of the withdrawal to ensure that the amount withdrawn is not included in your income for Québec tax purposes.

14.2.14 "FIRST HOME" REFUNDABLE TAX CREDIT

In late 1994, the Québec government announced the "**Premier Toit**" ("First Home") refundable tax credit. You must be a **"first-time" buyer**; this term is given the same meaning as under the Home Buyer's Plan (see 2.1.8). In general, you must not have owned a home earlier in the year or during the four previous calendar years. For a newly built home, you can receive up to 20% of your mortgage interest; for an existing home, you can receive up to 10% of the costs of renovation.

A **new home** must meet the following conditions:

- the home is built by a Québec-licensed general contractor and covered by the provincial new home warranty plan
- the home has never been lived in before
- you acquire ownership after December 20, 1994 but **by the end of 1995** (except for a condominium, for which you must have your offer to purchase accepted by the end of 1995 and acquire the unit by June 30, 1996)
- you and/or your spouse begin to live in it, as your **principal place of residence**, within **6 months** of acquisition (or, for condominiums, by the end of 1996)
- the value of the home including the land, when you acquire it, must not exceed **$150,000** (if you are in the Montreal Urban Community) or **$125,000** (outside Montreal)
- you obtain a first mortgage from a recognized financial institution (such as a bank, trust company or savings and credit union)

Once you meet these conditions, your credit is **20% of the first two years of mortgage interest**, to a limit of **$2,000 per year**.

For an **existing home**, your credit is **10% of your renovation expenses**, to a maximum of **$3,000**. In general, the renovation expenses must meet the following conditions:

- the renovations cost at least **$10,000**
- the value of the home including the land, when you acquire it, must not exceed **$135,000** (in Montreal) or **$110,000** (outside Montreal)
- the work involves only the home and is carried out by a Québec-licensed contractor
- the work is **completed within one year** of when you acquire the home
- you and/or your spouse begin to live in it, as your **principal place of residence**, within **6 months** of acquisition (note that this could be a problem if your renovations take a long time and you cannot move in)
- the following expenses are **excluded**: appliances, built-in furnishings, swimming pool, wallpaper, window coverings, fireplace, wood stove, generator, air conditioning system and heat pump.

14.2.15 Québec Sales Tax Credit

Québec offers a sales tax refund similar to the GST credit available to low-income families (see 1.5.2). The refund is $104 for each spouse living together, plus $31 for each dependent child. If you are single, an additional $18 is available if you live alone or with a dependant, plus $53 if you are a single parent with one or more dependants. The total credit is then reduced by 3% of you and your spouse's combined net income, subject to various adjustments. The credit is refundable and is claimed on your Québec tax return.

Québec also offers a sales tax rebate that parallels the GST rebate for employees and partners (see 17.9.4).

14.2.16 Cumulative Net Investment Loss

As we saw in 4.4.3.2, investment expenses and tax shelter writeoffs create a cumulative net investment loss (CNIL), which reduces your ability to claim the $500,000 capital gains exemption.

For Québec tax purposes, the special investment incentives, which we will discuss in 14.3, are *not* included in your CNIL calculation. That is, they will not affect your ability to claim the capital gains exemption on your Québec tax return.

The incentives in question are the deductions you claim under the Québec Stock Savings Plan, the Cooperative Investment Plan, Québec Business Investment Companies, certain scientific research and development expenses, certified Québec film and television productions, and resource exploration expenses incurred in Québec. These collectively form the "strategic economic investment account", or "compte d'investissements stratégiques pour l'économie" (CISE).

14.2.17 RESOURCE EXPLORATION EXPENSES

For Québec tax purposes, a 125% deduction is allowed for certain resource exploration costs incurred in Québec. In addition, a further 50% deduction is granted for certain surface mining exploration costs incurred in Québec. These deductions apply to costs incurred in Québec 60 days after year end. This terminates at the end of 1995.

As well, a portion of a corporation's financing costs (such as brokerage, legal and accounting fees) may be deducted by an individual who invests in flow-through shares of the corporation or in a partnership acquiring such shares.

Note that shares that entitle you to a QSSP deduction (see 14.3.1) are not eligible for a deduction for flow-through resource exploration expenses.

There is also a special exemption from Québec tax on the capital gain resulting from certain flow-through share expenses incurred by the end of 1995. Where flow-through shares are sold, any amount received normally gives rise to a capital gain. The details of the exemption are complex, and you should get professional advice if you are selling flow-through shares acquired between May 14, 1992 and the end of 1993.

14.2.18 EMPLOYER-PAID PRIVATE HEALTH INSURANCE

As we saw in 6.1.1, employer contributions to a private health services plan are non-taxable employee benefits for federal purposes. These contributions are, however, taxable for Québec tax purposes. Thus, if your employer pays for your group sickness, drug or dental plan, the value of the benefit will be included in your employment income on your Rélevé 1 and must be reported on your Québec tax return, even though it does not appear on your T4 for federal income tax purposes. You (or your spouse) can claim the taxable benefit as a medical expense on your Québec tax return.

14.2.19 OVERSEAS EMPLOYMENT TAX DEDUCTION

We discussed the federal overseas employment tax credit in 6.8. The Québec rules accomplish essentially the same goals of not taxing certain income earned while working on projects outside Canada, but do so rather differently.

First, the Québec system allows the overseas income as a deduction, rather than allowing a tax credit for a percentage of it. For each consecutive 30-day period that the employee works outside Canada on a qualified project, $^1/_{12}$ of the income earned abroad in the year can be deducted.

Second, foreign living allowances are completely tax exempt, provided they do not exceed one-half of the income earned abroad.

Third, the recognized activities for purposes of the deduction are broader than under the federal system. As well as the projects that qualify for federal purposes, the installation of computer or office automation systems or data communications systems, and the provision of scientific and technical services, entitle you to the deduction for Québec purposes.

14.2.20 ARTISTS' DEDUCTION FROM COPYRIGHT INCOME

If you are a painter, writer, performer or other artist, a new deduction is available as of 1995 that effectively exempts from Québec tax a portion of your income from your original copyrights. The deduction is limited to $15,000 a year, and is reduced by 1.5 times the amount of the eligible copyright income over $20,000. Thus, it is effectively eliminated for artists who earn over $30,000 in copyright income. To be eligible for this credit, you must be eligible for membership in one of several recognized associations of artists.

14.2.21 RENTAL EXPENSES—DOCUMENTATION

If you report rental income (or loss), and you claim any expenses for renovation, improvement, maintenance or repair of the property, you must include with your Québec income tax return form TP-1086.R.1.1-V ("Statement of Labour Costs with Respect to a Rental Building or Commercial Premises") with the contractor's name, address, social insurance number (if an individual) and QST registration number as well as the amount paid. This measure is designed to combat tax evasion in the contracting and renovation sectors.

14.2.22 MINIMUM TAX

The Québec alternative minimum tax (AMT) differs from the federal AMT (see Chapter 11) in two ways. First, the minimum tax rate is 20%, while the federal rate is 17%.

Second, certain tax benefits, such as deductions for resource exploration in Québec and investment tax credits for research and development, are not considered tax preferences for minimum tax purposes.

14.2.23 INSTALMENTS

Québec instalment requirements are parallel to those for federal tax described in 13.2.2, with some minor differences.

The penalty for late or insufficient instalments is an extra 10% in addition to the normal interest rate. This penalty is substantially higher than the federal penalty, so if you can only pay part of your instalments, you are better off to pay your Québec instalments on time.

The determination of who has to pay instalments is the same as under the federal system, as outlined in 13.2.2. Instalments are required where your balance of Québec tax owing at the end of the year exceeds $1,200 for both the current year and either of the previous two years.

For Québec residents, quarterly *federal* tax instalments are payable if you have federal taxes owing of $1,200 owing in the current year and either of the previous two years. Since Québec tax can be higher or lower than federal tax for any individual (depending on many factors including those outlined throughout 14.2 above), there can be cases where you must remit federal instalments but not Québec instalments, or vice versa.

14.2.24 HEALTH SERVICES FUND CONTRIBUTION

Your income from all sources (other than employment income) is subject to a "contribution" to the Health Services Fund (i.e., another tax). The income taxed is generally the total shown on your income tax return including business income, investment income, pension or retirement income and taxable capital gains, but not employment income or old age security. Certain specific deductions are permitted to arrive at the base amount for the contribution, and a further $5,000 exemption is allowed.

The Health Services Fund contribution is calculated on a graduated scale, which tops out at $1,000 once your income exceeds $125,000. In the top bracket, the contribution is $150 plus 1% of the excess of your income over $40,000 (but not over $125,000). Your contribution is then offset by a non-refundable tax credit of 20%.

If you are required to pay income tax instalments (see 14.2.23), you must also pay quarterly instalments on your Health Services Fund contribution. Instalments are based on the contribution paid for the preceding year or your estimated contribution for the year, whichever is lower.

14.3 SPECIAL QUÉBEC INCENTIVES

14.3.1 QUÉBEC STOCK SAVINGS PLANS (QSSP OR REA)

14.3.1.1 WHAT IS A QSSP?

A QSSP is a plan under which you invest in **new public share issues** of Québec-based corporations and receive a deduction for your investment for Québec tax purposes. Such a plan is also known as a RÉA (Régime d'Épargne Actions).

14.3.1.2 WHAT KINDS OF SHARES QUALIFY?

For you to be entitled to the deduction in respect of any given investment, it must meet the following conditions:

- the corporation is a "qualified corporation", essentially a Canadian corporation whose central management is in Québec (or which pays more than half its wages to employees in Québec), which has at least five full-time non-insider employees, and less than half of the assets of which are in passive investments
- the corporation has assets of at least $2 million and less than $250 million (referred to as a "growth corporation").
- you buy the shares as part of a public share issue
- the shares are common shares with voting rights in all circumstances, and there are no conditions entitling the corporation or anyone else to redeem or purchase the shares
- you pay for the shares in full (of course, you may borrow money for this purpose)
- the share certificate is sent directly to the dealer who maintains custody of your QSSP

As noted, QSSP shares must be common shares. Before 1995, unsecured preferred shares and debentures that were fully convertible into common shares could entitle you to a reduced deduction. As of 1995, there is no deduction for investing in convertible securities.

14.3.1.3 HOW MUCH CAN YOU DEDUCT?

The deduction for your QSSP investments applies for Québec tax purposes only. Its maximum value is therefore 26.4% of the amount you deduct, if your income is over about $60,000 (the exact threshold depends on the credits you can claim). **The total deduction claimed may not exceed 10% of your net income** for the year.

A special additional deduction of **25% of the investment** is available if you are an **employee** of the corporation in which you are investing. To qualify for this additional deduction, you must buy the shares through a stock ownership plan that offers financing and that is available only to employees who (together with their families) each own less than 5% of the shares of the corporation. Your total deduction is still subject to the limitation of 10% of your net income.

A further **50% or 100% deduction** is available where the qualifying corporation finances a Québec certified film or television production or is a "regional venture capital corporation" that finances businesses outside the Hull-Montreal-Sherbrooke-Québec City triangle. This additional deduction is *not* subject to the ceiling of 10% of net income. However, the total deduction can never exceed 200% of your investment.

14.3.1.4 WHAT HAPPENS WHEN YOU SELL THE SHARES?

If you sell QSSP shares in the year you acquire them or in the **next two calendar years**, the amount of your deduction will be included back in your income for Québec tax purposes. This is a strong incentive to hold the shares until at least the beginning of the third year.

You may, however, sell the shares and replace them with other qualifying shares, and to the extent the value of your investment is not reduced, you will not be taxed. The replacement shares may be purchased on the secondary market, provided they are shares of a "QSSP growth corporation" (between $2 million and $250 million in assets).

If you have shares of corporations with *over* $2.5 billion in assets in your QSSP account (as a result of investments made in earlier years), they were deemed for tax purposes to have been withdrawn from your account on January 1, 1994.

Shares in corporations with assets between $250 million and $2.5 billion are no longer eligible as QSSP investments. However, such shares can remain in your QSSP account if you acquired them when they were eligible (before May 20, 1993).

14.3.1.5 INVESTMENT CLUBS AND INVESTMENT FUNDS

The rules permit taxpayers to form groups, known as **investment clubs**, which pool their members' assets for investing in QSSP shares, thus reducing the risk. The deductions are granted to the investment club, and then allocated to the individual members.

QSSP investment funds (**QIFs**), which are similar to mutual funds, can also be formed for the purposes of investing in QSSP shares. When a QIF undertakes to invest at least 50% of its funds in common shares of QSSP growth corporations, you can claim a tax deduction for the year you invest in the QIF, even though the QIF might not invest in the QSSP shares until the following year. By investing in a QIF, you can receive the tax benefits of a QSSP while diversifying your investments.

14.3.2 QUÉBEC BUSINESS INVESTMENT COMPANIES (QBIC OR SPEQ)

14.3.2.1 WHAT IS A QBIC?

The QSSP, as we have seen, encourages investment in publicly-traded corporations. The QBIC, on the other hand, is a vehicle for investing capital in **private** corporations, typically ones that are newly formed and not yet ready to go public.

A QBIC is more commonly referred to as a SPEQ (Société de placements dans l'entreprise québécoise). It is a private investment corporation whose purpose is to invest in new shares of "eligible corporations" (see below). It must be registered with the Société de développement industriel.

14.3.2.2 WHAT CAN A QBIC INVEST IN?

To qualify as an "eligible corporation", any corporation in which the QBIC invests must:

- be a Canadian-controlled private corporation
- have assets of less than $25 million, or shareholders' equity of no more than $10 million
- operate mainly in one of the following sectors: manufacturing, tourism, tertiary growth, export, aquiculture, industrial incubator, environmental protection, or film or television production or distribution
- have its central management in Québec
- pay at least 75% of its total wages to employees of an establishment in Québec
- not be "related" to (meaning essentially under common or same-family control with) the QBIC
- issue common shares with full voting rights to the QBIC

The total invested by QBICs in any one eligible corporation (or group of associated corporations) may not exceed $5 million ($2.5 million for investments made before May 10, 1995). The QBIC is also required to hold the shares for at least two years before selling them.

14.3.2.3 HOW MUCH CAN YOU DEDUCT?

When you invest in a QBIC, you receive a basic deduction for 125% of the QBIC's eligible investments, in proportion to your interest in the QBIC. However, your deduction may not exceed 30% of your net income.

EXAMPLE

Jean and four of his friends get together and invest $20,000 each in a QBIC. The QBIC invests $60,000 (60% of its funds) in eligible corporations in 1995.

Jean's deduction for 1995 will be limited to $15,000, which is 125% of 60% of his investment. If Jean's net income is less than $50,000, his deduction will be reduced to 30% of his net income.

A QBIC deduction that cannot be used because of the net income limitation can be carried forward and used in any of the next five years, subject to the same limitation.

Additional deductions

A number of additional deductions, beyond the basic 125% of the investment, are available for incentive purposes. However, in no case can the total deduction exceed 200% of the investment.

First, where the investor is an employee of an eligible corporation, an additional 25% deduction is available for investments of the QBIC in that corporation or a subsidiary of it. Second, an additional 25% deduction is available for investments in a "regional QBIC", or a QBIC which invests exclusively in "regional corporations". ("Regional" refers to the remoter areas of Québec, and covers most of the province outside the Hull-Montreal-Sherbrooke-Québec City triangle.) Third, an additional 50% or 100% deduction is available where the eligible corporation finances Québec certified film or television productions.

In all of these cases, the additional deduction is available to you as an investor in the QBIC. However, the 30%-of-net-income limitation continues to apply, except in the case of Québec certified film and television production financing.

14.3.3 COOPERATIVE INVESTMENT PLANS (CIP OR RIC)

Cooperative Investment Plans, or Régimes d'investissement coopératif, are parallel to QBICs. They provide incentives to investment by members and workers in units issued by cooperatives governed by the *Cooperatives Act*—typically producing, processing, agricultural or workers' cooperatives. Various conditions and requirements must be met for the units to qualify.

14.3.4 LABOUR-SPONSORED VENTURE CAPITAL CORPORATIONS

Unlike the plans we have looked at so far, the FSTQ (Fonds de solidarité des travailleurs du Québec) is a labour-sponsored venture capital corporation that entitles you to tax benefits from both the federal and the Québec tax systems. The federal credit was discussed at 5.4.8.

If you invest in new common shares issued by the FSTQ (some publications use the acronym FTQ), you receive a 20% federal tax credit and a 20% Québec tax credit. Note that since this is a credit rather than a deduction (see 1.1.2), it is worth exactly that much to you regardless of your marginal tax rate, provided you otherwise have tax to pay.

The amount of either credit may not exceed $1,000 in any given year. This effectively limits your investment to a maximum of

$5,000, which will provide you with a combined $2,000 tax credit. You may, in addition, transfer your shares to an RRSP offered by the FSTQ.

You may not otherwise transfer or sell your shares in the FSTQ, unless you are in financial difficulty due to unusual circumstances. However, once you turn 60 and are retired, or once you turn 65, or after your death, the FSTQ will redeem the shares on request.

The Québec government announed in its May 1995 budget that the Confederation of National Trade Unions (**CNTU**) will be permitted to set up a fund similar to the FSTQ. It will operate under the same rules and will be eligible for both the 20% federal credit and the 20% provincial credit.

14.3.5 Worker gain sharing plans

Québec offers a credit and deduction for "worker gain sharing plans" (profit-sharing plans). Companies wanting these benefits must obtain a certificate from the ministère de l'Industrie, du Commerce et de la Technologie as well as registering their plan with the ministère du Revenu. The company must be a Canadian-controlled private corporation with less than $25 million in assets or no more than $10 million in shareholders' equity.

To qualify, a gain sharing plan must allow employees to receive cash compensation based on the results of the business as a whole. The formula must have been proposed to all employees and agreed to by a majority of them. As well, the business must have progressed through some of the stages of a "total quality approach" aimed at improving productivity.

Employees can deduct amounts received from the employer under the gain sharing plan, up to $3,000 per year, with a limit of $6,000 over five years. The **employer** can receive a 15% credit against Québec tax for the amounts paid to the employee, provided it has less than $25 million in assets or less than $10 million in net shareholder's equity. The credit for employers is also limited to a five-year period. Employees who own more than 5% of the shares of the employer do not qualify for the tax benefits.

14.4 Québec Sales Tax

As of July 1, 1992, Québec "harmonized" its retail sales tax with the federal Goods and Services Tax (GST), which is discussed in detail in Chapter 17. However, there are some differences. In an attempt to simplify the Québec Sales Tax ("QST") system, the Québec government announced significant changes in its 1995 budget. The main object of the new measures is to eliminate most of the differences between the GST and QST systems.

14.4.1 THE TAX RATE

The QST rate is nominally 6.5%, while the GST rate is 7%. However, the QST is calculated on the **GST-included price** of all supplies. As a result, the 6.5% rate is really 6.955%, leading to a combined GST/QST rate of 13.955%.

EXAMPLE

A store sells a radio priced at $100.

The GST of 7% is applied first, for a total of $107. The 6.5% QST then applies to the $107, and comes to $6.96. The combined tax is thus $13.96.

(Before May 13, 1994, the QST applied at two rates—8% for goods, and 4% for most services and real estate.)

14.4.2 CATEGORIES OF SALES

Like the GST, the QST has three categories of sales: taxable, zero-rated and exempt. Until July 31, 1995, the QST also had a fourth category, "non-taxable".

Taxable, zero-rated and exempt supplies are essentially the same as under the GST, except that **financial services** are zero-rated under the QST but exempt under the GST. (See 17.2.1 and 17.2.2.) As well, although the rules are the same, the zero-rating of sales to **non-residents** is different because "non-resident" under the QST means not resident in *Québec* rather than not resident in *Canada*.

Until July 31, 1995, **non-taxable supplies** were:

- movable property sold to a QST registrant for resale or rental in its existing form (say, sale of a television by a wholesaler to a retailer)
- goods sold to a registrant for incorporation into other goods for supply (say, sale of electronic parts to a manufacturer for use in a television it will sell)
- services acquired by a QST registrant for the purpose of re-supply
- real property sold to a registrant for resale purposes

The "non-taxable" category was eliminated as of August 1, 1995, meaning that, like the GST, the QST is charged at every stage of the production and distribution chain. Purchasers of these supplies are generally entitled to a full input tax refund of QST paid. The new measure will not increase the tax burden of most businesses, but it may adversely affect their cash flow.

14.4.3 INPUT TAX REFUNDS

Most businesses recover virtually all GST paid in the form of "input tax credits" (see 17.1 and 17.3.1). Similarly, QST paid by businesses can be recovered as an "input tax refund" (ITR) . However, for large businesses (annual taxable sales over $6 million) there are some very significant exceptions until December 1996. In general, no ITR can be claimed by large businesses for the following:

- road vehicles registered for use on public roads, and fuel for such vehicles
- electricity, gas, steam and combustibles (except where used directly in production activities)
- telephone and telecommunications services (except for 1-800 telephone services and related telecommunications services)
- meals and entertainment

These limitations used to apply to all businesses, but were eliminated as of August 1, 1995 for businesses with annual taxable sales under $6 million. For large businesses they will be eliminated as of December 1996, at which point the QST will be almost identical to the GST for most purposes.

Provincial taxes on insurance premiums are not QST as such, and so no ITR is available for them (for any size business).

14.4.4 ADMINISTRATION

The Québec government (Revenu Québec) administers and collects both the GST and the QST in Québec.

Before August 1995, larger businesses had to file QST returns monthly. Where the QST collected for the previous year was $20,000 or less, the business could file quarterly; where it was $2,500 or less, the business could file annually. Since these thresholds were lower than for the GST, many businesses that filed GST returns on a quarterly or annual basis were required to file monthly QST returns. When the GST and QST return were due on the same date, they could be filed on the same form (with any refund on one being usable as a credit against an amount owing on the other).

As of August 1995, businesses and organizations generally use the same filing period for QST purposes that they use for GST purposes. A registrant's QST filing period is now determined on the basis of taxable supplies made in Canada during the fiscal year, as under the GST system (see 17.5). Thus, most registrants can file combined GST/QST returns as of August 1, 1995. For now, however, combined GST/QST filing is not available for registrants with fiscal periods (i.e., accounting periods) that do not coincide with the calendar year or calendar quarter. According to Revenue Québec, these registrants will probably be able to file combined GST/QST returns by July, 1996.

14.4.5 MISCELLANEOUS RULES

Like the GST, sales are normally taxable only if made by a business. However, the sale of a road vehicle (such as an automobile) by a private individual, even where the vehicle was not used in a business, is taxed.

The value of a used road vehicle, for QST purposes, cannot be less than the *Canadian Red Book* (or for motorcycles: *Canadian Motorcycle Dealer's Blue Book*) price minus $500. Thus, if you buy a car privately, you cannot evade tax by reporting an artificially low sale price; QST on its fair market value will be collected when you register the transfer with the Société de l'assurance automobile du Québec.

For GST purposes, a supplier with less than $30,000 of annual sales need not register (see 17.2.3). As of August 1995, the same rule applies for QST purposes. Before August 1995, this rule applied for QST purposes, but only if 90% or more of the supplier's revenue was from services, immovables or incorporeal property (as opposed to corporeal movable property). Special rules will be adopted to ensure that persons no longer required to be QST registrants can cancel their registration without adverse effects (eg., regarding the remittance of previously claimed ITRs)

As with the GST, sales of new housing are taxable while used residential property is exempt. (Where the new home sale agreement was signed before May 13, 1994, the QST is 4% rather than 6.5%.) A rebate is available for homes priced $175,000 or less, to effectively reduce the QST from 6.5% to 4%. The rebate is phased out for more expensive homes and eliminated entirely for homes costing $200,000 or more. The rebate is similar to that under the GST (see 17.4), but the dollar thresholds are lower.

As with the GST, certain "selected public service bodies" are eligible for a partial rebate of QST paid. For QST paid after May 9, 1995, the rebate rates are:

Municipalities	43%
Hospitals	51.5%
Schools, public colleges, universities	47%
Other charities, qualifying non-profit organizations	50%

There are many other special rules and the 1995 Québec budget introduced a host of changes to the QST system. If you operate a business in Québec, you should obtain professional advice regarding the QST.

14.5 PLANNING OPPORTUNITIES

14.5.1 BE AWARE OF DIFFERENCES IN THE TAX SYSTEMS

You should review the differences between the federal and the Québec income tax systems, as highlighted in 14.2. Be cautious of the possible Québec tax implications of any step you take for federal tax purposes.

14.5.2 PURCHASE HOME FURNISHINGS WITH RHOSP FUNDS

If you still have a RHOSP and have not bought a house, consider buying furniture or appliances with the funds (see 14.2.13). No matter when in the year you withdraw the funds, you have until 60 days after the end of the year to take delivery of the goods without triggering tax on the RHOSP withdrawal.

14.5.3 INVEST IN FSTQ OR THE NEW CNTU FUND AND TRANSFER SHARES TO RRSP

Consider a $5,000 investment in the FSTQ or the CNTU fund once it is available (see 5.4.8 and 14.3.4), along with a simultaneous transfer of the FSTQ shares to an RRSP. The investment will generate a credit of $2,000 (combined federal and Québec). The contribution of $5,000 worth of shares to an RRSP will give you a $5,000 deduction, worth about $2,650 if you are in the top combined federal/Québec tax bracket. The net cost of the shares to you will only be about $350 (see 5.7.6).

This strategy will be particularly useful if you are not otherwise contributing the maximum to an RRSP, and, therefore, still have room to contribute. It may also be very attractive if you are nearing age 60 and close to retiring.

14.5.4 CLAIM CREDIT FOR HOUSING "DIRECT ASCENDANTS"

If you are eligible to claim a credit for an elderly parent, grandparent or great-grandparent living with you, make sure you claim this credit on your Québec tax return (see 14.2.7).

14.5.5 CLAIM REFUNDABLE CREDIT IF YOU ADOPT A CHILD

If you adopt a child, make sure to claim the credit of up to $2,000. Since it is refundable, it is available even if you have no tax to pay for the year. The credit was introduced to help finance the expenses associated with adopting children from overseas, but is available even for local adoptions. You will have to keep records of your expenses and claim only those that qualify.

14.5.6 SENIOR CITIZENS—CONSIDER HIRING DOMESTIC HELP

If you are over 65 and your income (combined with your spouse's) is well under $60,000, consider hiring someone to help with your domestic activities. Up to 30% of the domestic's salary can be refunded to you by Revenue Québec (see 14.2.3). This credit will make cleaning, cooking and personal care help much more affordable for seniors with modest incomes.

14.5.7 Claim refundable credit for "first-time" home buyers

If you acquire a home (or sign a deal to buy a new condominium) before the end of 1995, you may be able to recover up to 20% of the first two years' mortgage interest or up to 10% of renovation expenses under the "First Home" (Premier Toit) program. There are numerous conditions and restrictions, however; see 14.2.14. Be sure you understand all these rules, including the home value dollar thresholds and the deadlines, if you are shopping around for a new home.

Note that it is quite acceptable to use the First Home program and also use funds from your RRSP under the Home Buyer's Plan (see 2.1.8). Indeed, the definition of "first-time buyer" is the same for both plans so that the same taxpayers can use both.

14.6 References

Revenu Québec has offices in Hull, Jonquière, Montréal, Québec, Rimouski, Rouyn-Noranda, Sainte-Foy, Sept-Îles, Sherbrooke, Sorel, Trois-Rivières and Toronto.

Revenu Québec produces a number of publications to assist taxpayers, the most notable of which is the *Guide and General Information* book that accompanies the provincial income tax return.

15 U.S. Citizens in Canada

Planning Tips

- File joint return where appropriate
- Review income splitting arrangements to prevent double taxation
- Watch out for ownership of Canadian mutual funds, and other Canadian corporations earning passive income
- Keep records of expenses deductible on your U.S. return
- Claim foreign earned income exclusion if beneficial
- Aim for maximum foreign tax credit
- Watch out for U.S. AMT liability
- Elect out of instalment sale rules where appropriate
- Be cautious of using the $500,000 capital gains exemption
- Consider steps to take on departure from Canada
- Plan for U.S. estate and gift taxes
- Watch shareholder-corporation transactions
- Beware of differences between Canadian and U.S. rules governing retirement income
- Seek professional tax advice before moving to Canada

In this chapter we address the difficult and complicated tax problems of the United States citizen who lives in Canada. We can only scratch the surface, due to the interaction of two highly complex tax systems which are both subject to continual change.

The discussion in this chapter is based on current law. In 1995, the Democrats released a number of tax proposals that may retroactively affect U.S. estate and income taxes for Americans who renounce their citizenship or who are beneficiaries of foreign trusts. The Republicans issued a number of other tax proposals in 1995 which would, among other things, cut the maximum capital gains tax rate and introduce new child and marriage tax credits. Given Washington's current political mix, whether any of these proposals will become law is uncertain at the time of writing. You should seek professional advice if you are a U.S. citizen living in Canada.

15.1 Two systems of taxation

The income tax systems of the United States and Canada are similar in some general ways, but very different in their details. A U.S. citizen resident in Canada must deal with both systems.

The United States is one of the few countries in the world that taxes its **citizens** on their worldwide income, whether or not they are physically in the United States. Canada taxes only Canadian **residents** on their world income; non-residents (including Canadian citizens) are taxed by Canada only on certain income from Canadian sources.

The result is that U.S. citizens living in Canada must file returns under both systems, and often must pay tax to both governments. Safeguards exist to prevent double taxation: clearly, you could not afford to pay a large percentage of your income to each country! But the safeguards, which are outlined in 15.2 below, are not perfect. Much of this chapter deals with the double taxation problems that arise due to differences between the two systems' ways of calculating income and tax.

In general, you will find that U.S. taxation is lower than Canadian. U.S. federal tax currently reaches a maximum rate of 39.6%. Canadian federal tax reaches 31.32% (including surtaxes), but as a resident of Canada you also have a provincial tax liability, which raises the top rate to 50% or more, depending on your province of residence. As a U.S. citizen not resident in any state, you have no liability for any U.S. state tax except, perhaps, to the extent you have income arising in a state.

The 1995 U.S. income tax rates for single people with no dependants and for married couples filing joint returns (see 15.7.1) are:

Single (see 15.7.1) Taxable income	Federal tax
$ 0–$23,350	15%
$23,350–$56,550	$3,502.50 plus 28% of excess over $23,350
$56,550–$117,950	$12,798.50 plus 31% of excess over $56,550
$117,950–$256,500	$31,832.50 plus 36% of excess over $117,950
$256,500 and up	$81,710.50 plus 39.6% of excess over $256,500

Married filing joint returns (see 15.7.1) Taxable income	Federal tax
$ 0–$39,000	15%
$39,000–$94,250	$5,850 plus 28% of excess over $39,000
$94,250–$143,600	$21,320 plus 31% on excess over $94,250
$143,600–$256,500	$36,618.50 plus 36% of excess over $143,600
$256,500 and up	$77,262.5 plus 39.6% of excess over $256,500

(The rates for other types of taxpayers are different; see 15.7.1 for a discussion of the types of filers.)

The highest effective marginal rate is thus 39.6% for most taxpayers. Due to certain adjustments such as a phaseout of personal exemptions and a limitation on itemized deductions for high-income taxpayers, the effective marginal rate can be higher still in some cases.

The 39.6% marginal rate applies to taxable income over $250,000 regardless of filing status. However, married individuals filing separately (see 15.7.1) become subject to the surtax at taxable income in excess of $125,000.

15.2 BASIC MECHANISMS FOR AVOIDING DOUBLE TAXATION

There are three mechanisms in place to help you avoid paying tax twice on the same income.

15.2.1 FOREIGN EARNED INCOME EXCLUSION (U.S. TAX LAW)

The simplest way to avoid double taxation is the U.S. "foreign earned income exclusion". You may exclude from your income, on your U.S. tax return, up to US$70,000 of "earned income" (employment or services income) earned from services provided outside the United States.

If you do not have any income other than your employment or professional services income, and your annual income is under US$70,000, this exclusion will be all you need to escape U.S. tax entirely. You must still file a U.S. return (see 15.7.2 below) and claim the exclusion.

EXAMPLE

Gordon is a citizen of the United States who lives in Vancouver. He works as an accountant and earns Cdn$80,000 in 1995. (Assume the Canadian dollar is worth an average of U.S. 72 cents through 1995.) He has no other income.

On his U.S. tax return, Gordon will report his income of approximately US$57,600. He will then elect to use the foreign earned income exclusion, and will deduct the same $57,600, to show a total income of $0. As a result he will pay no tax to the United States. His Canadian tax return will not be affected by his U.S. citizenship.

Note that if you file as "married filing jointly" (see 15.7.1 below), you and your spouse can *each* claim up to US$70,000 for purposes of the exclusion against your respective earned incomes. This can be done even if your spouse is not a U.S. citizen.

The regulations make it possible to elect the foreign earned income exclusion on late-filed returns in a number of cases.

15.2.2 FOREIGN TAX CREDIT (BOTH U.S. AND CANADIAN LAW)

The foreign tax credit is a unilateral mechanism provided by many countries to prevent double taxation. Both the U.S. and Canada provide foreign tax credits. While the details differ, the concept is basically the same for both.

Consider the U.S. foreign tax credit as an example. If you are subject to U.S. taxation (because you are a citizen), but you have paid tax to Canada on **Canadian-source income**, you can, in general, claim a foreign tax credit to offset your U.S. tax on that income. Your credit cannot be greater than the Canadian tax you paid.

EXAMPLE

Ron is a U.S. citizen who lives and works in Winnipeg. He earns Cdn$1,389 (equivalent to US$1,000) in interest on his Winnipeg bank account in 1995. He also receives a salary in Canada and income from investments in the United States.

Ron will be required to include the US$1,000 in his income for U.S. tax purposes. (Because it is investment income and not earned income, it is not eligible for the foreign earned income exclusion.) Assume that he is in the 31% bracket (i.e., his taxable income is less than $117,950 and he is single), so his additional U.S. tax is US$310. If he is in a 50% tax bracket in Canada, so that he has paid the equivalent of US$500 to Canada (and Manitoba) on the income, he can receive a foreign tax credit for the full US$310 on his U.S. return. On the other hand, if his Canadian tax rate were lower and he paid only US$270 to Canada (and Manitoba), he could only claim US$270 as his foreign tax credit.

The above example is highly simplified, but it demonstrates the basic effect of the credit. When you total up the tax to both countries (including provincial and state tax) and the foreign tax credits of each, you should end up paying a total that is equal to the higher of the two countries' rates of tax.

The Canadian foreign tax credit follows essentially the same principles. Since Canada taxes Canadian residents on their worldwide income, Ron in our example will have to report his U.S.-source investment income on his Canadian tax return. He will then be eligible for a foreign tax credit for U.S. taxes paid on his U.S. source investment income to offset the Canadian tax that applies. (Note that each country's foreign tax credit applies only to foreign taxes on income from sources *outside* that country.)

The details of the foreign tax credit rules are very complicated. For U.S. foreign tax credit purposes, your non-U.S. income is grouped into several different "baskets", or pools, and a separate foreign tax credit is available for each. Expenses, deductions and Canadian taxes must be allocated to each basket using prescribed allocation rules. Canadian tax you have paid on your employment income, for example, generally cannot be used to create a foreign tax credit for tax on investment income or capital gains.

For U.S. foreign tax credit purposes, excess (non-creditable) foreign tax can be carried back two years and forward five years. For Canadian foreign tax credit purposes, excess foreign tax can, depending on the income to which it relates, be deducted from income in the current year or carried forward to be used as a credit in future years.

If you receive income for services performed in both the U.S. and Canada, it is a good idea to keep a diary to record U.S. and Canadian work days.

If you have various sources of income and need to claim a foreign tax credit under one or both systems, you should consult a professional adviser.

15.2.3 CANADA-U.S. TAX TREATY

The third safeguard against double taxation is the Canada-U.S. **tax treaty** (also known as a tax convention). Both Canada and the U.S. have such treaties with many countries. The purpose of a tax treaty is twofold: to prevent double taxation, and to reduce tax evasion by allowing exchange of taxpayer information between the two governments.

The Canada-U.S. treaty, for the most part, does not apply to United States citizens resident in Canada. However, a number of specific rules do apply.

For example, the treaty allows a U.S. citizen resident in Canada to defer U.S. taxation of funds accruing in an **RRSP**. Were it not for this provision, U.S. tax could apply to the accruing funds, which are specifically exempt from Canadian tax under the RRSP rules (see 2.1.5 and 15.3.4). A Protocol (amendment) to the Canada-U.S. Treaty signed on March 17, 1995 will extend the deferral election to RPPs, RRIFs and other retirement arrangements. If the Protocol is ratified (passed into law) before the end of 1995 as currently expected, this change will be effective for 1996 and later years.

Another treaty provision clarifies how to calculate the foreign tax credit (see 15.2.2) where you are claiming credits on both returns, and each one depends on the tax paid to the other country (which in turn depends on the credit available, leading to circularity). The rule is that you compute your U.S. tax first, without taking your U.S. foreign tax credit into account. Then you calculate your Canadian tax, and base the Canadian foreign tax credit on that U.S. tax figure. Finally, you go back to your U.S. return, and claim your U.S. foreign tax credit based on the Canadian tax actually paid. If you have U.S.-source interest, dividend or royalty income, this treaty provision may even result in a U.S. foreign tax credit for a portion of the Canadian and provincial taxes paid on your U.S. source income.

Yet another provision in the treaty deals with **child support** paid by a U.S. resident to a resident of Canada. For U.S. tax purposes, such support (as distinct from alimony or maintenance that goes to support the spouse) is not included in income. As a result, the treaty provides that child support will not be included in income for Canadian tax purposes either. This applies whether or not you are a U.S. citizen.

If you are using the treaty to reduce your U.S. tax liability, you are generally required to disclose the specific details on your U.S. tax return. If you do not, the treaty benefits can be denied.

15.3 Differences in Calculating Income

In theory, the foreign tax credit mechanism prevents you from paying tax twice. However, there are many differences between U.S. and Canadian calculations of income for tax purposes. These differences can lead to unexpected tax liabilities.

15.3.1 Deductions on U.S. Return That Are Not Available in Canada

Home mortgage interest may normally be deducted on your U.S. tax return, while it is not deductible in Canada, except where you took on the mortgage to make outside investments, or to the extent you can claim an office in your home (see 5.3 and 7.2.7). The same applies to **property taxes**.

State taxes, which may be imposed to the extent you reside in or having income arising in a U.S. state, are generally deductible for U.S. income tax purposes, while provincial income taxes are not deductible in Canada.

Certain employment-related expenses not available in Canada can also be deducted on your U.S. return.

15.3.2 Deductions on Canadian Return That Are Not Available in the U.S.

As we saw in 5.3, **interest paid** may be deducted for Canadian tax purposes where the funds were borrowed for the purposes of earning income from investments. There is no strict requirement that you actually earn more income from your investments than you spend in interest.

For U.S. tax purposes, your investment expense deduction is limited to your investment income. You cannot write off interest expense against other income such as employment or business income. This principle extends, under a separate set of complex rules, beyond interest expenses to all deductions relating to "passive" activities, including limited partnership writeoffs and most rental losses.

Certain other expenses and deductions permitted for Canadian purposes will not be allowed on your U.S. return.

15.3.3 Limitations on U.S. deductions for high-income taxpayers

Two limitations apply to high-income taxpayers.

First, **personal exemptions** ($2,500 for you, your spouse and each dependant) are phased out once adjusted gross income (AGI) exceeds a threshold. (Adjusted gross income is gross income minus certain deductions such as foreign earned income exclusion, alimony, and IRA or Keogh plan contributions.) For married persons filing jointly, the threshold is $172,050; for single taxpayers it is $114,700; for married filing separately, it is $86,025. For each $2,500 ($1,250 for married individuals filing separately) or part thereof by which AGI exceeds the threshold, *each* exemption is reduced by 2% (not to exceed 100%).

Second, **itemized deductions** are reduced once AGI exceeds a threshold, which is $114,700 for single taxpayers and married filing jointly, and $57,350 for married filing separately. For each dollar over the threshold, itemized deductions that could otherwise be claimed are reduced by 3% (other than medical expenses, investment interest, casualty or theft losses and gambling losses). However, even for very high-income taxpayers, a base amount of 20% of itemized deductions can always be claimed (i.e., the reduction cannot go beyond 80% of the deductions).

EXAMPLE

George is married and earns $202,050. His wife has no income. He will claim two personal exemptions worth $5,000. He has itemized deductions of $20,000 consisting of home mortgage interest and property taxes.

George's income is $30,000 (12 × $2,500) over the $172,050 threshold. Each of George's $2,500 personal exemptions is therefore reduced by 12 times 2%, or 24%. His total claim for exemptions is therefore $3,800 (that is, $5,000 – (5,000 × 24%)).

George's itemized deductions are reduced by 3% of $87,350 (which is the excess of his adjusted gross income over the $114,700 threshold), or $2,621. George may therefore deduct only $17,379 of his $20,000 in itemized deductions in determining his taxable income. (Note that the reduction can never exceed 80% of the itemized deductions, so no matter how high George's income was, he would always be able to deduct $4,000 of his $20,000 of itemized deductions.)

RRSPs, RPPs and DPSPs (see Chapter 2) can cause problems for U.S. citizens, because they are not given any special status in the U.S. Internal Revenue Code.

Employer contributions to a registered pension plan or a deferred profit sharing plan are exempt from immediate Canadian tax (see 6.1.1). As we saw in 2.2.1, you are taxed on the funds only when you receive them (usually on retirement).

For U.S. tax purposes, there is no such exemption. The amount contributed by your employer is treated as an employment benefit and is taxed, once the contributions have vested in you (that is, you are entitled to them even if you leave your employment). Furthermore, these amounts are explicitly excluded from the definition of "foreign earned income" under U.S. tax law, so you cannot make use of the foreign earned income exclusion (see 15.2.1). You may have to pay U.S. tax on these contributions, depending on the circumstances and the amount of your unused foreign tax credit carryover.

Your own contributions to an RRSP or RPP, which are deductible on your Canadian return, are not deductible for U.S. tax purposes.

Income accruing in your RRSP would normally be taxable in the U.S. However, as noted in 15.2.3, the Canada-U.S. tax treaty allows you to elect each year to defer the taxation of the accruing income until you actually receive the funds from the RRSP (or from a RRIF, if the RRSP is rolled into a RRIF). This allows you to report the income in the same year for Canadian and U.S. purposes. The rule applies only to earnings on contributions made while you were resident in Canada.

You should consult with an advisor if you are considering a "rollover" of your RPP entitlement. A distribution from your RPP, even if made directly into a locked-in RRSP (see 2.1.7.2), may be subject to U.S. tax with no relief available under the Canada-U.S. tax treaty. Later distributions out of your RRSP would be subject to Canadian tax with no credit for U.S. taxes previously paid—meaning double taxation.

If you contribute to an **IRA** (U.S. Individual Retirement Account) while resident in Canada, your contributions are deductible for U.S. tax purposes but not for Canadian tax purposes. Income accruing in an IRA is not taxed by Canada. When you withdraw funds from an IRA, Canada will tax the same amount that you would have had to include in your income under U.S. laws if you were a resident of the U.S. at the time of withdrawal. While you may be able to transfer lump-sum payments received from an IRA into an RRSP free of Canadian tax, the amount transferred would be subject to U.S. tax, so this is generally not a prudent strategy.

Contributions to a U.S. deferred income plan by a U.S. employer may be taxable in Canada as an employment benefit or "retirement compensation arrangement" (see 6.5).

15.3.5 DIVIDENDS

As we saw in 5.1.2, Canada taxes dividends from Canadian corporations using the "gross-up and credit" system, which results in less tax being levied than on other kinds of income. For U.S. purposes, dividends are taxed at the same rate as other income. The actual amount that you receive, rather than the grossed-up amount, is included in income for U.S. purposes.

Since Canadian tax rates (when provincial tax is counted) are normally higher than U.S. federal rates, the effect of the dividend tax credit roughly equalizes the tax rates of the two countries on dividends. The maximum U.S. rate is 39.6%; the maximum Canadian rate on dividends received is about 35%, depending on your province of residence.

15.3.6 CHARITABLE DONATIONS

As discussed in 1.3.4, charitable donations of up to 20% of your net income entitle you to a credit for Canadian tax purposes.

For Canadian tax purposes, charitable donations must normally be made to a Canadian charity to qualify (subject to certain specific exceptions). The Canada-U.S. tax treaty, however, provides that donations to U.S. charities will qualify, up to a limit of 20% of *U.S.-source* net income. You will need to obtain receipts from the U.S. charities and file them with your Canadian return.

Similarly, charitable donations are normally deductible in the U.S., subject to a limit of 50% of income for most charities. However, donations to Canadian charities may only be deducted for U.S. tax purposes to the extent of 50% of your *Canadian-source* "adjusted gross income". If you are excluding much or all of your Canadian-source income due to the foreign earned income exclusion (see 15.2.1), this limitation can cause problems.

15.3.7 MOVING EXPENSES

Moving expenses can present particular difficulties when dealing with the two tax systems. If you are posted to Canada and move to Canada, reimbursement by your employer of your moving expenses will normally be considered Canadian-source income for purposes of the U.S. foreign earned income exclusion and foreign tax credit. You may be able to claim certain moving expenses as a separate deduction on your U.S. tax return, but not if you have used the foreign earned income exclusion so that you have no Canadian-source employment income for tax purposes. Numerous special rules and restrictions apply to moving expenses claimed on a "foreign move" (a move *to* a non-U.S. home).

The deduction for moving expenses is limited to the costs of moving household goods and personal effects to the new residence and travel and lodging costs during the move. No deduction is allowed for meal expenses, expenses incurred while searching for a new home after obtaining employment, costs of selling the old residence or temporary lodging after obtaining employment. Reimbursement of moving costs by your employer is taxable income to you.

On a move back to the United States, a portion of your moving expenses may not be deductible, if the associated employer reimbursements are allocable to income eligible for the foreign earned income exclusion.

Under Canadian law, reimbursements of actual moving expenses are simply not taxed. A non-recoverable allowance for moving expenses is taxable if it exceeds $650, but the moving expenses themselves are deductible.

15.4 DIFFERENCES IN TAXATION OF CAPITAL GAINS

15.4.1 BASIC CALCULATION

It is in the field of capital gains that one finds the most glaring differences between the Canadian and U.S. tax systems. Not only are many details different, but the basic scheme of taxation of capital gains is itself fundamentally different. This area thus causes a large number of problems for U.S. citizens resident in Canada.

For Canadian tax purposes, only three-quarters of capital gains are taxed (see 4.2).

For U.S. tax purposes, capital gains are normally taxed like other income, at your marginal rate of 15%, 28%, 36% or 39.6% (see table in 15.1 above). However, the rate on *long-term* capital gains (generally from property held more than one year) is limited to 28%.

15.4.2 USE OF CAPITAL LOSSES

For Canadian purposes, allowable capital losses (three-quarters of your capital losses) can only be used to offset taxable capital gains, though they can be carried both forward and back against such gains (see 4.3.1). An exception exists for allowable business investment losses (on shares or debt of small business corporations), which can be used against any income (4.3.2).

For U.S. purposes, capital losses can be used against capital gains. In addition, US$3,000 of capital losses can be written off against other income ($1,500 for a married person filing separately). Unused capital losses can be carried forward, to be applied against capital gains or against $3,000 per year of other income in any future year.

15.4.3 THE CANADIAN CAPITAL GAINS EXEMPTION

As we saw in 4.4, a $100,000 lifetime capital gains exemption was available in Canada until 1994. The $500,000 capital gains exemption remains available for certain small business shares and farm property (see 4.4.1 and 4.4.2). No such exemption exists for U.S. tax purposes.

The Canadian foreign tax credit is calculated so as not to apply to any portion of a gain on foreign property for which the capital gains exemption was claimed. In other words, if you sell U.S. property and pay U.S. tax on the sale, you cannot claim a Canadian foreign tax credit for the portion of the U.S. tax that relates to the gain on which you or your spouse previously claimed the capital gains exemption for Canadian purposes.

The U.S. does have a limited form of capital gains exemption. U.S. citizens who invest in the shares of certain active small U.S. corporations after August 10, 1993, and hold the shares for at least five years, may be entitled to exclude up to 50% of any gains from income when the shares are sold. Numerous restrictions apply, however, and half of any excluded gain is treated as a "tax preference item" under the alternative minimum tax rules (see 15.5).

15.4.4 RESERVES VS. INSTALMENT SALES

Problems can arise when you sell capital property but do not receive full payment in the year of sale. As we saw in 4.5.2, a **reserve** is allowed for Canadian tax purposes, if you claim it. The reserve is based on the proportion of gain that has not yet been received, but at least one-fifth of the gain must be recognized cumulatively each year, so the reserve cannot be claimed for more than four years after the year of sale.

For U.S. tax purposes, **instalment sale** rules cover the same situation. However, the rules apply *unless* you elect to have them not apply. The basic concept is the same—a "gross profit ratio" will apply to include a portion of each payment into your income—but the five-year rule does not exist. This can lead to mismatching of Canadian and U.S. income, and thus foreign tax credits, in a given year.

There are further differences between Canadian reserves and U.S. instalment sale rules. In particular, the instalment sale method may not be available if the instalment obligation is pledged as security for a debt.

15.4.5 FOREIGN EXCHANGE GAINS OR LOSSES

When you sell Canadian property, your gain for U.S. tax purposes must be calculated using the U.S. dollar equivalent of your cost, as of the date you purchased the property. This can lead to a foreign exchange gain or loss that is independent of your (Canadian-dollar) gain or loss on the property.

EXAMPLE

You purchase 100 shares of XYZ Corporation on the Toronto Stock Exchange when the Canadian dollar is at 70 cents U.S. You pay $20 per share including commission, or Cdn$2,000 (US$1,400). You sell the shares several years later, when the Canadian dollar is at 78 cents U.S., for $19 each (after commission), or Cdn$1,900 (US$1,482).

For Canadian tax purposes, you have a $100 capital loss, three-quarters of which can be deducted against taxable capital gains. For U.S. tax purposes, however, you have an $82 capital gain, which is taxed. Since you do not pay any Canadian tax on the gain, no foreign tax credit is available to offset your tax (maximum 28%) on US$82.

A taxable foreign exchange gain can also arise on the sale of your principal residence, even though the entire gain is "rolled over" into a new principal residence within the required time frame (see 15.4.7). The problem is that the foreign exchange gain realized on the discharge of a Canadian-dollar-denominated mortgage is not a gain to which the U.S. principal residence rollover rules (see 15.4.7) apply.

Similarly, when you sell U.S. property, your gain for Canadian purposes must be calculated in Canadian dollars. The first $200 of your gain or loss on foreign currency in each year is ignored.

15.4.6 PRE-1972 HOLDINGS

As noted in 4.5.1, Canada taxes only capital gains accrued since 1972. The U.S. does not have any such rule. If you are a U.S. citizen and have owned property since before 1972, your gain for U.S. tax purposes could be substantially higher than your gain for Canadian tax purposes.

15.4.7 PRINCIPAL RESIDENCE

As we saw in 4.5.3, a gain on a "principal residence" is normally completely exempt from tax in Canada. The U.S. has two rules to deal with sales of a principal residence, but they are very different from the Canadian rules, and more restrictive.

First, if you are at least 55 years old, you may claim an exclusion of US$125,000 of gain on a principal residence. Certain requirements must be met; for example, you must have actually occupied the home for three of the past five years, and you and your spouse must not have claimed this exclusion in the past.

Second, you may defer the taxation of a gain on your principal residence if you buy another home (which may be outside the U.S.), except to the extent your new home costs less than what you sell the old home for. Your old home's cost will be transferred for tax purposes to your new home, so the gain may eventually be taxed. The time limitation for buying the new home is fairly generous: you must buy it within two years (before or after) of selling the old home. As well, the two-year period may be extended by a further two years during which your "tax home" (generally your place of employment) is outside the U.S. This means that you have up to four years after selling your old home to buy a new, more expensive one, if you are living in Canada.

Be careful if you buy more than one home during the two-year period. You will have to pay tax on any gain arising on the "middle" home.

A further difference between Canadian and U.S. exemptions for a principal residence lies in the definition of the term. As we saw in 4.5.3, a vacation property such as a cottage will generally qualify for Canadian tax purposes, although you can only designate one principal residence for each year. For U.S. purposes, a home will only qualify if it is the place where you "regularly reside".

15.4.8 IMMIGRATION TO AND EMIGRATION FROM CANADA

Most property you own is deemed to be acquired by you at its fair market value as of the date you immigrate to Canada. This means that Canada will tax only the capital gain that accrues while you are resident in Canada. The U.S., on the other hand, will use your actual cost for capital gains calculation purposes, resulting in a much higher capital gain in many cases.

When you emigrate from Canada (i.e., when you cease to be resident in Canada for Canadian tax purposes), you are generally deemed to have sold all of your property at its fair market value. This allows Canada to tax gains that accrued on your assets while you were resident in Canada. The principal exceptions are:

- "**taxable Canadian property**" — property on which any gain will normally be taxed by Canada even when you are non-resident. Essentially, this is Canadian real estate and shares in private corporations that are resident in Canada
- property that you already owned when you became resident in Canada, if your residence in Canada totalled no more than five years out of the last ten
- pension entitlements, including an RRSP or RRIF

You may elect to have some or all of your taxable Canadian property included in the assets that are deemed sold at their fair market value when you depart. This will be useful if you can claim the Canadian capital gains exemption on small business shares or farm property (see 4.4.1 and 4.4.2), which will not be available in respect of the property once you have become a non-resident. You can also elect under the treaty for the deemed disposition rules to apply for U.S. as well as Canadian tax purposes.

15.4.9 OTHER CAPITAL GAINS DIFFERENCES

Canada and the U.S. have very different rules with respect to the transfer of capital property to corporations, corporation reorganizations, mergers, windups, recapitalization, debt forgiveness, etc. If you are involved in such transactions, professional advice is essential, especially since there have been many changes to both systems.

15.5 MINIMUM TAX

Canada's minimum tax was discussed in Chapter 11. The U.S. alternative minimum tax ("AMT") has the same general structure, but there are a number of important differences.

First, the U.S. AMT exemption is US$45,000 for married taxpayers filing jointly (or a surviving spouse) and $33,750 for a single taxpayer. (The Canadian exemption is Cdn$40,000.) As well, the U.S. exemption is phased out for those with adjusted minimum taxable income over $150,000 if married filing jointly ($112,500 if filing as a single taxpayer).

Second, the U.S. AMT rate is calculated under a two-tier graduated rate schedule. A 26% rate applies to the first US$175,000 of alternative minimum taxable income over the AMT exemption amount, and a 28% rate applies to alternative minimum taxable income over US$175,000. The 28% rate comes into effect at an alternative minimum taxable income over US$87,500 for married individuals filing separate returns. (The Canadian rate, including provincial tax, is approximately 27%.)

Third, the list of "AMT adjustments"—items added back to income for AMT purposes—is, of course, different between the two countries. For U.S. tax purposes, the list includes the standard deduction, property and state taxes paid, oil and gas drilling costs, mining exploration and development costs, a portion of accelerated depreciation, and various other specific deductions.

Fourth, the U.S. foreign tax credit can only be used to offset 90% of your AMT payable. This means that if your income (not counting income eligible for the foreign earned income exclusion) is higher than the AMT exemption level, you will almost always end up paying at least some tax to the United States.

EXAMPLE

Pete is an unmarried U.S. citizen living and working in Canada. In 1995, his employment income is Cdn$65,000, and he makes Cdn$100,000 (US$72,000) in gains on the stock market.

Pete will pay Canadian tax on his employment income and on ¾ of his capital gain. For U.S. regular tax purposes, the employment income will be eligible for the foreign earned income exclusion, and the U.S. tax on the capital gain will be fully offset by a foreign tax credit for the Canadian tax he pays on the gain.

For U.S. AMT purposes, however, Pete's income will be US$72,000, minus his $33,750 AMT exemption. The AMT liability will therefore be 26% of $38,250, or $9,945. Only 90% of this amount can be offset by foreign tax credits, so Pete will have to pay $995 in U.S. tax. This will be in addition to his Canadian tax liability. No Canadian foreign tax credit will be available, since the gains are Canadian-source income even though they are being taxed by the U.S.

15.6 INCOME EARNED BY CHILDREN

15.6.1 EFFECT ON DEPENDANT DEDUCTION

If you claim a deduction for a dependent child (US$2,500) on your U.S. return, that child may not claim the regular personal exemption on his or her own tax return. The effect is that any income the child earns is taxed.

In Canada, there is no longer a credit for dependent children (see 1.3.1). Therefore, income earned by your children will not affect the tax you pay.

15.6.2 ATTRIBUTION RULES

We discussed the Canadian attribution rules with respect to minor children in 3.2.3. The basic rule is that if you give or lend funds to your child, the income from those funds will be taxed in your hands rather than the child's, until the child turns 18.

The U.S. tax system accomplishes the same general anti-income-splitting objective in a very different way. The income of the child is taxed in the child's hands, but may in part be taxed *at the parent's marginal tax rate*.

The first US$650 of **unearned income** (roughly equivalent in meaning to Canadian "income from property") of a child under 14 is not taxed. The next $650 is taxed as the child's income. Beyond US$1,300, if the child has no *earned* income (compensation for services rendered), any further unearned income will be taxed at the rate of the parent with the greater taxable income. So, beyond the $1,300 level, little is usually gained from a tax point of view by having a child under 14 earn investment income.

If certain requirements are met, the parent whose taxable income is used for calculating the child's tax rate may elect to include the child's income directly. This will eliminate the need to file a tax return for the child, and also lead to a better matching of incomes between the Canadian and U.S. tax systems.

15.7 U.S. FILING REQUIREMENTS

15.7.1 JOINT RETURN OR NOT?

For Canadian tax purposes, every taxpayer is distinct and must file separately. Combining the income of two spouses is only considered for certain specific purposes, such as eligibility for the Child Tax Benefit (1.5.1) and the GST Credit (1.5.2).

For U.S. tax purposes, you have the option of filing a **joint return** with your spouse. If one spouse has little or no income, this will usually result in less tax than if you file as "married filing separately". For U.S. purposes, spouses must be legally married; in Canada, spouses include common-law spouses (see 1.3.1).

For U.S. purposes, a joint return is mandatory (if you are married) if you wish to claim certain deductions and credits. The child-care credit is one example. Another is the $25,000 loss allowance for an owner who actively participates in rental real estate.

If you do not have a spouse, your filing status will be one of "unmarried", "head of household" or "surviving spouse", all of which have different implications for your U.S. tax return.

If your spouse is a U.S. citizen, the decision as to whether to file jointly can be made annually. If your spouse is not a U.S. citizen, the decision to file jointly can only be made once. If you file jointly, you must always file jointly unless the election to file jointly is revoked; but once revoked, the decision can never be made again (unless you have a new spouse).

15.7.2 TIME REQUIREMENTS FOR FILING

The requirements for filing Canadian tax returns were discussed in 13.1.

U.S. tax returns must normally be postmarked by April 15 each year.

If you are a U.S. citizen whose "tax home" (place of employment) and "abode" (place of residence) are *both* outside the U.S., your filing deadline is automatically extended to June 15 each year. You must attach a statement to your return identifying that you are eligible for this extension. You mail your U.S. tax return to the IRS in Philadelphia.

If you are unable to meet the June 15 deadline, you may file for an extension of the deadline to August 15. The extension will be granted automatically.

Even though you are permitted to file your return in June or August, interest on any balance of taxes owing will run from April 15. If more than 10% of your tax for the year is owing, a late payment penalty applies as well.

15.7.3 ESTIMATED TAXES

We discussed the Canadian tax instalment requirements in 13.2.2. The U.S. has parallel requirements, which are called payments of "estimated taxes".

Estimated tax payments are due quarterly, on April 15, June 15, September 15 and the following January 15. As with the Canadian system, you can generally choose either last year's tax or this year's tax as the basis for your quarterly estimated tax payments.

If you are basing your payments on the current year's tax, you need only pay 90% of the year's tax liability (regular tax or AMT) in estimated tax payments—22.5% each quarter. If you are using last year's tax, you must normally pay 25% of that amount each quarter. However, if you are using last year's tax and last year's gross adjusted income exceeded US$150,000 (US$75,000 if married filing separately), you must pay 27.5% each quarter (i.e., 110% of last year's tax). In order to use last year's tax, you must have filed a return in the previous year and the year must have been a 12 month-period.

In either case, any balance still owing will be due with your tax return. No estimated tax payments are required if your total tax for the year is less than US$500.

If you do not make your estimated tax payments on time, non-deductible late payment penalties will apply.

15.7.4 DISCLOSURE REQUIREMENTS

As well as filing a tax return, you must disclose a substantial amount of financial information under U.S. law.

First, you must disclose holdings in any non-U.S. corporations which you control directly or indirectly, or in which you have a substantial interest and which are controlled by other U.S. citizens or corporations. This information is filed with your tax return. The IRS uses this information, among other things, to help determine your liability for tax on any undistributed income of closely-held non-U.S. corporations that earn passive income.

In some cases, a Canadian corporation's reporting year must be the calendar year for U.S. reporting purposes.

Second, you are required to file annually a "Report of Foreign Bank and Financial Accounts" form with the U.S. Department of the Treasury. This form is mailed separately from your tax return and is due by June 30. It is required if the total value of your foreign bank accounts, brokerage accounts, RRSPs, etc. exceeds US$10,000 at any time in the year.

Severe penalties apply under U.S. law for not complying with these disclosure requirements.

15.7.5 U.S. PASSPORT RENEWALS

If you apply for a U.S. passport, or a renewal of your passport, while living outside the U.S., you will be required to provide your Social Security Number and file an IRS information return. If you have not been regularly filing U.S. tax returns, you will then likely receive a request to file from the Internal Revenue Service. Ignoring such requests can leave you liable to criminal penalties. In the future, the IRS hopes that legislation will be passed permitting the U.S. government to withhold renewal of your passport for non-filing of tax returns.

15.8 U.S. ESTATE AND GIFT TAXES

15.8.1 ESTATE TAX

The U.S. imposes estate tax on death of U.S. citizens, where the net value of the estate (when combined with certain taxable gifts) is over US$600,000. The tax applies at graduated rates, ranging from 18% for the value of an estate under US$10,000 to 55% of the value of an estate over US$3 million. See 16.4 for a more detailed discussion.

A deduction is allowed for any amounts left to your spouse on death, if your spouse is a U.S. citizen. As a result, leaving all of your estate to your spouse will result in no estate tax applying on your death. This will result, however, in losing your $600,000 exemption, since on your spouse's death only one $600,000 exemption is available on your combined estate.

If your spouse is not a U.S. citizen, the deduction is not available. However, a "qualified domestic trust" can be set up to defer tax (see 16.4.1).

As noted in 4.5.4 and 12.1.2, Canada effectively taxes accrued capital gains on death by deeming capital property to have been disposed of at fair market value immediately before death.

Since the U.S. tax on death is an estate tax and the Canadian tax is an income tax, neither one would normally permit a foreign tax credit in respect of the other. This can result in double taxation. The **Protocol** (amendment) to the Canada-U.S. Treaty signed on March 17, 1995 will change this, by allowing Canadian residents a credit against Canadian income tax on death for U.S. estate tax, and allowing U.S. citizens or residents a credit against U.S. estate tax for Canadian income tax imposed on the property on death. These rules are subject to various restrictions. As well, a limited rollover to a spouse will be allowed even where the surviving spouse is not a U.S. citizen. These changes will alleviate (but will not eliminate) the risk of double taxation. See 16.4.4.

The Protocol will be **retroactive** to deaths occurring after **November 10, 1988**. At time of writing the Protocol had not yet been ratified (passed into law); ratification is expected before the end of 1995. A claim for refund for a death from November 11, 1988 through to the day the Protocol enters into force will have to be filed within **one year** of the ratification date.

Note that although U.S. estate tax will only apply to the extent the *net* value of the estate exceeds US$600,000, an estate tax return must be filed whenever the *gross* value of the estate exceeds that figure. Furthermore, to the extent you have made taxable gifts (see 15.8.2) during your lifetime, the $600,000 threshold is reduced.

15.8.2 GIFT TAX

Canada does not have a gift tax, although the giver of a gift (except to a spouse) is deemed to have sold the property at its current fair market value, possibly leading to income tax on a resulting taxable capital gain (see 4.5.5).

The United States does have a gift tax, which applies only to those who make very substantial gifts. The *giver* is liable for the tax. Where the giver and recipient are spouses who are both U.S. citizens, no gift tax applies at all. Otherwise, if only the giver is a U.S. citizen, gift tax may apply.

Up to US$10,000 may be given tax-free each year to any one donee, and up to $100,000 to a spouse who is not a U.S. citizen. In addition, every U.S. citizen has a cumulative lifetime "unified credit" of $192,800 against gift and estate taxes; this can effectively exempt about $600,000 of gifts (over these $10,000 and $100,000 annual levels) over the course of your lifetime.

Beyond the $10,000 and $100,000 levels, gift tax applies at the same graduated rates as estate tax, ranging from 18% on taxable gifts under $10,000 to 55% on the portion of taxable gifts over $3.0 million.

As is the case with estate taxes, the Canadian tax (if any) that applies on a gift is an income tax, while the U.S. tax is not. As a result, no foreign tax credit applies in either system for taxes of the other system. Caution must therefore be exercised if you are giving large gifts. One further problem with gifts is that, for U.S. purposes, your cost base of property will be carried through to the recipient of a gift, whereas on death, any property left to your beneficiaries is treated as acquired by them at its fair market value.

You must also watch out for the Canadian attribution rules, as outlined in Chapter 3.

15.9 PLANNING OPPORTUNITIES

15.9.1 FILE JOINT RETURN WHERE APPROPRIATE

As discussed in 15.7.1, a joint return may be appropriate if you are married and both spouses are required to file U.S. tax returns. This will likely be the case if one spouse has very little income.

If your spouse is not an American citizen and has no U.S.-source income, and thus is not subject to U.S. tax, you may wish to file a "married filing separate" return. As a "non-resident alien", your spouse's Canadian income will not be relevant for U.S. tax purposes.

On the other hand, if your spouse has little income from any source but you are paying tax to the U.S., filing a joint return can be beneficial, as it will give you larger exclusions and wider tax brackets at the lower rates. The cost of doing this is that you bring your spouse's worldwide income within the U.S. tax system; and if you ever change your mind and choose not to file jointly, you can never file jointly again.

15.9.2 REVIEW INCOME SPLITTING ARRANGEMENTS TO PREVENT DOUBLE TAXATION

Because of the ability to file joint returns, income splitting (see Chapter 3) is not as much of an issue in the U.S. as it is in Canada. Income splitting arrangements that are set up for Canadian income tax purposes can result in double taxation if you are not careful.

For example, suppose you and your 13-year-old son are both U.S. citizens and your son has no income, and you lend funds to him with the intention of building up "secondary" income over time which will not be attributed back to you (see 3.3.6). The income on the funds you have loaned will be taxed in your hands under Canadian law, but in your son's hands (albeit at your marginal rate while the child is under 14—see 15.6.2) under U.S. law. Because different taxpayers are paying the tax, no foreign tax credit will be available and you may end up being taxed twice on the same income.

In this example, as long as your son is under 14, you can elect to include his unearned income on your return for U.S. tax purposes. That should solve the double taxation problem, since the income will be taxed in your hands under both systems.

15.9.3 WATCH OUT FOR CANADIAN OWNERSHIP OF CANADIAN MUTUAL FUNDS OR OTHER CANADIAN CORPORATIONS EARNING PASSIVE INCOME

Investing in Canadian mutual funds and similar corporations can result in unexpected U.S. tax liability. Under U.S. law, if you invest in a non-U.S. corporation that earns a substantial part of its income from investments (a "passive foreign investment corporation"), and then sell the stock or receive an "excess" distribution, there may be a theoretical deferral of U.S. tax (which would have applied if you had earned the investment income directly). In such a case, interest charged on this "deferred tax" may be imposed under U.S. tax law.

There is no minimum U.S. ownership required in a Canadian corporation to be subject to these rules. There are ways to avoid the interest charge, however; one way is to elect to include your *pro rata* share of the fund's earnings in your income on a current basis each year (which may result in a mismatching of income for Canadian and U.S. purposes).

15.9.4 KEEP RECORDS OF EXPENSES DEDUCTIBLE ON YOUR U.S. RETURN

If you are claiming deductions on your U.S. return that are not allowable in Canada (see 15.3.1), make sure to keep additional records sufficient to establish your claim.

15.9.5 CLAIM FOREIGN EARNED INCOME EXCLUSION IF BENEFICIAL

If you are eligible for the foreign earned income exclusion (see 15.2.1), you should normally claim it. It is by far the simplest and most straightforward way to avoid double taxation.

However, there are some unusual circumstances (mostly involving carryovers of foreign tax credits) where claiming a foreign tax credit can be more beneficial than claiming the exclusion. If you claim the exclusion and then, in a subsequent year, elect not to claim it, you cannot normally claim it again for five years. Because of this restriction, and on the off-chance that the foreign tax credit might be more valuable in some future year, many accountants will calculate tax both ways and not claim the exclusion if no tax is payable in either case.

15.9.6 AIM FOR MAXIMUM FOREIGN TAX CREDIT

You will wish to maximize your available foreign tax credit (see 15.2.2). Over the course of the year, you may be able to structure your income from various sources—U.S. and Canadian, employment and investment income, etc.—in such a way as to maximize your "pools" of foreign tax paid on foreign-source income for purposes of the foreign tax credits of both the U.S. and Canada.

While normally you cannot receive credit for all Canadian tax paid because Canadian taxes are higher than U.S. taxes, you may be able to take particular advantage of the credit if you are resident in Canada for a relatively short time before another foreign posting. That is because you may apply your excess Canadian taxes when determining the foreign tax credit on income earned in other foreign countries.

15.9.7 Watch out for U.S. AMT liability

As noted in 15.5, if your income is high enough, you may have to pay a certain amount of U.S. alternative minimum tax even though your income is fully taxed by Canada. One way to reduce this liability is to earn additional U.S.-source income. Canada will give you a foreign tax credit for regular U.S. tax paid on the U.S.-source income, but not for U.S. AMT payable on Canadian-source income.

15.9.8 Elect out of instalment sale rules where appropriate

If you are not claiming a reserve for Canadian tax purposes on the sale of a particular capital property, consider electing out of the automatic "instalment sale" provisions on your U.S. return (see 15.4.4). Otherwise you may have a mismatch of U.S. and Canadian income in any given year, leading to problems with the foreign tax credit.

Conversely, if you are claiming a reserve that can last only five years, but deferring a large portion of your proceeds beyond five years, the instalment sale rules will again lead to a mismatch of Canadian and U.S. income.

If the gain is taxed in the U.S. some years after it is taxed in Canada due to the instalment sale rules, Revenue Canada may allow you to reopen an earlier year's return (back to 1985) in order to claim a foreign tax credit.

15.9.9 Be cautious of using the $500,000 capital gains exemption

If you sell small business corporation shares or farm property, be aware that Canada's $500,000 capital gains exemption (see 4.4) won't protect you from U.S. tax on the gain, even if you are not subject to Canadian tax. Generally, you should steer clear of the planning ideas discussed in 8.8.6 to "crystallize" your gains and use up your exemption.

15.9.10 Consider steps to take on departure from Canada

When leaving Canada, consider both the U.S. and the Canadian income tax systems (see 15.4.8). It may be appropriate to sell certain assets before or after leaving Canada. Various elections may be worth making as well. For example, you might elect under the treaty to have the Canadian deemed disposition rules to apply for U.S. tax purposes, so that you can use the Canadian taxes arising as a foreign tax credit on your U.S. return to offset the resulting U.S. tax and give you a higher cost basis in the assets for U.S. tax purposes. Do not make this election without considering the state tax consequences, however.

15.9.11 PLAN FOR U.S. ESTATE AND GIFT TAXES

Be aware of the implications of U.S. estate and gift taxes, as outlined in 15.8, and in particular of the possible double taxation that can result from not planning properly. Be informed as to whether and when the Protocol to the Canada-U.S. tax treaty has been ratified (see 15.8.1).

15.9.12 WATCH SHAREHOLDER-CORPORATION TRANSACTIONS

If you control any private corporations, watch out for shareholder-corporation transactions which could result in a taxable benefit applying under Canadian or U.S. law or both. If investment income accumulates in a Canadian corporation that you control, you may be subject to the U.S. "Subpart F" rules, which will tax you on that income even though it is not distributed to you (see 15.7.4).

15.9.13 BEWARE OF DIFFERENCES IN RULES GOVERNING RETIREMENT INCOME

As discussed in 15.3.4, you can run into problems with retirement plans, since RRSPs and similar plans are not covered by U.S. tax law while deductions for contributions to IRAs and similar U.S. plans are not permitted by Canadian law.

If you have an RRSP, you will normally want to file the election under the Canada-U.S. tax treaty, as noted in 15.3.4, to defer taxation of the income in the RRSP until it is paid to you. This can only be done for the income accruing on contributions you have made while resident in Canada. Under the March 1995 Protocol (amendment) to the Canada-U.S. tax treaty, the deferral election will be extended to RPPs and to other Canadian retirement plans (see 15.2.3). As well, the limitation that the election can be made only on contributions made while a resident of Canada will be eliminated (effective 1996, if the Protocol is ratified during 1995).

15.9.14 SEEK PROFESSIONAL TAX ADVICE BEFORE MOVING TO CANADA

If you are a U.S. citizen moving to Canada, you should obtain professional advice regarding strategies for minimizing your tax burden. There may be steps you should take before you arrive in Canada.

If you have significant non-Canadian investments, it may be worthwhile to set up a foreign trust before you become resident in Canada. A foreign trust can be exempt from Canadian tax for up to five years after you become resident. This may be a useful strategy where your U.S. tax rate is lower than your Canadian rate.

If you own property that has gone down in value, you should consider selling it before becoming a Canadian resident. The current market value of the property at the time you become resident will be used as your cost base for Canadian capital gains calculation purposes.

If you are being relocated to Canada by your employer, you may wish to negotiate for a payment to cover the higher taxes imposed in Canada. See also 15.3.7 regarding moving expenses.

Under the Canada-U.S. Social Security Agreement, you can be exempted for up to five years from Canada Pension Plan contributions if you are a U.S. citizen temporarily transferred to Canada. You would continue to be covered under and pay contributions to the U.S. social security system. Your employer will need to obtain a certificate of coverage under the U.S. system for you to obtain this exemption.

15.10 References

The following publications can be obtained (in person or by telephone request) from your nearest Revenue Canada District Taxation Office:

- Interpretation Bulletin IT-122R2, "United States social security taxes and benefits"
- Interpretation Bulletin IT-221R2, "Determination of an individual's residence status"
- Interpretation Bulletin IT-270R2, "Foreign tax credit"
- Interpretation Bulletin IT-395R, "Foreign tax credit—capital gains and capital losses on foreign property"
- Interpretation Bulletin IT-506, "Foreign income taxes as a deduction from income"
- Interpretation Bulletin IT-520, "Unused foreign tax credits—carryforward and carryback"
- Form T2209, "Calculation of federal foreign tax credits"
- Form T2036, "Calculation of provincial foreign tax credit"
- Brochure, "Emigrants"
- Brochure, "Newcomers to Canada"

The following may be obtained from any office of the Internal Revenue Service, and are generally available at U.S. embassy and consular offices. Help is also available from the IRS office in Ottawa at (613) 563-1834, fax (613) 230-1376.

Publication 54, "Tax Guide For U.S. Citizens and Resident Aliens Abroad"

Publication 521, "Moving Expenses"

Publication 523, "Tax Information On Selling Your Home"

Publication 514, "Foreign Tax Credit For Individuals"

Form 1040, "U.S. Individual Income Tax Return"

Form 1116, "Computation of Foreign Tax Credit"

Form 2119, "Sale Of Your Home"

Form 2350, "Application For Extension Of Time to File U.S. Income Tax Return"

Form 2555, "Foreign Earned Income"

Form 3520, "Creation of or Transfers to Certain Foreign Trusts"

Form 3520A, "Annual Return of Foreign Trust With U.S. Beneficiaries"

Form 3903, "Moving Expenses"

Form 3903F, "Foreign Moving Expenses"

Form 4868, "Application for Automatic Extension of Time to File U.S. Individual Income Tax Return"

Form 5471, "Information Return With Respect To A Foreign Corporation"

Form 6251, "Alternative Minimum Tax—Individuals"

Form 8833, "Treaty-Based Return Position Disclosure under Section 6114 or 7701(b)

Form TD F 90-22.1, "Report of Foreign Bank and Financial Accounts".

16 U.S. Residency and Ownership of U.S. Property

Planning Tips

- Elect net rental income method
- File return on time to avoid losing deductions
- Sell real estate to buyer who will occupy it as principal residence
- Apply for U.S. "withholding certificate" on sale of real estate
- Be cautious about keeping artwork and other assets in the U.S.
- Be cautious when acquiring shares in U.S. corporations
- Hold property through Canadian corporation
- Leave property to spouse or qualified domestic trust
- Acquire property jointly with spouse or other person
- Sell U.S. property before death
- Take out life insurance to cover estate taxes
- Mortgage property (non-recourse) to reduce value of U.S. real estate
- Acquire U.S. property through irrevocable Canadian trust
- Consider the effects of the Protocol in your situation
- Avoid becoming a U.S. resident while visiting

In this chapter we discuss the United States taxes that apply to Canadian residents who are **not** *U.S. citizens and who acquire U.S. investments such as stocks and real estate. (Taxation of U.S. citizens resident in Canada was covered in Chapter 15.) Such investments are taxed in three ways: on the income they generate; on their sale; and on death of the owner. We also discuss the "snowbird" rules that can make you resident in the U.S. by spending too much time there.*

In general, the interaction between the U.S. and Canadian tax systems can be highly complex. Transactions in U.S. real estate should not be undertaken without qualified professional tax advice.

16.1 Income from U.S. properties

Certain U.S.-source income is subject to U.S. tax even if you are not resident in the U.S.

16.1.1 RENT FROM REAL ESTATE

A withholding tax of **30%** normally applies to the **gross** amount of any rent paid to a resident of Canada on real estate located in the United States. (Unlike withholding taxes on interest and dividends, this tax is not reduced by the Canada-U.S. tax treaty.)

EXAMPLE

You live in Canada and own a condominium in Texas. You rent out the condominium for the entire year, receiving US$10,000 in rent. Your mortgage interest, maintenance costs and property taxes total US$8,000.

30% of the rent paid to you, or US$3,000, should be withheld by your tenant over the course of the year and remitted to the IRS.

At the end of the year, you may elect to file a U.S. tax return and to pay U.S. tax on your *net* rental income. In the example above, your net rental income would be only US$2,000 rather than US$10,000. You can then receive a refund for the withholding tax, to the extent it exceeds the tax payable on your U.S. return. However, note that state tax (and possibly a small amount of city tax) will be payable on the rental income.

Once you have elected to file on a net basis, the election is permanent and you will be taxed on the net basis in future years. If you make the election, it applies to all of your rental real estate. The election can only be revoked in limited circumstances.

Once you have made the election, you can provide Form 4224 (see 16.6) to your tenant, and the 30% of the rent will not need to be withheld.

If you wish to file on a net basis, the IRS sets a deadline by which you must file. For the 1995 year, your return must normally be filed by October 15, 1997, or you will not be able to claim any deductions and tax will be assessed on the gross income. This rule applies not only to real estate rent, but to any U.S.-source income against which you may wish to claim deductions.

16.1.2 DIVIDENDS AND INTEREST FROM U.S. CORPORATIONS

Like rental payments, payments of dividends and interest by U.S. corporations to residents of Canada are subject to U.S. withholding tax. The Canada-U.S. tax treaty limits the tax to **15%** in most cases. Certain interest may qualify for a "portfolio debt" exemption from U.S. tax.

You do not file a U.S. income tax return in respect of dividend and interest income on which the correct tax is withheld.

16.2 SALE OF U.S. PROPERTIES

16.2.1 SALE OF REAL ESTATE

16.2.1.1 WITHHOLDING TAX (FIRPTA)

If you sell real estate located in the U.S., a withholding tax of **10%** of the sale price is normally payable under "**FIRPTA**" (the Foreign

Investment in Real Property Tax Act of 1980). The tax withheld can be offset against the U.S. income tax payable on any gain you realize on the sale, and refunded if it exceeds your U.S. tax liability.

Withholding under FIRPTA will not apply if the property is sold for less than US$300,000 and the purchaser intends to use it as a residence. For this exception to apply, the purchaser must have definite plans to reside at the property for at least half of the time that the property is in use during each of the two years following the sale. However, the gain on the sale will still be taxable in the U.S., and a U.S. tax return must therefore be filed.

Another way of reducing the FIRPTA withholding is to apply to the IRS before the sale for a "withholding certificate" on the basis that your expected U.S. tax liability will be less than 10% of the sale price.

Some states have state withholding tax provisions that parallel FIRPTA.

16.2.1.2 INCOME TAX

For income tax purposes, you must file a U.S. tax return and report the gain on the sale of U.S. real estate. (There is no reduced taxation of capital gains, as there is in Canada.) You can then claim a credit for the FIRPTA tax withheld.

If you have owned the property and have been resident in Canada since before September 27, 1980 and used it only for personal use, you can likely take advantage of the Canada-U.S. tax treaty (see 15.2.3) to reduce your gain. In such a case, only your gain accruing since January 1, 1985 will be taxed.

EXAMPLE

You bought a cottage in the U.S. for personal use in 1976 for US$10,000. On January 1, 1985 it was worth US$30,000. In 1995, you sell the cottage for US$60,000.

The U.S. will tax only your gain of US$30,000, being the increase in value of the property since the beginning of 1985. State income tax may be based on a gain of either US$30,000 or US$50,000, depending on whether the state adheres to the Canada-U.S. tax treaty.

If you cannot establish a January 1, 1985 valuation, the gain accrued to that date is determined by assuming that the entire gain accrued equally over each month in the holding period.

The above rules also apply to certain rental properties.

To claim the benefit under the treaty, you will need to make the claim on your U.S. return and include a statement containing certain specific information about the transaction.

U.S. tax on the sale of U.S. property will generate a foreign tax credit that can be used to reduce the Canadian tax on the sale. (See

15.2.2 for an explanation of the operation of foreign tax credits.) However, if the amount of the gain was taxed in Canada was reduced due to the capital gains exemption (see 4.4) or the principal residence exemption (see 4.5.3), the foreign tax credit available to you may be limited.

16.2.2 SALES OF U.S. STOCKS AND BONDS

As long as you are not a resident or citizen of the U.S., U.S. tax will normally not apply to sales of shares in U.S. corporations, whether public or private and no matter where they are traded.

However, if the majority of the corporation's assets are U.S. real estate, the corporation may be considered a "U.S. real property holding corporation" (unless it is a publicly traded company and you own less than 5% of the shares). In such a case, any gain on the sale of the shares of the corporation will be taxed by the U.S.

16.3 SNOWBIRDS—U.S. RESIDENCY RULES

If you spend a substantial portion of the year in the U.S., you may become a U.S. resident for tax purposes. If this happens you will be required to file U.S. tax returns and pay U.S. tax on your income from *all* sources, including Canada (except to the extent that you can claim foreign tax credits; see 15.2.2).

If you hold a "**green card**", you have the status of a U.S. permanent resident and will be considered resident in the U.S. for tax purposes.

If your "physical presence" in the U.S. totals **183 days** or more in the year, you will be deemed a U.S. resident. For this purpose, you must total up the number of days you spend in the U.S. in the current year, $1/3$ of the days from the previous year and $1/6$ of the days from the second previous year.

EXAMPLE

Simone spends the winter each year in Miami and the spring and summer in Montreal. For 1993, 1994 and 1995, she is physically in the U.S. for 150, 90 and 140 days respectively.

For 1995, Simone's "physical presence" calculation is 140 + ($1/3 \times 90$) + ($1/6 \times 150$), or 195. Since this figure exceeds 183, she is considered resident in the U.S. for 1995 (subject to the "closer connection" rule described below).

If you are deemed a U.S. resident under the "physical presence" test but the number of days you spend in the U.S. in the *current* year is less than 183, you can be treated as non-resident for purposes of U.S. tax if you can establish that you have a "**closer connection**" to Canada than to the U.S. This information is reported on Form 8840 (see 16.6), which is due by June 15 of the following year.

If your current year's days in the U.S. are 183 or more, or if you hold a green card, you can gain a measure of protection from the Canada-U.S. tax treaty if you can establish that under the treaty you are resident in Canada rather than the U.S. (This protection is not as broad as being treated as non-resident under the "closer connection" rule above, however.) For this purpose you would need to show that you have a permanent home in Canada and not in the U.S.; or, if you have a permanent home in both countries or neither, that your personal and economic relations are closer to Canada. You will have to file information with the IRS within certain time limits to be entitled to this treaty "tie-breaker" protection.

16.4 U.S. ESTATE TAXES ON DEATH

U.S. estate taxes can impose a very serious burden on the death of Canadians who own U.S. stocks and real estate. We shall discuss federal estate taxes only; many states also have estate taxes, and these must be considered as well.

16.4.1 DETERMINATION OF PROPERTY SUBJECT TO ESTATE TAX

U.S. estate tax applies to the deceased's "**property situated within the United States**". This includes:

- real property located in the U.S.
- certain tangible personal property located in the U.S.
- shares of U.S. corporations, *regardless of the location of the share certificates and regardless of where the shares are traded*
- debts of U.S. persons, including the U.S. government (such as U.S. Government Savings Bonds)
- interests in partnerships carrying on business in the U.S. (although this is not free from doubt)

Assets normally excluded from the definition include: shares of a non-U.S. corporation, regardless of where the corporation's assets are situated; U.S. bank deposits; certain U.S. corporate bonds that are publicly traded outside the U.S.; certain debt obligations that qualify for the "portfolio debt" exemption from U.S. tax; and life insurance proceeds payable on a non-resident alien's death.

The "**taxable estate**" for estate tax purposes is the gross value of all of the deceased's property situated in the U.S., minus certain allowable deductions. The most significant deductions are:

- amounts left to the deceased's spouse if the spouse is a U.S. citizen (and will therefore be subject to U.S. estate tax on death)

- amounts transferred to a "qualified domestic trust" (a trust which meets certain requirements, as set out below)
- a deduction for a non-recourse mortgage (see below) encumbering U.S. property
- a deduction for an allocable share of the deceased's liabilities at time of death in respect of which the estate becomes liable—including Canadian income taxes payable

To calculate and claim the allocable share of liabilities, the estate tax return must disclose the deceased's worldwide assets and liabilities.

A "non-recourse" mortgage is one that entitles the lender to have recourse only against the property mortgaged. That is, if you default on payment, the mortgagee can seize the mortgaged property, but cannot come after you for the balance if the property is not worth enough to pay off the debt.

Where property is left to a surviving spouse who is a U.S. citizen, or to a qualified domestic trust (QDOT), the estate tax can be deferred until the death of the surviving spouse.

To qualify as a QDOT, the trust instrument must provide that at least one trustee be a U.S. citizen or U.S. corporation, and that no distribution of capital may be made from the trust without the U.S. trustee being able to withhold U.S. estate tax. Any capital paid out of a QDOT will then become subject to estate tax.

16.4.2 U.S. FEDERAL ESTATE TAX RATES

Once the "taxable estate" has been determined, U.S. federal estate tax applies at 16 graduated rates ranging from 18% on the first US$10,000 to 55% on any amount over $3 million. A "unified credit" will then reduce this tax, as we shall see below.

Some examples of the U.S. federal estate tax payable at the graduated rates (all figures in U.S. dollars) are shown below:

Taxable estate	*Tax (before credit)*
$10,000	$1,800
$50,000	$10,600
$100,000	$23,800
$200,000	$54,800
$500,000	$155,800
$1,000,000	$345,800

16.4.3 UNIFIED CREDIT

Against the estate tax, one can apply a "unified credit" of US$13,000 for non-residents who are not U.S. citizens. This credit effectively exempts US$60,000 of the estate from taxation. (It is called "unified" because it also applies against any gift tax.)

EXAMPLE

George, a citizen and resident of Canada, dies in 1995. He owns a condominium in the U.S. worth US$150,000, on which there is US$50,000 in non-recourse mortgage outstanding.

George's "taxable estate" is US$100,000. His estate tax will be US$23,800 (see table above). From this tax is deducted the US$13,000 unified credit. George's estate will be liable to pay US$10,800 in federal estate taxes.

The estate will also be liable for state death taxes, but will receive a credit against federal estate tax for such state taxes. Most states limit their death taxes to the amount of this credit, so the total combined amount of tax is not increased by the application of state tax.

For U.S. citizens and U.S. residents, the unified credit is $192,800 rather than US$13,000. This effectively exempts US$600,000 of estate (and taxable gifts) rather than US$60,000. To be resident in the U.S. for estate tax purposes, one must generally be "domiciled" in the U.S.— that is, have one's permanent home and intention to stay in the U.S. The definition of "residence" for estate and gift tax purposes is different than it is for income tax purposes.

Both the graduated rates and the unified credit are phased out for certain large estates.

16.4.4 INTERACTION WITH CANADIAN TAX

On death, Canada will normally tax the accrued capital gains in the deceased's estate (see 12.1.2).

A foreign tax credit is available in Canada to offset foreign income taxes paid on foreign-source income. However, U.S. estate taxes are not income taxes. As a result, **no foreign tax credit is currently available** to offset estate taxes. This fact can result in substantial double taxation, although as we shall see below, the Protocol to the Canada-U.S. treaty will change this.

EXAMPLE

Judy, a citizen and resident of Canada, dies in 1995. Her single U.S. asset is a vacation home in Arizona, purchased in 1974 for US$100,000 and now worth US$500,000. (Assume Judy did not elect to use her entire Canadian capital gains exemption on this property during her lifetime.)

Judy's Canadian tax will be the equivalent of US$144,000, based on ¾ inclusion of the capital gain (see 4.2) and assuming a 48% combined federal/provincial tax rate, including surtaxes. Her U.S. estate tax will be $142,800. The combined taxes of US$286,800 represent over 57% of the value of the *property and over 71% of the accrued gain. In some cases the combined taxes will exceed 100% of the accrued gain.*

The Protocol: Relief for Canadians owning U.S. property at death

Officials have been negotiating an amendment to the Canada-U.S. tax treaty for several years, and this double taxation was high on the list of trouble spots. A Protocol (amendment) to the treaty was signed on March 17, 1995. When ratified, the Protocol's provisions will apply to deaths occuring after November 10, 1988.

The Protocol may reduce and, in some cases, eliminate the double tax exposure presently faced by Canadians who die owning U.S. property by potentially increasing the effective U.S. exemption amount, providing for a limited U.S. marital credit and by significantly narrowing the types of assets that are subject to U.S. estate tax for certain "small" estates. Also, Canada will (subject to certain limits) provide a tax credit for the estate tax payable in the U.S. as a result of a Canadian's death. However, if your net worth is high, you may be no better off than you were before the Protocol.

The Protocol must be ratified before any of its provisions take effect; this is expected to happen by the end of 1995. Tax refunds will be available after the Protocol comes into force provided that the claim is filed within one year of the coming into force of the Protocol or before any applicable filing deadline established in either country.

The Protocol will increase the U.S. estate tax credit for a Canadian from the present US$13,000 (which is the estate tax payable on US$60,000) to **US$192,800**. The credit must, however, be prorated by the value of the Canadian deceased's U.S. estate over the value of the deceased individual's world-wide estate.

The proration of the credit means that Canadians will not be subject to U.S. estate tax unless the value of their world-wide gross estate exceeds **US$600,000**. It also means that wealthy Canadians who hold a relatively small proportion of their total estate in the United States may not be in a much better position than they were prior to the Protocol. These Canadians may, therefore, choose to avail themselves of the planning techniques discussed in 16.5.4 through 16.5.12.

A deceased Canadian's world-wide estate will also include some surprising items that may erode the amount of the credit. The value of life insurance policies may be included if the deceased had the right to change beneficiaries at the time of death. This may be the case even though the deceased was not a named beneficiary under the policy. Similarly, the shares of a family holding corporation that are owned by a family trust (see 12.3.4 and 12.5.3) may be included if the deceased is the trustee (and regardless of whether the deceased is a beneficiary of the trust).

Credits previously claimed against U.S. gift tax will also reduce the credit available on death. As well, all information necessary for the computation and verification of the credit must be provided to the U.S. authorities or the credit will be denied.

An additional credit will be available if an estate tax marital deduction would have been available had the surviving spouse been a U.S. citizen. However, this credit will be capped at the lesser of the unified credit allowed to the deceased's estate and the U.S. estate tax payable after other credits. The executor of the estate must elect to take advantage of this provision and must irrevocably waive the benefit of any estate tax marital deduction which may have been allowable. The deadline for the election and waiver is the date on which a qualified domestic trust election could be made under U.S. law.

If the value at death of the world-wide estate of a Canadian resident individual (other than a U.S. citizen) is less than US$1.2 million, the Protocol will limit the U.S. assets on which estate tax may be levied to properties the gain on the sale of which would have been subject to U.S. income tax under the treaty. Normally, U.S. estate tax applies to the deceased's "property situated within the U.S.", including U.S. real estate, certain tangible personal property located in the U.S., shares of U.S. corporations (regardless of the location of the share certificates and of where the shares are traded), debts of U.S. persons, and interests in partnerships carrying on business in the U.S. Where this rule applies, the U.S. may only tax gains on U.S. real estate (including U.S. real property holding corporations) and personal property constituting business property.

For Canadian tax purposes, an individual is deemed to dispose of all capital property on death and is liable for Canadian tax on any resulting gain. Under the Protocol, Canada will permit U.S. estate tax to be deducted from a Canadian resident's Canadian tax otherwise payable for the year of death. The credit will, however, be limited to the Canadian tax attributable to the deceased's U.S. source income for the year.

16.5 PLANNING OPPORTUNITIES

As noted at the beginning of this chapter, you should be extremely cautious of taking any steps in this field without adequate professional advice. We have covered the details and interaction of the U.S. and Canadian tax systems at only the most general level. Remember also that the provisions of the Protocol are not yet law.

16.5.1 ELECT NET RENTAL INCOME METHOD

If you own U.S. rental property and your expenses are significant (mortgage interest, maintenance, insurance, property management, property taxes, etc.), you will almost always want to file a U.S. income tax return and elect the "net rental income" method, as outlined in 16.1.1. The amount subject to tax at your marginal rate will be substantially lower than the amount subject to 30% withholding. Make sure you take into account the fact that the election can only be revoked in limited circumstances.

Ensure you file the return by the "last chance" deadline for claiming the deductions (October 15, 1997 for 1995 returns).

16.5.2 Sell real estate to buyer who will occupy it as principal residence

If you are selling U.S. real estate for less than US$300,000, sell it to a buyer who intends to occupy it as a principal residence if possible. The buyer need not be a U.S. resident. This will allow the buyer to pay you the full purchase price rather than having to withhold 10% to remit to the IRS under FIRPTA (see 16.2.1.1). Make sure to take into account any state withholding tax rules.

16.5.3 Apply for U.S. withholding certificate on sale of real estate

As discussed in 16.2.1.1, you can apply to the IRS for a "withholding certificate" on the basis that the U.S. tax you will have to pay on the sale of your property will be less than 10% of the total sale price. The certificate will indicate what amount of tax should be withheld by the purchaser rather than the full 10%.

16.5.4 Be cautious about keeping artwork and other assets in the U.S.

U.S. estate tax could apply to any of your personal assets that are located in the U.S. at the time of your death. As long as you have no other U.S. assets, you will be able to exempt US$60,000 of assets via the unified credit (see 16.4.3). U.S. case law has established that the assets must be located in the U.S. with a degree of permanence, so the tax probably will not apply to jewellery or other items you might take with you on vacation.

If you own U.S. real estate, however, the unified credit will likely not wipe out all of your estate tax. In such a case, any personal assets could be subject to estate tax . You may wish to limit the value of the personal assets such as artwork which you keep in the U.S.

16.5.5 Be cautious when acquiring shares in U.S. corporations

As noted in 16.4.1, the definition of "property located in the U.S." includes shares of U.S. corporations, regardless of where they are traded.

If you buy shares of U.S. corporations, whether in the U.S. or on the Toronto Stock Exchange, those shares form part of your taxable estate for U.S. estate tax purposes. You should be aware of the implications of such investments.

16.5.6 HOLD PROPERTY THROUGH CANADIAN CORPORATION

An obvious solution to U.S. estate tax is to hold any U.S. stocks and real estate in a Canadian corporation rather than personally. When you die, your corporation does not, and no U.S. estate tax applies. You have effectively converted the "location" of your assets from the U.S. to Canada. While this solution is often useful, it is fraught with pitfalls, and qualified professional advice should be obtained. We shall highlight only a few of the possible problems that must be addressed.

First, beyond the initial setup costs, there are ongoing costs to maintaining a corporation. These include legal and accounting fees, and capital taxes in some Canadian provinces.

Second, the acquisition of the U.S. assets by the corporation must be legally complete, and all corporate formalities must be observed. If it is determined that the corporation was only acting as an agent or mere title holder for you, estate tax can still apply to the property on your death.

Third, any income earned by the corporation on its U.S. assets (interest, dividends, rent, etc.) will be subject to tax both when originally earned and when paid out to you in the form of dividends. The combined effect of the taxes may be higher than the tax you would pay if you held the assets directly.

Fourth, if the property is U.S. real estate that you *already* own personally, any accrued gain will normally be taxed by the U.S. when you transfer the property to the corporation. (As noted in 16.2.1.2, the tax can be reduced where you have owned the property since before September 27, 1980.) This suggests that the corporation route may only be useful for future acquisitions of U.S. real estate, and not for transfers of existing holdings.

Fifth, if you or members of your family will be using the property for personal purposes (e.g., a vacation property which you occupy for a few weeks each year), you may be taxed in Canada as having received a shareholder benefit from the corporation.

16.5.7 LEAVE PROPERTY TO SPOUSE OR QUALIFIED DOMESTIC TRUST

As discussed in 16.4.1, estate tax can be deferred until your spouse's death to the extent you leave your U.S. assets to your spouse (if a U.S. citizen) or a qualified domestic trust (QDOT).

A properly structured QDOT may qualify as a "spousal trust" for Canadian tax purposes (see 12.3.2).

A QDOT will have the effect of capping the estate tax liability if appreciating assets are sold shortly after death and invested in U.S. fixed-income securities. The income may then be paid out to the surviving spouse and taxed on an ongoing basis, but the amount of estate tax pending will not increase beyond the fixed value of the QDOT's assets.

Proposed regulations have been introduced which will apply more stringent rules to QDOTs with assets exceeding US$2 million in value.

16.5.8 ACQUIRE PROPERTY JOINTLY WITH SPOUSE OR OTHER PERSON

You can reduce your estate tax exposure by acquiring U.S. assets jointly with your spouse (or another person). For this to work, you and your spouse will each have to supply your own funds; you cannot simply give half of the interest in the property to your spouse, or give your spouse the funds to invest.

If you have each invested your own funds and you and your spouse jointly own a condominium worth US$200,000, for example, only US$100,000 of that value will form part of your estate on your death.

16.5.9 SELL U.S. PROPERTY BEFORE DEATH

If you sell your U.S. assets (say, to a family member) before your death, and receive in exchange assets that are not "located in the U.S." (e.g., cash or a promissory note situated in Canada), you will have no U.S. assets left to form a taxable estate.

This step may be useful when death is anticipated within a short time period. For example, property could be sold to a child to whom you intend to leave the property anyway, in exchange for a bona fide promissory note. The note might then be left to your spouse or to another family member. If the note were left to the child, the sale may be treated as a gift and subject to U.S. gift tax.

On such a sale, U.S. and Canadian income tax will apply to any gain (the Canadian tax applying to three-quarters of the capital gain: see 4.2). A foreign tax credit will normally be available in Canada to offset part or all of the U.S. tax paid. The U.S. instalment sale rules (see 15.4.4) may apply where you take back a promissory note rather than cash.

Be aware of the possible application of the Canadian attribution rules (see Chapter 3) where you have transferred property to your spouse or to a family member who is under 18.

Also, make sure you do not take back debt (such as a promissory note) from someone resident in the United States, since certain debts of U.S. residents are considered to be property located in the U.S.

Before undertaking any transaction, be sure to compare the tax consequences that will arise on death to the tax consequences that will arise on a transfer before death.

16.5.10 Take out life insurance to cover estate taxes

Life insurance proceeds will not form part of your estate on death, even if provided by a U.S. insurer. If you anticipate that substantial estate tax will apply on your death, consider taking out life insurance as a way of funding the payment of the tax without requiring the sale of your U.S. assets. Bear in mind, however, that premiums paid on a life insurance policy are not deductible for either Canadian or U.S. income tax purposes. Also, if the policy is with a U.S. insurer, have your professional adviser review the Canadian income tax implications of holding the policy.

16.5.11 Mortgage property (non-recourse) to reduce value of U.S. real estate

As noted in 16.4.1, a non-recourse mortgage outstanding on your U.S. real estate will reduce your equity in the property, and thus reduce the value of your taxable estate.

Consider taking out a substantial non-recourse mortgage on your U.S. property, even where it is already fully paid off.

EXAMPLE

You own a condominium in Florida, now worth US$200,000 and clear of all mortgages. Your worldwide assets are substantial. If you die, the U.S. estate tax will come to US$41,800.

Assume you borrow US$100,000 against the property at 11%, on a non-recourse basis, and invest the funds in Canada at 10%. Subject to currency fluctuations, your annual cost will be approximately US$1,000. If you die after taking out this mortgage, your taxable estate will be only US$100,000, and the estate tax will be US$10,800—a US$31,000 saving.

The mortgage should be obtained from a lender resident in Canada (however, Canadian financial institutions generally are reluctant to lend on a non-recourse basis, so you will have to seek out other sources). Canadian withholding tax (usually 15%) will apply to the interest payments you make to the non-resident lender if you are deducting the interest paid for Canadian tax purposes. In Canada, your interest expense will normally be denied to the extent it exceeds the investment income you earn from investing the loan proceeds. This has the effect of reducing the hoped-for estate tax savings.

Over time, the property's value may increase and the mortgage amount will decrease. Because of this, the potential U.S. estate tax will increase as time goes by.

16.5.12 Acquire U.S. property through irrevocable Canadian trust

It may be possible to acquire your U.S. property through a trust that is resident in Canada, thus removing the property from the ambit of U.S. estate tax. Extreme care must, however, be exercised in drafting the trust document, selecting the trustees, and setting out the powers of the trustees and the beneficiaries.

16.5.13 Consider the effects of the Protocol in your situation

Monitor the progress of the Protocol (see 16.4.4) through the Canadian Parliament and U.S. Congress. The Protocol will reduce the U.S. estate tax bite for many Canadians holding U.S. property. Nonetheless, many situations will remain where the Protocol will not provide complete relief (particularly for larger estates). Accordingly, you should put pencil to paper to calculate the impact of the Protocol on your situation, and to determine whether some of the other planning ideas described in the previous sections would be beneficial.

16.5.14 Avoid becoming a U.S. resident while visiting

If you regularly spend a large portion of each year in the U.S., make sure you understand the "physical presence" and "closer connection" rules described in 16.3. If you accidentally become a U.S. resident for tax purposes, the tax cost can be substantial.

16.6 References

Revenue Canada publishes a booklet titled "**Canadian Residents Going Down South**", available (in person or by phone) from any District Taxation Office. Written jointly with the IRS, it includes information on U.S. tax laws.

The following publications may be obtained by telephoning or writing to any office of the Internal Revenue Service. They may also be available at United States embassy and consular offices.

- Form 706NA, "United States Estate (and Generation Skipping Transfer) Tax Return: Estate of nonresident not a citizen of the United States"
- Form 1040NR, "U.S. Nonresident Alien Income Tax Return"
- Form 4224, "Exemption from Withholding of Tax on Income Effectively Connected with the Conduct of a Trade or Business in the United States"
- Form 8288-B, "Application for Withholding Certificate for Dispositions by Foreign Persons of U.S. Real Property Interests"

Form 8840, "Closer Connection Statement"HRPublication 515, "Withholding of Tax on Nonresident Aliens and Foreign Corporations"

Publication 519, "U.S. Tax Guide for Aliens"

Assistance and advice on completing U.S. tax returns can be obtained from the Internal Revenue Service in Ottawa at (613) 563-1834, fax (613) 230-1376.

17 THE GOODS AND SERVICES TAX

PLANNING TIPS

- Claim input tax credits for your business
- Consider GST when purchasing a home
- Consider GST if you own rental real estate
- Employees and partners should claim GST rebate
- Plan around GST on employment benefits
- Get credit for GST when trading in a used car
- Purchase from small suppliers
- Be aware of GST on food
- Non-residents should claim GST rebate after visiting Canada
- Claim the GST Credit

The Goods and Services Tax (GST) has been the subject of much controversy, both before and since its implementation on January 1, 1991. This tax applies to most purchases of goods and services. In this chapter we provide a brief overview of the GST and offer some suggestions for planning around it. The legislation and regulations that implement the tax are complex, and we will not cover all of the myriad exceptions and special rules.

The present Liberal government was elected with a mandate to abolish the GST. However, a parliamentary committee set up to study the GST recommended in June 1994 that it be retained though joined with the provincial sales taxes and hidden (buried in retail prices). At time of writing, no official proposals for change had been announced.

The Quebec Sales Tax (alone of the provincial sales taxes) is largely harmonized with the GST. See 14.4.

17.1 HOW DOES THE GST WORK?

The GST is a 7% tax on almost all goods sold and services provided in Canada. It has replaced the Federal Sales Tax (FST), which was in place from 1924 to 1990 and operated as a tax on the manufacturers' sale price of goods.

The GST is a tax on the **consumer**. Businesses pay GST up front but generally receive a full refund (an "input tax credit") for all GST paid. Ultimately, only the final consumer bears the burden of the GST. Businesses collect GST on sales, but since they receive full credit for GST paid on purchases, they remit only the difference to the federal government.

EXAMPLE

ABC Manufacturing Co. makes a refrigerator. It pays $100 for raw materials. The materials are subject to GST of $7. ABC pays the $7 to its supplier, who remits it to Revenue Canada. ABC now has an input tax credit of $7.

ABC sells the refrigerator to XYZ Appliances Co. for $300. On this amount, it collects $21 in GST. ABC remits $14 to Revenue Canada ($21 minus $7).

XYZ Appliances Co. sells the refrigerator to Fred Consumer for $700, and collects $49 in GST. XYZ remits $28 to Revenue Canada ($49 minus $21).

Fred Consumer has now paid $49 in GST, which is 7% of the final sales price. All of the GST paid at previous levels has been refunded. Both ABC and XYZ receive full refunds of their GST paid, since they deduct it from their GST collected before remitting the funds to the government.

Looking at the numbers:

	GST Paid	GST Collected	GST Remitted
Raw Materials Supplier		$ 7	$ 7
ABC Manufacturing	$7	$21	$14
XYZ Appliances	$21	$49	$28
Consumer	$49		

The total under "GST remitted" is $49, the same amount that the consumer has paid. The businesses simply act as collection agents, collecting the tax along each stage of the process. (The GST is thus a "value added" tax, or VAT, levied on the value added at each stage.)

If a business has more GST paid than GST collected, it will receive a refund of the difference from Revenue Canada.

Note that GST input tax credits (ITCs) are immediately or fully available to businesses for all GST paid, even where it is paid on capital equipment that is depreciated over many years for income tax purposes (see 7.2.4). However, there are some limitations to ITCs which parallel limitations in the income tax system. For example, only 50% of meal and entertainment expenses qualify for ITC purposes (see 7.2.6), and there is a $24,000 cap on the cost of a car when it comes to claiming an ITC (see 6.9.1 and 7.2.5). Also, small businesses that use the "Quick Method" of filing (see 17.3.2) can claim input tax credits only in respect of capital purchases.

A "GST credit" is available to offset the impact of the GST on low-income taxpayers. The credit is claimed and paid through the income tax system.

17.2 WHAT DOES GST NOT COVER?

GST generally applies to **taxable supplies,** which means most property and services—everything from appliances and new homes to restaurant meals, hotel accommodation, haircuts and lawyers' bills. Certain goods and services are not taxed, however. They fall into two distinct categories.

17.2.1 ZERO-RATED SUPPLIES

Zero-rated supplies are technically "taxable supplies", but they are taxed at 0%. Since they are, technically, taxable, the business selling them receives full credit for all GST paid on its costs of producing those supplies. As a result, no GST is built into the final price that the consumer pays. Zero-rated supplies include:

- most **groceries**
- **prescription drugs** and **medical devices**
- goods **exported** out of Canada
- most services rendered to **non-residents** of Canada
- travel or shipping to or from points **outside Canada**, *except* **air** travel to the continental U.S.
- most **farming and fishing products**

EXAMPLE

ABC Manufacturing buys raw materials for $100 and pays $7 in GST. It manufactures a refrigerator, which it sells for $300 to a retailer in the United States.

No GST applies on the sale to the U.S. retailer, since the goods have been exported. ABC Manufacturing receives a refund from the federal government of the $7 GST which it paid (and which the supplier of the raw materials has remitted to Revenue Canada). The price the U.S. retailer pays therefore has no GST built into it.

17.2.2 EXEMPT SUPPLIES

Supplies that are "exempt" are not subject to GST. From the consumer's point of view there is no apparent difference between a zero-rated supply and an exempt supply. However, the business receives no credit for GST paid on goods and services used in providing exempt supplies. The GST is thus buried and passed on to consumers in the final price, or absorbed by the business. Exempt supplies include:

- **medical, dental** and other health care services
- **day-care** and **educational** services

- residential **rent** for one month or more
- **used housing** (except where substantially renovated by a developer)
- most **land** sold by individuals, where the land was not used in a business
- most **farmland sold to relatives** for their personal use and enjoyment
- **financial services**, including **insurance**
- certain supplies made by **charities, non-profit organizations and governments**, including, for example, municipal public transit services and water

EXAMPLE

Jeff is a dentist. He spends $40,000 to buy equipment for his dental office, and pays $2,800 GST on that amount. He also pays $20,000 in rent for the year, plus $1,400 in GST.

Since Jeff's services are exempt, he does not collect GST from his patients. But, unlike businesses selling taxable or zero-rated supplies, Jeff receives no credit for the $4,200 GST he has paid. He must set his fees high enough to recover this GST.

Although water is exempt, other utilities such as electricity, gas, cable TV and telephone are all taxable.

Membership in many professional organizations, such as provincial law societies, accountants' institutes, etc., could be exempt, but most such organizations have elected to make their fees taxable. If they remained exempt they would have to absorb all GST on their purchases. By opting to be taxable they receive a refund for all GST they pay. The consequence is that they charge GST on fees to their members; but where most members are in business for themselves (e.g., lawyers and accountants), those members receive a refund for any GST they pay anyway. As a result, if you are a member of a professional organization, you can usually expect GST to apply to your fees.

Sales of **used goods** by private individuals are effectively like exempt supplies, since no GST is charged on them.

17.2.3 Small suppliers

Businesses with less than $30,000 in annual sales are not required to register under the GST (except for taxi operators, who must always register). If they do not register, they cannot claim input tax credits for their purchases; but they also do not charge GST to their customers. Many such small businesses whose customers are primarily consumers will therefore not register.

EXAMPLE

Jack washes windows for a living. He makes about $25,000 each year. He knocks on your door one day and offers to wash your windows for $50.

As long as Jack has not registered under the GST, no tax will apply to his window-washing services.

If Jack is washing your office windows rather than your home windows, you will not receive any input tax credit in respect of his bill—because you are not paying any GST on that bill. This is true even though Jack's price reflects the GST that he *has to pay on his washing fluid and squeegees.*

Where the customers of a business are themselves businesses, it makes sense to register. If Jack washes only office windows for a living, his clients will not object to him registering and collecting GST, since they will receive a full input tax credit for the GST they pay. (The only exceptions will be businesses that make exempt supplies, such as financial institutions and health care professionals.) Jack, in turn, will be able to recover the GST he pays on his materials and other costs of doing business.

17.3 GST AND BUSINESSES

17.3.1 CLAIMING INPUT TAX CREDITS

Claims for input tax credits must generally be supported by receipts or other documentation, not submitted with the GST return but held on file in case of audit. All documentation must show:

- the vendor's name
- the date (or, for a contract, the date amounts are payable)
- the total amount payable.

Where the total (including all taxes) is $30 or over, the receipt must also show:

- the amount of GST, or a statement that the total includes GST, and a clear indication of which items are taxable
- the supplier's GST registration number (the letter R followed by nine digits)

In addition, where the total is $150 or over, the receipt must also show:

- the purchaser's name
- the terms of payment
- a description sufficient to identify each item supplied

Failure to have this documentation will normally lead to a disallowance of any input tax credit claim if the return is audited.

Note that input tax credits can only be claimed where the expenses were incurred in the course of providing "taxable supplies" A business engaged in providing "exempt supplies"—such as a doctor, dentist or financial institution—cannot claim input tax credits in respect of the costs of making those supplies. Zero-rated supplies (including exports) are taxable supplies, however (see 17.2.1).

17.3.2 THE "QUICK METHOD" AND SIMPLIFIED ACCOUNTING

Small businesses may elect to use the "Quick Method" to simplify record-keeping for GST. It can be used by any business with annual sales under $200,000 (excluding sales of basic groceries). This method can be particularly useful for certain consultants. However, the Quick Method may not be used by anyone providing legal, accounting, actuarial, bookeeping, financial consulting, tax consulting or tax return preparation services.

Under the Quick Method, instead of remitting total GST collected minus total GST paid, the business remits to Revenue Canada a flat percentage of sales (including GST). Where sales are mostly services rather than goods, the flat percentage is **5%** (but only **4% on the first $30,000** of sales). For qualifying suppliers whose purchases of taxable personal property (other than basic groceries) for resale are at least 40% of sales (excluding basic groceries), the flat percentage is 2½% (but only 1½% on the first $30,000 of sales). Input tax credits can only be claimed for capital purchases.

EXAMPLE

John is a computer consultant. He bills his clients $100,000 in 1995, plus $7,000 GST, for his consulting services. Because he is able to use his clients' equipment and facilities, his cost of doing business is very low. He pays a total of $70 GST on $1,000 of business expenses during the year.

Normally, John would remit his GST collected minus his GST paid to Revenue Canada for the year. This would be $7,000 minus $70, or $6,930.

By electing to use the Quick Method, however, John will be required to remit a flat 4% of the first $30,000 of his GST-included sales and 5% on the remaining $77,000 (or, to put it another way, 5% of his total sales of $107,000, minus $300). He thus remits $5,050 instead of $6,930.

Clearly, the Quick Method can be useful for businesses that have few taxable expenses. If the business's taxable expenses are high, however, the loss of the ability to claim input tax credits will offset the benefit of the Quick Method's reduced remittance rate.

Simplified accounting

As an alternative to the Quick Method, you can total up your GST-bearing purchases — including GST, provincial sales tax, late payment penalties and tips — and claim $^{7}/_{107}$ of the total for input tax credit purposes. Your business's annual sales must not exceed $500,000 for you to use this method. Not only does it make accounting for input tax credits simpler, but it gives you a slightly larger claim than you can make by totalling up individual amounts of GST paid.

17.3.3 OTHER MISCELLANEOUS RULES

The GST rules are many and complex (the legislation and regulations run more than 600 pages). In this section we highlight just a few of the special rules.

Suppliers may price their goods and services "**GST included**" or "**GST extra**". It is entirely up to the supplier, as long as the status of the GST is clear. Most retailers price their goods GST-extra, so that they can advertise or display prices that appear more competitive. On the other hand, taxi drivers, movie theatres and many other businesses typically advertise or price their goods and services GST-included, to avoid customer resistance when the time comes to pay.

When a **business or part of a business is sold**, provided various requirements are met, one can avoid having GST apply to the sale.

There is no GST on **directors' fees**, since they are considered employment income.

Partnerships must register and account for GST directly (this is in contrast to the rule for income tax purposes: see 7.3.1). For **joint ventures** that are not partnerships, the individual participants must account for the GST; however, where the joint venture relates to certain activities such as real estate or oil and gas exploration, an election is available to allow the operator of the venture to handle all GST accounting on behalf of all participants.

Where a price is unconditionally **discounted** (e.g., $1,000, 30% off, you pay $700), the GST is paid on the discounted price. However, where an invoice provides a discount for early payment or a penalty for late payment, GST applies to the invoice price *before* the discount or penalty.

GST normally applies to **employee benefits** that would be taxable if acquired directly by the employee, such as the use of a car (see 6.1.2, 6.4 and 6.9.1). In general, an employer who is a GST registrant will be required to remit 7% GST on an employee's taxable benefit as if it had been collected on the last day of February of the following taxation year (the date when the T4 slip is due). If the employer is not a GST registrant or the employee drives the car 90% or more for personal use, the employer will not be required to remit GST on the taxable benefit (although it is still reported on employees' T4 slips). However, in such cases the employer cannot claim an input tax credit on the purchase of the car.

The "12¢ per personal-use kilometre" benefit for automobile operating costs (see 6.4) includes 0.6¢/km of GST on the taxable benefit (i.e., 5% of the benefit). This GST must be remitted by the employers who are GST registrants to Revenue Canada as though it had been collected on the last day of February after the end of the year.

17.4 REBATES

When GST applies to goods and services, it generally applies no matter who purchases them. (This simplifies things for the business collecting GST.) The only exceptions are the Governor General, Indians on reserves, provincial governments, and non-residents who are outside Canada.

In some cases, however, a purchaser who pays tax may obtain a refund of all or part of the GST paid. Businesses producing taxable goods and services, as already noted, receive a complete refund in the form of an input tax credit.

Employees and **partners** who are allowed to deduct certain expenses from employment or partnership income for income tax purposes can generally claim a rebate of GST paid on those expenses (see 6.9). Documentation must be kept to support the claim for the rebate: see 17.3.1. The rebate claim is filed with your personal income tax return.

EXAMPLE

Michelle is required to drive 10,000 km for employment-related purposes during the year. She also drives 10,000 km on personal trips. She spends $2,140 (including GST) over the course of the year in gas and repairs for her car, and does not receive any reimbursement from her employer. All the expenses are paid in Canada.

Since one-half of Michelle's expenses are required by her employment, she can claim $1,070 as a deduction from employment income. That figure, however, already includes $70 in GST that applied to the gas and repairs. Michelle can claim a rebate of the $70 on a form filed with her income tax return. If she deducts the full $1,070, the $70 rebate is taxable in the year she receives it. Alternatively, she can choose to claim only $1,000 in expenses net of the $70 rebate, and it will not be taxable when received.

Michelle can also claim a rebate of $^{7}/_{107}$ of the capital cost allowance she deducts in respect of her car. See the example in 6.9.1.

Note that a rebate is only available where GST was paid on the purchase. Michelle cannot receive a rebate in respect of the deductible portion of her car insurance, since insurance is not taxable. Similarly, there is no rebate for GST paid on gas purchased in the United States, because there is *no GST included in the price of such gas.*

Charities, non-profit organizations, municipalities, universities, colleges, hospitals and most **schools** receive a partial rebate ranging from 50% to 83% of most GST paid by them on the costs of making exempt supplies.

If you buy a **new home** as your principal place of residence for less than $450,000, a rebate is available either from Revenue Canada or directly from the vendor—in the latter case, you will pay the vendor less than the full 7% GST. For homes priced under $347,222 (before GST), the rebate is 2.52% of the purchase price and from that point to $350,000 it is capped at $8,750. For homes from $350,000 to $450,000, calculate the rebate as follows: subtract

$350,000 from the purchase price, multiply by 0.0875, and subtract the result from $8,750. Once the price hits $450,000 there is no rebate, and you pay the full 7% tax.

EXAMPLE

Joan buys a new home for $300,000.

The GST at 7% would normally be $21,000. Due to the rebate of 2.52%, however, Joan pays only $13,440 in GST to the vendor—a tax rate of 4.48%.

Non-residents who visit Canada are entitled to a full rebate of GST on goods they take out of the country with them, as well as on most hotel accommodation.

17.5 ADMINISTRATION

Generally, large businesses (over $6 million in annual taxable sales in Canada) are required to file GST returns monthly. Medium-sized businesses file quarterly, while those with less than $500,000 in annual taxable sales have the option of filing annually. Businesses can always file more frequently than required. Groups of associated companies base the frequency of their filing on the total taxable revenues of all the companies in the group.

For monthly and quarterly filers, GST must be remitted to Revenue Canada within **one month** after the end of the month or quarter in which it is invoiced (regardless of whether it has been collected).

Businesses filing annually make their payment of any outstanding GST **three months** after their year-end, having made quarterly instalments during the year. Instalments are based on the lower of the previous year's net GST and the estimated current year's net GST, as with the first two methods for calculating income tax instalments (see 13.2.2).

No instalments are required if the net GST owing for the year is less than $1,500.

Effective spring 1996, individuals filing annually can file their GST returns up to June 15, although the deadline for remittance of tax will likely still be March 31. This change allows income tax and GST returns to be filed together, since the deadline for income tax returns is also extended to June 15 for persons carrying on business (see 7.2.1).

Where GST or instalments are remitted late, interest and penalty apply. The interest rate varies with current commercial rates; as of the second quarter of 1995, the rate was 0.6% per month. The penalty is an additional 0.5% per month. The interest and penalty are compounded *daily*.

17.6 PROVINCIAL SALES TAXES

All provinces except Alberta have general retail sales taxes on most goods and certain services. Since the introduction of the GST, the federal government has encouraged the provinces to harmonize their retail sales tax bases with the GST, to simplify administration for businesses. Only Quebec has harmonized its sales tax system with the GST, however. The new Quebec system, which is virtually identical to the GST, came into effect in July 1992 and has been closely harmonized with the GST as of August 1995 (see 14.4).

In British Columbia, Saskatchewan, Manitoba and Ontario, retail sales tax applies to prices exclusive of GST. In the Atlantic provinces and Quebec, the sales tax applies to the price after GST is added.

EXAMPLE

You purchase a used car from a dealer in Ontario for $10,000.

GST of $700 will be added to the car's purchase price. Ontario sales tax of 8%, or $800, applies to the $10,000 cost. Your bill comes to $11,500.

Suppose you buy the same $10,000 car in Nova Scotia, where the sales tax rate is 11%. GST is still $700, but the provincial sales tax applies to the GST-included price of $10,700. Therefore, the provincial tax is $1,177 (an effective rate of 11.77% on the basic price of the car).

17.7 Importing goods

When you import goods from outside Canada, GST applies and is collected by Canada Customs (in addition to any customs duties), or by Canada Post where you order goods by mail. (Canada Post will charge you an extra $5 handling fee.)

There is an exemption from GST to parallel the exemption for customs duties for returning residents after a period outside Canada ($50 of goods after 24 hours, $200 after 48 hours, $500 after a week). There are a number of other exemptions, including one for goods under $20, excluding books and magazines, that are sent by mail order from outside Canada.

17.8 Transitional rules

A number of transitional rules applied to smooth the introduction of the GST. Only one is still relevant.

No GST applies to lease payments if the lease was signed before August 8, 1989 and has not been modified or extended since that date. A purchase option may be added to such a lease in many cases, allowing the purchase to escape GST as well.

17.9 Planning tips

17.9.1 If you own a business

If you are self-employed or the owner-manager of an incorporated business, the business can normally claim a full refund of the GST paid on most purchases. To be eligible for input tax credits, you must **register with Revenue Canada** to collect GST even if your sales are under $30,000. Make sure to keep accurate records so as to claim credits where possible (see 17.3.1). As is the case for income tax purposes, "personal or living expenses" are not eligible for input tax credits. Once you are registered, you *must* charge GST on all your taxable sales (though you can build it into your prices if you wish; see 17.3.3).

If you are running a small business, you should obtain professional advice in order to minimize the cost to your business of the GST. A number of special options and elections are available. In particular, you may be able to use the Quick Method or "simplified accounting" (see 17.3.2), under which the calculation of the GST you remit will be simplified.

17.9.2 Consider GST when purchasing a home

No GST applies to used housing, so a resale home may be cheaper than a new home.

The GST on a new home after the new housing rebate will be 4.48% as long as the total cost is under $347,222. Above that level, as noted in 17.4, it rises gradually to 7%, the level that applies if the home costs $450,000 or more. As long as you stay within this dollar limit, the rebate is available for all permanent parts of the home. If you are planning to add a swimming pool or landscaping, therefore, consider having them built as part of the construction price so that they become eligible for the 2.52% rebate.

If you buy land from an individual (exempt of GST) and then have a house built on it, the GST will apply only to the costs of building the house. (As well, there is a partial rebate of the GST on construction costs where the value of the house and land is less than $450,000, to parallel the 2.52% rebate on purchase of new homes.) Where land costs are high, therefore, it will be cheaper to buy the land from an individual owner and then contract with a builder than to buy the entire property from the builder.

Remember that GST will apply to lawyers' fees, real estate agents' commissions, moving expenses and other costs relating to real estate transactions, even those of resale homes.

17.9.3 If you own rental real estate

If you rent out residential real estate (whether a house or an apartment building), no GST will apply to the rent, since it is an "exempt supply" (see 17.2.2). As a result, you cannot use the input tax credit system to recover any of the GST that you pay on utilities, property management fees and other costs. You must set the rent high enough to cover your costs.

Rental of commercial real estate is taxable, unless your total revenue (including from any businesses you operate) is under $30,000 and you choose to remain outside the GST system as a "small supplier" (see 17.2.3). If you are renting to a business that makes taxable supplies (that is, just about any business other than a financial institution, health care professional, school or day care), you are likely better off to register, collect GST (which your tenant will recover in the form of an input tax credit), and claim input tax credits for GST paid on your costs, such as utilities and property management fees.

17.9.4 Employees and partners should claim GST rebates

Where employees and partners (who are not registered for GST purposes) have unreimbursed expenses such as automobile expenses that are deductible for income tax purposes, a rebate can generally be claimed for the GST paid. See 17.4 and 6.9.

Make sure to keep records through the year and obtain invoices that indicate the amount of GST paid. The rebate is claimed with your individual income tax return.

17.9.5 Planning around GST on employment benefits

Your T4 slip will normally reflect, as part of your employee benefits, a GST element of those benefits that are taxable to you. See 6.1.2 and 6.4. This GST element must be remitted by your employer as though it had been collected as GST.

In general, your employer receives an input tax credit for the GST originally paid on the purchase of the benefit, and the employer must remit GST for the related taxable benefit. However, certain input tax credits are restricted, such as where an automobile cost more than $24,000 (see 17.1). If you make use of a company car that is over the $24,000 threshold, there is an element of double GST due to the lack of a full input tax credit to your employer.

The impact of GST should be carefully considered on your existing employment benefits and on any new ones that are being contemplated.

17.9.6 Get credit for GST when trading in a used car

If you trade in a used car for, say, $5,000, and purchase a new car for $20,000, you will be charged 7% tax on the $20,000. The dealer, however, will receive a notional input tax credit of 7/107 of the $5,000 value of your trade-in. That is, even though you don't collect tax on the trade-in, the dealer receives a credit as if the trade-in price included GST.

Make sure that your final deal reflects this benefit that the dealer will receive. From your point of view, the price should be adjusted so that the effective GST you pay is on the difference in prices of the cars rather than on the total cost of the new car—since that difference is the amount of GST that the dealer must remit to Revenue Canada.

Note that if you used the car primarily for your business and you are a GST registrant, you must collect GST from the dealer when trading it in, and remit that GST to Revenue Canada. In such a case, the 7/107 of the total paid by the dealer to you, which the dealer claims as an input tax credit, is identical to the GST you remit.

17.9.7 PURCHASE FROM SMALL SUPPLIERS

Purchases from door-to-door vendors or other suppliers with less than $30,000 in sales per year will normally be free of GST (unless the vendor has registered, as noted in 17.2.3). Handymen or contractors who are not registered are not required to collect GST. You should therefore ensure that their prices do not include GST. If they collect GST from you, they must include their GST registration number on their invoice.

17.9.8 BE AWARE OF GST ON FOOD

Most groceries purchased in stores are not taxed. GST applies to most snack foods (potato chips, candies, soft drinks, etc.—if your kids like it, it's probably taxable). Restaurant meals are taxed, as are most take-out or delivered prepared foods, and food bought from vending machines.

In some cases you can avoid GST by buying food in large enough quantities to be considered bulk. Single servings of doughnuts or other pastries are taxable, but if you buy six or more (including in combinations) from a bakery, there is no GST. Similarly, a litre of ice cream bought at the supermarket is not taxable, but an ice-cream cone is. Apple juice packaged in multiple servings is not taxable, but a single small jar of juice is.

17.9.9 IF YOU HAVE FRIENDS OR RELATIVES VISITING FROM OUTSIDE CANADA

Non-residents are eligible for a full refund of GST paid on most goods they take back with them (but not alcohol and tobacco), as well as hotel accommodation while in Canada (see 17.4). They should keep receipts and apply for a refund once they get home.

They can also claim their refunds at duty-free stores at many land border points (all the airport duty-free shops have opted out of the refund program, not being able to handle the volume). Telephone 1-800-66VISIT from within Canada for information on this Visitors' Rebate Program.

The refund does not apply to purchases or services consumed in Canada, such as restaurant meals, gas or haircuts.

Many provinces also provide a refund of provincial sales tax on goods taken out of the province. For Quebec and Manitoba, this is handled by Revenue Canada on the same form on which the GST refund is claimed.

17.9.10 CLAIM THE GST CREDIT

As discussed in 1.5.2, a GST Credit is available through the income tax system for low and medium-income families. If your family income is under about $30,000-35,000 (depending on the number of children you have), make sure to apply for the GST Credit on your income tax return.

17.10 REFERENCES

A great deal of information is available (by phone or in person) from your nearest Revenue Canada Excise office. These include pamphlets, booklets, Guides and "GST Memoranda", which are comparable to Revenue Canada Taxation's Interpretation Bulletins dealing with income tax matters. The following is a small sample of publications that you may find useful:

Pamphlets and booklets

The Quick Method of Accounting Guide and Election Form
The Simplified Methods for Claiming Input Tax Credits and Rebates
Simplifying the GST for Small Businesses
Goods and Services Tax Refund for Visitors

Guides

Guide to the GST Tax Return for Registrants
Doing Business in Canada—A Guide for Non-Residents
Information for Health Care Professionals
Completion Guide and Form for General Rebate Application
Completion Guide and Form for Employee and Partner GST Rebate
Completion Guide and Form for New Housing Rebate
Information for Employers on Employee Benefits

APPENDIX I

1995 Personal Tax Credits

	Federal Tax Credit	Québec Tax Credit
Basic	$1,098	$1,180
Person living alone	N/A	210
Spousal	915[1]	1,180[2]
Income limit	538	
Dependent child 18 or under	—	520[3]
over 18 and full-time student	N/A	520[2,3]
over 18 and mentally or physically infirm	269[1]	1,180[3]
Income limit	2,690	
Other dependant over 18 General	N/A	480[2]
Mentally or physically infirm	N/A	1,180
Post-secondary student	N/A	330[2,4]
Income limit	N/A	
Person 65 or over	592[6]	440[5]
Direct ascendant	N/A	550
Adoption expenses	N/A	2,000[7]
Mental or physical impairment	720[6]	440

[1] Credit will be reduced by 17% of net income in excess of the amount stated below.

[2] The tax credit is reduced by 20% of the individual's net income.

[3] For the second and each subsequent child, the tax credit is decreased to $480. For single-parent families an additional tax credit of $260 is allowed for the first child.

[4] Tax credit is $330 per term, limited to two terms.

[5] This tax credit will not be affected by the taxpayer's employment and business income.

[6] This tax credit is transferable to a spouse. The credit available for transfer is reduced by the amount resulting from the application of the credit reduction rate to the transferor's net income in excess of $6,456. In 1994 the federal age amount ($3,482) used to determine the credit will be reduced by an amount equal to 7.5% of a taxpayer's net income in excess of $25,921. The rate will be increased to 15% in 1995.

[7] The maximum adoption expenses eligible for the credit is $10,000 for 1995 (see 14.2.9).

APPENDIX II

1995 Federal Income Tax Rates

If Taxable Income is:

Over—	But not over—	The tax is:	of the amount over—
$ 0	$29,590	$ 0 + 17%	$ 0
29,590	59,180	5,030 + 26%	29,590
59,180	—	12,724 + 29%	59,180

Federal Surtax

A surtax of 3% of federal tax is levied after taking into account any applicable credits. Where basic federal tax, after deducting any applicable credits and before adding the 3% surtax, exceeds $12,500, an additional surtax of 5% of the basic federal tax in excess of $12,500 is applicable.

1995 Provincial Income Tax Rates

	Percentage of Federal Tax		Percentage of Federal Tax
British Columbia	52.5%[1]	New Brunswick	64.0%[7]
Alberta	45.5%[2]	Nova Scotia	59.5%[8]
Saskatchewan	50.0%[3]	Prince Edward Island	59.5%[9]
Manitoba	52.0%[4]	Northwest Territories	45.0%
Ontario	58.0%[5]	Yukon	50.0%[10]
Québec	N/A[6]	Non-resident	52.0%
Newfoundland	69.0%		

1. A surtax of 30% applies to B.C. tax in excess of $5,300 (but not over $9,000) plus an additional surtax of 20% applies to B.C. tax in excess of $9,000.
2. A surtax of 8% of basic Alberta tax in excess of $3,500 and a flat tax rate of 0.5% of Alberta taxable income are also levied.
3. There is a flat tax of 2% of net income and a surtax of 15% on Saskatchewan tax (including flat tax) in excess of $4,000. A 10% "Deficit Surtax" applies to basic Saskatchewan tax plus the flat tax.
4. A surtax equal to 2% of net income in excess of $30,000 and a flat tax of 2% of net income are levied in Manitoba.
5. A surtax of 20% applies to basic Ontario tax in excess of $5,500 plus an additional surtax of 10% applies to Ontario tax exceeding $8,000.
6. For the Québec tax rate schedule, see Appendix III.
7. A surtax of 8% applies to New Brunswick tax in excess of $13,500.
8. A surtax of 10% applies to Nova Scotia tax in excess of $10,000.
9. A surtax of 10% applies to basic P.E.I. tax in excess of $12,500.
10. A surtax of 5% applies to basic Yukon tax in excess of $6,000.

APPENDIX III

1995 Québec Provincial Income Tax Rates*

Taxable Income	Québec Tax	On Next	Marginal Rate
NIL	NIL	$ 7,000	16%
$ 7,000	$ 1,120	7,000	19
14,000	2,450	9,000	21
23,000	4,340	27,000	23
50,000 and over	10,550	remainder	24

* Tax payable in Québec may be reduced by personal tax credits, any dividend tax credit (11.09% of actual amount of taxable Canadian dividends), foreign tax credits, credits for the acquisition of SODEQ shares, Class A shares relating to Fonds de solidarité des travailleurs du Québec or shares relating to the proposed "CNTU funds" and contributions to Québec provincial political parties.

Residents of Québec receive a reduction of federal taxes equal to 16.5% of basic federal tax

A surtax of 5% applies to Québec tax in excess of $5,000 plus an additional surtax of 5% applies to Québec tax in excess of $10,000.

A tax reduction is available in Québec which is equal to 2% of the excess of $10,000 over provincial taxes payable after deducting non-refundable tax credits. It declines as tax increases, reaching zero at $10,000 of taxes payable.

1995 Combined Federal and Québec Tax Rates[1]

Taxable Income	Combined Federal/Québec tax[2]		
$ 0–$ 6,459	Nil		
6,460– 8,349	Nil	plus 14.7% on excess over	$ 6,459
8,350– 14,000	$ 278	plus 34.1% on excess over	8,349
14,001– 23,000	2,205	plus 36.1% on excess over	14,000
23,001– 29,590	5,454	plus 38.2% on excess over	23,000
29,591– 31,000	7,971	plus 46.0% on excess over	29,590
31,001– 50,000	8,619	plus 47.1% on excess over	31,000
50,001– 52,625	17,568	plus 48.2% on excess over	50,000
52,626– 59,180	18,832	plus 48.9% on excess over	52,625
59,181– 62,195	22,037	plus 51.5% on excess over	59,180
62,196 and over	23,589	plus 52.9% on excess over	62,195

[1] Assumes a single tax filer.

[2] Assumes a single tax filer with ordinary income who is only entitled to the basic personal credit of $1,098 for federal purposes and to the basic personal credit of $1,180 for Québec purposes.

APPENDIX IV

Worksheets for Estimating 1995 Tax Liability

Schedule 1—Estimated 1995 Net Income

	1994 Actual	1995 Estimate	
Income			
Employment income	$	$	
Pensions—OAS/CPP/QPP			
—Other			
Taxable Canadian dividends (cash amount × 5/4)			
Interest			
Net rental income/(loss)			
Taxable capital gains net of allowable capital losses			
Net business and other self-employment income/(loss)			
Alimony or separation allowances received			
Workers' Compensation, social assistance and net federal supplements received (line 147 from 1994 federal tax return)			(A)
Other income			
Total Income	$	$	(T)
Deductions			
RPP/RRSP contributions	$	$	
Child care expenses			
Carrying charges—investments			
Moving expenses			
Alimony or separation allowances paid			
Tax shelter losses and deductions			
Other deductions			
Total Deductions	$	$	(D)
Income before deduction for tax on OAS benefits (T-D)	$	$	(F)
Deduction for tax on OAS benefits (from Schedule 3)	( )	( )	
Net Income	$	$	*

*Carry this amount forward to Schedule 2

Schedule 2—Estimated 1995 Tax Payable

	Federal Estimate	Québec Estimate
Calculation of taxable income		
Net income—from Schedule 1	$ ______	$ ______
Less:		
Québec deduction for strategic investments	N/A	(______)
Prior years' net capital losses	(______)	(______)
Other deductions from net income including amount (A) on Schedule 1	(______)	(______)
Taxable income	$ ______	$ ______

Calculation of tax (see rates in Appendices II and III)

				Federal	Québec
Federal taxable income (above)	$ ______				
Tax on first	______		is	______ (B)	
Tax on the remaining	______	@ _ %	is	______ (C)	
Federal tax on taxable income (B + C)				______ (D)	
Québec taxable income (above)	$ ______				
Tax on first	______		is		______ (E)
Tax on the remaining	______	@ _ %	is		______ (F)
Québec tax on taxable income (E + F)					______ (G)
Less total personal credits (see Schedule IV)				(______) (H)	(______) (I)
Basic federal tax (D – H)				$ ______ (J)	
Québec tax subtotal (G – I)					$ ______ (K)

	Federal Estimate	Québec Estimate
Basic federal and/or Québec tax (amounts (J) and/or (K) from previous page)	$______ (J)	$______ (K)
Federal surtax		
Regular surtax 3% x J	______ (L)	N/A
High income surtax 5% × (J – $12,500)	______ (M)	N/A
Québec surtax		
Regular surtax 5% × K	N/A	______ (N)
High income surtax 5% × (K – $10,000)	N/A	______ (O)
Québec tax reduction (2% × $10,000 – K)	N/A	(______) (P)
OAS clawback (see Schedule 3)	______ (Q)	N/A
Provincial tax (for provinces other than Québec; see Appendix II for rates)		
Basic—Amount (J) above × ______% $______		
Surtax ______		
Flat tax ______		
Total provincial tax	______ (R)	N/A
Plus CPP contributions for self-employed individuals (maximum $1701)	______ (S)	N/A
Plus QPP contributions for self-employed individuals (maximum $1701)	N/A	______ (T)
Estimated federal tax (J + L + M + Q + R + S)	______ (U)	
Estimated Québec tax (K + N + O – P + T)		______ (U)
Instalment payments and other credits		
Québec income tax abatement (16.5% × J)	(______) (V)	N/A
Tax deducted at source	______	______
Tax paid by instalments	______	______
Federal political contribution credit	______	N/A
Provincial political contribution credit	______	______
Other	______	______
Total instalment payments and credits	______ (W)	______ (X)
Estimated 1995 federal tax payable (U-V-W) and Québec tax payable (U-X)	$______	$______

Schedule 3—Calculation of Tax on OAS Benefits

	1995 Estimate
Limitation 1	
Old age security ("OAS") benefits received	$ ______ (Y)
Limitation 2	
Income before deductions for tax on OAS—Amount (F) from Schedule 1	$ ______
Deduct base amount	($53,215)
Amount in excess of base amount	$ ______
	× 15%
	$ ______ (Z)
Tax on OAS benefits	
Lesser of (Y) and (Z) above	$ ______ *

*Deduct this amount in arriving at your net income on Schedule 1 and also carry this amount forward to Schedule 2 in calculating estimated 1995 tax payable.

Schedule 4—Calculation of Estimated 1995 Personal Credits

	Federal Estimate	Québec Estimate
Personal tax credits (see Appendix I)		
Basic	$ ______	$ ______
Spousal or equivalent	______	______
Other dependants	______	______
Age	______ [1]	______
Mental or physical impairment	______	______
Person living alone	N/A	______
CPP/QPP and UI premium tax credits	______ [2]	______ [2]
Tuition and education tax credits	______ [3]	N/A
Post-secondary dependant student	N/A	______ [4]
Medical expenses tax credit	______ [5]	______ [5]
Charitable donations tax credit	______ [6]	______ [6]
Adoption expenses tax credit	N/A	______
Subtotal	$ ______(c)	$ ______(c)
Federal dividend tax credit—8.87% of taxable Canadian dividends)	______	N/A
Québec dividend tax credit—13.33% of taxable Canadian dividends	N/A	______
Pension income tax credit	______ [7]	______ [7]
Tax credits transferred from spouse (from Schedule 5)	______	______
Tax credits transferred from other dependants (from Schedule 5)	______	______
Total personal tax credits	$ ______(a)*	$ ______(b)*

*Carry this amount forward to Schedule 2 and deduct (a) from federal tax on taxable income, and (b) from Québec tax on taxable income.

[1] In 1995 the federal age amount ($3,482) is reduced by an amount equal to the lesser of $3,482 and 15% of a taxpayer's net income in excess of $25,921.

[2] The federal credit is calculated as 17% of the CPP/QPP contributions and UI premiums paid during the year. The Québec credit is calculated as 20% of the same amounts.

[3] The federal tuition credit is equal to 17% of the tuition fees paid during the year. The federal education credit is $13.60 for each month in full-time attendance in a qualifying educational program at a qualifying educational institution.

[4] The Québec credit for a dependant who is a student at a post-secondary institution is $330 per term over a maximum of two terms.

[5] Calculated as 17% (federal) or 20% (Québec) of total medical expenses (reduced by the lesser of $1,614 and 3% of the individual's net income).

[6] The federal credit is 17% of the first $200 of donations and 29% of any excess over $200. The Québec credit is 20% of total donations.

[7] Calculated as 17% (federal) or 20% (Québec) of the lesser of $1,000 and eligible pension income.

Schedule 5—Tax Credits Transferred from Other Taxpayers

	Federal	Québec
Spouse's taxable income	$______	______
Less: income limit	(6,456)	
Excess	______	
	× 0.17	× 0.20
Threshold amount	$______(d)	$______(e)

	Federal	Québec
Other dependant's taxable income	$______	$______
Less: income limit	(6,456)	
Excess	______	
	× 0.17	× 0.20
Threshold amount	$______(f)	$______(g)

Calculation of tax credits transferred from spouse

	Federal Estimate	*maximum*	Québec Estimate	*maximum*
Age tax credit	$______	*$592*	______	*$440*
Mental or physical impairment tax credit	______	*720*	______	*440*
Federal tuition and education tax credits	______	*680*		
Pension income tax credit (17% (federal) or 20% (Québec) of lesser of $1,000 and eligible pension income)	______	*170*	______	*200*
Less threshold amount (amount (d) or (e) from above)	______[1]	**(d)**	______[1]	**(e)**
Tax credits transferred from spouse	$______*		$______*	

Calculation of tax credits transferred from other dependants

	Federal Estimate	*maximum*	Québec Estimate	*maximum*
Mental or physical impairment tax credit	______	*720*	______	*440*
Federal tuition and education tax credits	______	*680*		
Other Québec Credits			______	
Less threshold amount (amount (f) or (g) from above)	______[1]	**(f)**	______[1]	**(g)**
Tax credits transferred from other dependants	$______*		$______*	*440*

*Carry forward these amount(s) to Schedule 4

[1] Where spouse or other dependant is entitled to CPP/QPP and UI premium tax credit amounts, (d), (e), (f) and (g) should be reduced by the amount of these credits.

Schedule 6—Estimated 1995 Minimum Tax Exposure

	Federal Estimate	Québec Estimate
Taxable income—Schedule 2	$	$
Add:		
Losses created by resource deductions		
Canadian films		
Québec stragegic investment deduction	N/A	
Untaxed portion of capital gains (1/4)		
RPP and RRSP contributions	[1]	[2]
Less: Gross-up on Canadian dividends (25% of cash dividends)	( )	( )
Adjusted taxable income		
Basic minimum tax exemption	(40,000)	(40,000)
Taxable income for minimum tax purposes		
Minimum tax rate	× 17%	× 20%
Minimum tax before personal tax credits	$	$
Basic minimum personal tax credits (subtotal (c) from Schedule 4)	( )	( )
Minimum federal tax	$	$
Basic federal/Québec tax—amounts (J) and (K) from Schedule 2	$ (J)	$ (K)
Less federal and/or Quebec political contribution credit (from Schedule 2)	( )	( )
Regular tax	$	$
Excess, if any, of Minimum tax over Regular tax	$ [2]	$ [2]

[1] Generally, only direct transfers of funds from one registered plan to another registered plan will be deductible for minimum tax purposes (i.e. not required to be added back here in arriving at adjusted taxable income). A single payment received from a superannuation or pension plan or a deferred profit sharing plan which has been transferred to a deferred income plan will be deductible for minimum tax purposes if it has been received as a result of withdrawal from the plan, termination of employment or death of a person; the winding-up of a plan in full satisfaction of all rights of the payee; or an amendment to the plan. Thus, where an individual receives property from a deceased taxpayer's RRSP as a consequence of being the spouse (or a mentally or physically infirm dependant of the deceased taxpayer) a deduction will be permitted for minimum tax purposes where the amount received is transferred to a deferred income plan.

[2] An excess of Minimum tax over Regular tax indicates that you will be subject to federal and/or Québec minimum tax for 1995. See Chapter 11 which explains this concept.

APPENDIX V

1995 Dividend/Interest Yield Comparison (Based on a 58% Provincial Tax Rate)

Before Tax Interest Rate	Before Tax Dividend Rate Required	After-Tax Yield Interest/Dividend
2.0%	1.5%	1.0%
4.0%	3.1%	2.1%
6.0%	4.6%	3.1%
8.0%	6.1%	4.1%
10.0%	7.7%	5.2%
12.0%	9.2%	6.2%

Notes:

This table shows the after-tax yield from six selected rates of interest and the equivalent rate of dividends, computed at the top federal tax bracket of 29%, plus the federal surtaxes and an "average" provincial tax rate of 58% of federal tax. Based on these assumptions, an interest rate of 6% produces an after-tax yield of 3.1%. A dividend rate of 4.6% will produce the same yield after tax. The rate comparisons are approximately the same for all income tax brackets, the dividend rate being slightly more than 3/4 of the interest rate. The after-tax yield will vary with the tax bracket that you are in. As a rule of thumb, multiply the dividend rate by 1.3 to find the approximate interest rate that will produce the same after-tax yield.

INDEX

AMT, *see* Alternative Minimum Tax

Accountant
incorporated, 163
modified accrual method of accounting, 161, 164
professional dues, 110

Accrual rules (interest), 86

Actor, *see* Artist

Administration, Chapter 13
GST, 277

Adjusted cost base, 62
of interest in partnership, 129

Adoption expenses (Quebec), 209, 224

Age credit, 11, 207

Agreement
shareholders', 143

Agriculture, *see* Farming

Alimony and maintenance, 5
child support received from U.S. resident, 231

Allowable business investment losses, 64
effect on capital gains exemption, 67

Allowance for newborns (Quebec), 209

Alternative Minimum Tax, Chapter 11
calculation of, 167
carryover, 168
death, year of, 171
planning tips, 169
Quebec, 214
U.S. citizens, 240, 248

Americans, *see* United States

Annual interest accrual, 230

Annuity
charitable insured, 184
purchased from charity, 184, 189
purchased with RRSP funds, 31

Anti-avoidance rules
attribution rules, 53
general, Introduction; 53, 96

Appealing an assessment
deduction for legal fees, 10
Federal Court of Canada, to, 200
Notice of Objection, 199, 202
planning tips, 201
Supreme Court of Canada, to, 200
Tax Court of Canada, to, 200

Appropriation of property by shareholder, 142

Architect
overseas projects, 106, 166, 213
professional dues, 110
self-employed, Chapters 6, 10

Art, donation of (Quebec), 207

Art gallery, *see* Museum

Artist
deduction from copyright royalties (Quebec), 214
expenses, deduction for, 111

Ascendants, housing of (Quebec), 208

Assessment of tax
partnership, 130
"quick" assessment, 198
reassessment, 199

Assistant
salary of, deductible for employee, 110

Attribution rules
anti-avoidance rules, 53
children over 18, 52
children under 18, 52
loans for interest, 55
loans to family members, 52
planning tips, 54
spouses, 50
reinvested income, 56
transfer for fair market value, 55
U.S. citizens, 241

Audit by Revenue Canada, 198

Author
deduction from copyright royalties (Quebec), 214
expenses, deduction for, 111

Automobile
business expenses, 124
employment benefit, 104
expenses, employees, 107, 115
loan, interest paid on
deductible as business expense, 124
deductible as employee expense, 107, 116
generally non-deductible, 87
$300 limit per month, *see* Luxury automobile
luxury, $24,000 cap, 107, 115, 116, 124
operating expenses benefit, 104, 115
planning tips, 112, 132

Avoidance of tax, Introduction; *see* Anti-avoidance rules
Baby bonus, *see* family allowance; Allowance for newborns
Becoming non-resident, *see* Emigration
Becoming resident, *see* Immigration
Beekeepers, *see* Farming
Benefits
CPP, assignment of, *see* Canada Pension Plan
employment, *see* Employees: benefits
pension, vesting of, 47
UI, clawback of, *see* Unemployment insurance
Bequests, *see* Charitable donations; Death
Blind, credit for, 11, 20
Boarding school expenses, 8
Bonds
accruing income on, 86, 87
capital gains on, 95
Bonus
accruing, for deferral purposes, 145
from employment, *see* Salary
Canada Savings Bonds, *see* Cash bonus
Building rental expenses, documentation needed (Quebec), 214
Business (*see also* Corporation)
calculation of income, 122
automobiles, 124
capital cost allowance, 124, 133, 134
capital gains, 127
entertainment, limitation, 125, 133
farming, 152
meals, limitation, 125, 133
farming, 151
investment tax credits, 15, 127, 155
losses, 130, 133
partnership, *see* Partnership
planning tips, 131
reasonable expectation of profit, 130, 157
sale of, 144
stub period income for 1995, 121, 131
succession of, 189
year-end, 121, 163
CCA, *see* Capital cost allowance
CIP, *see* Co-operative Investment Plan (Quebec)
CNIL, *see* Cumulative net investment loss
CNTU, *see* Confederation of National Trade Unions
CPP, *see* Canada Pension Plan
Camp expenses, 8
Canada Pension Plan
assignment of benefits to spouse, 59
contributions, credit for, 14
self-employed persons, 123
U.S. citizen temporarily transferred to Canada, 249
Canada Savings Bonds
accruing interest, 86
cash bonuses, 86
Canada-U.S. tax treaty, 231
Protocol of March 1995, 259, 266
Canadian development expense, 92
Canadian exploration expense, 92
Canadian oil and gas property expense, 92
Canadian securities election, 75
Capital
meaning of, 61, 74
repayment of, 140, 146
Canadian securities election, 75
Capital cost allowance, 124, 133, 134
Capital dividends, 57, 85, 140, 146
Capital gains, Chapter 4
basic rules, 62
business, of, 127
death, on, 72, 172
emigration, on, 73, 79
exemption, 65
crystallizing, 147
cumulative net investment loss, 67, 212
exempt capital gains balance, 69, 79, 97
multiplying, 148
planning tips, 75
qualified farm property, 66, 155, 157
qualified small business corporation shares, 65, 78, 147
U.S. citizens, 237, 248
foreign exchange, 237
immigration, 239
non-arm's length transfer, 73
options, 73
personal-use property, 73
8.8 tips, 74
pre-1972 property, 71, 238
principal residence, 71, 78, 237, 238
reserves, 71, 77, 237, 248
self-employed person, of, 127
U.S. taxation of, 236
Capital losses, 63
allowable business investment losses, 64
carryback and carryforward, 63
deducted against regular income, 67
superficial loss, 73
U.S. treatment of, 236

Car, *see* Automobile

Carryback, *see* Carryforward

Carryforward and carryback
  allowable business investment losses, 64, 75
  business losses, 130, 133
  farming losses, 154
  legal fees for retiring allowance or pension benefit, 110
  limited partnership losses, 89
  minimum tax, 168
  net capital losses, 63, 75
  non-capital losses, 130, 133
  restricted farm losses, 154

Carrying charges, *see* Interest: expense deduction

Carryover, *see* Carryforward

Cash bonus
  from Canada Savings Bonds, 87

Cash method
  for farmers, 152

Ceasing to be resident in Canada, *see* Emigration

Charitable donations or gifts, 181, 189
  artwork (Quebec), 207
  credit for, 12, 20, 181
  Crown foundations, 182
  cultural property, 183
  life insurance, of, 184
  in will, 181, 186
  planning tips, 189
  property, of, 182
  purchase of annuity from charity, 184, 189
  residual interest, of, 185, 189
  U.S. citizens, 235

Charitable insured annuity, 184

Charitable remainder trust, 185, 189

Chief source of income is farming, 151, 157

Children
  adoption expenses (Quebec), 209, 224
  attribution rules, 52
  child-care expenses, 8, 206
  child support, 5

Child Tax Benefit payments, 15
  consulting fees to, 54, 133, 145
  credit for dependant child, 11, 241
  family allowance clawback, 16
  family planning, 17
  gifts to, 52
  loans to, 52
  newborn allowance (Quebec), 209
  salary to, 54, 133, 145
  17 and older, 58, 59
  support payments, 5, 231
  taking over your business, 189
  trust for, 94, 95, 175, 187

Chiropractor
  modified accrual method of accounting, 161, 164
  professional dues, 110

Clawback
  old age security, family allowance and UI benefits, 16

Cleaning help, credit for (Quebec), 206

Clothing required for employment, 99

Club dues
  paid by employer, 99
  paid by partnership, 165

College fees, 13

Commission sales person
  expenses deductible, 109

Commodity straddles, 93

Common-law spouses, 11

Company car, *see* Automobile

Composer, *see* Author

Computer programmer, whether employee or contractor, 119

Confederation of National Trade Unions, 219, 224

Consultant, distinguished from employee, 119, 131

Contractor, distinguished from employee, 119, 131

Co-operative Investment Plan (Quebec), 219

Copyright royalties
  artist's deduction for (Quebec), 214

Corporation (*see also* Business; Shares)
  capital repayment, 140, 146
  dividends, *see* Dividends
  extracting profits from, 138
  investment income earned by, 144, 149
  professional, 163
  salary to shareholder, 139
  salary/dividend mix, 146
  shareholder appropriation, 142
  shareholders' agreement, 143
  taxation of, 137
  tax rates, 137

U.S., shares of, 254, 256, 257
U.S. citizens owning, 249

Counselling services provided by employer, 99

Coupons, from bonds, 87

Court appeal, *see* Appeal

Crown foundations, 182

Crystallizing capital gains exemption, 147

Cumulative net investment loss, 67, 208

Credits
adoption expenses (Quebec), 209, 224
Canada Pension Plan contributions, 14
charitable donations, 12, 20, 181, 235
child-care expenses (Quebec), 206
children, 11, 15, 241
dependants, 11
disability, 11, 20
distinction between credit and deduction, 4
domestic employees, 207, 224
educational, 13
effect on provincial tax, 10
GST credit, 16, 282
housing direct ascendants (Quebec), 208
medical expenses, 12, 18, 19, 171, 209
old age, 11, 207
pension income, 14, 20
person living alone (Quebec), 208
personal, 11, Appendix I
political contributions, 15, 20, 210
QST credit, 212
tax credits transferred to spouse, 10, 60, 85
tuition fees, 13
Unemployment Insurance premiums, 14

Crops, *see* Farming

Cultural property, donation of, 183

Dancer, *see* Artist

Day care expenses, 8

Death, Chapter 12
benefits paid by employer, 106, 174
capital gains on, 71, 172
deemed disposition on, 72, 172
estate freezing, 178, 187
estate taxes, 171, 189, 244, 249, 257, 261-266
family law, 177
foreign taxes, 189
life insurance, 180, 188
planning tips, 177
probate fees, 173, 188
RRSP planholder, 34
rollover to spouse or spousal trust, 172, 176
succession of your business, 189
taxes on, 171
will, 174, 186

Deductions, 5
alimony, maintenance and child support, 5
artist, from copyright royalties (Quebec), 214
attendant for disabled person, 9
business, *see* Business: calculation of income
child-care expenses, 8
distinction between deduction and credit, 4
interest expense, 87, 94
legal fees, 10
moving expenses, 7, 18, 235
Quebec, 208
U.S., 232

Deemed dividend, 142

Deferral of income
accruing bonuses, 145
RRSP, *see* Registered Retirement Savings Plan

Deferred profit-sharing plan, 39, 99, 105

Dental plan, *see* Employees: benefits

Dentist
modified accrual method of accounting, 161, 164
professional dues, 110

Dependants, 11
U.S. citizens, 241

Depreciation, *see* Capital cost allowance

Dinner, limitation on expense, 125, 133

Direct ascendants housing credit (Quebec), 208

Disability insurance plan, paid by employer, 99

Disabled person
attendant for, deduction, 9
credit for, 11, 20
part-time student, 13

Disclosure requirements (U.S.), 243

Dividend tax credit, 83

Dividends, 83, 138
capital dividend, 57, 85, 140, 146
deemed, 142
how taxed, 83, 138
intercorporate, 85, 142
meaning of, 83
stock dividend, 84
transfer from spouse, 85

U.S. citizens, 235
Doctor, *see* Physician
Domestic employees, credit for (Quebec), 207, 225
Donations, *see* Charitable donations
Drought-induced livestock sales, 153
Drug plan, *see* Employees: benefits
EHT, *see* Employer Health Tax
Earned income
exclusion (U.S. citizens), 229, 247
for child-care expenses, 8
for RRSP, 24
Education credit, 13
Elections
Canadian securities to be capital, 75
emigration, on, 73, 79, 239, 248
transfer dividends from spouse, 85
Emigration
capital gains tax on, 73, 79
U.S. citizens, 239, 248
Employee profit-sharing plan, 105, 113
Employees, Chapter 6
benefits
automobile, 104
death, 106
deferred, 105
home purchase loan, 101
health insurance, 99, 213
life insurance, 99
loans to, 101, 113
non-taxable, 99, 112
not available to self-employed, 131
phantom stock plan, 114
stock option plans, 103, 113
stock purchase plan, 114
taxable, 100
deductions, 107
assistant's salary, 110
automobile expenses, 107, 115
commission sales person's expenses, 109
home office, 110
supplies, 110
travelling expenses, 109
distinction from independent contractor, 119
domestic, credit for (Quebec), 207, 225
GST rebate, 16, 275, 280
overseas employment tax credit, 106, 213
planning tips, 112
U.S. citizen transferred to other country, 247
Employer Health Tax (Ontario), 123
Employment, *see* Employees
Engineer
overseas projects, 106, 166, 213
professional dues, 110
self-employed, Chapters 6, 10
Entering Canada, *see* Immigration
Entertainer, *see* Artist
Entertainment, limitation on expense, 125, 133
"Equivalent to married" credit, 11, 17
Estate freezing, 178, 187
Estate planning, Chapter 12 (*see also* Death)
Estate taxes, 171, 189, 244, 249, 257, 261-266
Estimated taxes (U.S.), *see* Instalments
Evasion, *see* Tax evasion
Executor (of will), 174, 186
Exempt capital gains balance, 69, 79, 97
Exempt supplies (GST), 271
Exempt life insurance contract, 94, 97
Exemption
capital gains, *see* Capital gains: exemption
principal residence, *see* Principal residence exemption
FIRPTA (U.S. withholding tax on real estate), 254, 262
FSTQ or FTQ, *see* Fonds de solidarité des travailleurs du Québec
Family allowance, *see* Child Tax Benefit
Family law, 177, 186, 187
Family members, loans to, 52
Family planning, 17
Family trusts, 94, 95, 175, 188
Farming, Chapter 9
calculation of income, 152
cash method, 152
chief source of income, 151, 157
drought-induced sale of livestock, 153
inventory valuation, 153
losses, 154
net income stabilization account, 154
planning tips, 157
transfer of property to children, 155, 158
whether a business, 151
Federal Court of Canada, appeal to, 200
Filing return, *see* Tax return
Films, as tax shelter, 91, 96
Financial disclosure requirements (U.S.), 243

First Home plan
federal, *see* Home Buyer's Plan
Quebec, 211, 225

Flow-through entities, capital gains exemption on, 69, 79

Flow-through shares, 92, 213

Fonds de solidarité des travailleurs du Québec, 219, 224

Food, GST treatment, 271, 281

Foreign earned income exclusion (U.S.), 229, 235, 247
Foreign estate taxes, 190, 244, 249, 257, 261

Foreign exchange gains or losses, 237

Foreign tax credit, 15, 230, 247, 259

Freezing an estate, 178, 187

Frequent-flyer plan, 100

Fruit growers, *see* Farming

GAAR, *see* General anti-avoidance rule

GST, *see* Goods and services tax

General anti-avoidance rule, Introduction; 53, 96

Gift
by will, 186
charitable, *see* Charitable donations
capital gain on, 73
tax on, U.S., 245, 249
to child, attribution rules, 52
to employee, whether taxable, 99
to museum or gallery, *see* Charitable donations
to spouse, attribution rules, 50

Goods and services tax (GST), Chapter 17
administration, 277
credit on income tax return, 16, 212, 282
employees, 16, 275, 280
exempt supplies, 271
food, 271, 281
importations, 278
input tax credits, 273
non-residents, 275, 281
partnerships, 274, 280
planning tips, 278
provincial sales tax, integration with, 277
Quebec version, 220
"Quick Method" of accounting, 273
real estate, 279
rebates, 275
small suppliers, 272, 281
streamlined accounting, 273
transitional rules, 278
zero-rated supplies, 271

Grandparents, credit for housing (Quebec), 208

Groceries, GST treatment, 271, 281

Group accident plan, paid by employer, 99

Group sickness plan, paid by employer, 99, 213

Group term life insurance, taxable, 99

Health care plan, *see* Employees: benefits

Health insurance provided by employer
public, taxable benefit, 100
private plan
non-taxable benefit (federal), 99
taxable benefit (Quebec), 213

Health Services Fund contribution (Quebec), 215

Health Tax (Ontario), 123

Holding company, 142, 147

Hobby farms, 151

Home
Buyer's Plan (RRSP), 35, 171
First Home (Quebec), 211, 225
office in, 110, 126
provided by employer, 100
purchase loan from employer, 101
purchase with RRSP funds, 35
sale of, *see* Principal residence exemption

Horses, for racing, *see* Farming

Hospital
charitable donation to, 181, 182
fees, credit for, 12

Hotel, capital cost allowance restrictions, 92

Housekeeper, credit for (Quebec), 207, 225

Husband, *see* Spouse

IPP, *see* Individual Pension Plan

IRA, *see* Individual Retirement Account

IRS, *see* Internal Revenue Service

Immigration to Canada, 239

Importations, GST on, 278

Incentives, Tax shelters

Income
from business, *see* Business
from employment, *see* Employees
net, 3
sheltering, *see* Tax shelters

taxable, 3
splitting, Chapter 3; 246
Incorporating, *see* Corporation
Independent contractor, distinguished from employee, 119, 131
Indirect payments, 50
Individual Pension Plan, 38, 46, 148
Individual Retirement Account (U.S.), 234, 249
Information circulars, *see* end of each chapter
Inheritance taxes, 171
Input tax credits, for GST, 273
Instalment sales (U.S. taxation), 237, 248
Instalments
Canada, 195, 202
Quebec, 214
U.S., 243
Instruments (musical), deduction for, 111
Insurance, *see* Life insurance
Intercorporate dividend
normally tax-free, 85, 142
Inter vivos trust, 176
Interest
accrual rules, 86
attribution, *see* Attribution rules
expense deduction, 87, 94
loss of source of income, 77
income, 86, 95
earned by corporation, 144, 149
late payment of tax, on, 197, 202
paid, deduction for, 87, 94
paid by partnership, whether deductible, 163, 165
paid on automobile, *see* Luxury automobile
prescribed rate, 197, 202
refund, on, 197, 202
reinvestment of, 56
Internal Revenue Service (U.S.)
advisor at U.S. embassy, 250, 266
International adoptions, credit for expenses (Quebec), 209, 224
Interpretation bulletins, *see* end of each chapter
Inventory purchases
for farmers, 153
Investment incentives, *see* Tax shelters
Investment income, *see* Interest; Dividends
Investment portfolio, incorporating, 149
Investment tax credit, 15, 127
agricultural investment, 155
of partnership, 129
Investments and tax shelters, Chapter 5
U.S. investments, Chapter 16
Job loss
payment on, *see* Retiring allowance
Joint filing (U.S. returns), 242, 246
LIF, *see* Life income fund
Labour-sponsored venture capital corporation, 93, 96, 219, 224
Land, *see also* Real estate
cost of improving, deduction for farming business, 153
Late payment of tax
interest on, 197, 202
Lawyer
fees paid to, *see* Legal fees
incorporated, 163
modified accrual method of accounting, 161, 164
professional dues, 110
Lease payments on automobile
limitations on, *see* Luxury automobile
Leaving Canada, *see* Emigration
Legal fees, 10
to adopt a child (Quebec), 209
to increase/decrease alimony or maintenance (Quebec), 206
to obtain pension benefits, 110
to obtain severance pay, 110
to recover unpaid wages, 110
Life annuity, 31, 184, 189
Life income fund (LIF), 32
Life insurance
contract, exempt, 94, 97
gift of, to charity, 183, 184, 189
planning, 180, 188
premiums
non-deductible, 180
taxable as employment benefit, 99
proceeds not taxable, 171, 180
Limited partnerships, 89, 92, 96, 213
to fund mutual fund selling commissions, 89
Livestock
drought-induced sale, 153
destruction where contagious, 154
Loan
business assets, to spouse, 54
to child, 52, 55

to corporation by shareholder, 139
to employee, 101
to family member, 52
to shareholder, 101
to spouse, 50, 54, 55

Locked-in RRSP, 32, 33

Losses
capital, *see* Capital losses
business, *see* Business: losses

Lunch, limitation on expense, 125, 133

Luxury automobile, $24,000 cap, 107, 115, 116, 124

MFLP, *see* Mutual funds: limited partnershipURB, *see* Multiple Unit Residential Building

Maintenance (spousal or child support), 5, 231

Maintenance (of rental building), in Quebec, 214

Marginal tax rates
Canada, 49
United States, 227

Marriage breakdown, 5, 19

Meals
limitations on expense, 125, 133
subsidized by employer, 99

Medical doctor, *see* Physician

Medical expenses, 12, 18, 19, 171, 209

Minimum tax, *see* Alternative minimum tax

Mining companies, as tax shelters, 92, 96, 213

Mortgage interest
deductible as home office expense, 126
generally non-deductible, 87

Moving expenses
deduction for, 7, 18
home purchase loan, 101
reimbursement of by employer, 99
U.S. citizens, 235

Multiple Unit Residential Building (MURB), 93

Museum
charitable donation to, 181-183

Musician
deduction from copyright royalties (Quebec), 214
expenses, deduction for, 111
instruments, deduction for, 111

Mutual funds, 85
exempt capital gains balance, 69, 79, 97
limited partnership to fund selling commissions, 89
U.S. citizens, 246

NISA, *see* Net income stabilization account

Net capital loss, carryover, 63, 75

Net family property, *see* Family law

Net income, 3

Net income stabilization account (farming), 154

Newborn allowance (Quebec), 209

Non-capital losses, 130, 133

Non-resident
becoming, *see* Emigration
ceasing to be, *see* Immigration
GST rebate for, 275, 281

Northern Canada
employees, special deduction, 111
resident of, credit, 10

Notice of Objection, 199, 202
appeal from, 200
time limit for filing, 199

Nurse, professional dues, 110

Nursing home, capital cost allowance restrictions, 92

Objection, *see* Notice of Objection

Office at home, 110, 126

Oil and gas, as tax shelter, 92, 96

Old age credit, 11, 207

Old age security clawback, 16

Ontario Employer Health Tax, 123

Options
capital gains on, 73
stock option plans, 103

Outside Canada, overseas employment tax credit, 106, 213

Overcontribution to RRSP, 34, 44

Overseas employment tax credit, 106, 213

Owner/manager, *see* Business; Corporation

Painter, *see* Artist

Painting, donation of (Quebec), 207

Parents (*see also* Dependants)
credit for housing (Quebec), 208

Part IV tax, 85

Partnership
adjusted cost base of, 129

allocation of income among partners, 128
assessment of, 130
capital gains of, 129
club dues, 165
exempt capital gains balance, 69, 79, 97
GST and, 274, 280
GST rebates to partners, 16, 275
how income taxed, 128
interest deductibility, 163, 165
interest, capital gain or loss on, 129
investment tax credits of, 129
of corporations, 148
payments to retired partners, 163, 165
planning tips, 164
with spouse, 54, 133

Passport renewals (U.S.), 244

Payment of tax
balance due with return, 196
late, interest on, 197, 202
source withholding, 194
instalments, 195, 202, 214

Payroll taxes, 123

Pension adjustment, 24

Pension income
credit for, 14, 20

Pension plan, *see* Registered pension plan

Performer, *see* Artist

Person living alone (Quebec), 208

Personal-use property, 73

Phantom stock plan, 114

Physician
incorporated, 163
modified accrual method of accounting, 161, 164
professional dues, 110
self-employes, Chapters 6, 10

Planning tips
administration, 201
appealing an assessment, 201
attribution rules, 54
automobiles, 112, 132
business income, 131
business succession, 189
corporations, 145
death, 185
employees, 112
estate planning, 185
farmers, 157
GST, 278
income splitting, 54, 246
investments, 94
minimum tax, 169, 248
partnerships, 164
professionals, 164
Quebec, 223
RRSPs, 41-46
self-employed persons, 131
small businesses, 131, 145
tax return, 17
tax shelters, 96
U.S. citizens, 246
U.S. investments, 261

Playwright, *see* Author

Political contributions, 15, 20, 210

Poultry raising, *see* Farming

Pre-1972 property
capital gain on, 73, 238

Preferred shares, 95

Premier Toit plan, 211, 225

Prescribed interest rate, 197, 202

Private health services plan, *see* Employees: benefits

Principal residence exemption, 71, 78
farm property, 155, 158
U.S. citizens, 238

Probate fees, 173, 188

Professionals, Chapter 10
dues deductible, 110
incorporated, 163
1971 receivables, 162, 164

Profit (*see also* Business)
reasonable expectation of, 130, 157

Property
gift of, to charity, 182
income from, 83, 86

Protocol to Canada-U.S. tax treaty, 259, 266

Provincial family law, 177, 186, 187

Provincial sales tax, integration with GST, 277

Provincial tax rates, Appendixes II, III

Purchase of inventory
for farmers, 153

QBIC, *see* Quebec Business Investment Company

QDOT, *see* Qualified domestic trust

QSSP, *see* Quebec Stock Savings Plan

QST, *see* Quebec taxation: sales tax

Qualified domestic trust (U.S.), 257, 263

Qualified farm property
capital gains exemption, 66, 155, 157

Qualified small business corporation shares
  capital gains exemption, 65, 78, 147
Quebec Stock Savings Plan, 215
Quebec taxation, Chapter 14
  artist's deduction from copyright royalties, 214
  differences from federal tax, 205, 223
  First Home (Premier Toit) plan, 211, 225
Health Services Fund contribution, 215
  instalments, 214
  investment incentives, 212, 215
  minimum tax, 214
  planning tips, 223
  real estate tax refund, 210
  sales tax (QST), 220
QST credit on income tax return, 212
  tax rates, 205, Appendix III
"Quick method" of GST accounting, 273
REA, *see* Quebec Stock Savings Plan
RESP, *see* Registered Education Savings Plan
RHOSP, *see* Registered Home Ownership Savings Plan
RIC, *see* Co-operative Investment Plan (Quebec)
RPP, *see* Registered Pension Plan
RRIF, *see* Registered Retirement Income Fund
RRSP, *see* Registered Retirement Savings Plan
Racehorses, *see* Farming
Rates of tax, Appendix II, III
Real estate
  GST on, 279
  investments, as tax shelter, 93
  tax refund (Quebec), 210
  U.S.
    rent from, 254, 261
    sale of, 254
Reasonable expectation of profit, 130, 157
Reassessment
  opening up return for other claims, 202
  time limit, 199
  waiver of time limit, 199, 202
Rebates of GST, 275 (*see also* GST: credit)
Recreational facilities provided by employer, 99
Recreational vehicle, capital cost allowance restrictions, 92
Reference information, *see* end of each chapter
Refund of tax
  interest on after June 14, 112, 197, 202
  real estate tax (Quebec), 210
  why not good planning, 112
Registered Education Savings Plan, 40, 47
Registered Home Ownership Savings Plan (Quebec), 210, 224
Registered Pension Plan (RPP), 38, 105
  contributions by employer non-taxable, 99
  Individual Pension Plan, 38, 46, 148
  small business owners, for, 144
  U.S. taxation of, 234, 249
  vesting of benefits, 47
Registered Retirement Income Fund (RRIF), 31, 46
Registered Retirement Savings Plan (RRSP)
  closing out, 28, 46
  contribution limits, 24, 171
  death of planholder, 34
  "earned income", 24
  getting money out of, 31
  Home Buyer's Plan, 35, 171
  locked-in, 32, 33
  overcontribution to, 34, 44
  pension adjustment, 24
  planning tips, 41-46
  retiring allowance, transfer to, 33, 43, 106, 113
  savings from, 27
  self-directed, 28, 41, 77
  setting up, 24
  spousal, 32, 43, 58
  tax-free growth, 28
  transfers to and from, 33
  U.S. taxation of, 234, 249
  what happens to the funds in, 28
Reinvestment of interest, 56
Relocation expenses, *see* Moving expenses
Renovation expense (Quebec)
  first home, refundable credit, 211, 225
  rental property, documentation required, 214
Rent from U.S. real estate, 254, 261
Rental expenses, documentation required (Quebec), 214
Reserve
  capital gains, 71, 77, 237, 248
Residence, *see* Principal residence exemption
Resident in Canada
  becoming, *see* Immigration
  ceasing to be, *see* Emigration

Resource exploration expenses, 92, 96, 213
Restaurant meals, limitation on expense, 125, 133
Restricted farm losses, 154
Retired partner, income payment to, 163, 165
Retirement compensation arrangement, 105
Retiring allowance (including severance pay, termination pay)
  legal fees incurred to obtain, 110
  taxable, 106
  transfer to RRSP, 33, 44, 106, 113
Revenue Canada publications, *see* end of each chapter
Rollover
  farming property to children or grandchildren, 155, 158
  property transferred to corporation, 78
  property transferred to spouse, 73
Royalties
  artist's, deduction for (Quebec), 214
SPEQ, *see* Quebec Business Investment Company
Salary
  from own corporation, 139
  of employee, Chapter 6
Salary deferral arrangement, 105
Salary/dividend mix, 146
Sale of a business, 144
Sales person, *see* Commission sales person
Sales tax
  federal, *see* Goods and services tax
  Quebec, 220
Sculptor, *see* Artist
Section 85 rollover, 78
Self-employed, Chapter 7 (*see also* Business income)
Selling a business, 144
Senior citizens, 11, 207, 208
Sentinels, 87
Separation from spouse, 5, 19
Severance pay, *see* Retiring allowance
Shareholder agreement, 143
Shareholder appropriation, 142
Shareholder loan
  from corporation, 101
  to corporation, 139
Shares
  capital gains exemption on, 65
  dividends on, *see* Dividends
  flow-through, 92, 213
  preferred, 95
  small business corporation, 65, 147
Shelters, *see* Tax shelters
Shows, limitation on expense, 125, 133
Singer, *see* Artist
Shelters, *see* Tax shelters
Small business corporation
  allowable business investment loss on, 64
  capital gains exemption on, 65
  meaning of, 64
  pension plan for owners, 144
  qualified, 65, 147
Small supplier (GST), 272, 281
Snowbirds, 256
Source withholdings
  credited on tax return, 194
  reduction of, 112
  where required, 194
Sports event, limitation on expense, 125, 133
Spousal RRSP, 32, 43, 58
Spouse
  attribution rules, 50
  consulting fees to, 54, 133, 145
  common-law, 11
  credit for, 11
  gift to, 50
  loan to, 50, 54
  partnership with, 54, 133
  paying taxes for, 57
  RRSP for, 32, 43, 58
  salary to, 54, 133, 145
  separation from, 5, 19
  transfer of property to, 73
  transfer of dividends, 85
  trust for, 172, 176
Stock dividend, 84
Stock option plans, 103, 114
Stock purchase plan, 114
Straddles, 93
Streamlined accounting (GST), 273
Stripped bonds, 87
Stub period business income for 1995, 121, 131
Students
  credit for, 13

Succession of business, planning for, 189

Superficial loss, 73

Supplies
payable by employee, deductible, 110

Support payments, 5
child support from U.S. resident, 231

Supreme Court of Canada, appeal to, 200

Symes court case, 8

Tax avoidance, Introduction; *see* Anti-avoidance rules

Tax convention, *see* Tax treaty

Tax Court of Canada, appeal to, 200

Tax credits, *see* Credits

Tax deferral plans, Chapter 2

Tax evasion, Introduction
countermeasures in Quebec, 214

Tax planning, Introduction; *see also* Planning tips

Tax rates, Appendixes I-VI

Tax return
filing deadline, 193
tips, Chapter 1
U.S., 242

Tax shelters, 88
commodity straddles, 93
identification number, 89
films and TV productions, 91
labour-sponsored venture capital corporation, 93, 96, 219, 224
limited partnerships, 89, 92, 213
minimum tax effect, 170
mining, 92, 96, 213
mutual fund limited partnerships, 89
oil and gas, 92, 96
planning tips, 94
Quebec, 215
real estate, 93
"tainted", effect on minimum tax, 170

Tax tables, Appendixes I-VI

Tax treaty, *see* Canada-U.S. tax treaty

Taxable benefits, *see* Employment

Taxable income, 3

Television production, as tax shelter, 91

Termination pay, *see* Retiring allowance

Testamentary trust, 176

Theatre, limitation on expense, 125, 133

Thibaudeau court case, 5

Tips, *see* Planning tips

Transitional rules for GST, 278

Transportation
expenses, *see* Travel expenses
passes given to employees, 99
to job by employer, 99

Travelling expenses (*see also* Automobile)
adoption (Quebec), 209
business, 122, 132
employees, 109

Treaty, *see* Canada-U.S. tax treaty

Trusts, 94, 95, 175, 188

Tuition fees, 13

USA, *see* United States

Unemployment insurance
benefits clawback, 16
not available to self-employed, 123
premiums, credit for, 14

Unified credit (U.S. estate and gift tax), 258

Uniform required for employment, 99

Union dues, 110

United States
citizens in Canada, Chapter 15
investment in, Chapter 16
real estate in, Chapter 16
residence in, 256

University
charitable donation to, 181, 182
tuition fees, 13

Vacation property
provided to employee, 100

Venture capital corporation, labour-sponsored, 93, 96, 219, 224

Veterinarian
modified accrual method of accounting, 161, 164
professional dues, 110

Waiver of reassessment period, 199, 202

Wife, *see* Spouse

Will, 174, 186

Withholding
tax on employment income, *see* Source withholdings

Work in progress
special rule for professionals, 161

Working outside Canada, *see* Overseas employment tax credit

Working Ventures fund, 93, 96

Writer, *see* Author

Wrongful dismissal award, *see* Retiring allowance

Yacht, capital cost allowance restrictions, 92

Year-end
  for business, 121
  for professional corporation, 163

Zero-rated supplies (GST), 271

1971 receivables, 162, 164

QUICK LOOKUP TABLE — DOLLAR AMOUNTS

Use this table if you know that a rule applies with a certain dollar amount, but can't remember exactly how the rule is described in the Index.

12¢/km taxable employee benefit re automobile operating costs, 104
31¢/km reasonable allowance paid by employer for employee's use of vehicle, 104
$7.50 per day deduction for residents of northern Canada, 10
$13.60 per month credit for full-time students, 13
$15 per day deduction for residents of northern Canada, 10
$90 per week child-care expenses per child age 7-14, 8
$100 employee Christmas or wedding gift not a taxable benefit, 99
$100 minimum fees for tuition credit, 13
$100 threshold for highest political credit, 15
$105 GST credit per child, 16
$150 per week child-care expenses per child under 7 or disabled, 8
$198 GST credit per adult, 16
$200 gain or loss on foreign currency ignored, 237
$200 maximum cost of tools, 100% capital cost allowance, 124
$200 threshold for high charitable donations credit, 12
$210 credit for person living alone (Quebec), 208
$269 credit for disabled dependent over 18, 11
$300 limit on automobile interest cost, 107, 124
$500 newborn allowance, first child (Quebec), 209
$550 credit for adult housing direct ascendant (Quebec), 208
$592 credit for age 65 or older, 11
$650 limit on automobile lease cost, 107, 124
$650 non-taxable allowance for moving expenses, 235
$680 maximum tuition/education credits transfer, 14
$720 credit for disability, 11
$915 credit for dependent spouse, 11
$1,000 deduction for employed artist's expenses, 111
$1,000 interest owing on late instalments, additional penalty, 196
$1,000 maximum credit for labour-sponsored venture capital fund, 93, 219
$1,000 maximum Health Services Fund contribution (Quebec), 215
$1,000 newborn allowance, second child (Quebec), 209
$1,000 pension income, credit for, 14
$1,000 threshold for capital gain on personal-use property, 73
$1,098 basic personal credit, 11
$1,200 per year balance of tax payable, instalments required, 214
$1,500 maximum RESP contribution per year, 40
$1,614 threshold for medical expenses, 12
$2,000 maximum credit for adoption expenses (Quebec), 209
$2,000 maximum credit for First Home mortgage interest (Quebec), 211
$1,000 maximum credit (federal+provincial) for labour-sponsored fund, 93, 219
$2,000 per year balance of tax payable, instalments required, 195
$2,000 per year of employment before 1996, retiring allowance into RRSP, 33, 106
$2,000 per year of pre-1986 capital loss, deduct against regular income, 63
$2,000 tax owing in April, instalments required for year, 195
$2,000 RRSP overcontribution limit, 18
$3,000 child-care expenses per child age 7-14, 8
$3,000 maximum credit for First Home renovations (Quebec), 211
$3,000 maximum credit for senior citizen's domestic employee (Quebec), 207
$3,000 maximum deduction from worker gain sharing plan (Quebec), 220
$4,000 maximum credit for First Home mortgage interest (Quebec), 211
$5,000 child-care expenses per child under 7 or disabled, 8, 206
$5,000 deduction for attendant for disabled person, 9
$5,000 maximum purchase of labour-sponsored venture capital fund, 93, 219
$5,000 newborn allowance, third child (Quebec), 209
$5,000 threshold for low withholding tax on RRSP withdrawal, 45
$6,750 maximum DPSP contribution by employer for 1996, 39
$7,750 maximum DPSP contribution by employer for 1995, 39
$8,000 former RRSP overcontribution limit, 18

$10,000 exemption for death benefits, 106
$10,000 maximum adoption expenses (Quebec), 209
$10,000 maximum expenses of senior citizen's domestic employee (Quebec), 207
$10,000 (U.S.) value of foreign assets, reporting requirement, 243
$12,000 federal tax in dispute, Tax Court general procedure required, 200
$13,500 RRSP contribution limit for 1994 and 1996-97, 24
$14,500 RRSP contribution limit for 1995 and 1998, 24
$15,000 artist's deduction from copyright royalties (Quebec), 214
$15,000 threshold for high withholding tax on RRSP withdrawal, 45
$20,000 loan from RRSP to purchase a home, 35
$24,000 limit on automobile capital cost, 107, 124
$25,921 threshold for phasing out Child Tax Benefit, 15
$25,921 threshold for phasing out GST credit, 15
$25,921 threshold for phasing out old age credit, 11
$29,590 low tax bracket, 4, 49
$31,500 maximum RESP contribution per child, 40
$40,000 minimum tax exemption, 167
$40,000 self-employment income, Ontario Employer Health Tax, 123
$53,215 income threshold for old age security clawback, 16
$59,180 high tax bracket, 4, 49
$60,000 (U.S.) value of estate subject to estate tax, 257
$60,840 income threshold for UI benefits clawback, 16
$70,000 (U.S.) foreign earned income exclusion, 229
$100,000 capital gains exemption, election, 69
$100,000 income eligible for overseas employment credit, 106
$110,000-$150,000 maximum home value for First Home credit (Quebec), 211
$175,000 maximum new home price for full QST housing rebate, 222
$200,000 minimum new home price for no QST housing rebate, 222
$200,000 active business income of corporation, low tax rate, 137
$350,000 maximum new home price for full GST housing rebate, 275
$450,000 minimum new home price for no GST housing rebate, 275
$500,000 capital gains exemption for farm property, 66
$500,000 capital gains exemption for small business shares, 65
$600,000 (U.S.) value of estate subject to estate tax, 244, 257
$2,000,000-$250,000,000 assets of "growth corporation" (Quebec), 216
$6,000,000 annual taxable sales, large business GST/QST, 221, 277
$10,000,000 of capital, phase-out of small business rate for corporations, 137